Reference Services and
Library Instruction

HANDBOOKS FOR LIBRARY MANAGEMENT

Reference Services and Library Instruction
A Handbook for Library Management

David F. Kohl

Foreword by Peter G. Watson

ABC·CLIO

Santa Barbara, California
Oxford, England

*This book is Smyth sewn and printed on acid-free paper to
meet library standards.*

Library of Congress Cataloging in Publication Data

Kohl, David F., 1942–
  Reference services and library instruction.

  (Handbooks for library management)
  Bibliography: p.
  Includes index.
  1. Reference services (Libraries) 2. Library
orientation. 3. Libraries and readers. 4. Library
administration. I. Title. II. Series: Kohl,
David F., 1942– . Handbooks for library
management.
Z711.K58 1985 025.5'2   85-13431
ISBN 0-87436-432-9

10 9 8 7 6 5 4 3 2 1

ABC-CLIO, Inc.
2040 Alameda Padre Serra, Box 4397
Santa Barbara, California 93103

Clio Press Ltd.
55 St. Thomas Street
Oxford OX1 1JG, England

Manufactured in the United States of America

CONTENTS

1.

Reference Services

v

2. _____

| **Library Instruction** |

FOREWORD

When the first volume of the *Handbooks for Library Management* was initially released at the 1985 Midwinter meeting of the American Library Association, it attracted increasing interest and a sense of happy recognition as the fundamental idea of the work was grasped: "Of course! How sensible." Upon leafing through the volume, one's interest soon turned to approbation as the organizing skill of the author became apparent—the promise of the author's central idea was indeed fulfilled in the succinct, consistent presentation of data in each of the summaries; the insight, precision, and depth of subject assignments; and the thoroughness of coverage. And then, as realization dawned that this was in fact only one part of a whole vast edifice comprising no less than *six* volumes and covering the entire range of the library profession, approbation became amazement.

Everyone to whom I showed my copy reacted in a similar fashion: they took it from me, ceased conversing, and started looking up information on a favorite topic or a particular concern. Many of them probably wondered, as did I, when the volume covering their own area of specialization would see publication. The answer to that question is "sooner than expected, thanks partly to judicious use of microcomputers in the publishing process." Here already is the third book of this splendid series: *Reference Services and Library Instruction*. The scope of this installment is commensurate with the first two. Dr. Kohl has successfully distilled almost the entire last quarter-century of quantitative library research on the subjects, as originally published in 34 key journals. In so doing, he has presented us with a remarkable picture of reference librarianship and how it has changed across the turbulent sweep of the last 25 years. (Let me alert new readers that, although the subject arrangement of each volume facilitates rapid look-up and consultation of specific data, these volumes are highly addictive. The user may soon be reading along for the sheer fascination of it!)

In this third volume, the field of reference work is accessible by over 200 subject access points, and the newer specialty, library instruction, by a further 25. Scanning these headings provides us librarians with an accurate conspectus of our affairs. Clearly, online searching has been the single greatest advance in direct reference service during these two-and-a-half decades, and Kohl's subheadings reflect that there exists substantial research on technique, sources, patron satisfaction, organizational impact, fees for service, etc. It is heartening to see, however, that a very creditable body of work assessing the quality of *standard* reference resources was also continuing to build, albeit with less fanfare. Indispensable tools of the trade such as encyclopedias, book review guides, national bibliographies, and dissertations were studied, as were the tools pertaining specifically to most major disciplines.

Of course, the reference librarian's most critical resource is the library catalog, and the 1960 start-date of the *Handbooks'* coverage allows the reader to travel from the landmark Yale catalog studies to the first generation of research in the present era of online catalogs. Through the chronological arrangement of summaries under each topic, one can easily follow the methodological maturing of this particular field of inquiry—most notably in the increasingly sophisticated application of statistical techniques. Online searching and library instruction, by contrast, are more recent additions to the panoply of direct patron service. Here, Kohl's summaries simply open up with a battery of detailed and well-researched statistical investigations in which (thanks largely to the advent of SPSS—perhaps the world's most widely-adopted computer program package) exact calculations of probability and significance and correlation are routinely included.

Another especially intriguing branch of reference practice, the behavioral component as distinct from the cognitive, is also beginning to be brought under the analytic lens of contemporary social science research technique. *Do* people respond differently to public desk staff who are standing than they do to those who are sitting? Assuming the librarians in question are employing the same non-verbal behavior, do library users *really* tend to approach females more readily than they do males? Look under Approachability—the precisely-chosen term for this topic.

The number of uses for this volume, as for the whole grand series, is infinite. Practitioners have a solid basis for improving practice (what is more valuable to the individual client of libraries whom we exist to help?). Managers can enhance their program-planning and decision-making; researchers (I think of working librarians and doctoral students—not only of teaching faculty) have here an efficient and reliable source to guide them in the framing of a project or topic, by displaying for them the context and direction of previous efforts. The *Handbooks* provide such a diversity of approaches to so many topics, that browsing through each volume will serve as a delightful stimulus to one's imagination in thinking about the job, the library, and the profession.

Without doubt, David Kohl has created an essential resource for the modern practice of librarianship. Gail Schlachter and her successors at ABC-CLIO are to be commended for having the vision to accept and produce this work, and for making their top priority the speedy issuance of all six volumes in a format of the highest possible quality.

—Peter G. Watson
California State University, Chico.

INTRODUCTION

The *Handbooks for Library Management* have been designed for library managers and decision makers who regularly need information, but who are chronically too short of time to do involved and time-consuming literature searches each time specific, quantitative information is desired. This unusual tool, rather than abstracting complete studies or providing only citations to research, instead presents summaries of individual research findings, grouped by subject. By looking under the appropriate subject heading in the *Handbook*, librarians can find summaries detailing the research findings on that topic. For example, what percentage of reference questions are answered correctly, and does it make a difference whether professional or nonprofessional staff are doing the answering? As a result, helpful information can be found in minutes and without an extensive literature review. Furthermore, if a more complete look at the study is desired, the user is referred to the bibliographic citation number so that the full study can be consulted.

Arrangement

The series consists of six volumes, with each volume covering two or more of the sixteen basic subject areas that divide the volumes into parts. While most of these basic subject divisions reflect such traditional administrative division of library work as administration, circulation, and reference, at least two subject areas go somewhat further. "Library Education" may be of interest, not just to library school administrators, but to faculty and students as well, and "Professional Issues" should be of interest to all career-oriented library professionals. Each basic subject division is further divided by specific subject headings, which are further subdivided by type of library: General (more than one library type), Academic, Public, School, and Special. For example, readers seeking information on book loss rates in academic libraries would consult the basic subject division "Collection Maintenance" and look under the specific subject heading "Loss Rates (Books)," in the "Academic" libraries subdivision. There they would find the summarized results of studies on book loss rates in academic libraries followed by the number referring to the full citation in the Bibliography of Articles.

Each volume in the series follows the same basic pattern: The introduction; a list of the journals surveyed; a detailed table of contents listing all subject headings used in that volume; the research findings arranged by subject; the complete bibliography of articles surveyed for the series with page numbers indicating locations of corresponding research summaries in the text; and an alphabetically arranged author index to the Bibliography of Articles.

The summaries of the research findings also tend to follow a standard format. First the study is briefly described by giving location, date, and, when appropriate, population or survey size and response rate. This information is provided to help users determine the nature, scope, and relevance of the study to their needs. The actual findings, signaled by an italicized *"showed that,"* follow and include, when appropriate, such supporting data as significance level and confidence interval. Information in brackets represents editorial comment, for example "[significance level not given]" or "[remaining cases not accounted for]," while information in parentheses merely represents additional data taken from the article.

The Sample Entries on page xxiii identify the elements and illustrate the interrelationships between the subject organization of the volume, research summaries of the text, corresponding article citations in the bibliography, and the author index entries.

Scope

In order to keep the *Handbook* series manageable, a number of scope limitations were necessary. The time period, 1960 through 1983, was selected since it covers the time when quantitative research began to come of age in library research. Only journal literature has been surveyed, because the bulk of quantitative library research is reported in that medium, and because the bulk of editorial and refereeing process required by most journals helps ensure the quality of the research reported. This limitation does ignore a number of important studies reported in monographic form, however, and we hope to cover this area at a later date. Further, only North American journals and research were reviewed since they constitute the main body of quantitative library research reported. Again, this ignores several journals reporting significant library research, particularly journals from Great Britain. We plan to expand our focus and include these in later editions or updates of the *Handbook* series.

Although we generally followed the principle that research good enough to publish was research worth including in the *Handbook* series, several caveats must be stated. First, no research findings with statistical significance exceeding .05 were reported. This follows general Social Science practice and, in recent years, almost universal library research practice. Second, occasional findings, and sometimes whole studies, were not reported in the *Handbook* series when there were serious problems with internal consistency and/or ambiguous and confusing text. At issue here is not the occasional typographical error or arithmetical miscalculation, but those situations where charts and text purportedly presenting the same information differed in substantial and unaccountable ways. Fortunately, such problems were not excessive. And third, as a general rule, only original and supported findings were used in the *Handbook* series. Findings that were reported second-hand, or where the study documentation was reported elsewhere (often the case with doctoral research), were generally not used in the series. Only in those instances when the second-hand data were used to show a pattern or otherwise resulted in new data by their juxtaposition, were such findings reported.

Finally, under the category of unsought limitations, we, like many library users, were not always able to find all the journal articles we needed in the time available to us. However, the excellent holdings and services of the University of Illinois Library Science Library provided us with access to almost all of the journal issues actually published and received by March 1984—a fact that should probably be listed as a record rather than as a limitation.

Acknowledgements

As might be expected, a project of this size required assistance from many quarters. Both the University of Illinois Library Research and Publication Committee and the University of Illinois Research Board provided invaluable assistance in the form of financial support for graduate assistants. The assistants themselves, Becky Rutter, Nicki Varyu, and Bruce Olsen, constituted a dedicated, bright, and hardworking team. The Undergraduate Library staff deserve special thanks for their support and cooperation, as do the Library Science Library staff, who were unfailingly courteous and helpful in making their truly outstanding collection available. The staff at ABC-Clio, particularly Gail Schlachter and Barbara Pope, provided much needed encouragement and good advice, even in the face of several delays and at least one nasty shock. And last, but by no means least, I would like to acknowledge the patience and support of my wife, Marilyn, and my son, Nathaniel, who have given up much in the way of a husband and father so that this *Handbook* series could be completed on schedule.

—*David F. Kohl*
Urbana, Illinois

SAMPLE ENTRIES

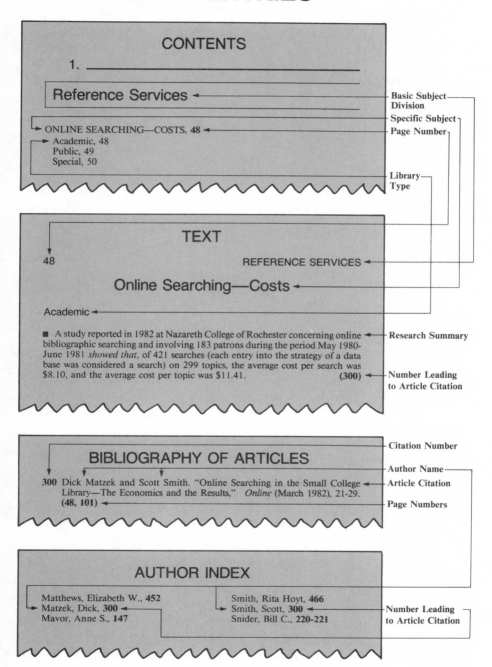

CONTENTS

1. _____

Reference Services ◄—————————————————— Basic Subject Division

————————————————————————— Specific Subject

► ONLINE SEARCHING—COSTS, 48 ◄———————— Page Number
► Academic, 48
Public, 49
Special, 50

Library Type

TEXT

48   REFERENCE SERVICES ◄————

Online Searching—Costs ◄————————————

Academic ◄————————————————————————————

■ A study reported in 1982 at Nazareth College of Rochester concerning online ◄— Research Summary
bibliographic searching and involving 183 patrons during the period May 1980-
June 1981 *showed that*, of 421 searches (each entry into the strategy of a data
base was considered a search) on 299 topics, the average cost per search was
$8.10, and the average cost per topic was $11.41.   **(300)** ◄— Number Leading to Article Citation

Citation Number

BIBLIOGRAPHY OF ARTICLES

Author Name

300 Dick Matzek and Scott Smith. "Online Searching in the Small College ◄— Article Citation
Library—The Economics and the Results," *Online* (March 1982), 21-29.
(48, 101) ◄————————————————————————— Page Numbers

AUTHOR INDEX

Matthews, Elizabeth W., **452**   Smith, Rita Hoyt, **466**
► Matzek, Dick, **300** ◄   ► Smith, Scott, **300** ◄———— Number Leading to Article Citation
Mavor, Anne S., **147**   Snider, Bill C., **220-221**

LIST OF JOURNALS SURVEYED

American Libraries. Chicago: American Library Association, 1970–. Monthly. LC 70-21767. ISSN 0002-9769. (Formerly *ALA Bulletin,* 1907–1969.)

American Society for Information Science. Journal. (JASIS) New York: John Wiley & Sons, 1970–. Bimonthly. LC 75-640174. ISSN 0002-8231. (Formerly *American Documentation,* 1950–1969.)

Canadian Library Journal. Ottawa: Canadian Library Association, 1969–. Bimonthly. LC 77-309891. ISSN 0008-4352. (Formerly *Bulletin,* 1944– March 1960; *Canadian Library,* 1960–1968.)

Catholic Library World. Haverford, PA: Catholic Library Association, 1929–. Monthly. LC 39-41. ISSN 0008-820X.

Collection Building. New York: Schuman, 1978–. Quarterly. LC 78-645190. ISSN 0160-4953.

Collection Management. New York: Haworth Press, 1975–. Quarterly. LC 78-640677. ISSN 0146-2679.

College and Research Libraries. Chicago: American Library Association, 1939–. Bimonthly. LC 42-16492. ISSN 0010-0870.

Drexel Library Quarterly. Philadelphia: Centrum Philadelphia, 1965–. Quarterly. LC 65-9911. ISSN 0012-6160.

Harvard Library Bulletin. Cambridge: Harvard University Library, 1947–. Quarterly. LC 49-1965//R802. ISSN 0017-8136.

International Journal of Legal Information. Camden, NJ: International Association of Law Libraries, 1982–. 6/yr. LC 82-643460. ISSN 0731-1265. (Formerly *Bulletin. International Association of Law Libraries,* 1960–1972; *International Journal of Law Libraries,* 1973–1979.)

International Library Review. London: Academic Press, 1969–. Quarterly. LC 76-10110. ISSN 0020-7837.

Journal of Academic Librarianship. Ann Arbor, MI: Mountainside Publishing, 1975–. Bimonthly. LC 75-647252. ISSN 0099-1333.

Journal of Education for Librarianship. State College, PA: Association of American Library Schools, 1960–. 5/yr. LC 63-24347. ISSN 0022-0604.

Journal of Library Administration. New York: Haworth Press, 1980–. Monthly. LC 80-644826. ISSN 0193-0826.

Journal of Library Automation. Chicago: American Library Association, 1968– . Quarterly. LC 68-6437//R82. ISSN 0022-2240.

Journal of Library History, Philosophy and Comparative Librarianship. Austin, TX: 1966– . Quarterly. LC 65-9989. ISSN 0275-3650. (Formerly *Journal of Library History,* 1966–1975.)

Law Library Journal. Chicago: American Association of Law Libraries, 1908– . Quarterly. LC 41-21688//R6. ISSN 0023-9283.

Library Acquisitions: Practice and Theory. Elmsford, NY: Pergamon Press, 1977– . Quarterly. LC 77-647728. ISSN 0364-6408.

Library Journal. New York: R.R. Bowker, 1876– . Semimonthly, except July–August. LC 76-645271. ISSN 0363-0277.

Library Quarterly. Chicago: University of Chicago, 1931– . Quarterly. LC 32-12448. ISSN 0024-2519.

Library Research. Norwood, NJ: Ablex Publishing, 1979– . Quarterly. LC 79-643718. ISSN 0164-0763.

Library Resources and Technical Services. Chicago: American Library Association, 1957– . Quarterly. LC 59-3198. ISSN 0024-2527. (Formed by the merger of *Serial Slants* and *Journal of Cataloging and Classification.*)

Library Trends. Champaign: University of Illinois at Urbana-Champaign, 1952– . Quarterly. LC 54-62638. ISSN 0024-2594.

Medical Library Association. Bulletin. Chicago: Medical Library Association, 1911– . Quarterly. LC 16-76616. ISSN 0025-7338.

Microform Review. Westport, CT: Meckler Publishing, 1972– . Quarterly. LC 72-620299. ISSN 0002-6530.

Notes. Philadelphia: Music Library Association, 1942– . Quarterly. LC 43-45299//R542. ISSN 0027-4380.

Online. Weston, CT: Online, 1977– . Quarterly. LC 78-640551. ISSN 0416-5422.

Public Libraries. Chicago: American Library Association, 1978– . 4/yr. ISSN 0163-5506. (Formerly *Just Between Ourselves,* 1962–1969; *PLA Newsletter,* 1962–1977.)

RQ. Chicago: American Library Association, 1960– . Quarterly. LC 77-23834. ISSN 0033-7072.

RSR Reference Services Review. Ann Arbor, MI: Perian Press, 1972– . LC 73-642283//R74. ISSN 0090-7324.

School Library Journal. New York: R.R. Bowker, 1954– . Monthly except June and July. LC 77-646483. ISSN 0362-8930.

School Library Media Quarterly. Chicago: American Library Association, 1981– . 4/yr. LC 82-640987. ISSN 0278-4823. (Formerly *School Libraries,* 1951–1972; *School Media Quarterly,* 1972–1980.)

Special Libraries. New York: Special Libraries Association, 1910– . 4/yr. LC 11-25280rev2*. ISSN 0038-6723.

Wilson Library Bulletin. Bronx, NY: H.W. Wilson, 1914– . Monthly except July and August. LC 80-9008(rev.42). ISSN 0043-5651.

1.

Reference Services

Approachability

Academic

■ A study of 4 academic libraries in the Southern California area *showed that* patrons almost always chose to approach a standing reference or circulation staff member rather than a seated one if both were exhibiting similar nonverbal behavior. **(050)**

Ibid. . . . *showed that* reference personnel exhibited positive nonverbal behavior a higher percentage of the time than circulation desk personnel. **(050)**

Ibid. . . . *showed that* patrons chose to approach a female rather than male staff member in reference or circulation if both were seated or standing and exhibiting similar nonverbal behavior. **(050)**

Clinical Medical Librarian Services

Academic

■ A 1974 survey by the University of Washington Health Sciences Library concerning the impact of the clinical medical librarianship program (2 reference librarians attended hospital rounds in order to provide physicians, students, nurses, etc. specialized literature on patient-related problems) in 2 hospital areas by surveying all staff who had been present on rounds in those areas (Neonatal Intensive Care Unit: survey size: 36; responding: 30 or 83%; Department of Orthopedics: survey size: 26; responding: 15 or 58%) *showed that* 73% of the NICU and 47% of the orthopedics preferred to have the CML present on rounds rather than available full-time within the library. **(710)**

Ibid. . . . *showed that* overall response to the program was good, with 100% of the NICU and 93% of the orthopedics "wishing to see the literature service continued." Further, 97% of NICU and 67% of orthopedics reported that the program "was of clinical importance in determining the diagnosis and treatment of patients." **(710)**

Ibid. . . . *showed that* 100% of the NICU and 93% of the orthopedics reported that the literature service had saved time for the recipients. Further, 53% of the NICU and 60% of the orthopedics reported that they would have looked the materials up on their own if the CML program had not done so.   **(710)**

Ibid. . . . *showed that* 97% of the NICU and 87% of the orthopedics reported that their awareness of the Health Sciences Library and its services and resources had increased as as a result of the CML program. Further, 50% of the NICU and 33% of the orthopedics were interested in more exposure to MEDLINE, while 63% of the NICU and 47% of the orthopedics reported an interest in more information on "specialized bibliographic resources and services."   **(710)**

■ A survey reported in 1978 at the Yale-New Haven Hospital of clinicians concerning their attitudes toward the clinical medical librarian program (4 reference librarians assigned to the departments of pediatrics, psychiatry, internal medicine, and surgery) (survey size: 98 hosptial clinicians; responding: 73 or 74%) *showed that* the program was primarily viewed as education-oriented rather than as supporting patient care.
                                                                              (723)

Ibid. . . . *showed that* respondents reported that the "information pro-vided was exceptionally relevant" (overall average of 3.45 on a scale of 1-4) and that the literature searches were highly accurate (overall average of 3.48 on a scale of 1-4).   **(723)**

Ibid. . . . *showed that* the degree to which respondents reported that the clinical medical librarian had been integrated into their unit was as follows:

not at all	0 (00%)	respondents
slightly	7 (10%)	respondents
mostly	36 (49%)	respondents
fully	30 (41%)	respondents **(723)**

Ibid. . . . *showed that* the methods by which 73 respondents wished to contact the clinical medical librarian were as follows:

in person at conferences in the hospital	38 (52%)	respondents
in person in the library	10 (14%)	respondents
by phone	22 (30%)	respondents

continued

through a third person 0 (0%) respondents
other (no preference) 3 (4%) respondents **(723)**

■ A survey/study reported in 1983 at the library of the University of Texas Health Science Center at San Antonio of a 3-month pilot clinical information consultation service (medical staff requested information they needed on a consultation form) *showed that* 126 clinical information consultation requests were received from 17 of the 26 residents on rotation in the medical service at the time. 124 requests were for 1-2 relevant articles, and 2 requests were for short bibliographies. **(751)**

Ibid. . . . *showed that* library staff spent an average of .9 hours in answering each request, with an average turnaround time of 6 hours.
(751)

Ibid. . . . *showed that* the kinds of articles requested were as follows (multiple responses allowed):

review articles 99 (78.6%) requests
case reports (with
literature review) 46 (36.5%) requests
clinical research 21 (16.7%) requests
case reports 5 (4.0%) requests
basic science research 2 (1.6%) requests **(751)**

Ibid. . . . *showed that,* of 37 (29%) user evaluation forms returned (1 was provided for each of the 126 requests), the 3 reasons given for using the service were: for diagnosis and/or treatment of patients (17 or 46% respondents), to provide general information or a review of a subject (18 or 48%), and to verify a belief (2 or 6%). **(751)**

Ibid. . . . *showed that,* of 37 (29%) user evaluation forms returned (1 was provided for each of the 126 requests), the following responses were given:

35 (94%) respondents reported they shared the information with their ward team;

34 (92%) respondents reported that the librarian accurately pinpointed the subject in the literature;

and 100% of the respondents felt the response time was

adequate, that the consultation service saved them time (an average of 2.2 hours time saved), and that the consultation service should be continued.   (751)

Special

■ A 1974 survey by the University of Washington Health Sciences Library concerning the impact of the clinical medical librarianship program (2 reference librarians attended hospital rounds in order to provide physicians, students, nurses, etc. specialized literature on patient-related problems) in 2 hospital areas by surveying all staff who had been present on rounds in those areas (Neonatal Intensive Care Unit: survey size: 36; responding: 30 or 83%; Department of Orthopedics: survey size: 26; responding: 15 or 58%) *showed that* 73% of the NICU and 47% of the orthopedics preferred to have the CML present on rounds rather than available full-time within the library.   (710)

Ibid. . . . *showed that* overall response to the program was good, with 100% of the NICU and 93% of the orthopedics "wishing to see the literature service continued." Further, 97% of NICU and 67% of orthopedics reported that the program "was of clinical importance in determining the diagnosis and treatment of patients."   (710)

Ibid. . . . *showed that* 100% of the NICU and 93% of the orthopedics reported that the literature service had saved time for the recipients. Further, 53% of the NICU and 60% of the orthopedics reported that they would have looked the materials up on their own if the CML program had not done so.   (710)

Ibid. . . . *showed that* 97% of the NICU and 87% of the orthopedics reported that their awareness of the Health Sciences Library and its services and resources had increased as as a result of the CML program. Further, 50% of the NICU and 33% of the orthopedics were interested in more exposure to MEDLINE, while 63% of the NICU and 47% of the orthopedics reported an interest in more information on "specialized bibliographic resources and services."   (710)

■ A survey reported in 1978 at the Yale-New Haven Hospital of clinicians concerning their attitudes toward the clinical medical librarian program (4 reference librarians assigned to the departments of pediatrics, psychiatry, internal medicine, and surgery) (survey size: 98 hosptial clinicians; responding: 73 or 74%) *showed that* the program was primarily viewed as education-oriented rather than as supporting patient care.

(723)

Ibid. . . . *showed that* respondents reported that the "information provided was exceptionally relevant" (overall average of 3.45 on a scale of 1-4) and that the literature searches were highly accurate (overall average of 3.48 on a scale of 1-4). (723)

Ibid. . . . *showed that* the degree to which respondents reported that the clinical medical librarian had been integrated into their unit was as follows:

not at all	0 (00%) respondents
slightly	7 (10%) respondents
mostly	36 (49%) respondents
fully	30 (41%) respondents (723)

Ibid. . . . *showed that* the methods by which 73 respondents wished to contact the clinical medical librarian were as follows:

in person at conferences in the hospital	38 (52%) respondents
in person in the library	10 (14%) respondents
by phone	22 (30%) respondents
through a third person	0 (0%) respondents
other (no preference)	3 (4%) respondents (723)

■ A survey/study reported in 1983 at the library of the University of Texas Health Science Center at San Antonio of a 3-month pilot clinical information consultation service (medical staff requested information they needed on a consultation form) *showed that* 126 clinical information consultation requests were received from 17 of the 26 residents on rotation in the medical service at the time. 124 requests were for 1-2 relevant articles, and 2 requests were for short bibliographies. (751)

Ibid. . . . *showed that* library staff spent an average of .9 hours in answering each request, with an average turnaround time of 6 hours.

(751)

Ibid. . . . *showed that* the kinds of articles requested were as follows (multiple responses allowed):

review articles	99 (78.6%) requests	
case reports (with		
literature review)	46 (36.5%) requests	
clinical research	21 (16.7%) requests	
case reports	5 (4.0%) requests	
basic science research	2 (1.6%) requests	**(751)**

Ibid. . . . *showed that*, of 37 (29%) user evaluation forms returned (1 was provided for each of the 126 requests), the 3 reasons given for using the service were: for diagnosis and/or treatment of patients (17 or 46% respondents), to provide general information or a review of a subject (18 or 48%), and to verify a belief (2 or 6%). **(751)**

Ibid. . . . *showed that*, of 37 (29%) user evaluation forms returned (1 was provided for each of the 126 requests), the following responses were given:

35 (94%) respondents reported they shared the information with their ward team;

34 (92%) respondents reported that the librarian accurately pinpointed the subject in the literature;

and 100% of the respondents felt the response time was adequate, that the consultation service saved them time (an average of 2.2 hours time saved), and that the consultation service should be continued. **(751)**

Collection Development

General

■ A report published in 1976 on a statewide Teletype reference service provided by library school students at the University of Iowa in an advanced reference course, involving 460 questions received in the first 6 months of 1974 from college libraries or public library regional centers *showed that* only 36 (7.8%) of the questions were answered using sources listed in *Reference Books for Small and Medium-Sized Libraries* and which theoretically should not have required referral of the question.   **(146)**

■ A study reported in 1978 of the 8th (1967) and 9th (1976) editions of *Guide to Reference Books showed that* the number of Canadian reference works had increased from a total of 113 to a total of 196, for an increase of 73.5%. **(550)**

Public

■ A study reported in 1978 concerning reference performance in Illinois public libraries (population: 530 libraries; sample size: 60; responding: 51 or 85%), using 1 reference librarian from each library to answer 25 test reference questions, *showed that*, based upon an analysis of each library's reference collection, at least 275 reference volumes were required before it was potentially possible to answer correctly 50% of the test reference questions, while at least 1,080 volumes would be required before it was potentially possible to answer correctly 70% of the questions. However, given that reference librarians did not work with 100% efficiency, the data suggests that at least 800 reference volumes would be required to answer 50% or more of the test questions correctly, and at least 2,463 reference volumes would be required to answer 70% or more of the questions correctly. **(259)**

Ibid. . . . *showed that* there was a statistically significant positive correlation (.49 at the .05 significance level) between reference collection size and average percentage of correct answers to the test reference questions, as well as a statistically significant positive correlation (.52 with no significance level given) between reference collection size and potential percentage of correct answers to the test reference questions. Both relationships, however, were shown to be nonlinear; i.e., a point of diminishing returns was reached at about the 3,500-volume point, where increasing the number of reference volumes led to smaller gains in the number of questions correctly answered. **(259)**

Ibid. . . . *showed that* perceived adequateness of size of reference collection was related to both percentage of correctly answered questions (.50 correlation with no significance level given) and percentage of those questions that, given the reference tools available, could have been answered correctly (.57 correlation with no significance level given) in a statistically significant manner. **(259)**

■ A 1980 survey of Canadian public libraries concerning the use and effectiveness (where effectiveness meant reliable, easy to use, clearly written, etc.) of 34 general English-language encyclopedias (survey size: 75 libraries; responding: 57 or 76%) *showed that*, of 54 respondents, 7

(13.0%) reported having a formal or written policy for encyclopedia replacement, while 47 (87.0%) reported they did not have such a policy.

(555)

Costs

Special

■ A study reported in 1980 at the National Library of Medicine concerning work patterns over a 2-month period (involving 8 reference librarians and 1,196 sampling points generated through the use of a random alarm mechanism) *showed that* reference costs were computed to be as follows (based on an average wage of $10.00/hour):

1-step or directional queries	$ .44 each
2-step or quick reference queries	$1.98 each
multiple-step or extended reference queries	$4.57 each **(730)**

Desk Staffing Patterns—Nonprofessional

Academic

■ A survey reported in 1969 of the 54 largest academic libraries in the U.S. with the addition of 7 other libraries from the University of California system and 4 libraries from the California State system (65 libraries total; 53 or 82% responding) *showed that* the number of nonprofessionals working at the reference desk ranged from 0-6 with a mode of 0 and an average of 1.5, while the average number of hours they spent at the reference desk each day ranged from 0-8 with a mode of 0 and an average of 1.6 hours. 29 libraries (55%) reported using nonprofessionals at the reference desk.

(136)

Ibid. . . . *showed that* the number of libraries using nonprofessionals in conjunction with professionals at certain hours was 17 (32%), while the number of libraries using nonprofessionals alone at certain hours was 22 (41%).

(136)

■ A mail survey of large (holdings of 500,000 volumes or more) academic and public libraries in 1972 (sample size: 197; usable returns: 102 academic and 47 public, for a total of 149) *showed that* respondents indicated that, of the time spent at the information desk, on the average 41.9% was taken with professional duties in academic libraries and 42.6% was reported taken with professional duties in public libararies. **(093)**

Ibid. . . . *showed that* 65% of the 48 academic libraries and 53% of the 30 public libraries with information desks reported that a professional librarian was needed at the information desk during the day, while 56% of the academic libraries and 50% of the public libraries reported that a professional librarian was needed during nights and weekends. **(093)**

■ A survey reported in 1975 of a stratified random sample of libraries of accredited 4-year colleges and universities to include small, medium, and large institutions based on student enrollment (sample size: 150; usable responses: 141 or 94%) *showed that* in 69% of the reporting libraries nonprofessionals were used at the reference desk, compared to 31% of the responding libraries that did not use nonprofessionals at the reference desk. No significant difference was found in the proportion of libraries reporting use/nonuse of nonprofessionals by institution size. **(105)**

Ibid. . . . *showed that*, of the nonprofessionals staffing the reference desk, 38% were reference assistants (nonprofessional staff) and 62% student assistants. 63.7% of the reference assistants had a college degree; 16.2% held a junior college degree; and 20.1% held no college degree of any kind. **(105)**

Ibid. . . . *showed that*, in libraries using nonprofesional staff at reference, 67% of the total reference desk hours were staffed by professional librarians, 19% by reference assistants (nonprofessional staff), and 14% by student assistants. **(105)**

■ A survey reported in 1979 of 49 university libraries (48 responding) in the North Central Association of Colleges and Universities *showed that* 58% reported using graduate or undergraduate assistants to help with night and weekend reference service. **(017)**

Public

■ A mail survey of large (holdings of 500,000 volumes or more) academic and public libraries in 1972 (sample size: 197; usable returns: 102 academic and 47 public, for a total of 149) *showed that* respondents indicated that, of the time spent at the information desk, on the average 41.9% was taken with professional duties in academic libraries and 42.6% was reported taken with professional duties in public libararies.   **(093)**

Ibid. . . . *showed that* 65% of the 48 academic libraries and 53% of the 30 public libraries with information desks reported that a professional librarian was needed at the information desk during the day, while 56% of the academic libraries and 50% of the public libraries reported that a professional librarian was needed during nights and weekends.   **(093)**

Desk Staffing Patterns—Professional

Academic

■ A survey reported in 1969 of the 54 largest academic libraries in the U.S. with the addition of 7 other libraries from the University of California system and 4 libraries from the California State system (65 libraries total; 53 or 82% responding) *showed that* the number of professionals working on the reference desk ranged from 2-11 with a mode of 5 and an average of 5.5, while the average number of daily hours each professional spent at the reference desk ranged from 2-8 hours with a mode of 3 hours and an average of 4.5 hours.   **(136)**

Ibid. . . . *showed that* the head of the reference department worked at the desk in 44 of the libraries (83%), with an additional 6 (11%) reporting that the head worked occasionally or in emergencies. The number of hours per day worked ranged from 1-7.5 hours with a mode of 2 and an average of 2.5 hours.   **(136)**

Ibid. . . . *showed that* the number of libraries using nonprofessionals in conjunction with professionals at certain hours was 17 (32%), while the number of libraries using nonprofessionals alone at certain hours was 22 (41%).   **(136)**

■ A mail survey of large (holdings of 500,000 volumes or more) academic and public libraries in 1972 (sample size: 197; usable returns: 102 academic and 47 public, for a total of 149) *showed that* respondents indicated that, of the time spent at the information desk, on the average 41.9% was taken with professional duties in academic libraries and 42.6% was reported taken with professional duties in public libararies.   **(093)**

Ibid. . . . *showed that* 65% of the 48 academic libraries and 53% of the 30 public libraries with information desks reported that a professional librarian was needed at the information desk during the day, while 56% of the academic libraries and 50% of the public libraries reported that a professional librarian was needed during nights and weekends.   **(093)**

■ A survey reported in 1975 of a stratified random sample of libraries of accredited 4-year colleges and universities to include small, medium, and large institutions based on student enrollment (sample size: 150; usable responses: 141 or 94%) *showed that* in 69% of the reporting libraries nonprofessionals were used at the reference desk, compared to 31% of the responding libraries that did not use nonprofessionals at the reference desk. No significant difference was found in the proportion of libraries reporting use/nonuse of nonprofessionals by institution size.   **(105)**

Ibid. . . . *showed that*, in libraries using nonprofesional staff at reference, 67% of the total reference desk hours were staffed by professional librarians, 19% by reference assistants (nonprofessional staff), and 14% by student assistants.   **(105)**

■ A survey reported in 1979 of 49 university libraries (48 responding) in the North Central Association of Colleges and Universities *showed that* 66% have 1 or 2 professionals on duty at night; 17% have 3 on duty; and 8% have from 3 to 7 on duty (6% report the number of professionals on duty at night varies, and 2% have none on duty).   **(017)**

Public

■ A mail survey of large (holdings of 500,000 volumes or more) academic and public libraries in 1972 (sample size: 197; usable returns: 102 academic and 47 public, for a total of 149) *showed that* respondents indicated that, of the time spent at the information desk, on the average 41.9% was taken with professional duties in academic libraries and 42.6% was reported taken with professional duties in public libararies.   **(093)**

Ibid. . . . *showed that* 65% of the 48 academic libraries and 53% of the 30 public libraries with information desks reported that a professional librarian was needed at the information desk during the day, while 56% of the academic libraries and 50% of the public libraries reported that a professional librarian was needed during nights and weekends.   **(093)**

Evaluation

General

■ A report published in 1976 on a statewide Teletype reference service provided by library school students at the University of Iowa in an advanced reference course, involving 460 questions received in the first 6 months of 1974 from college libraries or public library regional centers *showed that* 61% of the questions were answered completely successfully; 13% received nearly complete answers; 10% of the answers may have been minimally useful to the patron; and for 16% there were no available answers.   **(146)**

Ibid. . . . *showed that* only 36 (7.8%) of the questions were answered using sources listed in *Reference Books for Small and Medium-Sized Libraries* and which theoretically should not have required referral of the question.
                                                                      (146)

Academic

■ A report in 1974 on a statewide Teletype reference service provided by library school students at the University of Iowa in an advanced reference course, involving 460 questions received from college libraries or public library regional centers *showed that* 61% of the questions were answered completely successfully; 13% received nearly complete answers; 10% of the answers may have been minimally useful to the patron; and for 16% there were no available answers.   **(146)**

■ A study of reference questions (sample size: 5,588) encountered at the University of Nebraska, Omaha, during academic year 1975-76 *showed that* carefully trained nonprofessionals could competently answer 80% of the questions.   **(005)**

■ A study reported in 1977 comparing the performance of a reference unit staffed with nonprofessionals with that of a reference unit staffed with professionals, each in a different library in 2 medium-sized midwestern universities, *showed that*, of 25 questions deliberately containing faulty information, the professional librarians obtained correct information in 13 (52%) cases by themselves and in 15 (67%) cases with the help of referral or consultation. This compares to nonprofessionals, who obtained correct informtion in 5 (20%) cases by themselves and in 7 (28%) cases with the help of referral or consultation. **(456)**

Ibid. . . . *showed that*, of 21 deliberately indirect questions, professionals correctly solved 19 (90.5%), while nonprofessionals correctly solved 13 (61.9%). **(456)**

Public

■ A 1977-78 study of reference performance in the Suffolk Cooperative Library System involving a total of 57 libraries and branches, using a procedure of hidden testing consisting of proxies asking 20 identical reference questions at each library or branch over a period of 6 months for a total of 1,110 [sic] queries *showed that* about 56% of the time an actual answer was given the proxy; i.e., the proxy was given a document, fact, or citation. **(238)**

Ibid. . . . *showed that* "about 17%" of the time library respondents provided neither an answer to a query nor an idea where the proxy could find it. **(238)**

Ibid. . . . *showed that*, of the 56% of the queries to which library respondents gave actual answers, 84% of the time the answer was "correct" or "mostly correct." **(238)**

Ibid. . . . *showed that*, when special queries designed to test library respondents' willingness to negotiate the proxy's initial inquiry were posed, 67% of the library respondents made no effort to probe for the proxy's underlying need, while "about 20%" of the respondents did negotiate the query to its ultimate level. **(238)**

■ A study reported in 1978 concerning reference performance in Illinois public libraries (population: 530 libraries; sample size: 60; responding: 51

or 85%), using 1 reference librarian from each library to answer 25 test reference questions, *showed that* an average of 59% of the questions were answered correctly, with a range of 20% to 96%. Upon analysis of each library's reference collection and considering only those questions for which the library had appropriate sources, an average of 78% were answered correctly, with a range of 50% to 100%.   **(259)**

Ibid. . . . *showed that*, based upon an analysis of each library's reference collection, the potential range for answering the test questions with local tools ran from 20% to 100% with an overall average of 76%.   **(259)**

Ibid. . . . *showed that* contrary to expectation the reference experience of respondents at their present libraries was not correlated in a statistically significant way with either the percentage of test reference questions answered correctly or the percentage of questions which, given the reference tools available, could have been answered correctly. In fact, the slight direction of the relationship that did occur was negative.   **(259)**

Ibid. . . . *showed that* the correlation between the number of reference questions answered per week and the percentage of test reference questions answered correctly by respondent was strong ($r = .52$) and statistically significant (significance level not given). There was also a statistically significant relationship between number of reference questions answered per week and the percentage of test questions that, given the reference tools available, could have been answered correctly (strength and significance level not given).   **(259)**

Ibid. . . . *showed that* the percentage of test reference questions answered correctly and the percentage of questions that, given the reference tools available, could have been answered correctly did not correlate in a statistically significant way with either age of respondents or total length of reference experience, although the direction of this latter relationship was slightly negative.   **(259)**

Ibid. . . . *showed that* perceived adequateness of size of reference collection was related to both percentage of correctly answered questions ($r = .50$ with no significance level given) and percentage of those questions that, given the reference tools available, could have been answered correctly ($r = .57$ with no significance level given) in a statistically significant manner.   **(259)**

■ A 1981 comparison of obtrusive versus unobtrusive evaluation of reference services in 5 Illinois public libraries serving populations from 10,000 to 100,000, involving 15 obtrusive questions and 9-15 unobtrusive questions in each of the libraries *showed that* 85% of the obtrusive questions were answered completely and correctly, with a range among the 5 libraries of 67% to 100%, while 70% of the unobtrusive questions were answered completely and correctly, with a range of 33% to 92%. These differences were statistically significant at the .05 level.
(268)

Ibid. . . . *showed that* the following percentages of complete and correct answers were given in 7 unobtrusive studies: 54, 55, 40, 40, 50, 47, 70. The percentages of complete and correct answers given in 4 obtrusive studies were as follows: 50, 64, 59, and 85.
(268)

General Issues

Academic

■ A 1967 survey of medical school libraries concerning reference services (survey size: 93 libraries; responding: 85 or 91.4%) *showed that* 65 (76.5%) libraries reported that the reference department assumed "some degree of responsibility for book selection [presumably general, rather than reference book selection]," while 20 (23.5%) libraries reported no such responsibility.
(682)

Public

■ An informal survey in 1962 of the 50 state library extension agencies (38 responding) to assess trends of library service since 1954 *showed that* the 1 trend to which all respondents agreed was a movement away from the traditional emphasis on recreational reading to an increasing recognition of the importance of reference and informational services. The next highest rated trend was movement away from dependence on a limited library staff to provide all programming toward involving more community people in the library's program. The third highest was a trend away from local self-sufficiency toward greater intrastate library co-operation.
(063)

Special

■ A 1967 survey of medical school libraries concerning reference services (survey size: 93 libraries; responding: 85 or 91.4%) *showed that* 65 (76.5%) libraries reported that the reference department assumed "some degree of responsibility for book selection [presumably general, rather than reference book selection]," while 20 (23.5%) libraries reported no such responsibility.   **(682)**

Hours of Service

Academic

■ A 1967 survey of the 73 ARL members concerning their use of information desks (61 or 83.7% responding; 37 usable responses due to their reporting the presence of information desks) *showed that* 27 libraries reported staffing with librarians; 7 reported staffing with library assistants; and 3 reported staffing with clerical employees. Of these, 9 libraries reported staffing with 1 person on a full-time basis, while 28 reported personnel alternating hours. The average length of daily service was reported as 9 hours.   **(192)**

■ A 1967 survey of medical school libraries concerning reference services (survey size: 93 libraries; responding: 85 or 91.4%) *showed that* the libraries were open an average of 87.9 hours per week and provided reference services an average of 53.8 hours per week.   **(682)**

■ A survey reported in 1969 of the 54 largest academic libraries in the U.S. with the addition of 7 other libraries from the University of California system and 4 libraries from the California State system (65 libraries total; 53 or 82% responding) *showed that* night, weekend, or holiday reference work was expected in 37 libraries (70%), was scheduled only in emergencies in 5 (9%) libraries and not at all in 8 (15%) libraries.   **(136)**

■ A mail survey of large (holdings of 500,000 volumes or more) academic and public libraries in 1972 (sample size: 197; usable returns: 102 academic and 47 public, for a total of 149) *showed that*, of the 48 academic libraries with information desks, 98% staff the desk during the day, 73% during evenings, and 73% during weekends, while of the 30 public libraries 100%

staff the desk during the day, 97% staff during evenings, and 97% staff during weekends. **(093)**

Ibid. . . . *showed that* respondents indicated that, of the time spent at the information desk, on the average 41.9% was taken with professional duties in academic libraries and 42.6% was reported taken with professional duties in public libararies. **(093)**

Ibid. . . . *showed that* 65% of the 48 academic libraries and 53% of the 30 public libraries with information desks reported that a professional librarian was needed at the information desk during the day, while 56% of the academic libraries and 50% of the public libraries reported that a professional librarian was needed during nights and weekends. **(093)**

■ A random sampling of 196 public and private academic libraries in 4-year institutions (responding: 169) reported in 1974 *showed that* responding libraries were open an average of 90.3 hours a week, with a range of 114 hours to 56 hours a week. Of 159 responses to the question of evening professional staffing, 120 libraries (75%) reported professional staff were on duty until 10:00 p.m., while 25 libraries (16%) reported professional staff were on duty until 11:00 p.m. **(095)**

Public

■ A mail survey of large (holdings of 500,000 volumes or more) academic and public libraries in 1972 (sample size: 197; usable returns: 102 academic and 47 public, for a total of 149) *showed that*, of the 48 academic libraries with information desks, 98% staffed the desk during the day, 73% during evenings, and 73% during weekends, while of the 30 public libraries 100% staffed the desk during the day, 97% staffed during evenings, and 97% staffed during weekends. **(093)**

Ibid. . . . *showed that* respondents indicated that, of the time spent at the information desk, on the average 41.9% was taken with professional duties in academic libraries and 42.6% was reported taken with professional duties in public libararies. **(093)**

Ibid. . . . *showed that* 65% of the 48 academic libraries and 53% of the 30 public libraries with information desks reported that a professional librarian was needed at the information desk during the day, while 56% of the academic libraries and 50% of the public libraries reported that a professional librarian was needed during nights and weekends.   **(093)**

■ A random sampling of 196 public and private academic libraries in 4-year institutions (responding: 169) reported in 1974 *showed that* responding libraries were open an average of 90.3 hours a week, with a range of 114 hours to 56 hours a week. Of 159 responses to the question of evening professional staffing, 120 libraries (75%) reported professional staff were on duty until 10:00 p.m., while 25 libraries (16%) reported professional staff were on duty until 11:00 p.m.   **(095)**

Special

■ A 1967 survey of medical school libraries concerning reference services (survey size: 93 libraries; responding: 85 or 91.4%) *showed that* the libraries were open an average of 87.9 hours per week and provided reference services an average of 53.8 hours per week.   **(682)**

In-Service Training

Academic

■ A survey of a stratified random sample of libraries of accredited 4-year colleges and universities to include small, medium, and large institutions based on student enrollment (sample size: 150; usable responses: 141 or 94%) *showed that* of the responding libraries more than 80% reported that no formal in-service training was provided for the nonprofessional reference staff. However, 70% of responding libraries indicated that nonprofessionals could take classes during the working day (time had to be made up in 1/2 of those cases); 51% of the libraries indicated that tuition waivers were given nonprofessionals taking classes; and 74% of the libraries reported that nonprofessionals could attend professional library meetings during the working day.   **(105)**

Information Desks—General Issues

Academic

■ A 1967 survey of the 73 ARL members concerning their use of information desks (61 or 83.7% responding; 37 usable responses due to their reporting the presence of information desks) *showed that* 29 libraries reported providing simple telephone reference service at the information desk; 19 libraries reported that the information desk is responsible for public relations duties such as conducting tours, speaking to groups on library orientation, etc.; and 15 libraries reported no reference books were kept at the information desk, while 10 reported more than 100 books were kept at the information desk. **(192)**

■ A mail survey of large (holdings of 500,000 volumes or more) academic and public libraries in 1972 (sample size: 197; usable returns: 102 academic and 47 public, for a total of 149) *showed that*, of the 48 academic libraries with information desks, 98% staffed the desk during the day, 73% during evenings, and 73% during weekends, while of the 30 public libraries 100% staffed the desk during the day, 97% staffed during evenings, and 97% staffed during weekends. **(093)**

Ibid. . . . *showed that* respondents indicated that, of the time spent at the information desk, on the average 41.9% was taken with professional duties in academic libraries and 42.6% was reported taken with professional duties in public libararies. **(093)**

Ibid. . . . *showed that* 65% of the 48 academic libraries and 53% of the 30 public libraries with information desks reported that a professional librarian was needed at the information desk during the day, while 56% of the academic libraries and 50% of the public libraries reported that a professional librarian was needed during nights and weekends. **(093)**

Ibid. . . . *showed that* a larger percentage (64%) of public libraries had information desks than academic libraries (47%). **(093)**

Ibid. . . . *showed that* there was a statistically significant positive correlation at the .01 level for academic libraries and at the .10 [not generally accepted as statistically significant] level for public libraries between information desks and a decentralized system of reference. **(093)**

Ibid. . . . *showed that* 66% of the 48 academic libraries with information desks and 47% of the 30 public libraries with information desks also staffed general reference desks, while 27% of the academic libraries and 50% of the public libraries with information also had catalog assistance desks. **(093)**

Public

■   A mail survey of large (holdings of 500,000 volumes or more) academic and public libraries in 1972 (sample size: 197; usable returns: 102 academic and 47 public, for a total of 149) *showed that*, of the 48 academic libraries with information desks, 98% staffed the desk during the day, 73% during evenings, and 73% during weekends, while of the 30 public libraries 100% staffed the desk during the day, 97% staffed during evenings, and 97% staffed during weekends.   **(093)**

Ibid. . . . *showed that* there was a statistically significant positive correlation at the .01 level for academic libraries and at the .10 [not generally accepted as statistically significant] level for public libraries between information desks and a decentralized system of reference.   **(093)**

Ibid. . . . *showed that* respondents indicated that, of the time spent at the information desk, on the average 41.9% was taken with professional duties in academic libraries and 42.6% was reported taken with professional duties in public libararies.   **(093)**

Ibid. . . . *showed that* 65% of the 48 academic libraries and 53% of the 30 public libraries with information desks reported that a professional librarian was needed at the information desk during the day, while 56% of the academic libraries and 50% of the public libraries reported that a professional librarian was needed during nights and weekends.   **(093)**

Ibid. . . . *showed that* a larger percentage (64%) of public libraries had information desks than academic libraries (47%).   **(093)**

Ibid. . . . *showed that* 66% of the 48 academic libraries with information desks and 47% of the 30 public libraries with information desks also staffed general reference desks, while 27% of the academic libraries and 50% of the public libraries with information also had catalog assistance desks.
                                                                        (093)

Information Desks—Staffing Patterns, Nonprofessional

Academic

■ A 1967 survey of the 73 ARL members concerning their use of information desks (61 or 83.7% responding; 37 usable responses due to their reporting the presence of information desks) *showed that* 27 libraries reported staffing with librarians; 7 reported staffing with library assistants; and 3 reported staffing with clerical employees. Of these, 9 libraries reported staffing with 1 person on a full-time basis, while 28 reported personnel alternating hours. The average length of daily service was reported as 9 hours. **(192)**

Information Desks—Staffing Patterns, Professional

Academic

■ A 1967 survey of the 73 ARL members concerning their use of information desks (61 or 83.7% responding; 37 usable responses due to their reporting the presence of information desks) *showed that* 27 libraries reported staffing with librarians; 7 reported staffing with library assistants; and 3 reported staffing with clerical employees. Of these, 9 libraries reported staffing with 1 person on a full-time basis, while 28 reported personnel alternating hours. The average length of daily service was reported as 9 hours. **(192)**

Innovative Services

Academic

■ A 1975-77 study of the use of a drug information service (including closed-circuit TV capability for sending answers) originating from the Health Sciences Library at the University of Cincinnati to provide information about drugs, chemicals, and poisons to health professionals in 14 local hospitals (2,294 questions researched; TV used to help provide the answer in 460 instances) *showed that* types of users were as follows:

pharmacists accounted for 31.3% of the total queries and 29.3% of the queries with a TV response;

physicians accounted for 25.8% of the total queries and 22.6% of the queries with a TV response;

nurses accounted for 21.2% of the total queries and 24.8% of the queries with a TV response;

medical students accounted for 2.4% of the total queries and 3.5% of the queries with a TV response;

"other" accounted for 22.0% of the total queries and 24.1% of the queries with a TV response.   **(422)**

Ibid. . . . *showed that* the 3 main uses of the drug information system were to: select patient treatment approach (50.0% of all cases; 57.6% of the cases where TV response was used), explain observations in a patient (15.2% of all cases; 15.7% of the cases where TV response was used), and add to personal knowledge (13.0% of all cases; 9.2% of the cases where TV response was used).   **(422)**

Ibid. . . . *showed that* the time needed to provide an answer to the requester using TV transmission was under 5 minutes in 54.6% of the cases, 5-15 minutes in 30.0% of the cases, and more than 15 minutes in 15.4% of the cases.   **(422)**

Ibid. . . . *showed that*, of 523 questions studied, the librarian and the pharmacologist staffing the drug information service judged that 67% of the questions could have been handled by either person, 26% required the expertise of the pharmacologist, 2% required the expertise of the librarian, and 5% the cooperative efforts of both.   **(422)**

Ibid. . . . *showed that* 79% of the information providers rated the contribution of the television medium as "excellent" or "good," while 74% of the information users rated the television medium as "essential" or "very useful."   **(422)**

Ibid. . . . *showed that* information users rated the information received as "very helpful" in 75.9% of the cases, as "satisfactory" in 19.9% of the cases, and as "poor" in 4.2% of the cases.   **(422)**

■ A survey reported in 1978 at the University of Texas Medical Branch (Galveston) of the popularity of various elements of an in-house library publication as rated by UTMB faculty members (survey size: 489 faculty; responding: 295 or 60%) *showed that* the popularity of elements was as follows (in descending order of popularity):

1. new acquisitions
2. faculty publications
3. historical article
4. news and notes
5. meet our staff

Further, of the 4 faculty ranks the faculty rank most interested in the historical article was "full professors." **(721)**

■ A study and survey reported in 1983 to investigate the need for medical library services among rural physicians in southeastern Kentucky using a control group who were provided no special services (survey size: 60 physicians; responding: 36 or 60%) and an experimental group whose local technicians were provided special training in the use of basic library reference sources and whose physicians were provided with a toll-free number allowing access to the library services of the University of Kentucky's medical library (survey size: 33 physicians; responding: 29 or 89%) *showed that* there was a statistically significant difference between the 2 groups in their perception of how easy it was to access journal articles. Specifically, "all physicians in the experimental group reported that it was easy or very easy to obtain journal articles." In the control group, only 57% of the physicians reported that journal articles were easy or very easy to obtain, while 14% reported it was difficult and 20% reported it was very difficult. (Significant at the .05 level or better.) **(744)**

Ibid. . . . *showed that* there was a statistically significant difference between the 2 groups in their reports of how quickly they received materials. Specifically, 95% of the experimental group reported they received requested materials quickly enough to be useful either "most often" or "usually," compared to 70% of the control groups so reporting (significant at the .05 level). **(744)**

Ibid. . . . *showed that* the library service provided to the experimental group was generally reported to be satisfactory. 90% of the respondents reported themselves "very satisfied" or "satisfied," while only 3.3% reported "dissatisfied" and 6.7% reported "don't know." **(744)**

■ A survey/study reported in 1983 at the library of the University of Texas Health Science Center at San Antonio of a 3-month pilot clinical information consultation service (medical staff requested information they needed on a consultation form) *showed that* 126 clinical information consultation requests were received from 17 of the 26 residents on rotation in the medical service at the time. 124 requests were for 1-2 relevant articles, and 2 requests were for short bibliographies.   **(751)**

Ibid. . . . *showed that* library staff spent an average of .9 hours in answering each request, with an average turnaround time of 6 hours.
(751)

Ibid. . . . *showed that* the kinds of articles requested were as follows (multiple responses allowed):

review articles	99 (78.6%) requests	
case reports (with literature review)	46 (36.5%) requests	
clinical research	21 (16.7%) requests	
case reports	5 (4.0%) requests	
basic science research	2 (1.6%) requests	**(751)**

Ibid. . . . *showed that*, of 37 (29%) user evaluation forms returned (1 was provided for each of the 126 requests), the 3 reasons given for using the service were: for diagnosis and/or treatment of patients (17 or 46% respondents), to provide general information or a review of a subject (18 or 48%), and to verify a belief (2 or 6%).   **(751)**

Ibid. . . . *showed that*, of 37 (29%) user evaluation forms returned (1 was provided for each of the 126 requests), the following responses were given:

35 (94%) respondents reported they shared the information with their ward team;

34 (92%) respondents reported that the librarian accurately pinpointed the subject in the literature;

and 100% of the respondents felt the response time was adequate, that the consultation service saved them time (an average of 2.2 hours time saved), and that the consultation service should be continued.   **(751)**

Special

■ A 1975-77 study of the use of a drug information service (including closed-circuit TV capability for sending answers) originating from the Health Sciences Library at the University of Cincinnati to provide information about drugs, chemicals, and poisons to health professionals in 14 local hospitals (2,294 questions researched; TV used to help provide the answer in 460 instances) *showed that* types of users were as follows:

pharmacists accounted for 31.3% of the total queries and 29.3% of the queries with a TV response;

physicians accounted for 25.8% of the total queries and 22.6% of the queries with a TV response;

nurses accounted for 21.2% of the total queries and 24.8% of the queries with a TV response;

medical students accounted for 2.4% of the total queries and 3.5% of the queries with a TV response;

"other" accounted for 22.0% of the total queries and 24.1% of the queries with a TV response. **(422)**

Ibid. . . . *showed that* the 3 main uses of the drug information system were to: select patient treatment approach (50.0% of all cases; 57.6% of the cases where TV response was used), explain observations in a patient (15.2% of all cases; 15.7% of the cases where TV response was used), and add to personal knowledge (13.0% of all cases; 9.2% of the cases where TV response was used). **(422)**

Ibid. . . . *showed that* the time needed to provide an answer to the requester using TV transmission was under 5 minutes in 54.6% of the cases, 5-15 minutes in 30.0% of the cases, and more than 15 minutes in 15.4% of the cases. **(422)**

Ibid. . . . *showed that*, of 523 questions studied, the librarian and the pharmacologist staffing the drug information service judged that 67% of the questions could have been handled by either person, 26% required the expertise of the pharmacologist, 2% required the expertise of the librarian, and 5% the cooperative efforts of both. **(422)**

Ibid. . . . *showed that* 79% of the information providers rated the contribution of the television medium as "excellent" or "good," while 74% of the information users rated the television medium as "essential" or "very useful." **(422)**

Ibid. . . . *showed that* information users rated the information received as "very helpful" in 75.9% of the cases, as "satisfactory" in 19.9% of the cases, and as "poor" in 4.2% of the cases. **(422)**

■ A survey reported in 1978 at the University of Texas Medical Branch (Galveston) of the popularity of various elements of an in-house library publication as rated by UTMB faculty members (survey size: 489 faculty; responding: 295 or 60%) *showed that* the popularity of elements was as follows (in descending order of popularity):

1. new acquisitions
2. faculty publications
3. historical article
4. news and notes
5. meet our staff

Further, of the 4 faculty ranks, the faculty rank most interested in the historical article was "full professors."   **(721)**

■ A 1979 study and survey of physicians in nonmetropolitan areas of the Pacific Northwest who were offered an opportunity to receive, without charge, table of contents pages from 18 journals relating to cancer research as well as the option to request a photocopy of any article of interest identified through the service (1-day turnaround guaranteed) (study and survey size: 126 physicians, including 63 randomly selected physicians and 63 physicians identified as having a special interest in cancer research and patient care) *showed that* 18 (29%) of the randomly selected physicians chose to participate in the service, while 31 (49%) of the physicians with a special interest in cancer chose to participate.   **(735)**

Ibid. . . . *showed that* a small core of physicians in both groups made very active use of the service. Of the 31 physicians with a special interest in cancer issues who chose to participate in the service, 11 (35%) requested articles, while of the 18 randomly selected physicians who chose to participate in the service, 9 (50%) requested articles. Nevertheless, in a 6-month period 419 articles were requested by those who did request articles.   **(735)**

Ibid. . . . *showed that*, of the 419 articles requested, the 4 most frequently requested subject areas (out of 6) were as follows:

treatment/survival	230 (54.9%) articles
disease description/reviews	55 (13.1%) articles
laboratory/biologic/basic research	52 (12.5%) articles
epidemiology/occurrence/risk factors/etiology	50 (11.9%) articles **(735)**

Ibid. . . . *showed that,* of 56 physicians who had not responded to the original offer of the service but who did respond to a subsequent survey 6 months later, the reasons for not participating were as follows:

access to the journals elsewhere	38% physicians	
did not receive the letter offering the service (conjecture: thrown out by staff before seen by physician)	38% physicians	
too busy	16% physicians	
seldom saw cancer patients	9% physicians	**(735)**

Ibid. . . . *showed that,* of the 29 physicians who participated in the service but who did not request articles (96% did respond to a subsequent survey 6 months later), the following reasons were given for not requesting articles:

access to the journals elsewhere	11 (40%) physicians	
saw no journals of interest	8 (30%) physicians	
too busy	6 (22%) physicians	
seldom saw cancer patients	2 (7%) physicians	**(735)**

Ibid. . . . *showed that,* of the 18 physicians who participated in the service and requested articles and responded to a subsequent survey 6 months later, "at least half" read the articles they received in detail and "three-quarters" kept the article for future reference. Further, 17 of the 18 respondents thought that the service should be continued. **(735)**

Ibid. . . . *showed that,* including salaries, office supplies, mailing costs, and photocopying costs over the 6-month period, the average cost per person receiving tables of contents was $33.00 for the 6-month period; the average cost per person receiving articles was $80.00 for the 6-month period; and the average cost per article supplied during this time was $3.82. **(735)**

■ A study and survey reported in 1983 to investigate the need for medical library services among rural physicians in southeastern Kentucky, using a control group who were provided no special services (survey size: 60 physicians; responding: 36 or 60%) and an experimental group whose local technicians were provided special training in the use of basic library reference sources and whose physicians were provided with a toll-free number allowing access to the library services of the University of Kentucky's medical library (survey size: 33 physicians; responding: 29 or 89%) *showed that* there was a statistically significant difference between the 2 groups in their perception of how easy it was to access journal articles. Specifically, "all physicians in the experimental group reported that it was easy or very easy to obtain journal articles." In the control group, only 57% of the physicians reported that journal articles were easy or very easy to obtain, while 14% reported it was difficult and 20% reported it was very difficult. (Significant at the .05 level or better.)

(744)

Ibid. . . . *showed that* there was a statistically significant difference between the 2 groups in their reports of how quickly they received materials. Specifically, 95% of the experimental group reported they received requested materials quickly enough to be useful either "most often" or "usually," compared to 70% of the control groups so reporting (significant at the .05 level). **(744)**

Ibid. . . . *showed that* the library service provided to the experimental group was generally reported to be satisfactory. 90% of the respondents reported themselves "very satisfied" or "satisfied," while only 3.3% reported "dissatisfied" and 6.7% reported "don't know." **(744)**

■ A survey/study reported in 1983 at the library of the University of Texas Health Science Center at San Antonio of a 3-month pilot clinical information consultation service (medical staff requested information they needed on a consultation form) *showed that* 126 clinical information consultation requests were received from 17 of the 26 residents on rotation in the medical service at the time. 124 requests were for 1-2 relevant articles, and 2 requests were for short bibliographies. **(751)**

Ibid. . . . *showed that* library staff spent an average of .9 hours in answering each request, with an average turnaround time of 6 hours.

(751)

Ibid. . . . *showed that* the kinds of articles requested were as follows (multiple responses allowed) :

review articles	99 (78.6%) requests
case reports (with literature review)	46 (36.5%) requests
clinical research	21 (16.7%) requests
case reports	5 (4.0%) requests
basic science research	2 (1.6%) requests **(751)**

Ibid. . . . *showed that*, of 37 (29%) user evaluation forms returned (1 was provided for each of the 126 requests), the 3 reasons given for using the service were: for diagnosis and/or treatment of patients (17 or 46% respondents), to provide general information or a review of a subject (18 or 48%), and to verify a belief (2 or 6%). **(751)**

Ibid. . . . *showed that*, of 37 (29%) user evaluation forms returned (1 was provided for each of the 126 requests), the following responses were given:

35 (94%) respondents reported they shared the information with their ward team;

34 (92%) respondents reported that the librarian accurately pinpointed the subject in the literature;

and 100% of the respondents felt the response time was adequate, that the consultation service saved them time (an average of 2.2 hours time saved), and that the consultation service should be continued. **(751)**

Job Satisfaction

Academic

■ A comparison reported in 1978 of catalog and reference librarians in 91 university libraries in terms of overall job satisfaction *showed that* there was no statistically significant difference between the two groups. **(009)**

Ibid. . . . *showed that* there were statistically significant differences in 3 of 20 areas. Reference librarians were more satisfied in terms of creativity, social service, and variety than catalogers. **(009)**

■ A survey reported in 1983 of reference librarians in 75 U.S. universities with enrollments exceeding 20,000 (survey size: 380; responding: 262 or 69%) *showed that*, based on the Forbes Burnout Survey, reference librarians in academic libraries did not seem to have a burnout problem. Specifically, results of the Burnout Survey showed the following results:

librarians with burnout	none
librarians with mild burnout	1% of total
librarians who were candidates for burnout	12% of total
librarians with burnout under control	87% of total **(789)**

Length of Shift

Academic

■ A survey reported in 1969 of the 54 largest academic libraries in the U.S. with the addition of 7 other libraries from the University of California system and 4 libraries from the California State system (65 libraries total; 53 or 82% responding) *showed that* the number of professionals working on the reference desk ranged from 2-11 with a mode of 5 and an average of 5.5, while the average number of daily hours each professional spent at the reference desk ranged from 2-8 hours with a mode of 3 hours and an average of 4.5 hours.   **(136)**

Ibid. . . . *showed that* the number of nonprofessionals working at the reference desk ranged from 0-6 with a mode of 0 and an average of 1.5, while the average number of hours they spent at the reference desk each day ranged from 0-8 with a mode of 0 and an average of 1.6 hours. 29 libraries (55%) reported using nonprofessionals at the reference desk.
(136)

Ibid. . . . *showed that* the head of the reference department worked at the desk in 44 of the libraries (83%), with an additional 6 (11%) reporting that the head worked occasionally or in emergencies. The number of hours per day worked ranged from 1-7.5 hours with a mode of 2 and an average of 2.5 hours.   **(136)**

Online Searching—General Issues

General

■ A 1976 survey of RASD members (population: 4,062; sample size: 738; usable responses: 542 or 73.4%), concerning their attitudes towards automated information retrieval services *showed that* 61% of the respondents felt that automated information retrieval services should not be offered if no new funding were available, while 19% replied that it should be offered even if no new funding were available and 17% were undecided.
(148)

Ibid. . . . *showed that* the 3 greatest barriers to developing automated information retrieval sources in libraries reported by respondents were costs (88.2%), lack of trained library personnel (51.1%), and overworked staff (49.6%). **(148)**

Ibid. . . . *showed that* 15 (2.8%) respondents reported no personal involvement with such services; 291 (53.6%) had read about them or seen them demonstrated; 86 (15.9%) had used them in a trial mode; and 79 (14.6%) had used or are currently using one or more online services. **(148)**

Ibid. . . . *showed that* respondents felt that online, interactive access to automated bibliographic data bases should be offered in the following library departments: general reference or reader services (58.3%), separate unit devoted exclusively to such a service (19%), ILL unit (9.2%), subject branches (5.5%). **(148)**

■ A 12-month study of 1977-78 of online bibliographic literature searching of MINET (Kansas City Libraries Metropolitan Information Network, which includes 4 public libraries, 3 medical libraries, and 1 academic medical library), involving 403 paid search sessions and searches of 544 files or data bases, *showed that*, of 544 data bases searched, 229 (42%) had all citations printed online, while 315 (58%) had at least some citations printed offline. **(234)**

Academic

■ A 14-month study during 1972-73 at the Yale Medical Library (serving the Yale University School of Medicine, the Yale University School of Nursing, and the Yale-New Haven Hospital), involving 1,466 online search requests (MEDLINE) from 455 different individuals for the faculty and professional staff of the Yale-New Haven Medical Center, *showed that* the purposes of the requests were as follows:

research	1,140 (77.8%)	search requests
patient care	221 (15.0%)	search requests
education	105 (7.2%)	search requests	**(714)**

Ibid. . . . *showed that* the grant dollars received by departments were positively correlated with the number of comprehensive online searches generated by those departments ($r = .44$) and negatively correlated with the number of narrow searches processed by the departments ($i = -.44$) (significant at the .05 level). **(714)**

■ A 1975-76 study at the University of Utah Marriott Library of online bibliographic data base searching *showed that* a survey of 26 patrons using the online searching service revealed that (multiple responses allowed): 10 (32%) discovered the service through a librarian, 10 (32%) through a colleague, 7 (23%) through library fliers, 2 (6%) through campus news media, and 3 (9%) through other means. **(329)**

Ibid. . . . *showed that* a survey of 26 patrons using online bibliographic search services revealed that 18 (69%) desired search updates, 2 (8%) did not, and 6 (23%) were uncertain. **(329)**

■ A study reported in 1977, comparing an automatic algorithm that rank ordered the citations retrieved in 12 online bibliographic searches (using the Syracuse Information Retrieval Experiment system, SIRE) with the rank ordering of the citations by faculty and advanced physics students requesting the searches *showed that* the automatic algorithm was successful in moving an average document "about one-third of the way from its random location towards its perfect location" in a rank ordering of the citations. **(616)**

■ A study reported in 1977 by the University of Oklahoma Health Sciences Center Library of the literature searches performed during a 3-year period (1973-75) for physicians and fourth-year medical students serving a 5-week "preceptorship" with a rural physician (1,775 searches) *showed that* for both the physicians and students the subject category of most requests was "Diseases" (66% of the physicians' searches; 84% of the students' searches), while the subject category of the next most requests for both groups was "Chemicals and Drugs" (27.2% of the physicians' searches; 27.6% of the students' searches). **(716)**

■ A survey reported in 1977 by the University of Oklahoma Health Sciences Center Library to investigate the relationship between subjects for which physicians had requested literature searches and subjects for which physicians desired continuing education, based on a physician population that had requested at least 1 literature search from the Health Sciences Library during 1973-75 (survey size: 396 physicians; responding: 125 or 31.5%) *showed that* "literature searches alone could not be used to determine CME [continuing medical education] topics." Specifically, the 5 most frequently mentioned topics for CME and the 5 topics for which the most literature searches had been requested had only 3 (60%) topics in common. **(717)**

■ A survey reported in 1977 concerning online searching at the U.S. Army Construction Engineering Research Laboratory library (Cham-

paign, Illinois) and involving both users of the service (sample size: 27; responding: 26 or 96.3%) and nonusers of the service (sample size: 19; responding: 13 or 68.4%) *showed that*, of 25 user respondents, 7 (28%) indicated an interest in periodic update searches on their research topic, 11 (44%) indicated they would not, and 7 (28%) indicated they were uncertain. **(416)**

■ An analysis of records reported in 1978 on online bibliographic data base searching at Flordia State University Chemistry Department and Monsanto Textiles Company in Pensacola, Florida (353 searches conducted at FSU and 345 conducted at Monsanto) *showed that* the type of approach to the online search differed in a statistically significant way between FSU and Monsanto (significance level .001) in that 50% of the FSU searches were exhaustive (i.e., wanted everything available) compared to 33% at Monsanto, while 14% of the FSU searches wished specific facts or procedures compared to 39% of the Monsanto searches. **(155)**

Ibid. . . . *showed that* anticipated use of the search results between FSU and Monsanto differed in some statistically significant ways. 53% of the FSU searches compared to 41% of the Monsanto searches were to keep current in the researchers own field (significance level .002); 17% of the FSU searches compared to 10% of the Monsanto searches were to keep current in fields related to the researcher's field (significance level .02); 25% of the FSU searches compared to 53% of the Monsanto searches were concerned with procedures, apparatus, or methodology to support an ongoing project (significance level .001); and 33% of the FSU searches compared to 5% of the Monsanto searches were for papers for external dissemination (significance level .001). **(155)**

■ A 1978 survey of North American health sciences libraries that were users of the National Library of Medicine search services in November 1977 (survey size: 708 libraries; responding: 376; usable: 345 or 48.7%) *showed that* different types of health science libraries have offered online searches of NLM files, as follows:

in professional schools	5.0 years
in societies, foundations, and research institutes	3.5 years
in hospitals	3.2 years
in other colleges, universities, and commercial firms	3.0 years
in "other" (including, NLM, CISTI, state library, etc.)	4.8 years **(724)**

Ibid. . . . *showed that* online search services in addition to those offered by
the National Library of Medicine were provided by 199 (58%) respondents. Such additional services were provided by the following types of
institutions:

colleges and universities	91% of these libraries
commercial firms	88% of these libraries
professional schools	74% of these libraries
societies, foundations, and	
research institutes	60% of these libraries
hospitals	22% of these libraries
other	60% of these libraries **(724)**

■ A 1978 survey of publicly supported California libraries (primarily
public and academic) concerning fee-charging behavior for online bibliographic searching (survey size: 350 libraries; responding: 213 or 65%)
showed that the location of the actual search facility was within the
responding library for 35% of the respondents and elsewhere for 65% of
the respondents. On-site search facilities were reported in 93% of the
college/university libraries, in 50% of the community college libraries, in
50% of the "other" libraries, and in 3% of the public libraries.   **(570)**

■ A 1979 survey of libraries in accredited North American veterinary
schools (population: 25 libraries; responding: 23 or 92%) *showed that* all
respondents reported that online search services were available. 10
(43.5%) libraries reported they had their own terminals; 22 (95.7%)
reported direct or indirect access to the National Library of Medicine data
bases; and 19 (82.6%) reported access to Lockheed or Systems Development Corporation data bases.   **(740)**

■ A 1981 survey of U.S. depository libraries, both academic and public
(sample size: 221; responding: 171 or 77%), concerning their use of online
data bases (DIALOG, ORBIT, and BRS), particularly with regard to
government documents *showed that* 66% of the documents librarians in
responding institutions had received no online training; 19% had received
training in DIALOG; 4% had received training in ORBIT; 4% had
received training in BRS; and 7% had received training in some combination of all 3 online data bases.   **(317)**

Ibid. . . . *showed that* the 2 main reasons academic depository librarians
reported for not doing online searching were that other librarians do online
data base searching (53%) and no terminals (35%), while the 2 main
reasons public depository librarians reported for not doing online search-

ing were no terminals (60%) and no money available (38%).   **(317)**

Ibid. . . . *showed that* the top 3 reasons given by respondents for not ordering government documents microfiche as the result of an online search were library did not have computer terminals (academic depositories, 33%; public depositories, 59%), didn't know that microfiche government documents could be ordered online (academic depositories, 24%; public depositories, 25%), and preferred hard copy to microfiche copy (academic depositories, 27%; public depositories, 20%).   **(317)**

Public

■ A 1975 study of online searches provided free of charge in the DIALOG data bases over a 3-month period in 4 San Franscisco Bay area public libraries (411 usable requests; 429 searches undertaken, including some duplicates) *showed that* the reference interview averaged 10.5 minutes (295 cases); preparation averaged 10.48 minutes (223 cases); search averaged 22.72 minutes (408 cases); library follow-up (filling out reports, etc.) averaged 12.21 minutes (307 cases); patron follow-up (discussing results with patron) averaged 7.61 minutes (171 cases). In a limited number of cases where the actual search was conducted in another library the referring library preparation time averaged 18.65 minutes (46 cases), while their library follow-up time averaged 11.48 minutes (42 cases).   **(326)**

■ A 1978 survey of publicly supported California libraries (primarily public and academic) concerning fee-charging behavior for online bibliographic searching (survey size: 350 libraries; responding: 213 or 65%) *showed that* the location of the actual search facility was within the responding library for 35% of the respondents and elsewhere for 65% of the respondents. On-site search facilities were reported in 93% of the college/university libraries, in 50% of the community college libraries, in 50% of the "other" libraries, and in 3% of the public libraries.   **(570)**

■ A 1981 survey of U.S. depository libraries, both academic and public (sample size: 221; responding: 171 or 77%), concerning their use of online data bases (DIALOG, ORBIT, and BRS), particularly with regard to government documents *showed that* 66% of the documents librarians in responding institutions had received no online training; 19% had received training in DIALOG; 4% had received training in ORBIT; 4% had received training in BRS; and 7% had received training in some combination of all 3 online data bases.   **(317)**

Ibid. . . . *showed that* the 2 main reasons academic depository librarians reported for not doing online searching were that other librarians do online data base searching (53%) and no terminals (35%), while the 2 main reasons public depository librarians reported for not doing online searching were no terminals (60%) and no money available (38%).   **(317)**

Ibid. . . . *showed that* the top 3 reasons given by respondents for not ordering government documents microfiche as the result of an online search were library does not have computer terminals (academic depositories, 33%; public depositories, 59%), didn't know that microfiche government documents could be ordered online (academic depositories, 24%; public depositories, 25%), and prefer hard copy to microfiche copy (academic depositories, 27%; public depositories, 20%).   **(317)**

Special

■ A 14-month study during 1972-73 at the Yale Medical Library (serving the Yale University School of Medicine, the Yale University School of Nursing, and the Yale-New Haven Hospital), involving 1,466 online search requests (MEDLINE) from 455 different individuals for the faculty and professional staff of the Yale-New Haven Medical Center *showed that* the purposes of the requests were as follows:

research	1,140 (77.8%) search requests	
patient care	221 (15.0%) search requests	
education	105 (7.2%) search requests	**(714)**

Ibid. . . . *showed that* the grant dollars received by departments were positively correlated with the number of comprehensive online searches generated by those departments (r = .44) and negatively correlated with the number of narrow searches processed by the departments (i = −.44) (significant at the .05 level).   **(714)**

■ A study reported in 1977 by the University of Oklahoma Health Sciences Center Library of the literature searches performed during a 3-year period (1973-75) for physicians and fourth-year medical students serving a 5-week "preceptorship" with a rural physician (1,775 searches) *showed that* for both the physicians and students the subject category of most requests was "Diseases" (66% of the physicians' searches; 84% of the students' searches), while the subject category of the next most requests for both groups was "Chemicals and Drugs" (27.2% of the physicians' searches; 27.6% of the students' searches).   **(716)**

■ A survey reported in 1977 by the University of Oklahoma Health Sciences Center Library to investigate the relationship between subjects for which physicians had requested literature searches and subjects for which physicians desired continuing education, based on a physician population that had requested at least 1 literature search from the Health Sciences Library during 1973-75 (survey size: 396 physicians; responding: 125 or 31.5%) *showed that* "literature searches alone could not be used to determine CME [continuing medical education] topics." Specifically, the 5 most frequently mentioned topics for CME and the 5 topics for which the most literature searches had been requested had only 3 (60%) topics in common.

(717)

■ A survey reported in 1977, concerning online searching at the U.S. Army Construction Engineering Research Laboratory library (Champaign, Illinois) and involving both users of the service (sample size: 27; responding: 26 or 96.3%) and nonusers of the service (sample size: 19; responding: 13 or 68.4%), *showed that*, of 25 user respondents, 7 (28%) indicated an interest in periodic update searches on their research topic, 11 (44%) indicated they would not, and 7 (28%) indicated they were uncertain.

(416)

■ A 1978 survey of North American health sciences libraries that were users of the National Library of Medicine search services in November 1977 (survey size: 708 libraries; responding: 376; usable: 345 or 48.7%) *showed that* different types of health science libraries have offered online searches of NLM files, as follows:

in professional schools	5.0 years
in societies, foundations, and research institutes	3.5 years
in hospitals	3.2 years
in other colleges, universities, and commercial firms	3.0 years
in "other" (including, NLM, CISTI, state library, etc.)	4.8 years **(724)**

Ibid. . . . *showed that* online search services in addition to those offered by the National Library of Medicine were provided by 199 (58%) respondents. Such additional services were provided by the following types of institutions:

colleges and universities	91% of these libraries
commercial firms	88% of these libraries

continued

professional schools	74% of these libraries	
societies, foundations, and		
research institutes	60% of these libraries	
hospitals	22% of these libraries	
other	60% of these libraries	**(724)**

■ A study reported in 1978 of LEXIS subscribers in 4 different cities (Cleveland, Chicago, New York City, and Washington, D.C.) (sample size: 62; responding: 39; usable: 38 or 61.3%), involving 35 law firms, 2 law schools and 1 government agency, *showed that* the 3 most commonly reported ways librarians had heard about LEXIS for the first time were librarian (11 or 29.0% respondents), convention (6 or 15.8% respondents), and salesmen (4 or 10.5% respondents).   **(359)**

Ibid. . . . *showed that* the 3 main attitudes toward LEXIS by respondents were very receptive (21 or 55.4% respondents), curious (7 or 18.4% respondents), and neutral (6 or 15.8% respondents).   **(359)**

■ An analysis of records reported in 1978 on online bibliographic data base searching at Flordia State University Chemistry Department and Monsanto Textiles Company in Pensacola, Florida (353 searches conducted at FSU and 345 conducted at Monsanto) *showed that* the type of approach to the online search differed in a statistically significant way between FSU and Monsanto (significance level .001) in that 50% of the FSU searches were exhaustive (i.e., wanted everything available) compared to 33% at Monsanto, while 14% of the FSU searches wished specific facts or procedures compared to 39% of the Monsanto searches.   **(155)**

Ibid. . . . *showed that* anticipated use of the search results between FSU and Monsanto differed in some statistically significant ways. 53% of the FSU searches compared to 41% of the Monsanto searches were to keep current in the researchers own field (significance level .002); 17% of the FSU searches compared to 10% of the Monsanto searches were to keep current in fields related to the researcher's field (significance level .02); 25% of the FSU searches compared to 53% of the Monsanto searches were concerned with procedures, apparatus, or methodology to support an ongoing project (significance level .001); and 33% of the FSU searches compared to 5% of the Monsanto searches were for papers for external dissemination (significance level .001).   **(155)**

Online Searching—Availability

General

■ A 1976 survey of RASD members (population: 4,062; sample size: 738; usable responses: 542 or 73.4%), concerning their attitudes toward automated information retrieval services, *showed that* respondents felt that online, interactive access to automated bibliographic data bases should be offered in the following library departments: general reference or reader services (58.3%), separate unit devoted exclusively to such a service (19%), ILL unit (9.2%), subject branches (5.5%).   **(148)**

■ A survey reported in 1982 of the directors of 20 (19 or 95% responding) OCLC distributing networks (e.g., ILLINET, SOLINET, FEDLINK, etc.) *showed that* the 4 most common non-OCLC related information retrieval services contracted through the networks (either being offered as of May 1980 or planned for offering by mid-1981) reported by 12 respondents were (multiple responses allowed): BRS (8 respondents offering; 2 planning), Lockheed DIALOG (7 respondents offering; 2 planning), SDC ORBIT (6 offering; 2 planning), New York Times Information Service (5 offering; 4 planning).   **(343)**

Academic

■ A 1967 survey of medical school libraries concerning reference services (survey size: 93 libraries; responding: 85 or 91.4% libraries) *showed that* the following numbers of libraries provided the following services (multiple responses allowed):

MEDLARS searches	77 (90.6%) libraries
edit bibliographies for authors	37 (43.5%) libraries
current awareness service	15 (17.6%) libraries
recurring bibliographies	14 (16.5%) libraries
routing of current journals	11 (12.9%) libraries

Further, 3 (3.5%) libraries reported charging a fee for providing bibliographic services.   **(682)**

■ A 1979 survey of library automation in post-secondary educational institutions in Canada (survey size: 423 libraries; responding: 283 or 67%) *showed that*, of an average of 256 respondents for each of the following items, the distribution of automated activities was as follows (multiple responses allowed):

cataloging	47.2% respondents
online bibliographic searching	34.2% respondents
COM catalog	24.2% respondents
circulation	19.8% respondents
ordering	16.5% respondents
photo-sense ID	7.7% respondents
online catalog	3.2% respondents **(556)**

■ A 1979 survey of libraries in accredited North American veterinary schools (population: 25 libraries; responding: 23 or 92%) *showed that* all respondents reported that online search services were available. 10 (43.5%) libraries reported they had their own terminals; 22 (95.7%) reported direct or indirect access to the National Library of Medicine data bases; and 19 (82.6%) reported access to Lockheed or Systems Development Corporation data bases.   **(740)**

Special

■ A 1967 survey of medical school libraries concerning reference services (survey size: 93 libraries; responding: 85 or 91.4%) *showed that* the following number of libraries provided the following services (multiple responses allowed):

MEDLARS searches	77 (90.6%) libraries
edit bibliographies for authors	37 (43.5%) libraries
current awareness service	15 (17.6%) libraries
recurring bibliographies	14 (16.5%) libraries
routing of current journals	11 (12.9%) libraries

Further, 3 (3.5%) libraries reported charging a fee for providing bibliographic services.   **(682)**

■ A 1979 survey of libraries in accredited North American veterinary schools (population: 25 libraries; responding: 23 or 92%) *showed that* all respondents reported that online search services were available. 10 (43.5%) libraries reported they had their own terminals; 22 (95.7%) reported direct or indirect access to the National Library of Medicine data bases; and 19 (82.6%) reported access to Lockheed or Systems Development Corporation data bases.   **(740)**

Online Searching—Comparison to Manual Searching

Academic

■ A survey reported in 1974 at the University of Virginia Medical Center of MEDLINE users (primarily faculty, house staff, outside health professionals, and graduate students) during a 6-month period in 1972-73 (survey size: 428 users; responding: 246 or 58%) *showed that* 230 (93.5%) respondents reported that MEDLINE was a "substantial improvement of the traditional methods of searching through the printed indexes." However, 6 (2.4%) respondents felt MEDLINE was "no substantial improvement," and 10 (4.1%) felt it was a substantial improvement but had not found it helpful in either their clinical or research work. **(696)**

■ A 1975-76 study at the University of Utah Marriott Library of online bibliographic data base searching *showed that* a comparison between a manual and an online search for geology literature to be used in an annual bibliography on Utah geology revealed that the manual search required 12 hours and cost $61.04 while the online search required 1 hour and cost $43.69. **(329)**

■ A study of the University of Delaware during the 1976-77 academic year *showed that* students perceive the most important advantage of on-line searching is the time saved. Students reported average estimated saving of 10 hours each. **(001)**

■ A survey reported in 1977 concerning online searching at the U.S. Army Construction Engineering Research Laboratory library (Champaign, Illinois), involving both users of the service (sample size: 27; responding: 26 or 96.3%) and nonusers of the service (sample size: 19; responding: 13 or 68.4%), *showed that* of 13 nonuser respondents the main reason given for not using the online search service was (multiple responses allowed): found all the materials they needed for research on their own, 6 (46.2%). No respondents reported that expense was a problem. **(416)**

■ A 1978 survey of North American health sciences libraries that were users of the National Library of Medicine search services in November 1977 (survey size: 708 libraries; responding: 376; usable: 345 or 48.7%) *showed that* of 232 respondents the advent of online searching allowed a drop of 36% in the first year in FTE staff previously used for manual searching. By 1976-77 FTE staff for online searching had increased 10% over pre-online searching levels, while the number of searches for the same period had increased 241% (from an average of 247 searches per year to 842 searches per year per institution). **(724)**

Ibid. . . . *showed that*, of 310 respondents, 245 (79.0%) libraries "agreed" or "strongly agreed" that users have more confidence in online retrieval than in manual retrieval, while of 316 respondents, 277 (87.7%) libraries "agreed" or "strongly agreed" that "users have a more positive attitude about our staff's expertise since online searching has been available."

(724)

■ A study reported in 1978 comparing manual and online retrospective bibliographic searching at the Lawrence Livermore Laboratory (University of California, Livermore, California), involving 40 manual and 40 online searches in 7 abstracting-indexing publications and corresponding SDC/ ORBIT data bases (*Bibliography and Index of Geology*/GEOREF, *Chemical Abstracts*/CHEM7071/CHEMCON, *Congressional Information Service*/CIS, *Engineering Index*/COMPENDEX, *Government Reports Announcements*/NTIS, *Petroleum, Engineering, Business News Index*/P/E NEWS, and *Pollution Abstracts*/POLLUTION), *showed that*:

costs, including labor, subscription, reproduction, equipment, space, and telecommunications costs, averaged $30.15 per manual search compared to $26.05 per online search;

time required for a manual search averaged 119.5 minutes compared to 26.7 minutes for an online search;

turnaround time for manual searches averaged 60.5 hours compared to 95.5 hours (citations were printed offline and mailed to the laboratory) per online search. **(623)**

Ibid. . . . *showed that* the average time (in minutes) required per task for the 2 types of searches was as follows:

question analysis	5.1 manual;	8.3 online
searching	89.6 manual;	11.6 online
photocopying	5.1 manual;	0.0 online
shelving	4.9 manual;	0.0 online
output processing and distribution	14.8 manual;	6.8 online **(623)**

Ibid. . . . *showed that* the effectiveness of the 2 kinds of searches was as follows:

average number of citations retrieved per search	35.20 manual; 47.10 online
average number of relevant citations retrieved per search	35.20 manual; 39.80 online
recall ratio [not explained]	0.43 manual; 0.57 online
precision ratio (relevant citations divided by total citations)	1.00 manual; 0.84 online
cost per relevant citation	$ .86 manual; $ .65 online **(623)**

■ A 1979 study at the University of Michigan comparing 2 groups of graduate students in an educational psychology class who compiled required bibliographies in 2 different ways (6 students used online searching; 8 students used conventional manual methods) *showed that* there were substantial differences of opinion about the 2 search processes:

66% of the online group versus 100% of the manual group ranked the literature as "highly responsive to information needs";

12% of the online group versus 80% of the manual group reported a "high proportion of total productive time spent in literature search";

50% of the online group versus 100% of the manual group reported a "high level of confidence about being able to find information in future searches";

12% of the online group versus 40% of the manual group reported that "search techniques provide a great deal of insight into topics considered." **(651)**

■ A 1980 study at Washington University School of Medicine Library over a 13-week period to investigate the feasibility of substituting an online version of *Chemical Abstracts* for the print copy *showed that* such a substitution was not feasible. Specifically, of 53 times during this period when patrons began to use the print copy of *Chemical Abstracts* and were offered a free online search instead, on 32 (60.4%) occasions patrons indicated that they did not want an online search. Further, of the 21 (39.6%) occasions when patrons did take the free online search, 13 (61.9%) of these times patrons reported that they still planned to use the printed copies later for looking up the abstracts (which were available only in the printed copies). **(737)**

Ibid. . . . *showed that* the 4 most frequent reasons given for refusing the online search (out of 8) were:

wanted to browse printed copy	12 occasions
manual search quicker (searching for a specific citation or compound)	8 occasions
previous online searches unsatisfactory	4 occasions
did not want to wait for an online search (a wait of up to 24 hours was required)	4 occasions **(737)**

Special

■ A survey reported in 1974 at the University of Virginia Medical Center of MEDLINE users (primarily faculty, house staff, outside health professionals, and graduate students) during a 6-month period in 1972-73 (survey size: 428 users; responding: 246 or 58%) *showed that* 230 (93.5%) respondents reported that MEDLINE was a "substantial improvement of the traditional methods of searching through the printed indexes." However, 6 (2.4%) respondents felt MEDLINE was "no substantial improvement," and 10 (4.1%) felt it was a substantial improvement but had not found it helpful in either their clinical or research work.   **(696)**

■ A survey reported in 1977 concerning online searching at the U.S. Army Construction Engineering Research Laboratory library (Champaign, Illinois), involving both users of the service (sample size: 27; responding: 26 or 96.3%) and nonusers of the service (sample size: 19; responding: 13 or 68.4%) *showed that* of 13 nonuser respondents the main reason given for not using the online search service was (multiple responses allowed): found all the materials they needed for research on their own, 6 (46.2%). No respondents reported that expense was a problem.   **(416)**

■ A 1978 survey of North American health sciences libraries that were users of the National Library of Medicine search services in November 1977 (survey size: 708 libraries; responding: 376; usable: 345 or 48.7%) *showed that* of 232 respondents the advent of online searching allowed a drop of 36% in the first year in FTE staff previously used for manual searching. By 1976-77 FTE staff for online searching had increased 10% over pre-online searching levels, while the number of searches for the same period had increased 241% (from an average of 247 searches per year to 842 searches per year per institution).   **(724)**

Ibid. . . . *showed that*, of 310 respondents, 245 (79.0%) libraries "agreed" or "strongly agreed" that users have more confidence in online retrieval than in manual retrieval, while of 316 respondents, 277 (87.7%) libraries "agreed" or "strongly agreed" that "users have a more positive attitude about our staff's expertise since online searching has been available."

(724)

■ A study reported in 1978 comparing manual and online retrospective bibliographic searching at the Lawrence Livermore Laboratory (University of California, Livermore, California), involving 40 manual and 40 online searches in 7 abstracting-indexing publications and corresponding SDC/ORBIT data bases (*Bibliography and Index of Geology*/GEOREF, *Chemical Abstracts*/CHEM7071/CHEMCON, *Congressional Information Service*/CIS, *Engineering Index*/COMPENDEX, *Government Reports Announcements*/NTIS, *Petroleum, Engineering, Business News Index*/P/E NEWS, and *Pollution Abstracts*/POLLUTION), *showed that*:

costs, including labor, subscription, reproduction, equipment, space, and telecommunications costs, averaged $30.15 per manual search compared to $26.05 per online search;

time required for a manual search averaged 119.5 minutes compared to 26.7 minutes for an online search;

turnaround time for manual searches averaged 60.5 hours compared to 95.5 hours (citations were printed offline and mailed to the laboratory) per online search. **(623)**

Ibid. . . . *showed that* the average time (in minutes) required per task for the 2 types of searches was as follows:

question analysis	5.1 manual; 8.3 online
searching	89.6 manual; 11.6 online
photocopying	5.1 manual; 0.0 online
shelving	4.9 manual; 0.0 online
output processing and distribution	14.8 manual; 6.8 online **(623)**

Ibid. . . . *showed that* the effectiveness of the 2 kinds of searches was as follows:

average number of citations retrieved per search	35.20 manual; 47.10 online
average number of relevant citations retrieved per search	35.20 manual; 39.80 online

continued

recall ratio [not explained]   0.43 manual; 0.57 online
precision ratio (relevant
  citations divided by total
  citations)   1.00 manual; 0.84 online
cost per relevant citation $ .86 manual; $ .65 online   **(623)**

■ A 1980 study at Washington University School of Medicine Library over a 13-week period to investigate the feasibility of substituting an online version of *Chemical Abstracts* for the print copy, *showed that* such a substitution was not feasible. Specifically, of 53 times during this period when patrons began to use the print copy of *Chemical Abstracts* and were offered a free online search instead, on 32 (60.4%) occasions patrons indicated that they did not want an online search. Further, of the 21 (39.6%) occasions when patrons did take the free online search, 13 (61.9%) of these times patrons reported that they still planned to use the printed copies later for looking up the abstracts (which were available only in the printed copies).   **(737)**

Ibid. . . . *showed that* the 4 most frequent reasons given for refusing the online search (out of 8) were:

wanted to browse printed copy   12 occasions
manual search quicker (searching
  for a specific citation or compound)   8 occasions
previous online searches
  unsatisfactory   4 occasions
did not want to wait for an
  online search (a wait of up to 24
  hours was required)   4 occasions   **(737)**

Online Searching—Costs

Academic

■ A study reported in 1978 comparing manual and online retrospective bibliographic searching at the Lawrence Livermore Laboratory (University of California, Livermore, California), involving 40 manual and 40 online searches in 7 abstracting-indexing publications and corresponding SDC/ORBIT data bases (*Bibliography and Index of Geology*/GEOREF, *Chemical Abstracts*/CHEM7071/CHEMCON, *Congressional Information Service*/CIS, *Engineering Index*/COMPENDEX, *Government Reports Announcements*/NTIS, *Petroleum, Engineering, Business News Index*/P/E NEWS, and *Pollution Abstracts*/POLLUTION), *showed that*:

costs, including labor, subscription, reproduction, equipment, space, and telecommunications costs, averaged $30.15 per manual search compared to $26.05 per online search;

time required for a manual search averaged 119.5 minutes compared to 26.7 minutes for an online search;

turnaround time for manual searches averaged 60.5 hours compared to 95.5 hours (citations were printed offline and mailed to the laboratory) per online search. **(623)**

■ A 1979 survey of library automation in post-secondary educational institutions in Canada (survey size: 423 libraries; responding: 283 or 67%) *showed that*, of 31 respondents, total costs for online connect-time and offline prints averaged $9.27 per search. **(556)**

■ A study reported in 1982 at Nazareth College of Rochester concerning online bibliographic searching and involving 183 patrons during the period May 1980-June 1981 *showed that*, of 421 searches (each entry into the strategy of a data base was considered a search) on 299 topics, the average cost per search was $8.10, and the average cost per topic was $11.41. **(300)**

Public

■ A 1975 study of online searches provided free of charge in the DIALOG data bases over a 3-month period in 4 San Franscisco Bay area public libraries (411 usable requests; 429 searches undertaken, including some duplicates) *showed that* the average costs were:

data base charges	$17.29
off-line print charges	$ 9.16
search labor cost	$ 2.24
labor cost (all other tasks)	$ 5.02
telephone line charges (est.)	$ 5.68
TOTAL	$34.09 **(326)**

■ A 1975-76 study of 359 online searches over a 7-month period using DIALOG in 4 public libraries in the San Franscisco Bay area where patrons were charged half the connect costs (in contrast to a study the year before in the same libraries when searches were free) *showed that* the average costs for the various elements of the search were:

data base charges	$11.60
offline print charges	$10.87

continued

search labor cost $ 1.74
labor cost (all other tasks) $ 4.68
TOTAL $26.73

This compared to the total search costs for these same elements during the period of free searches (adjusted for inflation, price increases, etc.) of $28.78.   **(332)**

Special

■ A 1973 comparison of 48 manual and 66 online (DIALOG) bibliographic searches at the Lockheed-California Company Library *showed that* the average manual search took 22 hours for a total cost of $250, while the average online search took 45 minutes at a total cost of $47.00.   **(406)**

■ A study reported in 1978 comparing manual and online retrospective bibliographic searching at the Lawrence Livermore Laboratory (University of California, Livermore, California), involving 40 manual and 40 online searches in 7 abstracting-indexing publications and corresponding SDC/ORBIT data bases (*Bibliography and Index of Geology*/GEOREF, *Chemical Abstracts*/CHEM7071/CHEMCON, *Congressional Information Serivce*/CIS, *Engineering Index*/COMPENDEX, *Government Reports Announcements*/NTIS, *Petroleum, Engineering, Business News Index*/P/E NEWS, and *Pollution Abstracts*/POLLUTION) *showed that*:

costs, including labor, subscription, reproduction, equipment, space, and telecommunications costs, averaged $30.15 per manual search compared to $26.05 per online search;

time required for a manual search averaged 119.5 minutes compared to 26.7 minutes for an online search;

turnaround time for manual searches averaged 60.5 hours compared to 95.5 hours (citations were printed offline and mailed to the laboratory) per online search.   **(623)**

Online Searching—Effect on ILL

Academic

■ A 1974 study over a 4-month period (January-April) of free MEDLINE use at Oakland University (Rochester, Michigan), a university without a medical school, involving 21 faculty and students for a total of 36 searches, *showed that*, although 54% of the citations considered relevant by the user were not available in the university library, only 4.1% of the citations were requested through ILL. **(411)**

■ A survey reported in 1977 concerning online searching at the U.S. Army Construction Engineering Research Laboratory library (Champaign, Illinois), involving both users of the service (sample size: 27; responding: 26 or 96.3%) and nonusers of the service (sample size: 19; responding: 13 or 68.4%), *showed that*, of 25 user respondents, 11 (44%) reported ordering "many" of the documents for the citations from the online search through the library; 9 (36%) reported ordering "a few"; and 5 (20%) reported ordering "none." **(416)**

■ A 1978 survey of North American health sciences libraries that were users of the National Library of Medicine search services in November 1977 (survey size: 708 libraries; responding: 376; usable: 345 or 48.7%) *showed that*, of 337 respondents, 316 (93.8%) libraries "agreed" or "strongly agreed" that online searching had made it possible to serve more users, while of 330 respondents, 311 (94.2%) libraries "agreed" or "strongly agreed" that online searching had caused an increase in interlibrary loan borrowing. **(724)**

Special

■ A 1974 study over a 4-month period (January-April) of free MEDLINE use at Oakland University (Rochester, Michigan), a university without a medical school, involving 21 faculty and students for a total of 36 searches, *showed that*, although 54% of the citations considered relevant by the user were not available in the university library, only 4.1% of the citations were requested through ILL. **(411)**

■ A 1976-77 study at the Russell Research Center Library (USDA, Athens, Georgia) of the relationship between online literature searches and interlibrary loan activity *showed that*, during the 18-month period in which retrospective online seaching was initiated (314 searches), interlibrary loan requests compared to the 6-month period just prior to the online searching (858 requests) increased 167.7% (2,297 requests) during the first 6 months, 85.5% (1,592 requests) during the second 6 months, and 120.0% (1,888 requests) during the last 6 months. **(419)**

■ A survey reported in 1977 concerning online searching at the U.S. Army Construction Engineering Research Laboratory library (Cham-

paign, Illinois), involving both users of the service (sample size: 27; responding: 26 or 96.3%) and nonusers of the service (sample size: 19; responding: 13 or 68.4%), *showed that*, of 25 user respondents, 11 (44%) reported ordering "many" of the documents for the citations from the online search through the library; 9 (36%) reported ordering "a few"; and 5 (20%) reported ordering "none." **(416)**

■ A 1978 survey of North American health sciences libraries that were users of the National Library of Medicine search services in November 1977 (survey size: 708 libraries; responding: 376; usable: 345 or 48.7%) *showed that*, of 337 respondents, 316 (93.8%) libraries "agreed" or "strongly agreed" that online searching had made it possible to serve more users, while of 330 respondents, 311 (94.2%) libraries "agreed" or "strongly agreed" that online searching had caused an increase in interlibrary loan borrowing. **(724)**

■ A study reported in 1978 of LEXIS subscribers in 4 different cities (Cleveland, Chicago, New York City, and Washington, D.C.) (sample size: 62; responding: 39; usable: 38 or 61.3%), involving 35 law firms, 2 law schools and 1 government agency, *showed that* 6 (15.8%) respondents reported an increase in interlibrary loan borrowing since they began to use LEXIS; 1 (2.6%) reported that interlibrary loan borrowing decreased after they began to use LEXIS; 30 (79.0%) reported no change in interlibrary loan borrowing; and 1 did not reply to this question. **(359)**

Online Searching—Effectiveness

General

■ A 1971 study comparing MEDLINE bibliographic retrieval (data base of 1,100 journal titles) with SUNY Biomedical Communication Network bibliographic retrieval (data base of 2,300 journal titles) by duplicating 165 search requests on the 2 systems *showed that* the SUNY system retrieved 5,529 citations from 1,163 different journal titles compared to 4,353 citations from 641 unique journal titles for the MEDLINE system. MEDLINE retrieved 78.7% of the citations retrieved by the SUNY system. Further, "almost half" of the 21.3% citations not retrieved by the MEDLINE system were from foreign-language journals. **(693)**

■ A study reported in 1975 that involved searching 50 scientific profiles in a 6-month (October 1971-March 1972) section of COMPENDEX ("computer tape version of the *Engineering Index Monthly*") using 9 different data elements or combinations of data elements to search on [results of only 8 elements or combinations were reported] *showed that* the average success rate of each approach in retrieving all possible citations was as follows:

Title and Abstract elements combined	74.9% of possible citations
Abstract element only	61.2% of possible citations
Title, Free Language and Subject elements combined	47.0% of possible citations
Title and Subject elements combined	40.6% of possible citations
Subject and Free Language combined	29.9% of possible citations
Title and Free Language combined	26.9% of possible citations
Title element only	22.2% of possible citations
Subject element only	20.8% of possible citations (613)

■ A study reported in 1983 comparing the effectiveness of an automated intermediary (CONIT system) with a human intermediary in conducting an online bibliographic search, involving 16 patrons using 3 retrieval systems (NLM ELHILL, SDC ORBIT, and DIALOG) and 20 different data bases (mostly medical and biological) *showed that* patrons using the automated intermediary had a greater retrieval rate of relevant items. Specifically, searches using the human intermediaries (16 topics) retrieved from 6 to 144 relevant documents, with an average of 52 and a median of 31. This compared to the searches on 16 topics where patrons used the automated intermediary in which they retrieved an average of 172 items with a median of 41.5 items. **(661)**

Academic

■ A 1973 survey of patrons using MEDLINE at 7 information centers (University of Illinois Medical Center, Chicago; Indiana University; University of Chicago; University of Illinois, Urbana; Cleveland Health Sciences Library; Mayo Clinic; and Wayne State University) during April-September 1973 (survey size: 1,017 patrons; responding: 904 or 88.9%) *showed that* of 706 respondents there was a statistically significant relationship between the number of useful references received and the perception that the search was helpful (significant at the .001 level).

Specifically, 80% of the respondents who received a high number of useful references (6 or more) judged the search helpful, compared to 40% of the users so reporting who received a low number of references (less than 6).
                                                                    (715)

Ibid. . . . *showed that* of 795 respondents there was a statistically significant relationship between patron perception that relevant references were missed in a search and patron perception of the search as helpful (significant at the .001 level). Specifically, 70% of the patrons who perceived that no references had been missed in the search reported the search helpful, compared to 49.0% patrons so reporting who perceived that 1 or more references had been missed.   **(715)**

■ A 1974 study over a 4-month period (January-April) of free MED-LINE use at Oakland University (Rochester, Michigan), a university without a medical school, involving 21 faculty and students for a total of 36 searches, *showed that*, of 27 (75%) search evaluation forms returned, the precision values (number of unique relevant citations divided by total number of unique citations retrieved) averaged 53.9%.   **(411)**

Ibid. . . . *showed that*, of 27 (75%) search evaluation forms returned, the number of minutes of connect-time per relevant citation averaged 0.96 minutes with a median of 0.48 minutes. 74% of the searches generated at least 1 relevant citation per minute of connect-time.   **(411)**

■ A study reported in 1975 that involved searching 50 scientific profiles in a 6-month (October 1971-March 1972) section of COMPENDEX ("computer tape version of the *Engineering Index Monthly*") using 9 different data elements or combinations of data elements to search on [results of only 8 elements or combinations were reported] *showed that* the average success rate of each approach in retrieving all possible citations was as follows:

Title and Abstract elements combined	74.9% of possible citations
Abstract element only	61.2% of possible citations
Title, Free Language, and Subject elements combined	47.0% of possible citations
Title and Subject elements combined	40.6% of possible citations
Subject and Free Language combined	29.9% of possible citations

continued

Title and Free Language
   combined   26.9% of possible citations
Title element only   22.2% of possible citations
Subject element only   20.8% of possible citations **(613)**

■ A 1975-76 study at the University of Utah Marriott Library of online bibliographic data base searching *showed that* a survey of 26 patrons using the online searching service revealed that: 8 (31%) found 60-80% of the citations relevant; 6 (23%) found 80-100% of the citations relevant; 5 (19%) found 0-20% relevant; 4 (15%) found 40-60% relevant; and 3 (12%) found 20-40% relevant. **(329)**

■ A survey reported in 1976 of 10 academic and public libraries using the New York Times Information Bank *showed that* the average success rate in retrieving adequate information was between 70-80%. **(149)**

■ A study of the University of Delaware during the 1976-77 academic year *showed that*, of graduate and undergraduate students using on-line search services, there was a statistically significant relationship between patron satisfaction and both the absolute number of citations generated and the absolute number of relevant citations generated. Patron satisfaction was also statistically significantly correlated with patron estimate of time saved. **(001)**

Ibid. . . . *showed that*, of graduate and undergraduate students using on-line search services, there was no relationship between student status, purpose of the search, cost to the student, or percentage of relevant citations and student satisfaction with the search. **(001)**

■ A survey reported in 1977 concerning online searching at the U.S. Army Construction Engineering Research Laboratory library (Champaign, Illinois), involving both users of the service (sample size: 27; responding: 26 or 96.3%) and nonusers of the service (sample size: 19; responding: 13 or 68.4%), *showed that*, of 25 user respondents, 12 (48%) reported 0-20% of the search citations were relevant to their research topic; 6 (24%) reported 20-40% of the citations relevant; 3 (12%) reported 40-60% of the citations were relevant; and 4 (16%) reported that 60-80% of the citations were relevant. **(416)**

■ A study reported in 1978 comparing manual and online retrospective bibliographic searching at the Lawrence Livermore Laboratory (University of California, Livermore, California), involving 40 manual and 40 online searches in 7 abstracting-indexing publications and corresponding SDC/ORBIT data bases (*Bibliography and Index of Geology*/GEOREF, *Chemical Abstracts*/CHEM7071/CHEMCON, *Congressional Information Service*/CIS, *Engineering Index*/COMPENDEX, *Government Reports Announcements*/NTIS, *Petroleum, Engineering, Business News Index*/P/E NEWS, and *Pollution Abstracts*/POLLUTION), *showed that* the effectiveness of the 2 kinds of searches was as follows:

average number of citations retrieved per search	35.20 manual; 47.10 online
average number of relevant citations retrieved per search	35.20 manual; 39.80 online
recall ratio [not explained]	0.43 manual; 0.57 online
precision ratio (relevant citations divided by total citations)	1.00 manual; 0.84 online
cost per relevant citation	$ .86 manual; $ .65 online **(623)**

■ An analysis of records reported in 1978 on online bibliographic data base searching at Flordia State University Chemistry Department and Monsanto Textiles Company in Pensacola, Florida (353 searches conducted at FSU and 345 conducted at Monsanto) *showed that* there were no statistically significant differences of opinion on the currency of citations, with 44% of FSU researchers reporting "very satisfactory" compared to 35% of Monsanto researchers and 43% of FSU researchers reporting "satisfactory" compared to 49% of Monsanto researchers.   **(155)**

Ibid. . . . *showed that* there were no statistically significant differences of opinion on the utility of the searches, with 54% of the FSU researchers reporting "very useful" compared to 50% of the Monsanto researchers and 24% of the FSU researchers reporting "of some use" compared to 25% of the Monsanto researchers.   **(155)**

■ A study reported in 1982 at the University of Iowa Health Sciences Library concerning the effect of the patron's presence during MEDLINE searches, based on searches for 100 different patrons (each search was conducted twice by different staff members, once with and once without the patron) and subsequent survey (100% responding) of those patrons, *showed that*, although the precision rate (the number of relevant citations divided by the total number of citations found) increased with patrons present during the search process, the increase was not statistically significant. Specifically, the precision rate increased from an average of 40.3% per patron to an average of 45.3% per patron. (743)

Ibid. . . . *showed that* there was a statistically significant increase in recall rate (number of relevant citations retrieved out of the total relevant possibilities) and patron satisfaction rate when the patrons were present during the search process. Specifically, the recall rate increased from an average of 58.8% per patron to 74.6% per patron, and the satisfaction rate (based on a 5-point scale where a rating of 1 is least satisfied) increased from an average of 3.7 per patron to 4.3 per patron. (These differences were significant at the .001 level.) (743)

Ibid. . . . *showed that* a comparison of first-time search requesters with requesters who had requested previous online searches revealed that the experienced patrons had a statistically significantly higher satisfaction rate for both the user-present and the user-absent searches (significant at the .004 level). Further, it took statistically significantly less time to formulate a search for the experienced users (significant at the .04 level). There was no statistically significant difference in recall rate or in online search time between experienced and nonexperienced patrons. (743)

Ibid. . . . *showed that* there were no statistically significant differences among undergraduate, graduate, or faculty search requesters for precision, recall, or satisfaction rates. (743)

Public

■ A survey reported in 1976 of 10 academic and public libraries using the New York Times Information Bank *showed that* the average success rate in retrieving adequate information was between 70-80%. (149)

Special

■ A 1973 survey of patrons using MEDLINE at 7 information centers (University of Illinois Medical Center, Chicago; Indiana University; University of Chicago; University of Illinois, Urbana; Cleveland Health Sciences Library; Mayo Clinic; and Wayne State University) during April-September 1973 (survey size: 1,017 patrons; responding: 904 or 88.9%) *showed that* of 706 respondents there was a statistically significant relationship between the number of useful references received and the perception that the search was helpful (significant at the .001 level). Specifically, 80% of the respondents who received a high number of useful references (6 or more) judged the search helpful, compared to 40% of the users so reporting who received a low number of references (less than 6). **(715)**

Ibid. . . . *showed that* of 795 respondents there was a statistically significant relationship between patron perception that relevant references were missed in a search and patron perception of the search as helpful (significant at the .001 level). Specifically, 70% of the patrons who perceived that no references had been missed in the search reported the search helpful, compared to 49.0% patrons so reporting who perceived that 1 or more references had been missed. **(715)**

■ A study reported in 1974 that involved searching 228 SDI profiles from 104 industrial research chemists in *Basic Journal Abstracts* (from *Chemical Abstracts Services*) to compare the number of articles retrieved when a title data base was searched in contrast to the number of articles retrieved when a data base of abstracts was searched *showed that* the title data base produced only 27.0% (18.2% to 35.8% at a 95% confidence level) of the number of articles the data base of abstracts produced. Specifically, the title data base produced 5,133 articles compared to the 18,993 articles produced by a search of the abstracts data base. **(611)**

■ A survey reported in 1977 concerning online searching at the U.S. Army Construction Engineering Research Laboratory library (Champaign, Illinois), involving both users of the service (sample size: 27; responding: 26 or 96.3%) and nonusers of the service (sample size: 19; responding: 13 or 68.4%) *showed that*, of 25 user respondents, 12 (48%) reported 0-20% of the search citations were relevant to their research topic; 6 (24%) reported 20-40% of the citations relevant; 3 (12%) reported 40-60% of the citations were relevant; and 4 (16%) reported that 60-80% of the citations were relevant. **(416)**

■ A study reported in 1978 comparing manual and online retrospective bibliographic searching at the Lawrence Livermore Laboratory (University of California, Livermore, California), involving 40 manual and 40 online searches in 7 abstracting-indexing publications and corresponding SDC/ ORBIT data bases (*Bibliography and Index of Geology*/GEOREF, *Chemical Abstracts*/CHEM7071/CHEMCON, *Congressional Information Service*/CIS, *Engineering Index*/COMPENDEX, *Government Reports Announcements*/NTIS, *Petroleum, Engineering, Business News Index*/P/E

NEWS, and *Pollution Abstracts*/POLLUTION), *showed that* the effectiveness of the 2 kinds of searches was as follows:

average number of citations retrieved per search	35.20 manual; 47.10 online
average number of relevant citations retrieved per search	35.20 manual; 39.80 online
recall ratio [not explained]	0.43 manual; 0.57 online
precision ratio (relevant citations divided by total citations)	1.00 manual; 0.84 online
cost per relevant citation	$ .86 manual; $ .65 online **(623)**

■ An analysis of records reported in 1978 on online bibliographic data base searching at Flordia State University Chemistry Department and Monsanto Textiles Company in Pensacola, Florida (353 searches conducted at FSU and 345 conducted at Monsanto) *showed that* there were no statistically significant differences of opinion on the currency of citations, with 44% of FSU researchers reporting "very satisfactory" compared to 35% of Monsanto researchers and 43% of FSU researchers reporting "satisfactory" compared to 49% of Monsanto researchers. **(155)**

Ibid. . . . *showed that* there were no statistically significant differences of opinion on the utility of the searches, with 54% of the FSU researchers reporting "very useful" compared to 50% of the Monsanto researchers and 24% of the FSU researchers reporting "of some use" compared to 25% of the Monsanto researchers. **(155)**

■ A study reported in 1982 at the University of Iowa Health Sciences Library concerning the effect of the patron's presence during MEDLINE searches, based on searches for 100 different patrons (each search was conducted twice by different staff members, once with and once without the patron) and subsequent survey (100% responding) of those patrons *showed that* there was a statistically significant increase in recall rate (number of relevant citations retrieved out of the total relevant possibilities) and patron satisfaction rate when the patrons were present during the search process. Specifically, the recall rate increased from an average of 58.8% per patron to 74.6% per patron, and the satisfaction rate (based on a 5-point scale where a rating of 1 is least satisfied) increased from an average of 3.7 per patron to 4.3 per patron. (These differences were significant at the .001 level.) **(743)**

Ibid. . . . *showed that*, although the precision rate (the number of relevant citations divided by the total number of citations found) increased with patrons present during the search process, the increase was not statistically significant. Specifically, the precision rate increased from an average of 40.3% per patron to an average of 45.3% per patron. **(743)**

Ibid. . . . *showed that* a comparison of first-time search requesters with requesters who had requested previous online searches revealed that the experienced patrons had a statistically significantly higher satisfaction rate for both the user-present and the user-absent searches (significant at the .004 level). Further, it took statistically significantly less time to formulate a search for the experienced users (significant at the .04 level). There was no statistically significant difference in recall rate or in online search time between experienced and nonexperienced patrons. **(743)**

Ibid. . . . *showed that* there were no statistically significant differences among undergraduate, graduate, or faculty search requesters for precision, recall, or satisfaction rates. **(743)**

Online Searching—Equipment

Academic

■ A 1979 survey of libraries in accredited North American veterinary schools (population: 25 libraries; responding: 23 or 92%) *showed that* all respondents reported that online search services were available. 10 (43.5%) libraries reported they had their own terminals; 22 (95.7%) reported direct or indirect access to the National Library of Medicine data bases; and 19 (82.6%) reported access to Lockheed or Systems Development Corporation data bases. **(740)**

■ A 1981 survey of U.S. depository libraries, both academic and public (sample size: 221; responding: 171 or 77%), concerning their use of online data bases (DIALOG, ORBIT, and BRS), particularly with regard to government documents, *showed that* 35% of the academic libraries and 65% of the public libraries did not have online terminals in the library. **(317)**

Ibid. . . . *showed that* the 2 main reasons academic depository librarians reported for not doing online searching were other librarians do online data base searching (53%) and no terminals (35%), while the 2 main reasons public depository librarians reported for not doing online searching were no terminals (60%) and no money available (38%). **(317)**

Ibid. . . . *showed that* the top 3 reasons given by respondents for not ordering government documents microfiche as the result of an online search were library does not have computer terminals (academic depositories, 33%; public depositories, 59%), didn't know that microfiche government documents could be ordered online (academic depositories, 24%; public depositories, 25%), and prefer hard copy to microfiche copy (academic depositories, 27%; public depositories, 20%). **(317)**

Public

■ A 1981 survey of U.S. depository libraries, both academic and public (sample size: 221; responding: 171 or 77%), concerning their use of online data bases (DIALOG, ORBIT, and BRS), particularly with regard to government documents, *showed that* 35% of the academic libraries and 65% of the public libraries did not have online terminals in the library.
(317)

Ibid. . . . *showed that* the 2 main reasons academic depository librarians reported for not doing online searching were other librarians do online data base searching (53%) and no terminals (35%), while the 2 main reasons public depository librarians reported for not doing online searching were no terminals (60%) and no money available (38%). **(317)**

Ibid. . . . *showed that* the top 3 reasons given by respondents for not ordering government documents microfiche as the result of an online search were library does not have computer terminals (academic depositories, 33%; public depositories, 59%), didn't know that microfiche government documents could be ordered online (academic depositories, 24%; public depositories, 25%), and prefer hard copy to microfiche copy (academic depositories, 27%; public depositories, 20%). **(317)**

Special

■ A study reported in 1978 of LEXIS subscribers in 4 different cities (Cleveland, Chicago, New York City, and Washington, D.C.) (sample size: 62; responding: 39; usable: 38 or 61.3%), involving 35 law firms, 2 law schools, and 1 government agency, *showed that* 31 (81.6%) of the respondents had 1 LEXIS terminal; 6 (15.8%) had 2 LEXIS terminals; and 1 (2.6%) had more than 2 LEXIS terminals. **(359)**

Ibid. . . . *showed that* 15 (39.5%) respondents had had a LEXIS terminal for more than 2 years; 11 (28.9%) had had such a terminal for 1-2 years; 8 (21.1%) had had one for 1/2 to 1 year; and 4 (10.5%) had had one for less than 1/2 year. **(359)**

Ibid. . . . *showed that,* of 41 terminals, 32 (78.1%) were located in the library or adjacent office; 1 (2.4%) was located in the librarian's office; 6 (14.6%) were located in an assigned office; and 2 (4.9%) were located in branch offices. **(359)**

■ A 1979 survey of libraries in accredited North American veterinary schools (population: 25 libraries; responding: 23 or 92%) *showed that* all respondents reported that online search services were available. 10 (43.5%) libraries reported they had their own terminals; 22 (95.7%) reported direct or indirect access to the National Library of Medicine data bases; and 19 (82.6%) reported access to Lockheed or Systems Development Corporation data bases. **(740)**

Online Searching—Fees

General

■ A 1976 survey of RASD members (population: 4,062; sample size: 738; usable responses: 542 or 73.4%), concerning their attitudes toward automated information retrieval services *showed that* 23.4% of respondents felt patrons should not be charged any of the costs of an automated information retrieval system; 29.3% felt patrons should be charged less than half of the costs; and 36.5% felt that patrons should bear half or more of the costs. **(148)**

Academic

■ A 1967 survey of medical school libraries concerning reference services (survey size: 93 libraries; responding: 85 or 91.4%) *showed that* the following number of libraries provided the following services (multiple responses allowed):

MEDLARS searches	77 (90.6%) libraries
edit bibliographies for authors	37 (43.5%) libraries
current awareness service	15 (17.6%) libraries

continued

recurring bibliographies   14 (16.5%) libraries
routing of current journals   11 (12.9%) libraries

Further, 3 (3.5%) libraries reported charging a fee for providing bibliographic services.

(682)

■ A survey reported in 1974 at the University of Virginia Medical Center of MEDLINE users (primarily faculty, house staff, outside health professionals, and graduate students) during a 6-month period in 1972-73 (survey size: 428 users; responding: 246 or 58%) *showed that* 188 (76%) respondents reported they would continue to use MEDLINE even if charged for the service ($1.50 per simple search; $3.00 per more complex search); 5 (2%) reported they would not continue to use MEDLINE; and 53 (22%) were undecided.

(696)

■ A study of the University of Delaware during the 1976-77 academic year *showed that*, of graduate and undergraduate students using online search services, there was no relationship between student status, purpose of the search, cost to the student, or percentage of relevant citations and student satisfaction with the search.

(001)

Ibid. . . . *showed that* the percentage of undergraduates among users of online searching increased greatly when the library subsidized 50% of the total search costs.

(001)

Ibid. . . . *showed that* average online search cost at the University of Delaware in 1976-77 for library-subsidized searching was $20.25 and for non-library subsidized searching $18.57; average search cost reported for 4 public libraries in California was $21.15; average search cost in Bell Laboratories was reported as $44.04; all 505 users averaged a search cost of $23.83; an academic study reported an average search cost of $66.71.

(001)

■ Figures from the library at SUNY Albany *showed that* the number of online bibliographic searches dropped by 20% between 1976 and 1977, when the library began charging for the offline printing costs (15 cents per page), even though the number of data bases available to patrons was increased from 4 to 11.

(015)

■ A survey reported in 1977 concerning online searching at the U.S. Army Construction Engineering Research Laboratory library (Cham-

paign, Illinois), involving both users of the service (sample size: 27; responding: 26 or 96.3%) and nonusers of the service (sample size: 19; responding: 13 or 68.4%) *showed that* of 13 nonuser respondents the main reason given for not using the online search service was (multiple responses allowed): found all the materials they needed for research on their own, 6 (46.2%). No respondents reported that expense was a problem.   **(416)**

■ A 1978 survey of North American health sciences libraries that were users of the National Library of Medicine search services in November 1977 (survey size: 708 libraries; responding: 376; usable: 345 or 48.7%) *showed that* of 339 respondents some kind of online search fees were charged by 178 (52.50) libraries. The numbers of libraries charging some kind of online search fee by type of library were as follows:

in professional school	90 (89.11%) libraries
in other college or university	21 (91.30%) libraries
in commercial institution	9 (16.07%) libraries
in society, foundation, or research institute	17 (40.48%) libraries
in hospital	38 (33.93%) libraries
in "other"	3 (60.00%) libraries **(724)**

Ibid. . . . *showed that*, of 177 respondents who reported which users were charged, the following groups were identified as subject to an online search fee:

both outside and institutional users	98 (55.37%) libraries
outside users only	52 (29.38%) libraries
outside users and some institutional users	17 (9.60%) libraries
institutional users	8 (4.52%) libraries
some institutional users	2 (1.13%) libraries **(724)**

Ibid. . . . *showed that* the average MEDLINE search fee charged institutional users was $7.18, while the average MEDLINE search fee charged outside users was $9.23. By library type the average MEDLINE search fees for institutional users ranged from $6.29 for libraries in professional schools to $11.67 for libraries in societies, foundations, or research institutes, while for outside users the average MEDLINE search fees ranged from no charges for libraries in commercial institutions to $12.48 for libraries in societies, foundations, or research institutes.   **(724)**

Ibid. . . . *showed that* the average MEDLINE search fee for NLM region and Canada for institutional users ranged from $4.68 in region IX to $11.50 for region V (Canada averaged $9.25), while charges for outside users ranged from $4.76 in region IX to $16.00 in region V (Canada averaged $17.46). **(724)**

Ibid. . . . *showed that*, of the [178] libraries that charge user fees,the following elements were billed:

95% of the libraries billed for all the cost elements that appear on the vendor statement (computer connect-time, communication costs, and offline printing);

37% of the libraries included costs for terminal supplies;

26-29% of the libraries included costs for terminal maintenance, local telephone service, reruns, a share of the subscription costs or minimum charges by vendors;

22-23% of the libraries included costs for terminal rental/purchase and demonstrations;

15-19% of the libraries included costs for administrative expenses (billing, record keeping, postage, etc.);

8-10% of the libraries included costs for miscellaneous supplies or publicity materials;

and 4% of the libraries included costs for overhead or facilities.

(724)

■ A 1978 survey of publicly supported California libraries (primarily public and academic) concerning fee-charging behavior for online biblio-graphic searching (survey size: 350 libraries; responding: 213 or 65%) *showed that* 30% of the libraries charged fees for online bibliographic searching. This included 27% of 121 public libraries, 19% of 54 community college libraries, 78% of 18 college/university libraries, and 35% of 19 "other" libraries. **(570)**

Ibid. . . . *showed that* fee policy for online bibliographic searching was as follows:

no charge	43% of respondents
all users pay some fee	31% of respondents
some users charged; some not	3% of respondents
different fees for different user groups (all pay something)	7% of respondents

continued

other organization charges
    user (when search referred)   16% of respondents

Further, no online search fees were charged by 52% of the public libraries, 40% of the community college libraries, 21% of the college/university libraries, and 50% of the "other" libraries.   **(570)**

■ A 1979 survey of library automation in post-secondary educational institutions in Canada (survey size: 423 libraries; responding: 283 or 67%) *showed that* pricing policies for online searching were as follows [no total number of respondents given; percentages as provided in the article]:

30% of the respondents reported charging patrons only for connect-time, communication costs, and off-line prints;

14% of the respondents reported adding a flat surcharge for patrons outside their institution in addition to charging for connect-time, communications costs, and off-line prints;

12% of the respondents reported providing searches free for members of their own institution and did not provide searches for outsiders;

8% of the respondents reported charging flat fees for both insiders and outsiders, with a higher fee for outsiders;

31% of the respondents reported some other arrangement.   **(556)**

Public

■ A 1975-76 study of 359 online searches over a 7-month period using DIALOG in 4 public libraries in the San Franscisco Bay area where patrons were charged half the connect costs (in contrast to a study the year before in the same libraries when searches were free) *showed that* the total average time spent on a search request was 54.86 minutes when patrons were being charged for online searches, compared to 48.73 minutes when patrons were not being charged. In particular, reference interview time increased from 10.5 minutes for the free searches to 15.8 minutes for the paid searches; preparation time increased from 10.5 minutes for the free searches to 17.8 minutes for the paid searches; library follow-up time increased from 12.2 minutes to 14.2 minutes; and follow-up with the patron increased from 7.6 minutes to 10.3 minutes.   **(332)**

Ibid. . . . *showed that* the patron's presence during a search increased search time. This occurred both during the period of free searches, when the patron's presence increased the search time from 20.93 minutes to 33.85 minutes, and during the period of paid searches, when the patron's

presence increased the search time from 15.38 minutes to 16.51 minutes.
(332)

Ibid. . . . *showed that* the number of data bases used per search dropped from an average of 2.3 reported in an earlier study when the searches were free to an average of 1.9 in the present study when the patron was charged half the connect costs.
(332)

Ibid. . . . *showed that* the average costs for the various elements of the search were:

data base charges	$11.60
offline print charges	$10.87
search labor cost	$ 1.74
labor cost (all other tasks)	$ 4.68
TOTAL	$26.73

This compared to the total search costs for these same elements during the period of free searches (adjusted for inflation, price increases, etc.) of $28.78.
(332)

Ibid. . . . *showed that* the total search process (from patron interview to completion of follow-up) during the period of free searches took an average of 7.8 days, while during the pay period it took 4.4 days, a reduction of 44%. (Multiple causal factors may have been involved, including greater staff experience with online searching and proceedures.)
(332)

Ibid. . . . *showed that* the 3 most frequently used data bases were ERIC (159 or 22.78% searches), NTIS (119 or 17.05% searches), and PSY-CHOLOGY ABSTRACTS (107 or 15.33% searches). **(332)**

■ A 1978 survey of publicly supported California libraries (primarily public and academic) concerning fee-charging behavior for online bibliographic searching (survey size: 350 libraries; responding: 213 or 65%) *showed that* 30% of the libraries charged fees for online bibliographic searching. This included 27% of 121 public libraries, 19% of 54 community college libraries, 78% of 18 college/university libraries, and 35% of 19 "other" libraries.
(570)

Ibid. . . . *showed that* fee policy for online bibliographic searching was as follows:

no charge	43% of respondents
all users pay some fee	31% of respondents

continued

some users charged; some not	3% of respondents
different fees for different user groups (all pay something)	7% of respondents
other organization charges user (when search referred)	16% of respondents

Further, no online search fees were charged by 52% of the public libraries, 40% of the community college libraries, 21% of the college/university libraries, and 50% of the "other" libraries.   **(570)**

Special

■ A 1967 survey of medical school libraries concerning reference services (survey size: 93 libraries; responding: 85 or 91.4%) *showed that* the following number of libraries provided the following services (multiple responses allowed):

MEDLARS searches	77 (90.6%) libraries
edit bibliographies for authors	37 (43.5%) libraries
current awareness service	15 (17.6%) libraries
recurring bibliographies	14 (16.5%) libraries
routing of current journals	11 (12.9%) libraries

Further, 3 (3.5%) libraries reported charging a fee for providing bibliographic services.   **(682)**

■ A survey reported in 1974 at the University of Virginia Medical Center of MEDLINE users (primarily faculty, house staff, outside health professionals, and graduate students) during a 6-month period in 1972-73 (survey size: 428 users; responding: 246 or 58%) *showed that* 188 (76%) respondents reported they would continue to use MEDLINE even if charged for the service ($1.50 per simple search; $3.00 per more complex search); 5 (2%) reported they would not continue to use MEDLINE; and 53 (22%) were undecided.   **(696)**

■ A survey reported in 1977 concerning online searching at the U.S. Army Construction Engineering Research Laboratory library (Champaign, Illinois), involving both users of the service (sample size: 27; responding: 26 or 96.3%) and nonusers of the service (sample size: 19; responding: 13 or 68.4%), *showed that* of 13 nonuser respondents the main reason given for not using the online search service was (multiple responses allowed): found all the materials they needed for research on their own, 6 (46.2%). No respondents reported that expense was a problem.   **(416)**

■ A 1978 survey of North American health sciences libraries that were users of the National Library of Medicine search services in November 1977 (survey size: 708 libraries; responding: 376; usable: 345 or 48.7%) *showed that* of 339 respondents some kind of online search fees were charged by 178 (52.50) libraries. The numbers of libraries charging some kind of online search fee by type of library were as follows:

in professional school	90 (89.11%) libraries
in other college or university	21 (91.30%) libraries
in commercial institution	9 (16.07%) libraries
in society, foundation, or research institute	17 (40.48%) libraries
in hospital	38 (33.93%) libraries
in "other"	3 (60.00%) libraries **(724)**

Ibid. . . . *showed that,* of 177 respondents who reported which users were charged, the following groups were identified as subject to an online search fee:

both outside and institutional users	98 (55.37%) libraries
outside users only	52 (29.38%) libraries
outside users and some institutional users	17 (9.60%) libraries
institutional users	8 (4.52%) libraries
some institutional users	2 (1.13%) libraries **(724)**

Ibid. . . . *showed that* the average MEDLINE search fee charged institutional users was $7.18, while the average MEDLINE search fee charged outside users was $9.23. By library type the average MEDLINE search fees for institutional users ranged from $6.29 for libraries in professional schools to $11.67 for libraries in societies, foundations, or research institutes, while for outside users the average MEDLINE search fees ranged from no charges for libraries in commercial institutions to $12.48 for libraries in societies, foundations, or research institutes. **(724)**

Ibid. . . . *showed that* the average MEDLINE search fee for NLM region and Canada for institutional users ranged from $4.68 in region IX to $11.50 for region V (Canada averaged $9.25), while charges for outside users ranged from $4.76 in region IX to $16.00 in region V (Canada averaged $17.46). **(724)**

Ibid. . . . *showed that*, of the [178] libraries that charge user fees,the
following elements were billed:

> 95% of the libraries billed for all the cost elements that appear
> on the vendor statement (computer connect-time,
> communication costs, and offline printing);
>
> 37% of the libraries included costs for terminal supplies;
>
> 26-29% of the libraries included costs for terminal
> maintenance, local telephone service, reruns, a share of the
> subscription costs or minimum charges by vendors;
>
> 22-23% of the libraries included costs for terminal
> rental/purchase and demonstrations;
>
> 15-19% of the libraries included costs for administrative
> expenses (billing, record keeping, postage, etc.);
>
> 8-10% of the libraries included costs for miscellaneous supplies
> or publicity materials;
>
> and 4% of the libraries included costs for overhead or facilities.
>
> **(724)**

Online Searching—Follow-up

Public

■ A 1975 study of online searches provided free of charge in the
DIALOG data bases over a 3-month period in 4 San Franscisco Bay area
public libraries (411 usable requests; 429 searches undertaken, including
some duplicates) *showed that* the reference interview averaged 10.5
minutes (295 cases), preparation averaged 10.48 minutes (223 cases),
search averaged 22.72 minutes (408 cases), library follow-up (filling out
reports, etc.) averaged 12.21 minutes (307 cases), and patron follow-up
(discussing results with patron) averaged 7.61 minutes (171 cases). In a
limited number of cases where the actual search was conducted in another
library the referring library's preparation time averaged 18.65 minutes (46
cases), while their library follow-up time averaged 11.48 minutes (42
cases).   **(326)**

Ibid. . . . *showed that* the 4 libraries had statistically significant differences
in the amount of time which was spent on the reference interview, the
search itself, and the library follow-up (significance level greater than
.000). For example, average search time per library ranged from 19.74
minutes to 30.42 minutes.   **(326)**

■ A 1975-76 study of 359 online searches over a 7-month period using DIALOG in 4 public libraries in the San Francisco Bay area where patrons were charged half the connect costs (in contrast to a study the year before in the same libraries when searches were free) *showed that* the total average time spent on a search request was 54.86 minutes when patrons were being charged for online searches compared to 48.73 minutes when patrons were not being charged. In particular, reference interview time increased from 10.5 minutes for the free searches to 15.8 minutes for the paid searches; preparation time increased from 10.5 minutes for the free searches to 17.8 minutes for the paid searches; library follow-up time increased from 12.2 minutes to 14.2 minutes; and follow-up with the patron increased from 7.6 minutes to 10.3 minutes. **(332)**

Online Searching—General Impact

Academic

■ A survey reported in 1977 concerning online searching at the U.S. Army Construction Engineering Research Laboratory library (Champaign, Illinois), involving both users of the service (sample size: 27; responding: 26 or 96.3%) and nonusers of the service (sample size: 19; responding: 13 or 68.4%), *showed that,* of 25 user respondents, 11 (44%) reported ordering "many" of the documents for the citations from the online search through the library; 9 (36%) reported ordering "a few"; and 5 (20%) reported ordering "none." **(416)**

■ A 1978 survey of North American health sciences libraries that were users of the National Library of Medicine search services in November 1977 (survey size: 708 libraries; responding: 376; usable: 345 or 48.7%) *showed that,* of 337 respondents, 316 (93.8%) libraries "agreed" or "strongly agreed" that online searching had made it possible to serve more users, while of 330 respondents, 311 (94.2%) libraries "agreed" or "strongly agreed" that online searching had caused an increase in interlibrary loan borrowing. **(724)**

Ibid. . . . *showed that,* of 317 respondents, 194 (61.2%) libraries "agreed" or "strongly agreed" that it had been necessary to subscribe to new journals due to requests of online search users. Further, of 328 respondents, 311 (94.8%) "agreed" or "strongly agreed" that users' expectations for library services had increased since the advent of online searching. **(724)**

■ A 1981 survey of U.S. depository libraries, both academic and public (sample size: 221; responding: 171 or 77%), concerning their use of online data bases (DIALOG, ORBIT, and BRS), particularly with regard to government documents *showed that* none of the public depositories had ever ordered microfiche online as the result of a government document search, while only 3% of the academic libraries had ever done so. **(317)**

Public

■ A 1981 survey of U.S. depository libraries, both academic and public (sample size: 221; responding: 171 or 77%), concerning their use of online data bases (DIALOG, ORBIT, and BRS), particularly with regard to government documents *showed that* none of the public depositories had ever ordered microfiche online as the result of a government document search, while only 3% of the academic libraries had ever done so. **(317)**

School

■ A 1981 study of 53 ninth-grade honors students in science in a suburban Philadelphia public high school *showed that*, although all the students were required to undertake online bibliographic searches, 81% did not cite any materials so retrieved in their bibliographies. The 21 citations that were from online bibliographic searches accounted for less than 5% of all bibliographic citations. **(222)**

Special

■ A survey reported in 1977 concerning online searching at the U.S. Army Construction Engineering Research Laboratory library (Champaign, Illinois), involving both users of the service (sample size: 27; responding: 26 or 96.3%) and nonusers of the service (sample size: 19; responding: 13 or 68.4%), *showed that*, of 25 user respondents, 11 (44%) reported ordering "many" of the documents for the citations from the online search through the library; 9 (36%) reported ordering "a few"; and 5 (20%) reported ordering "none." **(416)**

■ A 1978 survey of North American health sciences libraries that were users of the National Library of Medicine search services in November 1977 (survey size: 708 libraries; responding: 376; usable: 345 or 48.7%) *showed that*, of 337 respondents, 316 (93.8%) libraries "agreed" or "strongly agreed" that online searching had made it possible to serve more users, while of 330 respondents, 311 (94.2%) libraries "agreed" or "strongly agreed" that online searching had caused an increase in interlibrary loan borrowing.

(724)

Ibid. . . . *showed that*, of 317 respondents, 194 (61.2%) libraries "agreed" or "strongly agreed" that it had been necessary to subscribe to new journals due to requests of online search users. Further, of 328 respondents, 311 (94.8%) "agreed" or "strongly agreed" that users' expectations for library services had increased since the advent of online searching.

(724)

Online Searching—Patron Interview

Academic

■ A study reported in 1982 at the University of Iowa Health Sciences Library concerning the effect of the patron's presence during MEDLINE searches, based on searches for 100 different patrons (each search was conducted twice by different staff members, once with and once without the patron) and subsequent survey (100% responding) of those patrons *showed that* increasing the depth of the interview with the patron during the formulation phase was not a good idea. Specifically, it did not increase the results for precision, recall, or user satisfaction to a statistically significant degree. It did, however, increase the online search time (from an average of 9.29 minutes per patron to an average of 10.62 minutes per patron) by a statistically significant amount (significant at the .05 level).

(743)

Public

■ A 1975 study of online searches provided free of charge in the DIALOG data bases over a 3-month period in 4 San Franscisco Bay area public libraries (411 usable requests; 429 searches undertaken, including some duplicates) *showed that* the reference interview averaged 10.5 minutes (295 cases), preparation averaged 10.48 minutes (223 cases), search averaged 22.72 minutes (408 cases), library follow-up (filling out reports, etc.) averaged 12.21 minutes (307 cases), patron follow-up (discussing results with patron) averaged 7.61 minutes (171 cases). In a limited number of cases where the actual search was conducted in another library, the referring library preparation time averaged 18.65 minutes (46 cases), while their library follow-up time averaged 11.48 minutes (42 cases).

(326)

Ibid. . . . *showed that* the 4 libraries had statistically significant differences in the amount of time spent on the reference interview, the search itself, and the library follow-up (significance level greater than .000). For example, average search time per library ranged from 19.74 minutes to 30.42 minutes.   **(326)**

■ A 1975-76 study of 359 online searches over a 7-month period using DIALOG in 4 public libraries in the San Franscisco Bay area where patrons were charged half the connect costs (in contrast to a study the year before in the same libraries when searches were free) *showed that* the total average time spent on a search request was 54.86 minutes when patrons were being charged for online searches, compared to 48.73 minutes when patrons were not being charged. In particular, reference interview time increased from 10.5 minutes for the free searches to 15.8 minutes for the paid searches; preparation time increased from 10.5 minutes for the free searches to 17.8 minutes for the paid searches; library follow-up time increased from 12.2 minutes to 14.2 minutes; and follow-up with the patron increased from 7.6 minutes to 10.3 minutes.   **(332)**

Special

■ A study reported in 1982 at the University of Iowa Health Sciences Library concerning the effect of the patron's presence during MEDLINE searches, based on searches for 100 different patrons (each search was conducted twice by different staff members, once with and once without the patron) and subsequent survey (100% responding) of those patrons *showed that* increasing the depth of the interview with the patron during the formulation phase was not a good idea. Specifically, it did not increase the results for precision, recall, or user satisfaction to a statistically significant degree. It did, however, increase the online search time (from an average of 9.29 minutes per patron to an average of 10.62 minutes per patron) by a statistically significant amount (significant at the .05 level).
                                                                            (743)

Online Searching—Patron Present

Academic

■ A 1975-76 study at the University of Utah Marriott Library of online bibliographic data base searching *showed that*, for a sample of 50 searches each in each of 4 major data bases, the patron chose to be present in 49 cases during ERIC searches, in 48 cases during PSYCHOLOGY AB-STRACTS searches, in 18 cases during NTIS searches and in 12 cases during CHEMICAL ABSTRACTS CONDENSATES searches.   **(329)**

■ A survey reported in 1977 concerning online searching at the U.S. Army Construction Engineering Research Laboratory library (Champaign, Illinois), involving both users of the service (sample size: 27; responding: 26 or 96.3%) and nonusers of the service (sample size: 19; responding: 13 or 68.4%), *showed that*, of 25 user respondents, 16 (64%) reported that they had been present at the terminal during the online search, and of these, 15 (93.8%) reported that they felt it was helpful while 1 (6.2%) was uncertain whether it was helpful or not.   **(416)**

■ A study reported in 1982 at the University of Iowa Health Sciences Library concerning the effect of the patron's presence during MEDLINE searches, based on searches for 100 different patrons (each search was conducted twice by different staff members, once with and once without the patron) and subsequent survey (100% responding) of those patrons, *showed that* there was a statistically significant increase in recall rate (number of relevant citations retrieved out of the total relevant possibilities) and patron satisfaction rate when the patrons were present during the search process. Specifically, the recall rate increased from an average of 58.8% per patron to 74.6% per patron, and the satisfaction rate (based on a 5-point scale where a rating of 1 is least satisfied) increased from an average of 3.7 per patron to 4.3 per patron. (These differences were significant at the .001 level.)   **(743)**

Ibid. . . . *showed that* although the the precision rate (the number of relevant citations divided by the total number of citations found) increased with patrons present during the search process, the increase was not statistically significant. Specifically, the precision rate increased from an average of 40.3% per patron to an average of 45.3% per patron.   **(743)**

Ibid. . . . *showed that* there was a statistically significant increase in the amount of time a search took when the patron was present. Specifically, the search time increased from an average of 10.1 minutes per patron to 11.7 minutes per patron (significant at the .05 level).   **(743)**

Ibid. . . . *showed that* patrons evaluated the 2 searches as follows: search 1 (without patron present) better (11%), search 2 (with patron present) better (58%), and no difference (31%).   **(743)**

Ibid. . . . *showed that* 80% of the patrons reported that the quality of the search where they were present was worth the extra time it cost them (17%

reported it was not worth the extra time, and 3% gave no response). Further, 80% of the patrons reported they preferred to be present during their next search, while 12% reported they preferred to be absent, and 8% did not respond or did not care either way.   **(743)**

Public

■ A 1975 study of online searches provided free of charge in the DIALOG data bases over a 3-month period in 4 San Franscisco Bay area public libraries (411 usable requests; 429 searches undertaken, including some duplicates) *showed that*, of 103 searches where the patron had the choice of being present, the patron chose to be present in only 43 (41.7%) instances. The average search time with patron present was 37.9 minutes, compared to 25 minutes when the patron was not present. (This difference was statistically significant at the .01 level.)   **(326)**

■ A 1975-76 study of 359 online searches over a 7-month period using DIALOG in 4 public libraries in the San Franscisco Bay area where patrons were charged half the connect costs (in contrast to a study the year before in the same libraries when searches were free) *showed that* the patron's presence during a search increased search time. This occurred both during the period of free searches, when the patron's presence increased the search time from 20.93 minutes to 33.85 minutes, and during the period of paid searches, when the patron's presence increased the search time from 15.38 minutes to 16.51 minutes.   **(332)**

Special

■ A survey reported in 1977 concerning online searching at the U.S. Army Construction Engineering Research Laboratory library (Champaign, Illinois), involving both users of the service (sample size: 27; responding: 26 or 96.3%) and nonusers of the service (sample size: 19; responding: 13 or 68.4%) *showed that*, of 25 user respondents, 16 (64%) reported that they had been present at the terminal during the online search, and of these, 15 (93.8%) reported that they felt it was helpful while 1 (6.2%) was uncertain whether it was helpful or not.   **(416)**

■ A 1977 survey of industrial clients' and NASA-Small Business Administration Technology Assistance Program clients' perception of costs and dollar benefits of online computer literature searches, involving 66 responding SBA clients and 71 responding regular industrial clients for a total of 137 responding clients *showed that* the interactive (i.e., client-present) search was the most cost-effective of 3 search techniques. The selected-search technique (i.e. a subject specialist does the online search) used by 31% of clients reporting dollar benefits for current or new products returned $11.27 for every dollar invested in an online search; the unselected-search technique (i.e., written request for a search and a written response) used by 9% of the clients reporting dollar benefits for current or new products returned $18.00 for each dollar invested; while the interactive search used by 25.6% of the clients reporting dollar benefits for current or new products returned $34.13 for each dollar invested. **(432)**

■ A study reported in 1982 at the University of Iowa Health Sciences Library concerning the effect of the patron's presence during MEDLINE searches, based on searches for 100 different patrons (each search was conducted twice by different staff members, once with and once without the patron) and subsequent survey (100% responding) of those patrons, *showed that* there was a statistically significant increase in recall rate (number of relevant citations retrieved out of the total relevant possibilities) and patron satisfaction rate when the patrons were present during the search process. Specifically, the recall rate increased from an average of 58.8% per patron to 74.6% per patron, and the satisfaction rate (based on a 5-point scale where a rating of 1 is least satisfied) increased from an average of 3.7 per patron to 4.3 per patron. (These differences were significant at the .001 level.) **(743)**

Ibid. . . . *showed that*, although the the precision rate (the number of relevant citations divided by the total number of citations found) increased with patrons present during the search process, the increase was not statistically significant. Specifically, the precision rate increased from an average of 40.3% per patron to an average of 45.3% per patron. **(743)**

Ibid. . . . *showed that* there was a statistically significant increase in the amount of time a search took when the patron was present. Specifically, the search time increased from an average of 10.1 minutes per patron to 11.7 minutes per patron (significant at the .05 level). **(743)**

Ibid. . . . *showed that* patrons evaluated the 2 searches as follows: search 1 (without patron present) better (11%), search 2 (with patron present) better (58%), and no difference (31%). **(743)**

Ibid. . . . *showed that* 80% of the patrons reported that the quality of the search where they were present was worth the extra time it cost them (17% reported it was not worth the extra time, and 3% gave no response). Further, 80% of the patrons reported they preferred to be present during their next search, while 12% reported they preferred to be absent, and 8% did not respond or did not care either way. **(743)**

Online Searching—Patron Satisfaction

Academic

■ A 1973 survey of patrons using MEDLINE at 7 information centers (University of Illinois Medical Center, Chicago; Indiana University; University of Chicago; University of Illinois, Urbana; Cleveland Health Sciences Library; Mayo Clinic; and Wayne State University) during April-September 1973 (survey size: 1,017 patrons; responding: 904 or 88.9%) *showed that* of 895 respondents the helpfulness of the search was judged as follows:

not helpful	9.7% respondents
moderately helpful	29.4% respondents
helpful	34.6% respondents
very helpful	26.3% respondents **(715)**

Ibid. . . . *showed that* of 706 respondents there was a statistically significant relationship between the number of useful references received and the perception that the search was helpful (significant at the .001 level). Specifically, 80% of the respondents who received a high number of useful references (6 or more) judged the search helpful, compared to 40% of the users so reporting who received a low number of references (less than 6).
(715)

Ibid. . . . *showed that* of 795 respondents there was a statistically significant relationship between patron perception that relevant references were missed in a search and patron perception of the search as helpful (significant at the .001 level). Specifically, 70% of the patrons who perceived that no references had been missed in the search reported the search helpful, compared to 49.0% patrons so reporting who perceived that 1 or more references had been missed.   **(715)**

■ A survey reported in 1974 at the University of Virginia Medical Center of MEDLINE users (primarily faculty, house staff, outside health professionals, and graduate students) during a 6-month period in 1972-73 (survey size: 428 users; responding: 246 or 58%) *showed that* 230 (93.5%) respondents reported that MEDLINE was a "substantial improvement of the traditional methods of searching through the printed indexes." However, 6 (2.4%) respondents felt MEDLINE was "no substantial improvement," and 10 (4.1%) felt it was a substantial improvement but had not found it helpful in either their clinical or research work.   **(696)**

Ibid. . . . *showed that* 125 (51%) reported that MEDLINE had been helpful "in both their clinical and research activities," while 79 (32.1%) reported MEDLINE helpful only in research, and 26 (10.6%) reported it helpful only in clinical work.   **(696)**

Ibid. . . . *showed that* 188 (76%) respondents reported they would continue to use MEDLINE even if charged for the service ($1.50 per simple search; $3.00 per more complex search); 5 (2%) reported they would not continue to use MEDLINE; and 53 (22%) were undecided.   **(696)**

■ A 1974 study over a 4-month period (January-April) of free MEDLINE use at Oakland University (Rochester, Michigan), a university without a medical school, involving 21 faculty and students for a total of 36 searches, *showed that*, of 27 (75%) search evaluation forms returned, 25 indicated the search to be of "major" or "considerable" value to the user; 2 searches were reported to be of "minor" value to the user.   **(411)**

■ A study of the University of Delaware during the 1976-77 academic year *showed that*, of graduate and undergraduate students using online search services, there was a statistically significant relationship between patron satisfaction and both the absolute number of citations generated and the absolute number of relevant citations generated. Patrons satisfaction was also statistically significantly correlated with patron estimate of time saved.   **(001)**

Ibid. . . . *showed that* graduate and undergraduate students using online search services revealed no relationship between student status, purpose of the search, cost to the student, or percentage of relevant citations and student satisfaction with the search.   **(001)**

■ A survey reported in 1977 concerning online searching at the U.S. Army Construction Engineering Research Laboratory library (Champaign, Illinois), involving both users of the service (sample size: 27; responding: 26 or 96.3%) and nonusers of the service (sample size: 19; responding: 13 or 68.4%), *showed that*, of 24 user respondents, 21 (87.5%) reported that it was worth sorting through the irrelevant citations to get to the relevant ones; 1 (4.2%) reported that it was not worth it; and 2 (8.3%) reported themselves undecided.   **(416)**

Ibid. . . . *showed that*, of 26 user respondents, 25 (96.2%) reported that they felt the online search service was a useful addition to other library services; none reported feeling it was not; and 1 (3.8%) reported they were uncertain.   **(416)**

■ A survey reported in 1978 of the literature *showed that* 70-91% of the patrons in all types of libraries (academic, special, public) reported satisfaction with their online search results. **(001)**

■ An analysis of records reported in 1978 on online bibliographic data base searching at Flordia State University Chemistry Department and Monsanto Textiles Company in Pensacola, Florida (353 searches conducted at FSU and 345 conducted at Monsanto) *showed that* there were no statistically significant differences of opinion (.02 level) on the currency of citations, with 44% of FSU researchers reporting "very satisfactory" compared to 35% of Monsanto researchers and 43% of FSU researchers reporting "satisfactory" compared to 49% of Monsanto researchers. **(155)**

Ibid. . . . *showed that* there were no statistically significant differences of opinion on the utility of the searches, with 54% of the FSU researchers reporting "very useful" compared to 50% of the Monsanto researchers and 24% of the FSU researchers reporting "of some use" compared to 25% of the Monsanto researchers. **(155)**

■ A study reported in 1982 at the University of Iowa Health Sciences Library concerning the effect of the patron's presence during MEDLINE searches, based on searches for 100 different patrons (each search was conducted twice by different staff members, once with and once without the patron) and subsequent survey (100% responding) of those patrons *showed that* there was a statistically significant increase in recall rate (number of relevant citations retrieved out of the total relevant possibilities) and patron satisfaction rate when the patrons were present during the search process. Specifically, the recall rate increased from an average of 58.8% per patron to 74.6% per patron, and the satisfaction rate (based on a 5-point scale where a rating of 1 is least satisfied) increased from an average of 3.7 per patron to 4.3 per patron. (These differences were significant at the .001 level.) **(743)**

Ibid. . . . *showed that* patrons evaluated the 2 searches as follows: search 1 (without patron present) better (11%), search 2 (with patron present) better (58%), and no difference (31%). **(743)**

Ibid. . . . *showed that* a comparison of first-time search requesters with requesters who had requested previous online searches revealed that the experienced patrons had a statistically significantly higher satisfaction rate for both the user-present and the user-absent searches (significant at the .004 level). Further, it took statistically significantly less time to formulate a search for the experienced users (significant at the .04 level). There was no statistically significant difference in recall rate or in online search time between experienced and nonexperienced patrons. **(743)**

Ibid. . . . *showed that* there were no statistically significant differences among undergraduate, graduate, or faculty search requesters for precision, recall, or satisfaction rates. **(743)**

Special

■ A 1973 survey of patrons using MEDLINE at 7 information centers (University of Illinois Medical Center, Chicago; Indiana University; University of Chicago; University of Illinois, Urbana; Cleveland Health Sciences Library; Mayo Clinic; and Wayne State University) during April-September 1973 (survey size: 1,017 patrons; responding: 904 or 88.9%) *showed that* of 895 respondents the helpfulness of the search was judged as follows:

not helpful	9.7% respondents
moderately helpful	29.4% respondents
helpful	34.6% respondents
very helpful	26.3% respondents **(715)**

Ibid. . . . *showed that* of 706 respondents there was a statistically significant relationship between the number of useful references received and the perception that the search was helpful (significant at the .001 level). Specifically, 80% of the respondents who received a high number of useful references (6 or more) judged the search helpful, compared to 40% of the users so reporting who received a low number of references (less than 6). **(715)**

Ibid. . . . *showed that* of 795 respondents there was a statistically significant relationship between patron perception that relevant references were missed in a search and patron perception of the search as helpful (significant at the .001 level). Specifically, 70% of the patrons who perceived that no references had been missed in the search reported the search helpful, compared to 49.0% patrons so reporting who perceived that 1 or more references had been missed. **(715)**

■ A survey reported in 1974 at the University of Virginia Medical Center of MEDLINE users (primarily faculty, house staff, outside health professionals, and graduate students) during a 6-month period in 1972-73 (survey size: 428 users; responding: 246 or 58%) *showed that* 230 (93.5%) respondents reported that MEDLINE was a "substantial improvement of the traditional methods of searching through the printed indexes." However, 6 (2.4%) respondents felt MEDLINE was "no substantial improvement," and 10 (4.1%) felt it was a substantial improvement but had not found it helpful in either their clinical or research work. **(696)**

Ibid. . . . *showed that* 125 (51%) reported that MEDLINE had been helpful "in both their clinical and research activities," while 79 (32.1%) reported MEDLINE helpful only in research, and 26 (10.6%) reported it helpful only in clinical work. **(696)**

■ A survey reported in 1977 concerning online searching at the U.S. Army Construction Engineering Research Laboratory library (Champaign, Illinois), involving both users of the service (sample size: 27; responding: 26 or 96.3%) and nonusers of the service (sample size: 19; responding: 13 or 68.4%), *showed that*, of 24 user respondents, 21 (87.5%) reported that it was worth sorting through the irrelevant citations to get to the relevant ones; 1 (4.2%) reported that it was not worth it; and 2 (8.3%) reported themselves undecided. **(416)**

Ibid. . . . *showed that*, of 26 user respondents, 25 (96.2%) reported that they felt the online search service was a useful addition to other library services; none reported feeling it was not; and 1 (3.8%) reported they were uncertain. **(416)**

■ A 1977 survey of industrial clients' and NASA-Small Business Administration Technology Assistance Program clients' perception of costs and dollar benefits of online computer literature searches, involving 66 responding SBA clients and 71 responding regular industrial clients for a total of 137 responding clients, *showed that* 34 (51.5%) of the SBA clients and 39 (55.0%) of the regular industrial clients reported dollar benefits from the search results. The remaining clients reported that no application of the search information was or would be attempted. **(432)**

Ibid. . . . *showed that* 13 (19.7%) of the SBA clients and 7 (9.9%) of the regular industrial clients reported dollar benefits related to current products; 4 (6.1%) of the SBA clients and 11 (15.5%) of the regular industrial clients reported dollar benefits related to new products; and 17 (25.7%) of the SBA clients and 21 (29.6%) of the regular industrial clients reported significant time savings in the information-gathering process. Additional 5-year follow-on benefits were estimated for both groups. **(432)**

Ibid. . . . *showed that* of those reporting dollar benefits the overall cost/ benefit ratio in dollars of online searching for SBA clients was 1 to 2.7 ($124,481 invested for $364,605 in benefits), while for regular industrial clients the ratio was 1 to 3.0 ($87,808 invested for $263,550 in benefits). 5-year follow-on benefits were estimated by respondents to be $373,500 for SBA clients (c/b ratio of 1 to 10.2) and $500,000 for regular industrial clients (c/b ratio of 1 to 5.7). **(432)**

Ibid. . . . *showed that* the interactive (i.e., client-present) search was the most cost-effective of 3 search techniques. The selected-search technique (i.e., a subject specialist does the online search) used by 31% of clients reporting dollar benefits for current or new products returned $11.27 for every dollar invested in an online search; the unselected-search technique (i.e., written request for a search and a written response) used by 9% of the clients reporting dollar benefits for current or new products returned $18.00 for each dollar invested; while the interactive search used by 25.6% of the clients reporting dollar benefits for current or new products returned $34.13 for each dollar invested. **(432)**

■ An analysis of records reported in 1978 on online bibliographic data base searching at Flordia State University Chemistry Department and Monsanto Textiles Company in Pensacola, Florida (353 searches conducted at FSU and 345 conducted at Monsanto) *showed that* there were no statistically significant differences of opinion (.02 level) on the currency of citations, with 44% of FSU researchers reporting "very satisfactory" compared to 35% of Monsanto researchers and 43% of FSU researchers reporting "satisfactory" compared to 49% of Monsanto researchers. **(155)**

Ibid. . . . *showed that* there were no statistically significant differences of opinion on the utility of the searches, with 54% of the FSU researchers reporting "very useful" compared to 50% of the Monsanto researchers and 24% of the FSU researchers reporting "of some use" compared to 25% of the Monsanto researchers. **(155)**

■ A study reported in 1982 at the University of Iowa Health Sciences Library concerning the effect of the patron's presence during MEDLINE searches, based on searches for 100 different patrons (each search was conducted twice by different staff members, once with and once without the patron) and subsequent survey (100% responding) of those patrons *showed that* there was a statistically significant increase in recall rate (number of relevant citations retrieved out of the total relevant possibilities) and patron satisfaction rate when the patrons were present during the search process. Specifically, the recall rate increased from an average of 58.8% per patron to 74.6% per patron, and the satisfaction rate (based on a 5-point scale where a rating of 1 is least satisfied) increased from an average of 3.7 per patron to 4.3 per patron. (These differences were significant at the .001 level.)   **(743)**

Ibid. . . . *showed that* patrons evaluated the 2 searches as follows: search 1 (without patron present) better (11%), search 2 (with patron present) better (58%), and no difference (31%).   **(743)**

Ibid. . . . *showed that* a comparison of first-time search requesters with requesters who had requested previous online searches revealed that the experienced patrons had a statistically significantly higher satisfaction rate for both the user-present and the user-absent searches (significant at the .004 level). Further, it took statistically significantly less time to formulate a search for the experienced users (significant at the .04 level). There was no statistically significant difference in recall rate or in online search time between experienced and nonexperienced patrons.   **(743)**

Online Searching—Preparation

Public

■ A 1975 study of online searches provided free of charge in the DIALOG data bases over a 3-month period in 4 San Franscisco Bay area public libraries (411 usable requests; 429 searches undertaken, including some duplicates) *showed that* the reference interview averaged 10.5 minutes (295 cases), preparation averaged 10.48 minutes (223 cases), search averaged 22.72 minutes (408 cases), library follow-up (filling out reports, etc.) averaged 12.21 minutes (307 cases), patron follow-up (discussing results with patron) averaged 7.61 minutes (171 cases). In a limited number of cases where the actual search was conducted in another library, the referring library preparation time averaged 18.65 minutes (46 cases), while their library follow-up time averaged 11.48 minutes (42 cases).   **(326)**

■ A 1975-76 study of 359 online searches over a 7-month period using DIALOG in 4 public libraries in the San Franscisco Bay area where patrons were charged half the connect costs (in contrast to a study the year before in the same libraries when searches were free) *showed that* the total average time spent on a search request was 54.86 minutes when patrons were being charged for online searches, compared to 48.73 minutes when patrons were not being charged. In particular, reference interview time increased from 10.5 minutes for the free searches to 15.8 minutes for the paid searches; preparation time increased from 10.5 minutes for the free searches to 17.8 minutes for the paid searches; library follow-up time increased from 12.2 minutes to 14.2 minutes; and follow-up with the patron increased from 7.6 minutes to 10.3 minutes.   **(332)**

Online Searching—Response Time

General

■ A 1979 study of response time variations in the National Library of Medicine's ELHILL bibliographic search system over a 5-week period, involving 35,972 measurements of response time, *showed that* overall the average response time was 2.2 seconds. Specifically, 44.5% of the response times were less than 1 second; 74.4% of the response times were less than 2 seconds; 91.2% of the response times were less than 4 seconds; and only 1.1% of the response times were more than 10 seconds.   **(660)**

Ibid. . . . *showed that* before 9:00 a.m. the response time averaged less than 1.5 seconds, while after 6:00 p.m. the response time averaged less than 1.7 seconds. Between 9:00 a.m. and 6:00 p.m. the response time slowed down, but the hourly average never exceeded 3.9 seconds during this period.   **(660)**

Ibid. . . . *showed that* the only significant variable explaining response time variations was "volume of transactions" (significant at the .02 level). There were no significant differences in response time due to the file being used or the command issued.   **(660)**

Special

■ A 1979 study of response time variations in the National Library of Medicine's ELHILL bibliographic search system over a 5-week period, involving 35,972 measurements of response time *showed that* overall the average response time was 2.2 seconds. Specifically, 44.5% of the response times were less than 1 second; 74.4% of the response times were less than 2 seconds; 91.2% of the response times were less than 4 seconds; and only 1.1% of the response times were more than 10 seconds.   **(660)**

Ibid. . . . *showed that* before 9:00 a.m. the response time averaged less than 1.5 seconds, while after 6:00 p.m. the response time averaged less than 1.7 seconds. Between 9:00 a.m. and 6:00 p.m. the response time slowed down, but the hourly average never exceeded 3.9 seconds during this period.   **(660)**

Ibid. . . . *showed that* the only significant variable explaining response time variations was "volume of transactions" (significant at the .02 level). There were no significant differences in response time due to the file being used or the command issued.   **(660)**

Online Searching—Specific Data Bases/Vendors Used

General

■ A 12-month study in 1977-78 of online bibliographic literature searching of MINET (Kansas City Libraries Metropolitan Information Network, which includes 4 public libraries, 3 medical libraries, and 1 academic medical library), involving 403 paid search sessions and searches of 544 files or data bases, *showed that* the 4 most used data bases were ERIC with 181 (33.1%) searches, PSYCHOLOGICAL ABSTRACTS with 77 (14.1%) searches, SOCIAL SCISEARCH with 51 (9.3%) searches, and MEDLARS/MEDLINE with 32 (5.8%) searches.   **(234)**

Ibid. . . . *showed that*, of the 544 data bases searched, the vendors most used were Lockheed, 296 uses of its files (54.3% of total data base use); BRS, 182 uses of its files (33.5% of total data base use); and National Library of Medicine, 34 uses (6.2% of total data base use).   **(234)**

■ A survey reported in 1983 of librarians/information specialists at 2 Philadelphia area online users meetings and at the SLA annual conference in Detroit (sample size: 300; responding: 80) *showed that* the 3 top-ranked online vendors out of 7 were (in order of descending importance): (1) DIALOG, (2) BRS, and (3) SDC.   **(442)**

Ibid. . . . *showed that* 77.2% of the respondents reported that they used DIALOG frequently; 32.9% reported they used BRS frequently; and 13.9% reported they used SDC frequently. There was a statistically significant correlation between the number of respondents reporting frequent use of a data base and the overall ranking of that vendor, i.e., the greater the number of frequent users of a vendor the higher the vendor's ranking (significant at the .05 level). **(442)**

Academic

■ A 1975-76 study at the University of Utah Marriott Library of online bibliographic data base searching *showed that* the number of searches and average length per search were as follows:

CHEMICAL ABSTRACTS CONDENSATES (254 searches averaging 7.47 minutes each)

ERIC (341 searches averaging 14.03 minutes each)

NTIS (120 searches averaging 6.30 minutes each)

PSYCHOLOGY ABSTRACTS (227 searches averaging 11.45 minutes each)

other (447 searches averaging 6.58 minutes each) **(329)**

■ A survey reported in 1976 of 10 academic and public libraries using the New York Times Information Bank *showed that* the areas in which the most requests for information were made were politics (9 libraries), news reports (7 libraries), and biography (6 libraries). **(149)**

■ A 1978 survey of major biomedical libraries (primarily those serving accredited medical schools) (survey size: 120 libraries; responding: 88 or 73%) *showed that* respondents reported access to the following vendors of bibliographic data bases:

National Library of Medicine (MEDLINE, et al.)	85 (97%) libraries
Bibliographic Retrieval Service	52 (59%) libraries
Lockheed	50 (57%) libraries
Systems Development Corporation	44 (50%) libraries **(726)**

■ A 1979 survey of libraries in accredited North American veterinary schools (population: 25 libraries; responding: 23 or 92%) *showed that* all respondents reported that online search services were available. 10 (43.5%) libraries reported they had their own terminals; 22 (95.7%) reported direct or indirect access to the National Library of Medicine data bases; and 19 (82.6%) reported access to Lockheed or Systems Development Corporation data bases. **(740)**

■ A 1979 survey of library automation in post-secondary educational institutions in Canada (survey size: 423 libraries; responding: 283 or 67%) *showed that* the 5 most frequently identified online data bases (out of 53) listed as "among the five most searched" were [no total number of respondents given]:

ERIC	43 respondents
PSYCHOLOGY ABSTRACTS	41 respondents
BIOSIS	36 respondents
MEDLINE	23 respondents
SOCIAL SCIENCE CITATION	
INDEX	22 respondents **(556)**

Ibid. . . . *showed that* the 4 search services most frequently used (out of 12) based on data base searches conducted were [no total number of respondents given]:

LRS DIALOG	165 respondents
CAN/OLE	32 respondents
INFOMART/SDC ORBIT	32 respondents
BRS	31 respondents **(556)**

■ A 1981 survey of U.S. depository libraries, both academic and public (sample size: 221; responding: 171 or 77%), concerning their use of online data bases (DIALOG, ORBIT, and BRS), particularly with regard to government documents *showed that* the 2 online government document data bases most frequently searched by academic depository librarians were ERIC (average of 1 search per month) and MONTHLY CATALOG (average of .6 of a search per month), while the government document data bases most frequently searched by public depository librarians were CIS/INDEX (average of .3 of a search per month) and AMERICAN STATISTICS INDEX (average of .3 of a search per month). **(317)**

Public

■ A 1975 study of online searches provided free of charge in the DIALOG data bases over a 3-month period in 4 San Franscisco Bay Area public libraries (411 usable requests; 429 searches undertaken, including some duplicates) *showed that* the top 3 data bases searched were: NTIS, 168 searches or 17.84% of the total number of searches; PSYCHOLOGY

ABSTRACTS, 155 searches or 16.57% of the total; and ERIC, 125 searches or 13.35% of the total. **(326)**

■ A 1975-76 study of 359 online searches over a 7-month period using DIALOG in 4 public libraries in the San Franscisco Bay area where patrons were charged half the connect costs (in contrast to a study the year before in the same libraries when searches were free) *showed that* the 3 most frequently used data bases were ERIC (159 or 22.78% searches), NTIS (119 or 17.05% searches), and PSYCHOLOGY ABSTRACTS (107 or 15.33% searches). **(332)**

■ A survey reported in 1976 of 10 academic and public libraries using the New York Times Information Bank *showed that* the areas in which the most requests for information were made were: politics (9 libraries), news reports (7 libraries), and biography (6 libraries). **(149)**

■ A 1981 survey of U.S. depository libraries, both academic and public (sample size: 221; responding: 171 or 77%), concerning their use of online data bases (DIALOG, ORBIT, and BRS), particularly with regard to government documents *showed that* the 2 online government document data bases most frequently searched by academic depository librarians were ERIC (average of 1 search per month) and MONTHLY CATALOG (average of .6 of a search per month), while the government document data bases most frequently searched by public depository librarians were CIS/INDEX (average of .3 of a search per month) and AMERICAN STATISTICS INDEX (average of .3 of a search per month). **(317)**

Special

■ A 1978 survey of North American health sciences libraries that were users of the National Library of Medicine search services in November 1977 (survey size: 708 libraries; responding: 376; usable: 345 or 48.7%) *showed that* the average number of NLM searches per data base per respondent during 1976-77 was as follows:

MEDLINE (274 respondents)	842.0 searches per library
AVLINE (242 respondents)	4.7 searches per library
CANCERLIT (250 respondents)	14.2 searches per library
TOXLINE (250 respondents)	30.7 searches per library
SDI profiles (276 respondents)	24.7 profiles per library **(724)**

Ibid. . . . *showed that*, of the 199 respondents providing online search services in addition to those offered by NLM, the 3 most frequently used vendors were:

Lockheed	144 (72.4%)	respondents
SDC	134 (67.3%)	respondents
BRS	67 (33.7%)	respondents

Further, on the average, respondents reported using SDC for 2.7 years, Lockheed for 2.4 years, and BRS for 1.0 years.   **(724)**

Ibid. . . . *showed that*, of the 199 respondents providing online services in addition to those offered by NLM, the average number of searches per institution for the 6 most frequently searched data bases in 1976-77 were as follows:

CA CONDENSATES	121.1 searches
BIOSIS PREVIEWS	52.2 searches
NTIS	43.7 searches
PSYCHOLOGICAL ABSTRACTS	36.0 searches
ERIC	32.2 searches
AGRICOLA	26.0 searches **(724)**

■ A 1978 survey of major biomedical libraries (primarily those serving accredited medical schools) (survey size: 120 libraries; responding: 88 or 73%) *showed that* respondents reported access to the following vendors of bibliographic data bases:

National Library of Medicine (MEDLINE, et al.)	85 (97%) libraries
Bibliographic Retrieval Service	52 (59%) libraries
Lockheed	50 (57%) libraries
Systems Development Corporation	44 (50%) libraries **(726)**

■ A 1979 survey of libraries in accredited North American veterinary schools (population: 25 libraries; responding: 23 or 92%) *showed that* all respondents reported that online search services were available. 10 (43.5%) libraries reported they had their own terminals; 22 (95.7%) reported direct or indirect access to the National Library of Medicine data bases; and 19 (82.6%) reported access to Lockheed or Systems Development Corporation data bases.   **(740)**

Online Searching—Staffing

General

■ A 1978 survey of North American health sciences libraries that were users of the National Library of Medicine search services in November 1977 (survey size: 708 libraries; responding: 376; usable: 345 or 48.7%) *showed that* of 232 respondents the advent of online searching allowed a drop of 36% in the first year in FTE staff previously used for manual searching. By 1976-77 FTE staff for online searching had increased 10% over pre-online searching levels, while the number of searches for the same period had increased 241% (from an average of 247 searches per year to 842 searches per year per institution). **(724)**

Ibid. . . . *showed that* increased workloads due to online searching were handled as follows: reassigning duties among existing staff (47.2% respondents), adding staff (34.6% respondents), and combination of reassignment and adding staff (18.1% respondents). **(724)**

Academic

■ A 1978 survey of North American health sciences libraries that were users of the National Library of Medicine search services in November 1977 (survey size: 708 libraries; responding: 376; usable: 345 or 48.7%) *showed that* of 232 respondents the advent of online searching allowed a drop of 36% in the first year in FTE staff previously used for manual searching. By 1976-77 FTE staff for online searching had increased 10% over pre-online searching levels, while the number of searches for the same period had increased 241% (from an average of 247 searches per year to 842 searches per year per institution). **(724)**

Ibid. . . . *showed that* increased workloads due to online searching were handled as follows: reassigning duties among existing staff (47.2% respondents), adding staff (34.6% respondents), and combination of reassignment and adding staff (18.1% respondents). **(724)**

■ A 1981 survey of U.S. depository libraries, both academic and public (sample size: 221; responding: 171 or 77%), concerning their use of online data bases (DIALOG, ORBIT, and BRS), particularly with regard to government documents *showed that* there was a statistically significant relationship between the number of FTE professionals and the hours of online searching, i.e., the larger the staff the more hours of online searching done (significant at the .02 level); between number of FTE professionals and the likelihood of having an online terminal in the library, i.e., the larger the staff the greater the chance of having an online terminal (significant at the .001 level); and between the number of FTE professionals and the number of documents librarians trained for online data base searching, i.e., the larger the staff the more documents librarians trained in online searching (significant at the .001 level).   **(317)**

Public

■ A 1981 survey of U.S. depository libraries, both academic and public (sample size: 221; responding: 171 or 77%), concerning their use of online data bases (DIALOG, ORBIT, and BRS), particularly with regard to government documents *showed that* there was a statistically significant relationship between the number of FTE professionals and the hours of online searching, i.e., the larger the staff the more hours of online searching done (significant at the .02 level); between number of FTE professionals and the likelihood of having an online terminal in the library, i.e., the larger the staff the greater the chance of having an online terminal (significant at the .001 level); and between the number of FTE professionals and the number of documents librarians trained for online data base searching, i.e., the larger the staff the more documents librarians trained in online searching (significant at the .001 level).   **(317)**

Special

■ A 1978 survey of North American health sciences libraries that were users of the National Library of Medicine search services in November 1977 (survey size: 708 libraries; responding: 376; usable: 345 or 48.7%) *showed that* of 232 respondents the advent of online searching allowed a drop of 36% in the first year in FTE staff previously used for manual searching. By 1976-77 FTE staff for online searching had increased 10% over pre-online searching levels, while the number of searches for the same period had increased 241% (from an average of 247 searches per year to 842 searches per year per institution).   **(724)**

Ibid. . . . *showed that* increased workloads due to online searching were handled as follows: reassigning duties among existing staff (47.2% respondents), adding staff (34.6% respondents), and combination of reassignment and adding staff (18.1% respondents).   **(724)**

Online Searching—Time

General

■ A study reported in 1983 comparing the effectiveness of an automated intermediary (CONIT system) with a human intermediary in conducting an online bibliographic search, involving 16 patrons using 3 retrieval systems (NLM ELHILL, SDC ORBIT, and DIALOG) and 20 different data bases (mostly medical and biological) *showed that* the human intermediaries (expert searchers) requried less time to conduct the searches than did patrons using the automated intermediary. Specifically, in all 16 cases the human intermediaries spent at least 20% less time than patrons using the automated intermediary. However, if interview time was included with the time required to actually conduct the search, the automated intermediary searches required slightly less time than the searches using human intermediaries, namely 154 minutes compared to 159 minutes.   **(661)**

Academic

■ A 1974 study over a 4-month period (January-April) of free MED-LINE use at Oakland University (Rochester, Michigan), a university without a medical school, involving 21 faculty and students for a total of 36 searches, *showed that* the average search took 32 minutes of terminal connect-time and generated an average of 185 unique citations per search.   **(411)**

■ A 1975-76 study at the University of Utah Marriott Library of online bibliographic data base searching *showed that* the number of searches and average length per search were as follows:

CHEMICAL ABSTRACTS CONDENSATES (254 searches averaging 7.47 minutes each)

ERIC (341 searches averaging 14.03 minutes each)

NTIS (120 searches averaging 6.30 minutes each)

PSYCHOLOGY ABSTRACTS (227 searches averaging 11.45 minutes each)

other (447 searches averaging 6.58 minutes each)   **(329)**

■ A 1978 survey of North American health sciences libraries that were
users of the National Library of Medicine search services in November
1977 (survey size: 708 libraries; responding: 376; usable: 345 or 48.7%)
showed that, for the average MEDLINE search performed in 1976-77 [total
number not given]: 9.3 minutes was spent interviewing the requester; 12.8
minutes was spent on preterminal formulation time; and 12.7 minutes
spent at the terminal. Together, these 3 processes required an overall
average of 34.8 minutes and ranged from a low of 28 minutes for hospital
libraries to a high of 42 minutes for libraries in colleges and universities,
societies, foundations, and research institutes.   **(724)**

Ibid. . . . *showed that* the average turnaround time (from acceptance of
search to completion of terminal work) for MEDLINE searches [total
number not given] including weekend days and holidays was 1.0 days
overall, with hospitals averaging .86 days and commercial firms averaging
1.8 days.   **(724)**

■ A study reported in 1978 comparing manual and online retrospective
bibliographic searching at the Lawrence Livermore Laboratory (University
of California, Livermore, California), involving 40 manual and 40 online
searches in 7 abstracting-indexing publications and corresponding SDC/
ORBIT data bases (*Bibliography and Index of Geology*/GEOREF, *Chemical Abstracts*/CHEM7071/CHEMCON, *Congressional Information Service*/CIS, *Engineering Index*/COMPENDEX, *Government Reports Announcements*/NTIS, *Petroleum, Engineering, Business News Index*/P/E
NEWS, and *Pollution Abstracts*/POLLUTION), *showed that*:

> costs, including labor, subscription, reproduction, equipment,
> space, and telecommunications costs, averaged $30.15 per
> manual search compared to $26.05 per online search;

> time required for a manual search averaged 119.5 minutes
> compared to 26.7 minutes for an online search;

> turnaround time for manual searches averaged 60.5 hours
> compared to 95.5 hours (citations were printed offline and
> mailed to the laboratory) per online search.   **(623)**

Ibid. . . . *showed that* the average time (in minutes) required per task for
the 2 types of searches was as follows:

question analysis	5.1 manual; 8.3 online
searching	89.6 manual; 11.6 online
photocopying	5.1 manual; 0.0 online

continued

shelving   4.9 manual;   0.0 online
output processing and
    distribution   14.8 manual;   6.8 online   **(623)**

■ A study reported in 1982 at the University of Iowa Health Sciences Library concerning the effect of the patron's presence during MEDLINE searches, based on searches for 100 different patrons (each search was conducted twice by different staff members, once with and once without the patron) and subsequent survey (100% responding) of those patrons *showed that* there was a statistically significant increase in the amount of time a search took when the patron was present. Specifically, the search time increased from an average of 10.1 minutes per patron to 11.7 minutes per patron (significant at the .05 level). **(743)**

Ibid. . . . *showed that* a comparison of first-time search requesters with requesters who had requested previous online searches revealed that the experienced patrons had a statistically significantly higher satisfaction rate for both the user-present and the user-absent searches (significant at the .004 level). Further, it took statistically significantly less time to formulate a search for the experienced users (significant at the .04 level). There was no statistically significant difference in recall rate or in online search time between experienced and nonexperienced patrons. **(743)**

Public

■ A 1975 study of online searches provided free of charge in the DIALOG data bases over a 3-month period in 4 San Franscisco Bay area public libraries (411 usable requests; 429 searches undertaken, including some duplicates) *showed that* the reference interview averaged 10.5 minutes (295 cases), preparation averaged 10.48 minutes (223 cases), search averaged 22.72 minutes (408 cases), library follow-up (filling out reports, etc.) averaged 12.21 minutes (307 cases), patron follow-up (discussing results with patron) averaged 7.61 minutes (171 cases). In a limited number of cases where the actual search was conducted in another library, the referring library preparation time averaged 18.65 minutes (46 cases), while their library follow-up time averaged 11.48 minutes (42 cases). **(326)**

Ibid. . . . *showed that*, of 103 searches where the patron had the choice of being present, the patron chose to be present in only 43 (41.7%) instances. The average search time with patron present was 37.9 minutes compared to

25 minutes when the patron was not present. (This difference was statistically significant at the .01 level.)   **(326)**

Ibid. . . . *showed that* the 4 libraries had statistically significant differences in the amount of time spent on the reference interview, the search itself, and the library follow-up (significance level greater than .000). For example, average search time per library ranged from 19.74 minutes to 30.42 minutes.   **(326)**

■ A 1975-76 study of 359 online searches over a 7-month period using DIALOG in 4 public libraries in the San Franscisco Bay area where patrons were charged half the connect costs (in contrast to a study the year before in the same libraries when searches were free) *showed that* the total average time spent on a search request was 54.86 minutes when patrons were being charged for online searches, compared to 48.73 minutes when patrons were not being charged. In particular, reference interview time increased from 10.5 minutes for the free searches to 15.8 minutes for the paid searches; preparation time increased from 10.5 minutes for the free searches to 17.8 minutes for the paid searches; library follow-up time increased from 12.2 minutes to 14.2 minutes; and follow-up with the patron increased from 7.6 minutes to 10.3 minutes.   **(332)**

Ibid. . . . *showed that* the patron's presence during a search increased search time. This occurred both during the period of free searches, when the patron's presence increased the search time from 20.93 minutes to 33.85 minutes, and during the period of paid searches, when the patron's presence increased the search time from 15.38 minutes to 16.51 minutes.
                                                              (332)

Ibid. . . . *showed that* the total search process (from patron interview to completion of follow-up) during the period of free searches took an average of 7.8 days, while during the pay period it took 4.4 days, a reduction of 44%. (Multiple causal factors may have been involved, including greater staff experience with online searching and procedures.)
                                                              (332)

Special

■ A 1973 comparison of 48 manual and 66 online (DIALOG) bibliographic searches at the Lockheed-California Company Library *showed that* the average manual search took 22 hours for a total cost of $250, while the average online search took 45 minutes at a total cost of $47.00.   **(406)**

■ A 1978 survey of North American health sciences libraries that were users of the National Library of Medicine search services in November 1977 (survey size: 708 libraries; responding: 376; usable: 345 or 48.7%) *showed that*, for the average MEDLINE search performed in 1976-77 [total number not given]: 9.3 minutes was spent interviewing the requester; 12.8 minutes was spent on preterminal formulation time; and 12.7 minutes spent at the terminal. Together, these 3 processes required an overall average of 34.8 minutes and ranged from a low of 28 minutes for hospital libraries to a high of 42 minutes for libraries in colleges and universities, societies, foundations, and research institutes.   **(724)**

Ibid. . . . *showed that* the average turnaround time (from acceptance of search to completion of terminal work) for MEDLINE searches [total number not given] including weekend days and holidays was 1.0 days overall, with hospitals averaging .86 days and commercial firms averaging 1.8 days.   **(724)**

■ A study reported in 1978 comparing manual and online retrospective bibliographic searching at the Lawrence Livermore Laboratory (University of California, Livermore, California), involving 40 manual and 40 online searches in 7 abstracting-indexing publications and corresponding SDC/ORBIT data bases (*Bibliography and Index of Geology*/GEOREF, *Chemical Abstracts*/CHEM7071/CHEMCON, *Congressional Information Service*/CIS, *Engineering Index*/COMPENDEX, *Government Reports Announcements*/NTIS, *Petroleum, Engineering, Business News Index*/P/E NEWS, and *Pollution Abstracts*/POLLUTION), *showed that*:

   costs, including labor, subscription, reproduction, equipment, space, and telecommunications costs, averaged $30.15 per manual search compared to $26.05 per online search;

   time required for a manual search averaged 119.5 minutes compared to 26.7 minutes for an online search;

   turnaround time for manual searches averaged 60.5 hours compared to 95.5 hours (citations were printed offline and mailed to the laboratory) per online search.   **(623)**

Ibid. . . . *showed that* the average time (in minutes) required per task for the 2 types of searches was as follows:

question analysis	5.1 manual; 8.3 online
searching	89.6 manual; 11.6 online
photocopying	5.1 manual; 0.0 online
shelving	4.9 manual; 0.0 online
output processing and distribution	14.8 manual; 6.8 online **(623)**

■ A study reported in 1982 at the University of Iowa Health Sciences Library concerning the effect of the patron's presence during MEDLINE searches, based on searches for 100 different patrons (each search was conducted twice by different staff members, once with and once without the patron) and subsequent survey (100% responding) of those patrons *showed that* there was a statistically significant increase in the amount of time a search took when the patron was present. Specifically, the search time increased from an average of 10.1 minutes per patron to 11.7 minutes per patron (significant at the .05 level).   **(743)**

Ibid. . . . *showed that* a comparison of first-time search requesters with requesters who had requested previous online searches revealed that the experienced patrons had a statistically significantly higher satisfaction rate for both the user-present and the user-absent searches (significant at the .004 level). Further, it took statistically significantly less time to formulate a search for the experienced users (significant at the .04 level). There was no statistically significant difference in recall rate or in online search time between experienced and nonexperienced patrons.   **(743)**

Online Searching—Type of Patron

General

■ A 12-month study in 1977-78 of online bibliographic literature searching of MINET (Kansas City Libraries Metropolitan Information Network, which includes 4 public libraries, 3 medical libraries, and 1 academic medical library), involving 403 paid search sessions and searches of 544 files or data bases, *showed that*, of the 544 databases searched, 231 (42.0%) were requested by graduate or advanced professional students; 108 (19.7%) were requested by college or university faculty; 67 (12.2%) were requested by the business community; and 26 (4.7%) were requested by undergraduate students.   **(234)**

Academic

■ A 14-month study during 1972-73 at the Yale Medical Library (serving the Yale University School of Medicine, the Yale University School of Nursing, and the Yale-New Haven Hospital), involving 1,466 online search requests (MEDLINE) from 455 different individuals for the faculty and professional staff of the Yale-New Haven Medical Center *showed that* there were substantial differences in the number of individuals (455) requesting online searches by professorial rank. The number of individuals requesting online searches and their percentage of the faculty at that rank were as follows:

professor (112 faculty)	32 (28.6%) individuals
associate professor (160 faculty)	70 (43.8%) individuals
assistant professor (215 faculty)	81 (37.7%) individuals
instructor (94 faculty)	29 (30.9%) individuals
lecturer (134 faculty)	2 (1.5%) individuals
postdoctoral fellow (319 faculty)	102 (32.0%) individuals
research associate (192 faculty)	28 (14.9%) individuals

Clinical faculty and staff:

clinical professor (23 faculty)	1 (4.4%) individuals
associate clinical professor (105 faculty)	8 (7.6%) individuals
assistant clinical professor (291 faculty)	11 (3.8%) individuals
clinical professor [sic, lecturer?] (105 faculty)	1 (1.0%) individuals
clinical instructor (85 faculty)	4 (4.9%) individuals
resident (257 staff)	79 (30.7%) individuals
intern (25 staff)	7 (28.0%) individuals **(714)**

Ibid. . . . *showed that* there was generally little difference in per capita use by faculty/staff rank for those who used online searches. Specifically, the per capita number of searches requested by those who requested searches in terms of faculty or staff rank was as follows:

professor	2.7 searches each
associate professor	2.8 searches each
assistant professor	3.2 searches each
instructor	2.6 searches each
lecturer	2.5 searches each
postdoctoral fellow	3.4 searches each
research associate	5.9 searches each

Clinical faculty and staff:

clinical professor	3.0 searches each
associate clinical professor	2.5 searches each
assistant clinical professor	5.3 searches each

continued

clinical professor [sic,
  lecturer?]   2.0 searches each
clinical instructor   4.8 searches each
resident   2.7 searches each
intern   2.0 searches each   **(714)**

■ A 1975-76 study at the University of Utah Marriott Library of online bibliographic data base searching *showed that* a survey of 26 patrons using the online searching service revealed that (multiple responses allowed): 10 (36%) were faculty, 9 (33%) were doctoral students, 2 (8%) were master's students, 2 (8%) were undergraduate students, and 4 (15%) were professional researchers.   **(329)**

■ A study of the University of Delaware during the 1976-77 academic year *showed that* the percentage of undergraduates among users of online searching increased greatly when the library subsidized 50% of the total search costs.   **(001)**

■ A 1978 survey of North American health sciences libraries that were users of the National Library of Medicine search services in November 1977 (survey size: 708 libraries; responding: 376; usable: 345 or 48.7%) *showed that*, based on replies from 251 respondents, 16.3% of all MEDLINE searches in 1966-67 were for outside users.   **(724)**

■ A study reported in 1982 at the University of Iowa Health Sciences Library concerning the effect of the patron's presence during MEDLINE searches, based on searches for 100 different patrons (each search was conducted twice by different staff members, once with and once without the patron) and subsequent survey (100% responding) of those patrons, *showed that* there were no statistically significant differences among undergraduate, graduate, or faculty search requesters for precision, recall, or satisfaction rates.   **(743)**

■ A study reported in 1982 at Nazareth College of Rochester concerning online bibliographic searching and involving 183 patrons during the period May 1980-June 1981 *showed that* distribution of users was as follows:

undergraduates   40 (21.9% of total)
graduates   105 (57.4% of total)
faculty   28 (15.3% of total)

continued

library	6 (3.3% of total)
administration	4 (2.2% of total) **(300)**

Special

■ A 14-month study during 1972-73 at the Yale Medical Library (serving the Yale University School of Medicine, the Yale University School of Nursing, and the Yale-New Haven Hospital), involving 1,466 online search requests (MEDLINE) from 455 different individuals for the faculty and professional staff of the Yale-New Haven Medical Center *showed that* there were substantial differences in the number of individuals (455) requesting online searches by professorial rank. The number of individuals requesting online searches and their percentage of the faculty at that rank were as follows:

professor (112 faculty)	32 (28.6%) individuals
associate professor (160 faculty)	70 (43.8%) individuals
assistant professor (215 faculty)	81 (37.7%) individuals
instructor (94 faculty)	29 (30.9%) individuals
lecturer (134 faculty)	2 (1.5%) individuals
postdoctoral fellow (319 faculty)	102 (32.0%) individuals
research associate (192 faculty)	28 (14.9%) individuals

Clinical faculty and staff:

clinical professor (23 faculty)	1 (4.4%) individuals
associate clinical professor (105 faculty)	8 (7.6%) individuals
assistant clinical professor (291 faculty)	11 (3.8%) individuals
clinical professor [sic, lecturer?] (105 faculty)	1 (1.0%) individuals
clinical instructor (85 faculty)	4 (4.9%) individuals
resident (257 staff)	79 (30.7%) individuals
intern (25 staff)	7 (28.0%) individuals **(714)**

Ibid. . . . *showed that* there was generally little difference in per capita use by faculty/staff rank for those who used online searches. Specifically, the per capita number of searches requested by those who requested searches in terms of faculty or staff rank was as follows:

professor	2.7 searches each
associate professor	2.8 searches each
assistant professor	3.2 searches each
instructor	2.6 searches each

continued

lecturer	2.5 searches each
postdoctoral fellow	3.4 searches each
research associate	5.9 searches each

Clinical faculty and staff:

clinical professor	3.0 searches each	
associate clinical professor	2.5 searches each	
assistant clinical professor	5.3 searches each	
clinical professor [sic, lecturer?]	2.0 searches each	
clinical instructor	4.8 searches each	
resident	2.7 searches each	
intern	2.0 searches each	**(714)**

■ A 1978 survey of North American health sciences libraries that were users of the National Library of Medicine search services in November 1977 (survey size: 708 libraries; responding: 376; usable: 345 or 48.7%) *showed that*, based on replies from 251 respondents, 16.3% of all MED-LINE searches in 1966-67 were for outside users.   **(724)**

■ A study reported in 1982 at the University of Iowa Health Sciences Library concerning the effect of the patron's presence during MEDLINE searches, based on searches for 100 different patrons (each search was conducted twice by different staff members, once with and once without the patron) and subsequent survey (100% responding) of those patrons *showed that* there were no statistically significant differences among undergraduate, graduate, or faculty search requesters for precision, recall, or satisfaction rates.   **(743)**

Online Searching—Workload

General

■ A 12-month study in 1977-78 of online bibliographic literature search-ing of MINET (Kansas City Libraries Metropolitan Information Network, which includes 4 public libraries, 3 medical libraries, and 1 academic medical library), involving 403 paid search sessions and searches of 544 files or data bases, *showed that*, of the 403 search sessions, 296 (73.6%) searched 1 database; 77 (19.1%) searched 2 databases; 22 (5.4%) searched 3 databases; and 7 (1.7%) searched 4 databases. **(234)**

Ibid. . . . *showed that*, of 544 data bases searched, 229 (42%) had all citations printed online, while 315 (58%) had at least some citations printed offline. **(234)**

Academic

■ A 14-month study during 1972-73 at the Yale Medical Library (serving the Yale University School of Medicine, the Yale University School of Nursing, and the Yale-New Haven Hospital), involving 1,466 online search requests (MEDLINE) from 455 different individuals for the faculty and professional staff of the Yale-New Haven Medical Center *showed that* there was generally little difference in per capita use by faculty/staff rank for those who used online searches. Specifically, the per capita number of searches requested by those who requested searches in terms of faculty or staff rank was as follows:

professor	2.7 searches each
associate professor	2.8 searches each
assistant professor	3.2 searches each
instructor	2.6 searches each
lecturer	2.5 searches each
postdoctoral fellow	3.4 searches each
research associate	5.9 searches each

Clinical faculty and staff:

clinical professor	3.0 searches each	
associate clinical professor	2.5 searches each	
assistant clinical professor	5.3 searches each	
clinical professor [sic, lecturer?]	2.0 searches each	
clinical instructor	4.8 searches each	
resident	2.7 searches each	
intern	2.0 searches each	**(714)**

Ibid. . . . *showed that* the grant dollars received by departments was positively correlated with the number of comprehensive online searches generated by those departments (r = .44) and negatively correlated with the number of narrow searches processed by the departments ($i = -.44$). (Significant at the .05 level.)   **(714)**

■ A 1975-76 study at the University of Utah Marriott Library of online bibliographic data base searching *showed that* a survey of 26 patrons using the online searching service revealed that: 17 (64%) had used the service once; 3 (12%) had used the service twice; 6 (24%) had used the service 3 times or more.   **(329)**

■ A 1978 survey of North American health sciences libraries that were users of the National Library of Medicine search services in November 1977 (survey size: 708 libraries; responding: 376; usable: 345 or 48.7%) *showed that* in libraries in hospitals and professional schools 1 FTE "might be expected to handle roughly 1,400-1,600 searches per year" based on the number of MEDLINE searches performed by existing staff in 1976-77.   **(724)**

■ A 1979 survey of library automation in post-secondary educational institutions in Canada (survey size: 423 libraries; responding: 283 or 67%) *showed that* the annual volume of online bibliographic searches conducted by type of library was as follows [search categories given as printed in article]:

of 24 main university libraries:

1-30 searches per year	4.2% libraries
31-100 searches per year	29.2% libraries
100-500 searches per year	37.5% libraries
500+ searches per year	29.2% libraries

of 25 branch university libraries:

1-30 searches per year	16.0% libraries
31-100 searches per year	12.0% libraries
100-500 searches per year	32.0% libraries
500+ searches per year	40.0% libraries

of 10 community college libraries:

1-30 searches per year	30.0% libraries
31-100 searches per year	50.0% libraries
100-500 searches per year	20.0% libraries
500+ searches per year	0.0% libraries

        (556)

■ A 1981 survey of U.S. depository libraries, both academic and public (sample size: 221; responding: 171 or 77%), concerning their use of online data bases (DIALOG, ORBIT, and BRS), particularly with regard to government documents, *showed that* academic librarians spent a total of 12 minutes a week per institution searching government document data bases online, while public librarians spent a total of 6 minutes a week conducting such searches. Depository librarians themselves conducted an average of 3.1 government document data base searches a month per academic institution, while public library depository librarians conducted .7 government document data base searches per month per institution. **(317)**

Ibid. . . . *showed that* the 2 online government document data bases most frequently searched by academic depository librarians were ERIC (average of 1 search per month) and MONTHLY CATALOG (average of .6 of a search per month), while the government document data bases most frequently searched by public depository librarians were CIS/INDEX (average of .3 of a search per month) and AMERICAN STATISTICS INDEX (average of .3 of a search per month). **(317)**

Public

■ A 1975-76 study of 359 online searches over a 7-month period using DIALOG in 4 public libraries in the San Franscisco Bay area where patrons were charged half the connect costs (in contrast to a study the year before in the same libraries when searches were free) *showed that* the number of data bases used per search dropped from an average of 2.3 reported in an earlier study when the searches were free to an average of 1.9 in the present study when the patron was charged half the connect costs. **(332)**

■ A 1981 survey of U.S. depository libraries, both academic and public (sample size: 221; responding: 171 or 77%), concerning their use of online data bases (DIALOG, ORBIT, and BRS), particularly with regard to government documents, *showed that* academic librarians spent a total of 12 minutes a week per institution searching government document data bases online, while public librarians spent a total of 6 minutes a week conducting such searches. Depository librarians themselves conducted an average of 3.1 government document data base searches a month per academic institution, while public library depository librarians conducted .7 government document data base searches per month per institution. **(317)**

Ibid. . . . *showed that* the 2 online government document data bases most frequently searched by academic depository librarians were ERIC (average of 1 search per month) and MONTHLY CATALOG (average of .6 of a search per month) while the government document data bases most frequently searched by public depository librarians were CIS/INDEX

(average of .3 of a search per month) and AMERICAN STATISTICS
INDEX (average of .3 of a search per month).   **(317)**

Special

■ A 14-month study during 1972-73 at the Yale Medical Library (serving
the Yale University School of Medicine, the Yale University School of
Nursing, and the Yale-New Haven Hospital), involving 1,466 online search
requests (MEDLINE) from 455 different individuals for the faculty and
professional staff of the Yale-New Haven Medical Center, *showed that*
there was generally little difference in per capita use by faculty/staff rank
for those who used online searches. Specifically, the per capita number of
searches requested by those who requested searches in terms of faculty or
staff rank was as follows:

professor	2.7 searches each
associate professor	2.8 searches each
assistant professor	3.2 searches each
instructor	2.6 searches each
lecturer	2.5 searches each
postdoctoral fellow	3.4 searches each
research associate	5.9 searches each

Clinical faculty and staff:

clinical professor	3.0 searches each
associate clinical professor	2.5 searches each
assistant clinical professor	5.3 searches each
clinical professor [sic, lecturer?]	2.0 searches each
clinical instructor	4.8 searches each
resident	2.7 searches each
intern	2.0 searches each **(714)**

■ A 1978 survey of North American health sciences libraries that were
users of the National Library of Medicine search services in November
1977 (survey size: 708 libraries; responding: 376; usable: 345 or 48.7%)
showed that in libraries in hospitals and professional schools 1 FTE "might
be expected to handle roughly 1,400-1,600 searches per year" based on the
number of MEDLINE searches performed by existing staff in 1976-77.
                                                                (724)

Ibid. . . . *showed that* of 232 respondents the advent of online searching
allowed a drop of 36% in the first year in FTE staff previously used for
manual searching. By 1976-77 FTE staff for online searching had increased
10% over pre-online searching levels, while the number of searches for the

same period had increased 241% (from an average of 247 searches per year to 842 searches per year per institution).   **(724)**

Ibid. . . . *showed that* increased workloads due to online searching were handled as follows: reassigning duties among existing staff (47.2% respondents), adding staff (34.6% respondents), and combination of reassignment and adding staff (18.1% respondents).   **(724)**

■ A study reported in 1978 of LEXIS subscribers in 4 different cities (Cleveland, Chicago, New York City, and Washington, D.C.) (sample size: 62; responding: 39; usable: 38 or 61.3%), involving 35 law firms, 2 law schools and 1 government agency, *showed that* 2 (5.3%) respondents ran more than 20 searches a week; 5 (13.2%) ran 5 to 9 searches a week; and 29 (76.3%) ran 0 to 4 searches a week. 1 respondent reported that the number of searches ran depended on the number of new users, while 1 did not reply to the question.   **(359)**

Organization

General

■ A 1976 survey of RASD members (population: 4,062; sample size: 738; usable responses: 542 or 73.4%) concerning their attitudes toward automated information retrieval services *showed that* respondents felt that online, interactive access to automated bibliographic data bases should be offered in the following library departments: general reference or reader services (58.3%), separate unit devoted exclusively to such a service (19%), ILL unit (9.2%), subject branches (5.5%).   **(148)**

Patron Use of Services

General

■ A 1970 survey of psychiatrists randomly selected from the 1968 membership of the American Psychiatric Association (survey size: 394; responding: 290 or 74%) *showed that* the 4 most frequently mentioned prime methods of searching the literature (out of 11) were:

library reference services	23% respondents
abstracts and indexes	17% respondents
bibliographies	17% respondents
review articles	16% respondents

Use of the card catalog as a prime method of searching the literature was reported by 5% of the respondents, while browsing as a prime method was reported by 4% of the respondents.   **(690)**

Academic

■ A 1975 study at the University of Nebraska, Omaha, concerning student perceptions of academic librarians and involving a stratified sample of full-time students (sample size: 700; responding: 362 or 51.7%) *showed that* only 16.1% reported "frequently" or "always" seeking assistance immediately when searching for library materials or information.   **(449)**

Public

■ A 1966 survey of 21,385 adult (12 years old or older) public library users in the Baltimore-Washington metropolitan region of Maryland conducted during a 6-week period, entering the library (79.1% of patrons approached filled out the survey instrument) *showed that* the use made of the library was as follows (multiple responses allowed): browsing (43.1%), reference books (22.1%), library catalogs (19.0%), help from a librarian (16.0%), consulting books or magazines (12.4%), read new magazines or newspapers (8.7%), periodical indexes (5.7%), recordings (2.7%), films (0.7%), other (2.0%), and no response (11.1%).   **(301)**

■ A 1979 telephone survey of 1,046 New Orleans residents over the age of 12 *showed that* the central library was used more for reference and research, while the branches were used more for recreational reading. 43.7% of the central library's use was for information other than school, 34% for school, and 19.3% for pleasure, while the branches were used 26.9% for information other than school, 38.7% for school, and 33.4% for pleasure.   **(166)**

Patron Use of Tools—General Issues

Academic

■ A 1964 study at the Yale Medical Library involving patron use of books (survey size: 831 borrowers; responding: 430) during a 5-month period

showed that respondents reported learning about library books from the
following sources (multiple responses allowed):

library	117 (24.2%) respondents
chance	104 (21.5%) respondents
citations from another	
published source	97 (20.0%) respondents
previous use	72 (14.9%) respondents
personal recommendation	60 (12.4%) respondents
miscellaneous	34 (7.0%) respondents

Further, a breakdown of the library sources was as follows:

card catalog	77 (16.0%) respondents	
monthly accessions list	22 (4.6%) respondents	
new book shelf	15 (3.0%) respondents	
asked librarian for help	3 (0.6%) respondents	**(672)**

■ A 1979 study at the University of Illinois, Urbana, involving parton use
of an online circulation system for known-item searching (interviews with
240 faculty, staff, students, and visiting patrons conducting 310 searches)
showed that, of 235 known-item searches, 8% of the location searches (call
number previously looked up in card catalog and departmental library
location sought only) and 16% of the original searches (online search was
first attempt to find out if the library had an item) failed because of an error
in using LCS. **(626)**

Ibid. . . . *showed that*, of 120 original known-item searches (original
search was the first attempt to find out whether the library had the item
desired), the library owned the item in 91% of the cases; the patron could
find the item LCS (Library Circulation System, an online system) in 66%
of the cases; and the copy was uncharged in 90% of the cases. **(626)**

Ibid. . . . *showed that* the length of 156 successful known-item searches
was as follows:

0.2 minutes or less	16 (10%) searches	
1.0 minutes or less	82 (53%) searches	
2.0 minutes or less	117 (75%) searches	
3.7 minutes or less	139 (89%) searches	
7.5 minutes or less	156 (100%) searches	**(626)**

Ibid. . . . *showed that*, of 222 searches, there was no statistically significant
difference in success rate between more experienced users (5 or more

previous uses) of the online system and less experienced users (less than 5 previous uses) of the system. Specifically, both groups had the same number of unsuccessful seraches (33), while the more experienced patrons had 83 successful searches compared to 73 for the less experienced patrons. However, experienced patrons did complete their successful searches more quickly than inexperienced patrons to a statistically significant degree with a correlation of r = .24 (significant at the .01 level).   **(626)**

School

■   A 1981 study of 53 ninth-grade honors students in science in a suburban Philadelphia public high school *showed that*, although all the students were required to undertake online bibliographic searches, 81% did not cite any materials so retrieved in their bibliographies. The 21 citations that were from online bibliogaphic searches accounted for less than 5% of all bibliographic citations.   **(222)**

Special

■   A 1964 study at the Yale Medical Library involving patron use of books (survey size: 831 borrowers; responding: 430) during a 5-month period *showed that* respondents reported learning about library books from the following sources (multiple responses allowed):

library	117 (24.2%) respondents
chance	104 (21.5%) respondents
citations from another published source	97 (20.0%) respondents
previous use	72 (14.9%) respondents
personal recommendation	60 (12.4%) respondents
miscellaneous	34 (7.0%) respondents

Further, a breakdown of the library sources was as follows:

card catalog	77 (16.0%) respondents
monthly accessions list	22 (4.6%) respondents
new book shelf	15 (3.0%) respondents
asked librarian for help	3 (0.6%) respondents

(672)

■   A 1970 study of physicians in 14 hospitals and medical institutions in the Toronto metropolitan area concerning self-education (survey size:

1,050 physicians; responding: 390 or 37.1%) *showed that* the following numbers were *not* acquainted with the following tools:

Index Medicus	6.0% of total
Excerpta Medica	21.0% of total
Science Citation Index	84.0% of total
Pandex	91.5% of total **(634)**

■ A 1970 survey of psychiatrists randomly selected from the 1968 membership of the American Psychiatric Association (survey size: 394; responding: 290 or 74%) *showed that* the 4 most frequently mentioned prime methods of searching the literature (out of 11) were:

library reference services	23% respondents
abstracts and indexes	17% respondents
bibliographies	17% respondents
review articles	16% respondents

Use of the card catalog as a prime method of searching the literature was reported by 5% of the respondents, while browsing as a prime method was reported by 4% of the respondents. **(690)**

Patron Use of Tools—Catalogs, Card

Academic

■ A 1963 study of 501 searches in the card catalog of the Yale Medical library during 1 working week in fall 1963 (a historically busy period) *showed that*, of 501 searches, 64 or 12.8% were subject searches. **(171)**

■ A 1964 study at the Yale Medical Library involving patron use of books (survey size: 831 borrowers; responding: 430) during a 5-month period *showed that* respondents reported learning about library books from the following sources (multiple responses allowed):

library	117 (24.2%) respondents
chance	104 (21.5%) respondents
citations from another published source	97 (20.0%) respondents
previous use	72 (14.9%) respondents
personal recommendation	60 (12.4%) respondents
miscellaneous	34 (7.0%) respondents

Further, a breakdown of the library sources was as follows:

card catalog	77 (16.0%) respondents
monthly accessions list	22 (4.6%) respondents
new book shelf	15 (3.0%) respondents
asked librarian for help	3 (0.6%) respondents **(672)**

■ A 1967 study comparing a dictionary catalog at 1 university with a divided catalog (author/title and subject) at another university by using undergraduates to search entries *showed that* there was no statistically significant difference in average success rates between the 2 catalogs in subject searching or known-item searching. **(199)**

■ A survey of 12 university libraries (11 responding) during a 3-month period in 1965 and a survey of 11 public libraries during a similar period in 1967 to determine the kinds of reference assistance needed at the card catalog (647 problems reported with 284 from university libraries and 363 from public libraries), reported together in 1968 *showed that* the 3 most frequent problems with the card catalog in university libraries were subject headings (18% of university total), filing arrangement (17% of university total), and see or see also references (15% of university total). In public libraries the 3 most frequent problems were filing arrangement (23% of public total), call number (15% of public total), and subject headings (13% of public total). **(134)**

■ A survey reported in 1970 at the University of Michigan, based on random interviews of catalog users in the General Library, Undergraduate Library, and Medical Library (2,167 users interviewed; 1,489 usable interviews, i.e., users searching for a particular item), *showed that*, of the known-item searches, 67.9% of the respondents entered the catalog with an author's or editor's name; 26.2% entered with a title; and 5.9% with a subject heading. **(321)**

Ibid. . . . *showed that*, of the 925 searches involving single, personal authorship or editorship that could be verified, 470 (50.8%) had complete and correct author/editor entries, while 455 did not. Of the incomplete/incorrect entries, 348 (76.5%) had mistakes and/or omissions in the first or middle name or in the initials (although the last name was accurate); 87 (19.1%) had mistakes and/or omissions in the last name; and 20 (4.4%)

had the identity of the author/editor wrong (i.e., the error was not in incompleteness or misspelling). (321)

Ibid. . . . *showed that*, of 87 errors in the last name, 49.4% involved errors in one of the first 4 letters of the name. (321)

Ibid. . . . *showed that*, of the 925 searches involving single, personal authorship or editorship that could be verified, more errors were made with longer names than with shorter names. For example, 4.9% of the short names (names 5 or less letters long) had errors; 10.5% of the medium names (names 6 to 8 letters long) had errors; and 14.3% of the long names (9 to 12 letters long) had errors. (321)

Ibid. . . . *showed that*, of the 104 errors contained in the 87 searches that had errors in the last name, 50 (48.1%) of the errors were replacement errors (i.e., where 1 letter or string of letters was replaced by an incorrect letter or string of letters); 34 (32.7%) of the errors were omission errors (i.e., a letter or string of letters was omitted); 18 (17.3%) of the errors were addition errors (i.e., where a letter or string of letters was added); and 2 (1.9%) of the errors were transposition errors. (321)

■ A 1967-70 study in the Main Library at Yale University, involving 2,100 interviews at the card catalog during a 1-year period, *showed that* known-item searches to determine if the library held the item and, if so, where, accounted for 73% of the catalog use; subject searches accounted for 16%; author searches (to determine what works are available for a known author or publishing body) accounted for 6%; and bibliographic searches (to make use of data on the catalog card rather than locate a book) accounted for 5%. Follow-up questioning about known-item searches suggested that many of these are really subject searches using a known item to identify an appropriate call number or subject heading. The real or "underlying" percentage of known-item and subject searches in the card catalog may be more like 56 and 33, respectively. (248)

Ibid. . . . *showed that* 84% of the card catalog searches were successful; that 5% of the searches were unsuccessful for the patron even though library staff later located the document in the card catalog; that 10% of the searches were for documents that probably exist but that were not in the card catalog at the time; and that 1% of the searches were for documents too vaguely or inaccurately described to follow up on.   **(248)**

Ibid. . . . *showed that* the 4 most popular approaches to searching the card catalog were author name (personal or corporate, 62.0%), title (28.5%), subject (4.5%), and editor (4.0%).   **(248)**

Ibid. . . . *showed that* use of the card catalog during the academic year was as follows: Yale freshmen (8.3% of catalog use), other Yale undergraduates (27.7%), graduate/postgraduate students (35.6%), Yale faculty (7.3%), Yale staff (2.9%), and other (18.1%).   **(248)**

■   A study reported in 1970 at the University of Chicago concerning the use of nonstandard catalog access points (104 individuals selected and read 440 books in the general area of psychology that they had not previously read and then were tested on what they remembered about the book 2 weeks later) *showed that* standard author/title/subject information sufficient to look the book up in a conventional card catalog was recalled in only 18% of the cases.   **(606)**

■   A survey in 1976 of 999 library users at San Jose State Library *showed that* the biggest barrier to locating library materials was difficulty in using the card catalog and finding desired items already in circulation. 42% of the items not found by patrons in the card catalog were in the card catalog, and 42% of the books not locateable on the shelves were in circulation or in the Reserve Book Room.   **(010)**

Ibid. . . . *showed that* there was a 77.52% success rate in locating desired items in the card catalog and a 76% success rate in locating the book in the book stacks, for an overall success rate of 58.9%.   **(010)**

Ibid. . . . *showed that*, of 288 card catalog users, only 74 (26%) asked for help, and of individuals who had only partial or no success in locating materials in the catalog, only 34% had requested help.   **(010)**

■   A study reported in 1977 at the University of California, Berkeley, comparing the importance of subject familiarity (knowledge of a specified academic field) versus catalog familiarity (knowledge of the structure of the Library of Congress subject headings) in thinking of an appropriate term for subject searching in the library catalog when presented an abstract and book title and involving 22 psychology students (subject familiarity), 22 economics students (subject familiarity) and 17 library students (catalog familiarity) *showed that* catalog familiarity was more important than subject familiarity to a statistically significant degreee in selecting an appropriate subject term [significance level not given]. Specifically, scores for library students in determining subject terms for psychology and economics materials were higher than scores for students in those disciplines determining subject terms in their own discipline.

(615)

Ibid. . . . *showed that*, although the difference was not statistically significant, psychology and economics students scored higher in selecting appropriate subject terms for the opposite discipline than they did in their own discipline.

(615)

Ibid. . . . *showed that* students were more likely to achieve the illusion of success in using the library catalog than real success. This was demonstrated by the discrepancy between basic matching (exact matches between subject heading assigned by the library to a particular item and the subject heading chosen by the student) and "existence matching" (a marginal match in which the subject heading chosen by the student existed in the catalog but was not the subject heading assigned by the library). Specifically, the numbers of terms which constituted basic matches versus existence matches for the 3 groups were as follows:

economics students	21% basic; 62% existence matches
psychology students	22% basic; 60% existence matches
library students	35% basic; 64% existence matches **(615)**

■ A 1981 survey of faculty, students, staff, and community users of the University of Cincinnati Libraries (sample size: 4,074; responding: 912 or 22.4%, including 436 or 39% faculty response and 218 or 11% student response) *showed that* the faculty and student success rate (those reporting "always" or "often" successful) in using the 3 elements of the periodical records was as follows:

PERIODICAL RECORD	FACULTY	STUDENTS	
public card catalog (shows standing orders)	90%	75%	
Kardex (shows if item received)	75%	58%	
serial record (shows bound holdings)	73%	63%	**(522)**

Ibid. . . . *showed that* the success rate (those reporting the card catalog "easy" or "very easy" to use) was 71% for faculty, 61% for students, and

40% for librarians. Further, those who reported that they "never" or "sometimes" fail to find material in the card catalog was 84% for faculty, 74% for students, and 85% for librarians.   **(522)**

Ibid. . . . *showed that*, when asked their most frequent access point used in the public card catalog, faculty and library staff reported "author," while community users, university administrators, and students reported "subject." Further, subgroups among the faculty reported differently from the 57% overall report of author access. For example, 74% of the arts and sciences faculty reported "author" as the most frequent point of access, while 60% of the faculty in the College of Business Administration and College of Education reported "subject" as the most frequent point of access.   **(522)**

Public

■ A 1973 study in the Burnaby Public Library (British Columbia) involving patron use of the card catalog (survey size: 367 patrons) *showed that* 152 (42%) were looking for a specific publication (about which they knew something); 208 (57%) were looking for information on a topic or something to read but without a specific item in mind; 6 (1%) were using the catalog to find something out about a book rather than looking for a book; and none were using the catalog to find out something about an author.   **(542)**

Ibid. . . . *showed that*, of the 152 patrons who were looking for a specific publication about which they knew something, the information brought to the card catalog was as follows:

subject only	197 (54%) patrons
title only	59 (16%) patrons
author only	55 (15%) patrons
author and title	34 (9%) patrons
title and subject	11 (3%) patrons
author and subject	8 (2%) patrons
author, title, and subject	3 (1%) patrons **(542)**

Ibid. . . . *showed that*, for those patrons who had completed successful searches (282 patrons), the information they reported looking at on the catalog card was as follows:

call number only	180 (64%) patrons
call number, author, and title	20 (7%) patrons
author only	19 (7%) patrons
call number and title	17 (6%) patrons
call number and author	16 (6%) patrons
author and title	15 (5%) patrons
title only	10 (3%) patrons

Further, no patron reported looking for "subtitle, edition statement, publisher, place or date of publication, number of pages, or other information on the catalog card." **(542)**

■ A 1980 survey of card catalog and information desk patrons in the Pikes Peak Library District Library over a 2-week period (sample size: 97; responding: 91) *showed that* 85.4% reported a preference for online catalog searching over the traditional manual approach to the card catalog. The main reason given for preferring the online catalog was its ease of use and the speed with which searches could be conducted. **(345)**

Special

■ A 1964 study at the Yale Medical Library involving patron use of books (survey size: 831 borrowers; responding: 430) during a 5-month period *showed that* respondents reported learning about library books from the following sources (multiple responses allowed):

library	117 (24.2%) respondents
chance	104 (21.5%) respondents
citations from another published source	97 (20.0%) respondents
previous use	72 (14.9%) respondents
personal recommendation	60 (12.4%) respondents
miscellaneous	34 (7.0%) respondents

Further, a breakdown of the library sources was as follows:

card catalog	77 (16.0%) respondents
monthly accessions list	22 (4.6%) respondents
new book shelf	15 (3.0%) respondents
asked librarian for help	3 (0.6%) respondents

(672)

Ibid. . . . *showed that* 11% of the books were reported used in lecture preparation, while 89% appeared to be "associated with research activities." Further, 28% of the books were reported used to "acquire general information to keep up with the field." **(672)**

■ A 1970 survey of psychiatrists randomly selected from the 1968 membership of the American Psychiatric Association (survey size: 394; responding: 290 or 74%) *showed that* the 4 most frequently mentioned prime methods of searching the literature (out of 11) were:

library reference services	23% respondents
abstracts and indexes	17% respondents
bibliographies	17% respondents
review articles	16% respondents

Use of the card catalog as a prime method of searching the literature was reported by 5% of the respondents, while browsing as a prime method was reported by 4% of the respondents. **(690)**

Patron Use of Tools—Catalogs, Microform

General

■ A 1979 study comparing lookup time of the same catalog (Anoka County, Minnesota, with a collection size of 110,000 titles with almost 500,000 entries) in fiche format (using a nmi-90 fiche reader) versus microfilm format (ROM 3 mechanized reader) *showed that* an arbitrarily selected group of 36 UC Berkeley patrons (an additional 3 did not complete enough of the lookups to be included) carrying out 252 trials revealed that the fiche catalog required an average of 7.6% longer lookup time. A lookup task that would take 20 minutes using a ROM film reader would take 21 to 22 minutes in a fiche reader. **(267)**

Ibid. . . . *showed that* 40 library staff at UC Berkeley carrying out 240 trials revealed that the fiche catalog required on average a 5.7% longer lookup time. **(267)**

Ibid. . . . *showed that*, of 39 respondents in the patron group and 31 respondents in the library staff group, 10 (26%) of the patron group favored the fiche reader versus 14 (45%) of the library staff group; 10 (26%) of the patron group had no preference versus 1 (3%) of the library staff group; and 19 (49%) of the patron group favored the ROM versus 16 (52%) of the library staff group. **(267)**

Academic

■ A study reported in 1981 at San Jose State University Library comparing graduate library school students' lookup speeds of 16 entries (3 author, 8 title/added entries, and 5 subject entries) in fiche vs. microfilm forms of a dictionary public library catalog with 436,791 entries (using a Micro-Desing 4020 fiche reader and an Information Design ROM 3 film reader) *showed that* the average speed of the film users was 16.7 minutes compared to 25.3 minutes for the fiche users. (This was a statistically significant difference at the .01 level.) **(340)**

Patron Use of Tools—Catalogs, Online

Academic

■ A 1982 online survey of MELVYL patrons from all 9 UC campuses conducted over a 2-month period for each 25th user of the system (1,259 questionnaires collected; 72.2 questionnaires complete and usable) *showed that* the average length of time a patron spent at the terminal was 8 minutes, 41 seconds, while the average number of commands issued during a session was 22.297. **(349)**

Ibid. . . . *showed that* the patrons conducted an average of 5.66 searches per session. **(349)**

Ibid. . . . *showed that* the help facilities were used in 14.28% of the sessions, with those patrons who did use the help facilities averaging 1.59 unqualified help requests and 2.63 help requests with a specific glossary term. Only 2.6% of the patrons made the same error 3 times in a row. **(349)**

Ibid. . . . *showed that* 75.22% of the patrons made no errors at all during their sessions (this includes command syntax errors, logical errors, and unrecognizable commands). The remaining 24.77% of the patrons made an average of 2.85 errors during their sessions. **(349)**

Ibid. . . . *showed that* the 3 most frequently used searches in the COM-MAND mode were subject (51.6%), personal author (21.5%), and title (18.8%), while the 3 most frequently used searches in the LOOKUP mode were subject/title (63.4%), personal author/corporate author (15.4%), and title/personal author/corporate author (13.2%).   **(349)**

Ibid. . . . *showed that*, in relation to what they were looking for during the search in which they were queried, 32.7% of the respondents judged MELVYL "very satisfactory," 33.5% judged it "somewhat satisfactory," 14.9% judged it "somewhat unsatisfactory," and 18.9% judged it "very unsatisfactory."   **(349)**

Ibid. . . . *showed that* respondents' university affiliation was:

freshman/sophmore	23.2% respondents
junior/senior	39.0% respondents
graduate, master's level	6.4% respondents
graduate, doctoral level	7.6% respondents
graduate, professional school	1.9% respondents
faculty	3.2% respondents
staff	2.6% respondents
other	16.1% respondents **(349)**

Ibid. . . . *showed that* respondents were in the following academic areas:

art/humanities	24.2% respondents
physical/biological sciences	22.7% respondents
social sciences	19.3% respondents
engineering	14.1% respondents
medical and health sciences	5.8% respondents
business management	4.7% respondents
major undeclared	4.0% respondents
law	2.9% respondents
education	2.0% respondents
interdisciplinary	0.2% respondents **(349)**

Public

■ A 1980 survey of card catalog and information desk patrons in the Pikes Peak Library District Library over a 2-week period (sample size: 97; responding: 91) *showed that* 85.4% reported a preference for online catalog searching over the traditional manual approach to the card catalog.

The main reason given for preferring the online catalog was its ease of use and the speed with which searches could be conducted.   **(345)**

Patron Use of Tools—Catalogs, Serial Record

Academic

■   A 1980 study of patron use of the serial card catalog at the University of Illinois, Urbana (sample size: 452 patrons; usable responses: 445 patrons), involving faculty, students, and staff, *showed that* 94% of the materials sought were English-language materials, with 27 (6%) in other languages.
(505)

Ibid. . . . *showed that* the top 2 sources of 192 serial citations patrons obtained through use of an index, abstract, or bibliography were *Readers' Guide* (accounting for 54 or 28% of the citations) and *Business Periodicals Index* (accounting for 17 or 9% of the citations).   **(505)**

Ibid. . . . *showed that* the sources of the 445 serial citations patrons brought to the serial card catalog were as follows:

class reading list	42 (9%) citations
index, abstract, or bibliography	192 (43%) citations
bibliography or footnote in book or journal	127 (29%) citations
online literature search	40 (9%) citations
other/no answer	44 (10%) citations **(505)**

Ibid. . . . *showed that* 366 (83%) of the searches undertaken by patrons in the serial card catalog were successful, i.e., a citation was matched to a catalog entry. Further, the success rate of the frequent catalog user (daily or once/twice per week) was not statistically significantly better than the success rate of the infrequent catalog user. Specifically, 167 (46%) of the frequent catalog users and 199 (54%) of the infrequent catalog users were successful in their searches.   **(505)**

Ibid. . . . *showed that*, of 427 searches, there was no statistically significant difference in success rates between patrons who wrote their citation down (or Xeroxed them) and those who did not. For example, 246 (70%) of the patrons who found their citations in the card catalog had written them down, compared to 52 (69%) of the patrons who did not find their citations in the card catalog but who had written them down. Conversely, 93 (26%) of the patrons found their citations in the card catalog without writing them down, compared to 20 (27%) of the patrons who did not find their citations in the card catalog but also did not write the citation down.   **(505)**

Ibid. . . . *showed that*, of the 79 (18%) unsuccessful searches in the serial card catalog, the reasons for failure were as follows:

not owned by the library	24 (5%) citations
patron missed the entry	22 (5%) citations
patron had incomplete entry	5 (1%) citations
serial record failures	28 (6%) citations

Of those not owned by the library, 20 of the 24 titles were verified as correct in spelling and existing in print, i.e., not simply incorrect citations.
                                                                        (505)

■ A 1981 survey of faculty, students, staff, and community users of the University of Cincinnati Libraries (sample size: 4,074; responding: 912 or 22.4%, including 436 or 39% faculty response and 218 or 11% student response) *showed that* the faculty and student success rate (those reporting "always" or "often" successful) in using the 3 elements of the periodical records was as follows:

PERIODICAL RECORD	FACULTY	STUDENTS	
public card catalog (shows standing orders)	90%	75%	
Kardex (shows if item received)	75%	58%	
serial record (shows bound holdings)	73%	63%	**(522)**

Patron Use of Tools—Government Documents

Academic

■ A 1982 survey of economics and political science faculty members in 9 colleges and universities serving as academic depository institutions in Massachusetts for the Government Printing Office (federal) (sample size: 216, including 105 economists and 111 political scientists; responding: 155 or 71.8%, including 86 economists and 69 political scientists) *showed that* the top 6 methods used by the 125 respondents to locate federal documents were (multiple responses allowed): finding citations in the general litera- ture of the subject discipline (97 respondents), receiving assistance from librarians (84 respondents), being on the mailing lists of federal agencies (70 respondents), finding citations in indexes, abstracts, and subject bibliographies (68), receiving citations from colleagues (53 respondents), and contacting federal agencies (46 respondents). The difference between the responses given by economists and political scientists was not great, with a Spearman rank correlation coefficient showing a strong relationship between the responses of the two groups (rho = .97). **(316)**

Patron Use of Tools—Instruction in

General

■ A survey reported in 1978 of 74 North American libraries providing point-of-use library instruction ("any presentation that informs the patron about the use of a particular reference/research tool and is found at the location of that tool") *showed that* the 4 most frequently mentioned tools with which point-of-use instruction was used were card catalog (34 or 45.9% libraries), *Readers' Guide* (12 or 16.2% libraries), and *Science Citation Index*, and *Psychological Abstracts* (11 or 14.9% libraries each).
(753)

Ibid. . . . *showed that*, in response to the question of whether or not point-of-use instruction saved time for librarians, the following responses were given:

it saved time	28 (38%) libraries
it saved time under certain conditions	9 (12%) libraries
doubted that it saved time	17 (23%) libraries
it did not save time	13 (18%) libraries
[not accounted for]	7 (9%) libraries

(753)

Patron Use of Tools—Periodical Indexes

Academic

■ A study reported in 1979 at Temple University comparing retrieval of specific articles by subject and title keyword terms in the *Social Science*

Index and the *Humanities Index showed that* retrieval of 19 specific articles using 53 subject terms (developed by social science faculty to fit these specific articles) and 51 significant title keyword terms (developed by an undergraduate from the titles of these articles) was more effective using the title keyword terms (68% success rate) than using the subject terms (47% success rate). This suggests that searching these indexes by remembered title words may be more effective than a topical approach when searching for specific articles. **(475)**

■ A 1982 survey of patrons using periodical indexes in an urban university library (survey size: 104 patrons; usable responses: 98, including 53 undergraduates, 41 graduates, 3 faculty, and 1 alumnus) *showed that* the 3 most frequently used indexes (out of 22) were:

Readers' Guide	32 (32.7%) respondents
Business Periodicals Index	14 (14.3%) respondents
Psychology Abstracts	10 (10.2%) respondents **(805)**

Public

■ A survey reported in 1968 of Michigan public libraries (559 libraries or branches queried; 462 or 82% responding) receiving periodicals from the state, *showed that*, while most libraries (252) reported that their periodicals are used about equally for current reading and for reference, a substantial number revealed a trend for increasingly larger libraries to report their periodicals used more for reference, starting with libraries serving populations in excess of 5,000. **(133)**

Patron Use of Tools—Subject Area (Agricultural Economics)

Academic

■ A survey reported in 1969 of a representative sample of agricultural economists in universities and the USDA (sample size: 590; response rate: 379 or 64%) *showed that* 23.9% reported that they never used the *Bibliography of Agriculture*; 40.8% reported never using *Index of Economic Journals*; 41.1% reported never using *Journal of Economic Abstracts*; 50.0% reported never using *Biological and Agricultural Index*; 58.0% reported never using *World Agricultural Economics and Rural*

Sociology Abstracts; 72.7% reported never using *International Bibliography of Economics*; 76.2% reported never using *Biological Abstracts*; and 79.8% reported never using *PAIS Bulletin*. **(245)**

Patron Use of Tools—Subject Area (Business)

Academic

■ A 1968 survey concerning purchase and use of loose-leaf business services by 92 public libraries specializing in business reference service and 47 graduate business school libraries (139 total; 67 or 73% of public libraries responding and 39 or 83% of business school libraries responding) *showed that* over half of the responding business school libraries took and reported frequent use of the following services:

SERVICE	% TAKING
U.S. Dept. of Commerce Overseas Business Reports	69
Funk and Scott Financial Index	69
Moody's Investors Service	97
Standard and Poor's Corporation Records	67
Standard and Poor's Industry Surveys	95
Standard and Poor's Trade and Securities Stats.	87
Value Line Service	71
Wiesenberger Investment Report	62
BNA Labor Relations Reporter	67
BNS Collective Bargaining Negotiations & Contracts	62
BNA Labor Relations Expediter	51
CCH Standard Federal Tax Reporter	69
CCH State Tax Guide	51
Prentice-Hall Federal Tax Service (complete)	71 **(138)**

Public

■ A 1968 survey concerning purchase and use of loose-leaf business services by 92 public libraries specializing in business reference service and 47 graduate business school libraries (139 total; 67 or 73% of public libraries responding and 39 or 83% of business school libraries responding) *showed that* over half of the responding public libraries took and reported frquent use of the following services:

SERVICE	% TAKING	
U.S. Dept. of Commerce Overseas Business reports	70	
Moody's Investors Service	96	
Standard and Poor's Corporation Records	51	
Standard and Poor's Industry Surveys	63	
Standard and Poor's Stock Reports OTC	52	
Value Line Service	61	
Wiesenberger Investment Report	56	
CCH State Tax Guide	57	**(138)**

Patron Use of Tools—Subject Area (History)

Academic

■ A survey reported in 1981 of historians listed in the 1978 *Directory of American Scholars* concerning their use of and attitudes toward periodicals (survey size: 767 historians, although not all questionnaires could be delivered; responding: 360 or 46.9%, with respondents tending to be younger and with a higher scholarly productivity record than nonrespondents) *showed that* the 5 most frequently reported indexing and abstracting services (out of 8) used for current research were (multiple responses allowed):

Readers' Guide	132 (36.7%) respondents	
Historical Abstracts	113 (31.4%) respondents	
America: History and Life	86 (23.9%) respondents	
Social Sciences Index	73 (20.3%) respondents	
Humanities Index	66 (18.3%) respondents	**(780)**

Ibid. . . . *showed that* respondents clearly preferred bibliographic tools providing abstracts over those providing simple author and title entries. Specifically, when asked to compare the value of bibliographic tools providing abstracts in contrast to simple author and title entries, 23.7% reported the abstracts "about the same," 46.4% reported the abstracts "somewhat more satisfactory," and 29.9% reported the abstracts "much more satisfactory." **(780)**

Ibid. . . . *showed that* the invisible college was also not important in making accidental discoveries. For example, the 3 most frequently reported ways of making frequent accidental discoveries (out of 6) were:

scanning current periodicals	173 (48.1%) respondents
looking up a given reference and spotting something else	151 (41.9%) respondents
wandering along library shelves	108 (30.0%) respondents

"In conversation with colleagues" ranked fourth with 78 (21.7%) respondents.   **(780)**

Patron Use of Tools—Translations

Academic

■ A survey reported in 1979 of a large plant pathology department at the University of Minnesota concerning language skills (sample size: 100; responding: 43 or 42%) *showed that*, although *Translations Register Index* and *World Transindex* were readily available in the library, only 7% of the respondents were familiar with either index.   **(426)**

Perception of Service

Academic

■ A 1973 survey of physicists in 6 universities of the greater Boston area (Boston University, Brandeis, Brown, Harvard, MIT, and Northeastern) to determine how they meet their information needs (sample size: 339; responding: 179 or 52.8%) *showed that* 83.2% reported always or usually finding what they want when assisted by a librarian, compared to 76.6% who reported always or usually finding what they want without assistance from a librarian.   **(404)**

■ A 1975 study at the University of Nebraska, Omaha, concerning student perceptions of academic librarians and involving a stratified sample of full-time students (sample size: 700; responding: 362 or 51.7%) *showed that* 40.7% of the students were unsure or did not think that academic reference librarians had subject specialities, although 41.4% reported that librarians "frequently" or "always" had the same "mastery of research methodology in subject areas as instructors." **(449)**

Ibid. . . . *showed that* only 31.6% felt that the verbal interchange between student and librarian was "frequently" or "always" a learning experience; 22.5% of the students felt that librarians should not locate answers and materials for them (59.4% answered "sometimes"); and 11.6% "frequently" or "always" wished their questions answered briefly without additional information. **(449)**

Ibid. . . . *showed that* 61.6% believed that librarians performed a teaching function while 38.4% did not. No statistically significant differences were found in the response to this question by sex, age, subject area, or class level. **(449)**

Ibid. . . . *showed that* 70.1% of the students did not perceive the reference desk as a major barrier, while 20.1% "sometimes" felt it was. Further, 34.4% of the students stated that they were bothered about asking the same librarian for further information. **(449)**

■ A 1977 survey of faculty at Clark University, the College of the Holy Cross, and the Worcester Polytechnic Institute (population: 474; sample size: 121; responding: 87 or 72%) concerning faculty perception of academic libraries *showed that* faculty length of time at an institution tended to be correlated with positive attitudes toward the library. Specifically (not all respondents answered all questions):

43 (89.6%) of the faculty with 7 or more years of service at their institution felt their students' library needs were being satisfied, compared to 19 (55.9%) of the faculty with less than 7 years of service (a statistically significant difference at the .001 level);

37 (86.0%) of the faculty with 7 or more years of service at their institution ranked the helpfulness of the library staff high in terms of importance to their use of the library, compared to 21 (63.6%) of the faculty with less service (a statistically significant difference at the .04 level);

of the faculty with 7 or more years of service at their institution, 38 (92.7%) gave high ratings to the adequacy of the speed of cataloging while 40 (83.3%) gave high ratings to the adequacy of the quality of the collection in their field, compared to 18 (69.2%) and 13 (43.3%), respectively, of the faculty with less service (a statistically significant difference at the .04 and .03 levels respectively). **(478)**

■ A 1978 survey of North American health sciences libraries that were users of the National Library of Medicine search services in November 1977 (survey size: 708 libraries; responding: 376; usable: 345 or 48.7%) *showed that*, of 310 respondents, 245 (79.0%) libraries "agreed" or "strongly agreed" that users have more confidence in online retrieval than in manual retrieval, while of 316 respondents, 277 (87.7%) libraries "agreed" or "strongly agreed" that "users have a more positive attitude about our staff's expertise since online searching has been available." **(724)**

Public

■ A survey reported in 1977 based on a stratified random sample of 300 households (response rate: 251 or 83%) in the Piedmont area of North Carolina *showed that* 97 or 39% (10 or 30% of respondents who had never used a library) of the full sample of respondents reported they would turn to the library for the names, locations, and phone numbers for health services (e.g., hospitals, clinics, prenatal care) were such information available through the library. **(225)**

Ibid. . . . *showed that* 71 or 28% (8 or 24% of respondents who had never used a library) of the full sample of respondents reported they would turn to the library for the names, locations, and phone numbers of emergency services (e.g., fire and police departments, civil defense, poisonings) were such information available through the library. **(225)**

Ibid. . . . *showed that* 60 or 24% (5 or 15% of respondents who had never used a library) of the full sample of respondents reported they would turn to the library for the names, locations, and phone numbers for social services (e.g., foster homes, food stamps, Medicare) were such information available through the library. **(225)**

Special

■ A 1976 survey of physicians associated with hospitals in a 17-county region of upstate New York (Health Service Area V) based on a systematic sample of "approximately 40%" of the physicians in each county (survey size: 592 physicians; responding: 258 or 45.6%) *showed that* the 3 most frequently used sources of information as reported by the physicians were (in descending order of importance):

1. papers in journals
2. personal contact with colleagues
3. books

As an information source used by physicians "library reference services" ranked 7 out of a list of 19.   **(720)**

Ibid. . . . *showed that*, of the 61% physicians who had asked a medical librarian for work-related information within the past year, 61.8% rated the information received as "adequate," 28.9% as "more than adequate," and 9.2% as "less than adequate." Further, 84.9% of the physicians had requested the information themselves, while 15.1% had used an intermediary (e.g., secretary).   **(720)**

■ A 1978 survey of North American health sciences libraries that were users of the National Library of Medicine search services in November 1977 (survey size: 708 libraries; responding: 376; usable: 345 or 48.7%) *showed that*, of 310 respondents, 245 (79.0%) libraries "agreed" or "strongly agreed" that users have more confidence in online retrieval than in manual retrieval, while of 316 respondents, 277 (87.7%) libraries "agreed" or "strongly agreed" that "users have a more positive attitude about our staff's expertise since online searching has been available." **(724)**

Quality of Tools—General Issues

General

■ A 1962 survey of 1,750 librarians (1,090 responding; 1,078 used) in academic, school, and public libraries who were asked to sort a list of 352 basic reference titles into 1 of 3 use categories (constant, regular, infrequent) *showed that* librarians from the 57 Ph.D.-granting institutions gave a unanimous "constant" rating to 9 titles. These were: *Books in Print, CBI, Winchell, Current Biography, Who's Who, Webster's New International* (2nd ed.), *Americana, Government Organization Manual*, and *Reader's Guide*.   **(132)**

■ A 1967 study comparing *Cumulative Book Index* (CBI) with *Canadiana* in terms of its coverage of English-language books published in Canada (209 titles from the first 3 months of 1966 *Canadiana* searched in CBI for

1965-66-67) *showed that* 154 titles (74%) were located in CBI, while 55 (26%) were not found. Of the 55 titles not found in CBI, 26 (12.4% of the total) were the products of publishers not on CBI's list of publishers, while 29 (13.9% of the total) *were* on CBI's list of publishers. **(595)**

Ibid. . . . *showed that*, of the 154 titles located in CBI, 17 (11%) of the titles appeared in CBI before they appeared in *Canadiana*, 22 (14%) titles appeared in CBI within a month or 2 of their appearance in *Canadiana* and 115 (75%) appeared in CBI at least 2 months after appearing in *Canadiana*. Further, 93 (60.4%) of the titles found in CBI appeared 4-5 months after appearing in *Canadiana*. **(595)**

■ An analysis reported in 1970 of listings in the 1969 edition of *Books in Print*, which serves as an index to *Publishers Trade List Annual* (sample size: 2,000 listings from PTLA checked in both author and title volumes of BIP, for a total of 4,000 entries), *showed that* there were 351 discrepancies, for an error rate of 8.8% or a range of expected errors 8.3 to 9.3% with a 95% confidence interval. If only author and title discrepancies that make it difficult to locate items in BIP were considered, the error range dropped to 2.1 to 3.1%. Other discrepancies involved prices and dates. **(087)**

■ A study in 1978 comparing 2,600 book reviews in *Library Journal* and *Choice showed that* 55% of the *Choice* reviews and 70% of the *Library Journal* reviews compared the book neither to another book nor to the literature in general. **(039)**

Ibid. . . . *showed that* there was little evidence that *Choice* reviews were more substantive or critical than those in *Library Journal*, nor was there much evidence of a qualitative difference between reviews by college teachers and those by librarians. The latter point held true whether comparing *Library Journal* reviews as a group with *Choice* reviews as a group or *Library Journal* reviews by college teachers with *Library Journal* reviews by librarians. **(039)**

Ibid. . . . *showed that* the judgment used by editors of these 2 journals in selecting which books to review was substantially sound in that 90% of the books given negative reviews in either of the journals were not reviewed by the other journal. **(039)**

Ibid. . . . *showed that* the main issue for a new book was not the quality of the review but getting reviewed at all—a decision made by the editors of reviewing journals. For example, *Library Journal* reviews approximately

6,000 books a year from a pool of 25-30,000 submitted books and manuscripts, whereas of the reviewed books, only 9% of the *Library Journal* books and 6% of the *Choice* books were given negative recommendations. **(039)**

■ A study reported in 1978 of the 8th (1967) and 9th (1976) editions of *Guide to Reference Books showed that* the number of Canadian reference works had increased from a total of 113 to a total of 196 for an increase of 73.5%. **(550)**

■ A study reported in 1981 comparing 6 "commonly used library tools" (*American Book Publishing Record, Books in Print, Cumulative Book Index, Micrographic Catalog Retrieval Systems, National Union Catalog*, and the OCLC online service) as to their effectiveness for verification of monographs before acquisition, using a sample of 360 books from 9 subject areas (including some foreign imprints) *showed that* the success in locating the 360 titles was as follows:

OCLC online service	97.5% of the books	
MCRS	94.4% of the books	
NUC	93.0% of the books	
BIP	83.6% of the books	
CBI	81.7% of the books	
BPR	73.9% of the books	**(767)**

Ibid. . . . *showed that*, of the combinations of 2 tools, the highest find rate was 98.9% using CBI and OCLC, while of the combinations of 3 tools, the highest find rate was 99.4% using BIP, OCLC, and MCRS. Further addition of tools did not increase the find rate; even using all 6 tools the last 0.6% could not be found. **(767)**

Ibid. . . . *showed that*, when searching for books only in the imprint year of the book, BIP was as effective a tool as OCLC. 70% of the books were located in both. Further, using both tools together increased the find rate to 83.3% of the sample. Other effective combinations which used only print tools were NUC + BIP (find rate = 79.2%) and BPR + BIP (find rate = 77.5%). Finally, even when using all 6 tools to search for books during the imprint year, 13.1% of the books could not be found. **(767)**

Ibid. . . . *showed that* when searching for books in the imprint year plus the following year, OCLC was the most effective tool (find rate = 92.5%), followed by MCRS (find rate = 90.6%) and NUC (find rate = 88.9%).

However, combinations of printed tools were also effective for this period. NUC + BIP had a find rate of 94.7%; NUC + CBI had a find rate of 93.6%; and NUC + BPR had a find rate of 92.5%. Further, searching more than 1 year after the imprint year resulted in only a very small increase in the effectiveness of any of the tools, ranging from 0.3% for BPR to 5.0% for OCLC.

(767)

Ibid. . . . *showed that* the speed of searching for each of the tools was as follows:

OCLC online service	1.15 minutes per item
MCRS	1.31 minutes per item
BPR	2.10 minutes per item
CBI	2.17 minutes per item
BIP	2.25 minutes per item
NUC	2.94 minutes per item (767)

Academic

■ A study reported in 1975 of the reading level of abstracts compared to the reading level of the source document of 48 ERIC documents (12 each from 4 different clearinghouses) as determined by the Flesch Reading Ease formula *showed that* the abstracts had a statistically significantly higher reading level than their source documents (significant at the .001 level). Nevertheless, the reading levels of even the most highly scoring abstracts (score of 14.59) appeared within the range of the intended audience (new teachers, graduate students, and librarians) as described in the *ERIC Operating Manual.*

(612)

■ A study reported in 1979 at Temple University comparing *Social Science Index* and *Humanities Index* with *Social Science Citation Index*, involving 45 journals randomly selected from Carl White's identification of core social science journals in *Sources of Information in the Social Sciences* and 38 journals selected from citations in the 45 core journals, *showed that* 42 (93%) of the 45 core journals were indexed in the SSCI and 33 (73%) were indexed in either *Social Science Index* or *Humanities Index.* Of the 38 less central journals, 30 (78%) were indexed in the SSCI and 18 (47%) were indexed in either *Social Science Index* or *Humanities Index.*   (475)

Ibid. . . . *showed that,* of 45 articles taken from the 45 core journals (1 each), the hit rate in SSCI was 33 (73%) articles, while the hit rate for *Social Science Index* and *Humanities Index* combined was 16 (35%) articles. For 38 articles taken from the 38 less central journals, 25 (65%)

were found in SSCI, while 10 (26%) were found in *Social Science Index* and *Humanities Index* combined.   **(475)**

Ibid. . . . *showed that*, if only articles from those core journals that SSCI indexes (42 journals) were considered, the hit rate increased to 78%, while for *Social Science Index* and *Humanities Index* (33 journals) the hit rate increased to 48%. If only those articles from the less central journals indexed in SSCI (30 journals) were considered, the hit rate increased to 83%, while for *Social Science Index* and *Humanities Index* (18 journals) the hit rate increased to 55%.   **(475)**

Ibid. . . . *showed that*, of all the articles found [no number given], the average time lag between publication date of an article and the date it appeared in an index was 2.7 months for *Social Science Citation Index* and 5.5 months for *Social Science Index* and *Humanities Index* combined.
(475)

Ibid. . . . *showed that*, of 33 articles located in core journals and 25 articles located in less central journals that were found in *Social Science Citation Index*, the average lookup time was 1.36 minutes and 2.92 minutes per item, respectively; for 16 articles located in core journals and 10 articles located in less central journals that were found in *Social Science Index* and *Humanities Index* combined, the average lookup time was 3.25 minutes and 10.1 minutes per item, respectively.   **(475)**

■ A 1980 study comparing the Library Computer System (University of Illinois) and the Washington Library Network by searching 152 periodical titles in both systems (the former a circulation system; the latter an acquisitons system) *showed that* 90 titles were found on the first screen generated by LCS, while 87 titles were found on the first screen generated by WLN. This was a statistically significant difference at the .04 level. Furthermore, 62 LCS searches with 11 or more matches were concluded by using fewer than 10 screens (each screen could show 10 matches), while 51 WLN searches with 11 or more matches were concluded by using fewer than 10 screens.   **(348)**

■ A study reported in 1981 investigating the adequacy of the *Science Citation Index* as a data source for international scientific activity by comparing journal counts between SCI and the British Library Lending Division on a country-by-country basis (for 1973) as well as a country-by-country comparison of the number of papers indexed in SCI compared to other abstracting services *showed that* coverage of relevant research activity was relatively unbiased as to country except for the USSR, where there were "indicators of an underrepresentation of its journal literature in every field," ranging from extreme (clinical medicine, biology, psychology, and mathematics) to slight (chemistry, physics, and biomedical research). **(652)**

■ A study reported in 1982 comparing the descriptors of *The Political Science Thesaurus* and *The Thesaurus of Engineering and Scientific Terms* on the basis of type-token ratio (where "type" is the number of unique words occurring in the text and "token" is the total number of words in the same text) *showed that* the retrieval language of the social sciences consisted of fewer unique descriptors in relation to the total number of descriptors than was the case in the sciences. This suggested that a larger proportion of the social science descriptors were used repeatedly than was the case in the sciences. Specifically, the type-token ratio in *The Political Science Thesaurus* was .21 (2,632 unique descriptors out of a total of 12,425 descriptors) compared to .27 (13,039 unique descriptors out of a total of 47,642 descriptors) in *The Thesaurus of Engineering and Scientific Terms*. This was a statistically significant difference in type-token ratios at the .05 level. **(653)**

Special

■ A study reported in 1982 of the number of cases received by West Publishing Company annually during the period 1900 to 1980 *showed that* the number of cases had increased from 18,937 in 1900 to 52,214 in 1980, with the greatest increase coming in the last 20 years. 26,241 cases were received in 1960; 36,892 were received in 1970; and 52,214 in 1980. **(373)**

Quality of Tools—Book Reviews

General

■ A study in 1978 comparing 2,600 book reviews in *Library Journal* and *Choice showed that* 55% of the *Choice* reviews and 70% of the *Library Journal* reviews compared the book neither to another book nor to the literature in general. **(039)**

Ibid. . . . *showed that* there was little evidence that *Choice* reviews were more substantive or critical than those in *Library Journal*, nor was there much evidence of a qualitative difference between reviews by college teachers and those by librarians. The latter point held true whether comparing *Library Journal* reviews as a group with *Choice* reviews as a group or *Library Journal* reviews by college teachers with *Library Journal* reviews by librarians. **(039)**

Ibid. . . . *showed that* the judgment used by editors of these 2 journals in selecting which books to review was substantially sound in that 90% of the books given negative reviews in either of the journals were not reviewed by the other journal. **(039)**

Ibid. . . . *showed that* the main issue for a new book was not the quality of the review but getting reviewed at all—a decision made by the editors of reviewing journals. For example, *Library Journal* reviews approximately 6,000 books a year from a pool of 25-30,000 submitted books and manuscripts, whereas of the reviewed books, only 9% of the *Library Journal* books and 6% of the *Choice* books were given negative recommendations. **(039)**

■ A study reported in 1979 of the *Book Review Digest, Book Review Index*, and *Current Book Review Citations* (1975-76-77) cumulated editions, which compared their coverage of 62 fiction and nonfiction best sellers reported in *Publishers Weekly* during January/December 1976, *showed that Book Review Index* had covered all 62 titles by its 1976 cumulation; that *Current Book Review Citations* had covered all 62 titles by its 1977 cumulation; and *Book Review Digest* had covered only 52 titles (81%) by its 1977 cumulation. **(158)**

Ibid. . . . *showed that* the number of citations per title in *Book Review Digest* ranged from 2 to 20 with an average of 9.46; those in *Book Review Index* ranged from 2 to 57 with an average of 20.10; and those in *Current Book Review Citations* ranged from 1 to 34 with an average of 9.69. Further, although more than 90% of the citations in CBRC were also listed in BRI, still CBRC did list for 29 of the titles citations that were not given in BRI. **(158)**

■ A study reported in 1980 comparing the *Book Review Digest, Book Review Index*, and *Current Book Review Citations showed that* the number of journals covered by each tool was as follows:

Current Book Review Citations	1,261 journals
Book Review Index	270 journals
Book Review Digest	69 journals **(790)**

Ibid. . . . *showed that Book Review Digest* reviewed no journals that CBRC and BRI did not together review. Of the total journals reviewed by all 3 tools, *Current Book Review Citations* was the sole reviewer of 1,022 (78.9%) journals, while *Book Review Index* was the sole reviewer for 34

(2.6%) journals. The amount of overlap between BRI and CBRC was 170 (13.1%) journals, while the number of journals reviewed in all 3 tools was 66 (5.1%) journals.

(790)

Ibid. . . . *showed that*, based on a sample check of 30 reviews in each of the tools, there were no errors due to faulty citations in any of the 3 tools.

(790)

Academic

■ A study reported in 1969 comparing 1,336 (adult) nonfiction reviews in *Kirkus* for the year 1962 with books listed in *Books for College Libraries* (1967 edition) *showed that Kirkus* was a good reviewing medium for college libraries. Specifically, 450 (33.7%) of the *Kirkus* reviews were found in *Books for College Libraries*.

(589)

■ A study reported in 1974 of 3,347 biomedical book reviews (2,067 titles) taken from the 1970 issues of 54 English-language biomedical journals (excluding *Science* and *Nature*) that contained "bona fide" book reviews *showed that* the average time lag (difference between publication date of a book and the date of the journal issue containing the review of the book) for the 54 journals varied widely, ranging from 5.8 months for *Lancet* to 42 months for *Acta Radiologica: Therapy, Physics, Biology*. 29.7% of the 3,347 reviews appeared in the same year as the book was published.

(700)

Ibid. . . . *showed that* the length of the reviews ranged from 50 words to 1,650 words with "most . . . over 265 words." Further, reviews in all but 3 of the 54 journals were signed.

(700)

Ibid. . . . *showed that* the lag time for individual reviews ranged from 0 months to 108 months (9 years). The modal lag for individual reviews was 8 months, while the average lag was 10.43 months.

(700)

■ A study reported in 1974 of 3,347 biomedical book reviews (2,067 titles) taken from the 1970 issues of 54 English-language biomedical journals (excluding *Science* and *Nature*) that contained "bona fide" book reviews *showed that* 5 journals covered 680 (93.53%) of the books reviewed more than once and 1,131 titles (54.71%) of the total titles reviewed. These journals were:

British Medical Journal	375 (18.1%) total titles
Annals of Internal Medicine	243 (11.8%) total titles
Lancet	212 (10.3%) total titles
Journal of the American Medical Association	184 (8.9%) total titles
New England Journal of Medicine	117 (5.7%) total titles

(703)

Public

■ A comparison of the number of U.S. juvenile books published in the period 1972-74 (7,160 titles) with the number of reviews published in 5 major reviewing media for the same period *showed that School Library Journal* reviews 97% of the new titles; *Booklist* reviews 40% of the new titles; *Bulletin of the Center for Children's Books* reviews 32% of the new titles; *Horn Book* reviews 17% of the new titles; and the *New York Times Book Review* reviews 13% of the new titles.   **(218)**

■ A study reported in 1980 of a sample of 30 titles selected at random from the 1972-73-74 lists of Notable Children's Books and checked in *Book Review Index* to locate reviews *showed that* the *Bulletin of the Center for Children's Books* had reviewed 29 of the books (97%); *Booklist* and *School Library Journal* had each reviewed 28 of the books (93%); *Horn Book* had reviewed 23 of the books (77%); and the *New York Times Book Review* had reviewed 17 (57%).   **(218)**

Ibid. . . . *showed that* 11 of the sample titles were reviewed by all 5 periodicals; 14 of the titles were reviewed by 4 periodicals; 4 of the titles were reviewed by 3 periodicals; and 1 title was reviewed by 2 periodicals.   **(218)**

Ibid. . . . *showed that* the time lag between publication date and review averaged 54.6 days for the *New York Times Book Review*, 64.2 days for *Booklist*, 80.7 days for *School Library Journal*, 118.6 days for *Horn Book*, and 136 days for the *Bulletin of the Center for Children's Books*.   **(218)**

Ibid. . . . *showed that* the number of critical themes (evaluative, subjective comments such as "well-written") per title reviewed in *Booklist* averaged 4.89; for the *Bulletin of the Center for Children's Books* averaged 5.24; for the *School Library Journal* averaged 5.64; for *Horn Book* averaged 6.3; and for the *New York Times Book Review* averaged 6.64. **(218)**

■ A study reported in 1982 to investigate the reviewing of the 81 books on the 1980 list of the Outstanding Science Trade Books for Children in 7 periodicals (*Appraisal, Booklist, Bulletin of the Center for Children's Books, Horn Book, Kirkus Reviews, School Library Journal*, and *Science Books and Films*) *showed that* the 81 titles received 378 reveiws in these journals, for an average of 4.66 reviews per title. The number of titles reviewed in each journal was as follows:

School Library Journal	69 (85%) titles
Booklist	68 (84%) titles
Science Books and Films	61 (75%) titles
Kirkus Reviews	53 (65%) titles
Appraisal	50 (62%) titles
Bulletin of the Center for Children's Books	34 (42%) titles
Horn Book	32 (40%) titles **(779)**

Ibid. . . . *showed that* the average time lag between publication date of the book and appearance of the review for each of the 7 journals was as follows:

Booklist	9 days time lag
Kirkus Reviews	52 days time lag
Bulletin of the Center for Children's Books	121 days time lag
School Library Journal	128 days time lag
Horn Book	140 days time lag
Science Books and Films	231 days time lag
Appraisal	238 days time lag **(779)**

Ibid. . . . *showed that* the number of reviews in each of the 7 reviewing journals that referred to the accuracy of the book was as follows:

Appraisal	54% of the reviews
Science Books and Films	46% of the reviews
Horn Book	22% of the reviews
Bulletin of the Center for Children's Books	21% of the reviews
School Library Journal	19% of the reviews

continued

Kirkus Reviews   13% of the reviews
Booklist   12% of the reviews   **(779)**

Ibid. . . . *showed that* the number of reviews in each of the 7 reviewing journals that referred to the readability (e.g., such issues as clarity, simplicity, appeal, or style) of the book was as follows:

Appraisal   98% of the reviews
Bulletin of the Center for
    Children's Books   88% of the reviews
Science Books and Films   84% of the reviews
Kirkus Reviews   77% of the reviews
Booklist   76% of the reviews
School Library Journal   75% of the reviews
Horn Book   63% of the reviews   **(779)**

Ibid. . . . *showed that* the number of reviews in each of the 7 reviewing journals that referred to the format (e.g., mention of illustrations, print style or size, paper quality, or page layout) of the book was as follows:

Appraisal   94% of the reviews
School Library Journal   87% of the reviews
Booklist   84% of the reviews
Science Books and Films   82% of the reviews
Horn Book   69% of the reviews
Bulletin of the Center for
    Children's Books   65% of the reviews
Kirkus Reviews   62% of the reviews   **(779)**

Ibid. . . . *showed that* the number of reviews in each of the 7 reviewing journals that contained 3 or 4 of the 4 central reviewing elements (description, evaluation of accuracy, evaluation of readability, and evaluation of format) was as follows:

Appraisal   49 (98%) of the reviews
Science Books and Films   50 (82%) of the reviews
School Library Journal   50 (72%) of the reviews
Bulletin of the Center for
    Children's Books   22 (65%) of the reviews
Booklist   43 (63%) of the reviews
Kirkus Reviews   31 (59%) of the reviews
Horn Book   18 (56%) of the reviews   **(779)**

School

■   A comparison of the number of U.S. juvenile books published in the period 1972-74 (7,160 titles) with the number of reviews published in 5 major reviewing media for the same period *showed that School Library Journal* reviews 97% of the new titles; *Booklist* reviews 40% of the new titles; *Bulletin of the Center for Children's Books* reviews 32% of the new titles; *Horn Book* reviews 17% of the new titles; and the *New York Times Book Review* reviews 13% of the new titles.   **(218)**

■   A study reported in 1980 of a sample of 30 titles selected at random from the 1972-73-74 lists of Notable Children's Books and checked in *Book Review Index* to locate reviews *showed that* the *Bulletin of the Center for Children's Books* had reviewed 29 of the books (97%); *Booklist* and *School Library Journal* had each reviewed 28 of the books (93%); *Horn Book* had reviewed 23 of the books (77%); and the *New York Times Book Review* had reviewed 17 (57%).   **(218)**

Ibid. . . . *showed that* 11 of the sample titles were reviewed by all 5 periodicals; 14 of the titles were reviewed by 4 periodicals; 4 of the titles were reviewed by 3 periodicals; and 1 title was reviewed by 2 periodicals.   **(218)**

Ibid. . . . *showed that* the time lag between publication date and review averaged 54.6 days for the *New York Times Book Review*, 64.2 days for *Booklist*, 80.7 days for *School Library Journal*, 118.6 days for *Horn Book*, and 136 days for the *Bulletin of the Center for Children's Books*.   **(218)**

Ibid. . . . *showed that* the number of critical themes (evaluative, subjective comments such as "well-written") per title reviewed in *Booklist* averaged 4.89; for the *Bulletin of the Center for Children's Books* averaged 5.24; for the *School Library Journal* averaged 5.64; for *Horn Book* averaged 6.3; and for the *New York Times Book Review* averaged 6.64.   **(218)**

■   A study reported in 1982 to investigate the reviewing of the 81 books on the 1980 list of the Outstanding Science Trade Books for Children in 7 periodicals (*Appraisal, Booklist, Bulletin of the Center for Children's Books, Horn Book, Kirkus Reviews, School Library Journal*, and *Science Books and Films*) *showed that* the 81 titles received 378 reveiws in these journals, for an average of 4.66 reviews per title. The number of titles reviewed in each journal was as follows:

School Library Journal	69 (85%) titles	
Booklist	68 (84%) titles	
Science Books and Films	61 (75%) titles	
Kirkus Reviews	53 (65%) titles	
Appraisal	50 (62%) titles	
Bulletin of the Center for Children's Books	34 (42%) titles	
Horn Book	32 (40%) titles	**(779)**

Ibid. . . . *showed that* the average time lag between publication date of the book and appearance of the review for each of the 7 journals was as follows:

Booklist	9 days time lag	
Kirkus Reviews	52 days time lag	
Bulletin of the Center for Children's Books	121 days time lag	
School Library Journal	128 days time lag	
Horn Book	140 days time lag	
Science Books and Films	231 days time lag	
Appraisal	238 days time lag	**(779)**

Ibid. . . . *showed that* the number of reviews in each of the 7 reviewing journals that referred to the accuracy of the book was as follows:

Appraisal	54% of the reviews	
Science Books and Films	46% of the reviews	
Horn Book	22% of the reviews	
Bulletin of the Center for Children's Books	21% of the reviews	
School Library Journal	19% of the reviews	
Kirkus Reviews	13% of the reviews	
Booklist	12% of the reviews	**(779)**

Ibid. . . . *showed that* the number of reviews in each of the 7 reviewing journals that referred to the readability (e.g., such issues as clarity, simplicity, appeal, or style) of the book was as follows:

Appraisal	98% of the reviews
Bulletin of the Center for Children's Books	88% of the reviews
Science Books and Films	84% of the reviews

continued

Kirkus Reviews	77% of the reviews	
Booklist	76% of the reviews	
School Library Journal	75% of the reviews	
Horn Book	63% of the reviews	**(779)**

Ibid. . . . *showed that* the number of reviews in each of the 7 reviewing journals that referred to the format (e.g., mention of illustrations, print style or size, paper quality, or page layout) of the book was as follows:

Appraisal	94% of the reviews	
School Library Journal	87% of the reviews	
Booklist	84% of the reviews	
Science Books and Films	82% of the reviews	
Horn Book	69% of the reviews	
Bulletin of the Center for Children's Books	65% of the reviews	
Kirkus Reviews	62% of the reviews	**(779)**

Ibid. . . . *showed that* the number of reviews in each of the 7 reviewing journals that contained 3 or 4 of the 4 central reviewing elements (description, evaluation of accuracy, evaluation of readability, and evaluation of format) was as follows:

Appraisal	49 (98%) of the reviews	
Science Books and Films	50 (82%) of the reviews	
School Library Journal	50 (72%) of the reviews	
Bulletin of the Center for Children's Books	22 (65%) of the reviews	
Booklist	43 (63%) of the reviews	
Kirkus Reviews	31 (59%) of the reviews	
Horn Book	18 (56%) of the reviews	**(779)**

Special

■ A study reported in 1974 of 3,347 biomedical book reviews (2,067 titles) taken from the 1970 issues of 54 English-language biomedical journals (excluding *Science* and *Nature*) that contained "bona fide" book reviews *showed that* the average time lag (difference between publication date of a book and the date of the journal issue containing the review of the book) for the 54 journals varied widely, ranging from 5.8 months for

Lancet to 42 months for *Acta Radiologica: Therapy, Physics, Biology.* 29.7% of the 3,347 reviews appeared in the same year as the book was published.   **(700)**

Ibid. . . . *showed that* the length of the reviews ranged from 50 words to 1,650 words with "most . . . over 265 words." Further, reviews in all but 3 of the 54 journals were signed.   **(700)**

Ibid. . . . *showed that* the lag time for individual reviews ranged from 0 months to 108 months (9 years). The modal lag for individual reviews was 8 months, while the average lag was 10.43 months.   **(700)**

■ A study reported in 1974 of 3,347 biomedical book reviews (2,067 titles) taken from the 1970 issues of 54 English-language biomedical journals (excluding *Science* and *Nature*) that contained "bona fide" book reviews *showed that* 5 journals covered 680 (93.53%) of the books reviewed more than once and 1,131 titles (54.71%) of the total titles reviewed. These journals were:

British Medical Journal	375 (18.1%) total titles
Annals of Internal Medicine	243 (11.8%) total titles
Lancet	212 (10.3%) total titles
Journal of the American Medical Association	184 (8.9%) total titles
New England Journal of Medicine	117 (5.7%) total titles **(703)**

Quality of Tools—Catalogs, Card

Academic

■ A study reported in 1972 of the author/title section of the card catalog in the Norlin Library of the University of Colorado (population: 1,000,000 cards; sample size: 2,500 cards) *showed that* there was a filing error in the sample of 1.1%. 52% of the errors were due to lack of knowledge of the filing rules, and 48% were mechanical or simple alphabetical mistakes.
                                                                    (210)

Ibid. . . . *showed that* in the sample 10.14% of the cross-references were blind.   **(210)**

Ibid. . . . *showed that* in the sample 1.48% of the cards were judged to be mutilated, i.e., call numbers or other essential information was torn off or completely obscured by dirt and wear. **(210)**

Quality of Tools—Catalogs, Online

General

■ A study reported in 1977 of a sample of titles with 1974, 1975, and 1976 imprint dates *showed that* OCLC was substantially more effective as a verification tool (with a 92.7% verification rate) than Library of Congress depository cards (73.2%), *American Book Publishing Record* (69.9%), *National Union Catalog* (44.6%), and *Cumulative Book Index* (32.8%). **(048)**

■ A 1978 study of OCLC's Online Union Catalog preparatory to converting to AACR 2 form of name headings and uniform titles, involving a 1% test file (41,212 records) and a thorough review of AACR 2 rules, *showed that* 39% of the total records in the Online Union Catalog were ultimately converted to AACR 2 form. **(337)**

Ibid. . . . *showed that* AACR 2 contained 454 "significant" rule changes or new rules, of which 56% would benefit neither librarian nor patron, 23% of which would benefit librarians, and 21% of which would benefit patrons. **(337)**

■ A study reported in 1981 comparing 6 "commonly used library tools" (*American Book Publishing Record, Books in Print, Cumulative Book Index, Micrographic Catalog Retrieval Systems, National Union Catalog,* and the OCLC online service) as to their effectiveness for verification of monographs before acquisition using a sample of 360 books from 9 subject areas (including some foreign imprints) *showed that* the success in locating the 360 titles was as follows:

OCLC online service	97.5% of the books	
MCRS	94.4% of the books	
NUC	93.0% of the books	
BIP	83.6% of the books	
CBI	81.7% of the books	
BPR	73.9% of the books	**(767)**

Ibid. . . . *showed that*, of the combinations of 2 tools, the highest find rate was 98.9% using CBI and OCLC, while of the combinations of 3 tools, the highest find rate was 99.4% using BIP, OCLC, and MCRS. Further addition of tools did not increase the find rate; even using all 6 tools the last 0.6% could not be found.   (767)

Ibid. . . . *showed that*, when searching for books only in the imprint year of the book, BIP was as effective a tool as OCLC. 70% of the books were located in both. Further, using both tools together increased the find rate to 83.3% of the sample. Other effective combinations that used only print tools were NUC + BIP (find rate = 79.2%) and BPR + BIP (find rate = 77.5%). Finally, even when using all 6 tools to search for books during the imprint year, 13.1% of the books could not be found.   (767)

Ibid. . . . *showed that*, when searching for books in the imprint year plus the following year, OCLC was the most effective tool (find rate = 92.5%), followed by MCRS (find rate = 90.6%) and NUC (find rate = 88.9%). However, combinations of printed tools were also effective for this period. NUC + BIP had a find rate of 94.7%, NUC + CBI had a find rate of 93.6%; and NUC + BPR had a find rate of 92.5%. Further, searching more than 1 year after the imprint year resulted in only a very small increase in the effectiveness of any of the tools, ranging from 0.3% for BPR to 5.0% for OCLC.   (767)

Ibid. . . . *showed that* the speed of searching for each of the tools was as follows:

OCLC online service	1.15 minutes per item
MCRS	1.31 minutes per item
BPR	2.10 minutes per item
CBI	2.17 minutes per item
BIP	2.25 minutes per item
NUC	2.94 minutes per item (767)

■ A survey reported in 1982 of 144 libraries contracting for OCLC services through the Bibliographic Center for Research (126 or 87.5% responding) *showed that*, when 2 or more copies of a work are acquired at one time, 44.4% of the respondents reported they would not indicate multiple-copy ownership in the OCLC record if all copies went into the same collection, while 30.2% reported they would not indicate multiple-copy ownership even if copies went into different collections.   (342)

Ibid. . . . *showed that*, when a subsequent copy of a title cataloged earlier on OCLC was purchased, 70.6% of the respondents reported they would not enter information on the subsequent copy into the OCLC record if the copy were going into the same collection as the earlier copy, while 30.2% reported they would not enter information on the subsequent copy even if it were going into a different collection than the earlier copy.   **(342)**

Ibid. . . . *showed that*, when the only copy of a work in the library was withdrawn, 70.6% of the respondents reported canceling the holdings recorded in the OCLC data base, while 19.8% reported they did not, 6.4% reported varying practices, and 3.2% did not reply to the question. **(342)**

Ibid. . . . *showed that*, when 1 of several copies of a work in the library that were previously cataloged on OCLC was withdrawn, 21.4% of the respondents reported that the OCLC holdings were updated, while 65.9% of the respondents reported that the holdings were not, 4.8% reported that their practice varied, and 7.9% did not answer.   **(342)**

■ A 1982 study of the OCLC union catalog to investigate the extent of record duplication, based on 100 records randomly selected from the OCLC database and subsequently searched in the OCLC database for duplicates by using the alphabetic and numeric search keys generated from the selected record, *showed that* 17 (17%) records had duplicate entries, some more than 1 duplicate, for a total of 40 duplicate records (an average of 2.4 duplicate entries for each of the 17 duplicated records).   **(772)**

Ibid. . . . *showed that*, based on an average of 3.6 alphabetic searches per record, 23% of the search keys evoked the response "[search key] produces more than 50 entries."   **(772)**

■ A study reported in 1983 comparing the OCLC database and *New Serial Titles* as information resources for serials, based on searching 200 titles randomly selected from OCLC in *New Serial Titles* and 200 titles randomly selected from *New Serial Titles* in OCLC *showed that* there was only a moderate amount of overlap between the 2 tools. Specifically, a total of 217 (54.3%) titles were found in both. Further, 96 (48%) of the OCLC titles were found in *New Serial Titles*, while 121 (60.5%) of the *New Serial Titles* were found in OCLC.   **(776)**

Ibid. . . . *showed that* different information appeared to be contributed by OCLC and NST for the 217 serial titles they reported in common. For example, bibliographic information present in the NST record but absent in the OCLC record was as follows:

ISSN	21 (9.7%) records	
Dewey number	127 (58.5%) records	
beginning date/number	21 (9.7%) records	
place of publication	4 (1.8%) records	
publisher's address	24 (11.1%) records	
price	10 (4.6%) records	
frequency	9 (4.1%) records	**(776)**

Ibid. . . . *showed that* information absent from both the OCLC and NST for the 217 records held in common was as follows:

ISSN	absent from 108 (49.8%) records	
beginning date/number	absent from 76 (35.0%) records	
publisher's address	absent from 119 (54.8%) records	
price	absent from 161 (74.2%) records	
frequency	absent from 89 (41.0%) records	**(776)**

Ibid. . . . *showed that*, of the 217 titles held in common, OCLC records contained 273 notes, while NST records held 220 notes. 102 (37.4%) of the OCLC notes supplied information not contained in the NST notes, while 15.9% [no raw number given] of the NST notes provided information not contained in the OCLC notes.   **(776)**

Quality of Tools—Doctoral Dissertations

Academic

■ A study reported in 1972 of the bibliographic control of doctoral dissertations in the areas of sociology, psychology, biology, and education, involving 3,012 dissertations selected from *American Doctoral Dissertations*, *showed that* 1,665 (55.3%) dissertations were abstracted in either *Microfilm Abstracts* or the following *Dissertation Abstracts* during the period 1934-69.   **(400)**

Ibid. . . . *showed that*, of those dissertations abstracted in *Dissertation Abstracts* and available on microfilm, 1,604 (90.5%) were abstracted within

2 years of the date of degree issuance. However, this comprised only
53.4% of the total number of dissertations issued.   **(400)**

Ibid. . . . *showed that* 2,452 (81.4%) dissertations were never published;
457 (15.2%) resulted in journal articles; 62 (2.0%) resulted in books; and
41 (1.4%) resulted in chapters in books.   **(400)**

Ibid. . . . *showed that* the subject of the dissertation as determined by the
author for *Dissertation Abstracts* and the subject field assigned in *American
Doctoral Dissertations* varied in their degree of agreement from a high of
88.9% agreement in psychology to a low of 45.1% agreement in health
sciences.   **(400)**

Quality of Tools—Encyclopedias

General

■ A study reported in 1983 of 10 major adult encyclopedias concerning
presence of sexism, based on inclusion/exclusion rates, use of language,
and use of illustrations, *showed that* all of the encyclopedias contained "a
measure of sexist treatment." For example, a search of a random list of
names *showed that* men were included more frequently than women and
that, with the dubious exception of *Encyclopedia Britannica*, 1980, entries
for males were longer than entries for women. Of 19 sample topics, there
were only 8 topics for which more than half of the encyclopedias had
neutral [sexist-free] language. Also, of the 19 sample topics, only 3 had
illustrations predominating that showed women only; 3 had illustrations
predominating that showed mixed gender groups; and 13 had illustrations
predominating that showed men only.   **(803)**

Public

■ A study reported in 1973 of 5 sets of encyclopedias recommended for
children's home use by the Reference and Subscription Books Committee
of the American Library Association (*Britannica Junior*, 1972; *Compton's
Encyclopedia and Fact Index*, 1972; *Merit Students Encyclopedia*, 1970;
World Book Encyclopedia, 1972; and *The New Book of Knowledge: The
Children's Encyclopedia*, 1971) *showed that* a list of notable women
generated from Ireland's book *Index to Women of the World from Ancient
to Modern Times* (1970) and searched in the above encyclopedias for
individual biographies or an appearance in 4 or more collective biographies

revealed the following success rate: *Compton's* (40%), *World Book* (36%), *New Book of Knowledge* (29%), *Merit Students* (28%), and *Britannica Junior* (22%). **(278)**

■ A 1978 survey of 100 (77 or 77% responding) U.S. public libraries of varying sizes concerning 37 general English-language encyclopedias *showed that* the 3 "most effective all-around" encyclopedias were reported to be *World Book Encyclopedia* by 56 (75%) respondents, *Encyclopedia Americana* by 25 (32%), and *Collier's Encyclopedia* by 5 (6%). **(232)**

Ibid. . . . *showed that*, of 3 major multivolume adult encyclopedias, *Encyclopedia Americana* was rated most effective (i.e., reliable, easy to use, clearly written, etc.) by 54 (70%) respondents, *Collier's Encyclopedia* by 17 (22%), and *Encyclopedia Britannica* by 5 (6%). **(232)**

Ibid. . . . *showed that*, of 6 small-volume adult encyclopedias, *New Columbia* was rated most effective (i.e., reliable, easy to use, clearly written, etc.) by 29 (38%) respondents, *Lincoln Library* by 19 (25%) respondents, and *Random House* by 13 (17%) respondents. **(232)**

Ibid. . . . *showed that*, of 4 young adult encyclopedias, *World Book* was rated most effective (i.e., reliable, easy to use, clearly written, etc.) by 71 (92%) respondents, *Compton's Encyclopedia* by 5 (6%) respondents, and *Merit Students Encyclopedia* by 4 (5%) respondents. **(232)**

Ibid. . . . *showed that*, of 3 multivolume children's encyclopedias, *New Book of Knowledge* was rated most effective (i.e., reliable, easy to use, clearly written, etc.) by 41 (53%) respondents and *Britannica Junior Encyclopedia* by 19 (25%). **(232)**

Ibid. . . . *showed that* the general encyclopedia most commonly included in a ready reference collection was *World Book Encyclopedia* (29 or 38% respondents), followed by *Encyclopedia Americana* (11 or 14% respondents) and *New Encyclopedia Britannica* (6 or 8% respondents). **(232)**

■ A 1980 survey of Canadian public libraries concerning the use and effectiveness (where effectiveness meant reliable, easy to use, clearly written, etc.) of 34 general English-language encyclopedias (survey size: 75 libraries; responding: 57 or 76%) *showed that* the 3 most frequently mentioned encyclopedias rated as "most effective all-around general reference work" were:

World Book	27 (47.4%) respondents
New Encyclopedia Britannica	10 (17.5%) respondents
Encyclopedia Americana	10 (17.5%) respondents **(555)**

Ibid. . . . *showed that*, of [42] respondents, the rating of 3 major multivolume encyclopedias as most "effective sources of encyclopedic information" was as follows:

Americana	21 (50.0%) respondents
New Encyclopedia Britannica	14 (33.3%) respondents
Collier's Encyclopedia	7 (16.7%) respondents **(555)**

Ibid. . . . *showed that*, of [28] respondents, the 2 most frequently rated small-volume adult encyclopedias as most "effective sources of encyclopedic information" out of 6 such encyclopedias was as follows:

New Columbia Encyclopedia	13 (46.4%) respondents
Random House Encyclopedia	13 (46.4%) respondents **(555)**

Ibid. . . . *showed that*, of [45] respondents, *World Book* was rated as the most "effective source of encyclopedia information" of 4 young adult encyclopedias by 43 (95.6%) respondents. *Merit Students Encyclopedia* was rated second most effective by 20 (44.4%) respondents, and *Compton's Encyclopedia* was rated second most effective by 18 (40%) respondents. **(555)**

Ibid. . . . *showed that*, of [32] respondents, the 2 most frequently rated multivolume children's encyclopedias as most "effective sources of encyclopedic information" out of 3 were as follows:

New Book of Knowledge	27 (84.4%) respondents
Britannica Junior Encyclopedia	5 (15.6%) respondents **(555)**

Ibid. . . . *showed that*, of [27] respondents, the 4 most frequently mentioned general encyclopedias included in a ready reference collection were:

World Book	8 (29.6%) respondents
Encyclopedia Britannica	6 (22.2%) respondents

continued

> *Encyclopedia Americana*   5 (18.5%) respondents
> *New Book of Knowledge*   5 (18.5%) respondents   **(555)**

School

■ A study reported in 1973 of 5 sets of encyclopedias recommended for children's home use by the Reference and Subscription Books Committee of the American Library Association (*Britannica Junior*, 1972; *Compton's Encyclopedia and Fact Index*, 1972; *Merit Students Encyclopedia*, 1970; *World Book Encyclopedia*, 1972; and *The New Book of Knowledge: The Children's Encyclopedia*, 1971) *showed that* a list of notable women generated from Ireland's book *Index to Women of the World from Ancient to Modern Times* (1970) and searched in the above encyclopedias for individual biographies or an appearance in 4 or more collective biographies revealed the following success rate: *Compton's* (40%), *World Book* (36%), *New Book of Knowledge* (29%), *Merit Students* (28%), and *Britannica Junior* (22%).   **(278)**

Quality of Tools—Government Documents

General

■ A study reported in 1982 comparing U.S. government projections (taken from *Projections of Educational Statistics*) for the number of graduates from library science degree programs with actual numbers of graduates from such programs *showed that*, for all 3 kinds of library degrees, the long-term projections were extremely inaccurate and even the shortest-term projections were quite inaccurate except for doctoral candidates. For example:

> in 1979-80, 73 doctoral degrees in library science were actually granted, while the projected number of doctoral degrees for 1979-80 in 1971 was 40, in 1973 was 60, in 1976 was 90, and in 1978 was 80;

> in 1979-80, 5,374 master's degrees in library science were actually granted, while the projected number of master's degrees for 1979-80 in 1971 was 19,280, in 1973 was 10,940, in 1976 was 10,250, and in 1978 was 8,920;

> in 1979-80, 398 bachelor's degrees in library science were actually granted, while the projected number of bachelor's

degrees for 1979-80 in 1971 was 1,580, in 1973 was 1,520, in 1976 was 1,410, and in 1978 was 940. **(665)**

Ibid. . . . *showed that* the number of doctoral degrees granted in library science rose from 14 in 1960-61 to a high of 102 in 1972-73 and declined to 73 in 1979-80. **(665)**

Quality of Tools—Media

Academic

■ A study reported in 1977 of audiovisual catalogs in the Learning Resources Center of the University of Connecticut Health Center Library (64 catalogs selected randomly from a total collection of 640 domestic and foreign catalogs) *showed that*:

the catalogs provided a title 100% of the time and a summary and physical description at least 75% of the time;

the catalogs provided information about intended audience 44-47% of the time, date of production 31-53% of the time, and producer 47-53% of the time;

the catalogs provided a title index 25% of the time and a subject index 16-22% of the time. **(713)**

Special

■ A study reported in 1977 of audiovisual catalogs in the Learning Resources Center of the University of Connecticut Health Center Library (64 catalogs selected randomly from a total collection of 640 domestic and foreign catalogs) *showed that*:

the catalogs provided a title 100% of the time and a summary and physical description at least 75% of the time;

the catalogs provided information about intended audience 44-47% of the time, date of production 31-53% of the time, and producer 47-53% of the time;

the catalogs provided a title index 25% of the time and a subject index 16-22% of the time. **(713)**

Quality of Tools—Microforms

General

■ A study reported in 1981 of 45 monographs in microform format (randomly selected from the 1979 *Microforms in Print*) and searched in RLIN, OCLC, and the *National Union Catalog showed that*:

> exact copy was found for 17.7% of the microform items searched, of which 4.4% was Library of Congress cataloging and 13.3% was shared cataloging;

> variant copy was found for 22.3% of the microform items searched, of which 6.7% was Library of Congress cataloging and 15.6% was shared cataloging;

> exact copy was found for 55.5% of the hard copy editions of the items, of which 31.1% was Library of Congress cataloging and 24.4% was shared cataloging.

> variant copy was found for 17.7% of the hard copy editions of the items, of which 13.3% was Library of Congress cataloging and 4.4% was shared cataloging.   **(768)**

Quality of Tools—National Bibliographies

General

■ A study reported in 1971 to evaluate the success of the National Program for Acquisitions and Cataloging (also known as the Shared Cataloging Program) by comparing Australian, British, and French publications entered in the *National Union Catalog* before (1962) and after (1967) the program began (180 titles from *British National Bibliography, Australian National Bibliography*, and *Bibliographie de la France* for 1962; 200 titles from the same 3 works for 1967) *showed that* the number of titles from these 3 countries appearing in the NUC had substantially increased. Specifically, searching each of the 380 titles in the 14 monthly issues of NUC after the title appeared in the foreign bibliography revealed that 118 (66%) of the 1962 sample titles were found in NUC, compared to 173 (87%) of the 1967 sample titles. This was an increase of 21% after the program began.   **(594)**

Ibid. . . . *showed that* the amount of cataloging for foreign titles contributed by foreign libraries after the start of the shared cataloging program began was substantial. Specifically, of 118 book titles in the 1962 sample from Australia, Britain, and France found in the NUC, 53 (45%) were

cataloged by the Library of Congress, while 65 (55%) were cataloged by other U.S. libraries through union cataloging. Of 173 titles found in the NUC from the 1967 sample, 9 (5%) were cataloged by the Library of Congress; 8 (5%) were cataloged by other U.S. libraries through union cataloging; and 156 (90%) were cataloged by foreign libraries through the shared cataloging program.
(594)

Ibid. . . . *showed that* foreign titles appear to show up more quickly in the NUC since the shared cataloging program began. Specifically, of the 118 book titles from the 3 countries found in NUC before the shared cataloging program began, 13 (11.0%) titles appeared in NUC within 4 months of appearing in their national bibliography. Of the 173 titles from the 3 countries found in the NUC after the shared cataloging program began, 102 (59.0%) appeared in the NUC within 4 months of appearing in their national bibliography.
(594)

Quality of Tools—OCLC

General

■ A study reported in 1977 of a sample of titles with 1974, 1975, and 1976 imprint dates *showed that* OCLC was substantially more effective as a verification tool (with a 92.7% verification rate) than Library of Congress depository cards (73.2%), *American Book Publishing Record* (69.9%), *National Union Catalog,*(44.6%) and *Cumulative Book Index* (32.8%).
(048)

■ A 1978 study of OCLC's Online Union Catalog preparatory to converting to AACR 2 form of name headings and uniform titles, involving a 1% test file (41,212 records) and a thorough review of AACR 2 rules, *showed that* 39% of the total records in the Online Union Catalog were ultimately converted to AACR 2 form.
(337)

Ibid. . . . *showed that* AACR 2 contained 454 "significant" rule changes or new rules, of which 56% would benefit neither librarian nor patron, 23% of which would benefit librarians, and 21% of which would benefit patrons.
(337)

■ A study reported in 1981 comparing 6 "commonly used library tools" (*American Book Publishing Record, Books in Print, Cumulative Book Index, Micrographic Catalog Retrieval Systems, National Union Catalog*, and the OCLC online service) as to their effectiveness for verification of monographs before acquisition using a sample of 360 books from 9 subject areas (including some foreign imprints) *showed that* the success in locating the 360 titles was as follows:

OCLC online service	97.5% of the books
MCRS	94.4% of the books
NUC	93.0% of the books
BIP	83.6% of the books
CBI	81.7% of the books
BPR	73.9% of the books **(767)**

Ibid. . . . *showed that*, of the combinations of 2 tools, the highest find rate was 98.9% using CBI and OCLC, while of the combinations of 3 tools, the highest find rate was 99.4% using BIP, OCLC, and MCRS. Further addition of tools did not increase the find rate; even using all 6 tools the last 0.6% could not be found. **(767)**

Ibid. . . . *showed that*, when searching for books only in the imprint year of the book, BIP was as effective a tool as OCLC. 70% of the books were located in both. Further, using both tools together increased the find rate to 83.3% of the sample. Other effective combinations that used only print tools were NUC + BIP (find rate = 79.2%) and BPR + BIP (find rate = 77.5%). Finally, even when using all 6 tools to search for books during the imprint year, 13.1% of the books could not be found. **(767)**

Ibid. . . . *showed that*, when searching for books in the imprint year plus the following year, OCLC was the most effective tool (find rate = 92.5%), followed by MCRS (find rate = 90.6%) and NUC (find rate = 88.9%). However, combinations of printed tools were also effective for this period. NUC + BIP had a find rate of 94.7%; NUC + CBI had a find rate of 93.6%; and NUC + BPR had a find rate of 92.5%. Further, searching more than 1 year after the imprint year resulted in only a very small increase in the effectiveness of any of the tools, ranging from 0.3% for BPR to 5.0% for OCLC. **(767)**

Ibid. . . . *showed that* the speed of searching for each of the tools was as follows:

OCLC online service	1.15 minutes per item
MCRS	1.31 minutes per item
BPR	2.10 minutes per item
CBI	2.17 minutes per item
BIP	2.25 minutes per item
NUC	2.94 minutes per item **(767)**

■ A survey reported in 1982 of 144 libraries contracting for OCLC services through the Bibliographic Center for Research (126 or 87.5% responding) *showed that*, when 2 or more copies of a work are acquired at one time, 44.4% of the respondents reported they would not indicate multiple-copy ownership in the OCLC record if all copies went into the same collection, while 30.2% reported they would not indicate multiple-copy ownership even if copies went into different collections. **(342)**

Ibid. . . . *showed that*, when a subsequent copy of a title cataloged earlier on OCLC was purchased, 70.6% of the respondents reported they would not enter information on the subsequent copy into the OCLC record if the copy were going into the same collection as the earlier copy, while 30.2% reported they would not enter information on the subsequent copy even if it were going into a different collection than the earlier copy. **(342)**

Ibid. . . . *showed that*, when the only copy of a work in the library was withdrawn, 70.6% of the respondents reported canceling the holdings recorded in the OCLC data base, while 19.8% reported they did not, 6.4% reported varying practices, and 3.2% did not reply to the question. **(342)**

Ibid. . . . *showed that*, when 1 of several copies of a work in the library that were previously cataloged on OCLC was withdrawn, 21.4% of the respondents reported that the OCLC holdings were updated, while 65.9% of the respondents reported that the holdings were not, 4.8% reported that their practice varied, and 7.9% did not answer. **(342)**

■ A 1982 study of the OCLC union catalog to investigate the extent of record duplication, based on 100 records randomly selected from the OCLC database and subsequently searched in the OCLC database for duplicates by using the alphabetic and numeric search keys generated from the selected record, *showed that* 17 (17%) records had duplicate entries, some more than 1 duplicate, for a total of 40 duplicate records (an average of 2.4 duplicate entries for each of the 17 duplicated records). **(772)**

Ibid. . . . *showed that*, based on an average of 3.6 alphabetic searches per record, 23% of the search keys evoked the response "[search key] produces more than 50 entries." **(772)**

■ A study reported in 1983 comparing the OCLC database and *New Serial Titles* as information resources for serials, based on searching 200 titles randomly selected from OCLC in *New Serial Titles* and 200 titles randomly selected from *New Serial Titles* in OCLC *showed that* there was only a moderate amount of overlap between the 2 tools. Specifically, a total of 217 (54.3%) titles were found in both. Further, 96 (48%) of the OCLC titles were found in *New Serial Titles*, while 121 (60.5%) of the *New Serial Titles* were found in OCLC.   **(776)**

Ibid. . . . *showed that* different information appeared to be contributed by OCLC and NST for the 217 serial titles they reported in common. For example, bibliographic information present in the NST record but absent in the OCLC record was as follows:

ISSN	21 (9.7%) records
Dewey number	127 (58.5%) records
beginning date/number	21 (9.7%) records
place of publication	4 (1.8%) records
publisher's address	24 (11.1%) records
price	10 (4.6%) records
frequency	9 (4.1%) records **(776)**

Ibid. . . . *showed that* information absent from both the OCLC and NST for the 217 records held in common was as follows:

ISSN	absent from 108 (49.8%) records
beginning date/number	absent from 76 (35.0%) records
publisher's address	absent from 119 (54.8%) records
price	absent from 161 (74.2%) records
frequency	absent from 89 (41.0%) records **(776)**

Ibid. . . . *showed that*, of the 217 titles held in common, OCLC records contained 273 notes, while NST records held 220 notes. 102 (37.4%) of the OCLC notes supplied information not contained in the NST notes, while 15.9% [no raw number given] of the NST notes provided information not contained in the OCLC notes.   **(776)**

Academic

■ A review of use statistics of an OCLC public-access terminal (3,307 publications searched) during the period January-August 1979 at the University of Michigan, Ann Arbor *showed that* searches for patrons were successful in locating a bibliographic record 61% of the time and of that number only 17% were listed as housed in the University of Michigan Libraries.   **(034)**

Ibid. . . . *showed that* of the 3,978 searches for patrons 48% required use of the author/title search key, 43% title search key, and 5% author search key. (The author search key could not be used much of the heaviest patron use time.) **(034)**

■ A study reported in 1982 of retrospective conversion of 3 library collections at the University of South Carolina, involving a main collection (Thomas Cooper Library, 47,514 records), a rare book collection (1,985 records), and a historical collection (the South Caroliniana Library, 16,281 records), *showed that* the hit rate for finding records in the data base (OCLC) was 92.7% for the main collection, 78.0% for the rare book collection, and 48.5% for the historical collection. **(344)**

Quality of Tools—Online Bibliographic Data Bases

General

■ A 1982 investigation to identify a core group of business journals, by selecting those periodicals that were listed in at least 3 of 4 business reference tools (ABI/INFORM, *Business Index*, *Business Periodicals Index*, and the *F and S Index United States*) or that were cited more than the median number of times business and business-related journals were cited in the 1981 *Social Sciences Citation Index Journal Reports*, *showed that* the percentage of the 283 business periodicals indexed in each of the 4 tools was as follows:

Business Index	91% of the core periodicals
Business Periodicals Index	84% of the core periodicals
ABI/INFORM	81% of the core periodicals
F and S Index United States	43% of the core periodicals **(561)**

Ibid. . . . *showed that* the number of the core periodicals as a percentage of the total periodicals indexed in each of the 4 tools was as follows:

Business Periodicals Index	78% of total periodicals indexed
Business Index	46% of total periodicals indexed
ABI/INFORM	42% of total periodicals indexed
F and S Index United States	22% of total periodicals indexed **(561)**

Ibid, . . . *showed that* the number of unique titles in each of the 4 tools, i.e., the number of titles indexed by each of the tools that were not indexed in any of the other tools, was as follows:

F And S Index United States	71% of periodicals indexed
ABI/INFORM	30% of periodicals indexed
Business Index	26% of periodicals indexed
Business Periodicals Index	8% of periodicals indexed **(561)**

Academic

■ A study reported in 1970 comparing *Epilepsy Abstracts* (a monthly journal) with monthly bibliographies on epilepsy from MEDLARS over the period of a year (1968) *showed that Epilepsy Abstracts* provided more citations more quickly than MEDLARS. Specifically, *Epilepsy Abstracts* retrieved 1,116 citations with an average delay (based on a subset of 100 abstracts) between publication date of the article and appearance of the abstract of 5.41 months, while MEDLARS retrieved 1,006 citations (no more than 1 year old) with an average delay of 6.45 months. **(684)**

Ibid. . . . *showed that* the overlap between the citations retrieved by the 2 services was relatively small. Only citations to 316 articles were duplicated by the 2 services, representing 28.3% of the citations retrieved by *Epilepsy Abstracts* and 31.4% of the citations retrieved by MEDLARS. This lack of overlap was not due to indexing or abstracting a different set of journals, since only 37% of the citations not retrieved by MEDLARS and 20% of the citations not retrieved by *Epilepsy Abstracts* were due to the journals not being covered by that particular service. The main reason for lack of more overlap was conjectured to be indexing or abstracting and retrieval procedures. **(684)**

Ibid. . . . *showed that* "approximately 10%" of the MEDLARS citations were irrelevant, compared to .1% of the *Epilepsy Abstracts* citations.
(684)

■ A 1971 study comparing MEDLINE bibliographic retrieval (data base of 1,100 journal titles) with SUNY Biomedical Communication Network bibliographic retrieval (data base of 2,300 journal titles) by duplicating 165 search requests on the 2 systems *showed that* the SUNY system retrieved 5,529 citations from 1,163 different journal titles, compared to 4,353 citations from 641 unique journal titles for the MEDLINE system.

MEDLINE retrieved 78.7% of the citations retrieved by the SUNY system. Further, "almost half" of the 21.3% citations not retrieved by the MEDLINE system were from foreign-language journals. **(693)**

■ A study reported in 1981 comparing the duplication rates of periodical titles among 3 agricultural data bases (AGRICOLA, U.S. National Agricultural Library; CAB, Commonwealth Agricultural Bureaux, United Kingdom; and AGRIS, International Information for the Agricultural Sciences and Technology, Food and Agriculture Organization, United Nations) *showed that* only 10.01% of the combined periodical titles were common to all 3 data bases. **(644)**

Ibid. . . . *showed that* AGRICOLA covered 6,079 periodical titles (97 countries), from which 120,000 articles a year were indexed; that AGRIS covered 5,365 periodical titles (97 countries), from which 180,000 articles a year were indexed; and that CAB covered 8,500 periodical titles (115 countries), from which 120,000 articles a year were indexed. **(644)**

■ A study reported in 1982 of time lag between receipt of indexed journal issue and receipt of the index that covered the first article (or in the case of the online index the time lag between receipt of the journal issue and the date when the first article in that issue became available online) involving 4 indexes (*Current Contents: Life Sciences, Science Citation Index*, SDILINE/MEDLINE, and *Index Medicus*) and 51 journals *showed that* the lag was:

Current Contents: Life Sciences	31 day lag
SDILINE/MEDLINE	86 day lag
Science Citation Index	110 day lag
Index Medicus	129 day lag **(439)**

■ A study reported in 1983 investigating consistency of indexing in MEDLINE, based on 760 articles published between 1974 and 1980 that were indexed twice in *Index Medicus*, *showed that* MeSH headings and subheadings were applied with more consistency to central concepts than to peripheral points, that the addition of subheadings to main headings lowered consistency, and that "floating" subheadings were more consistent than attached subheadings. The degree of consistency for different types of headings and subheadings was as follows:

checktags	74.7% consistency
central concept main headings	61.1% consistency

continued

geographics	56.6% consistency
descriptors	55.4% consistency
central concept subheadings	54.9% consistency
subheadings	48.7% consistency
main headings	48.2% consistency
central concept main headings/ subheadings combinations	43.1% consistency
main heading/subheading combinations	33.8% consistency **(748)**

Ibid. . . . *showed that* inconsistency in the use of geographic terms was not caused by different geographic terms applied to the same item but whether a geographic term was used at all. In other words, some indexers would use a geographic heading for an article, and some would not. In order to retrieve all relevant articles, therefore, care should be taken when using a geographic heading.   **(748)**

Ibid. . . . *showed that* length of article, language of article, and journal indexing priority had no statistically significant effect on consistency. Further, in all 9 categories of index terms, the average number of terms used (depth of indexing) showed no statistically significant differences.
                                                                                    (748)

Special

■ A study reported in 1970 comparing *Epilepsy Abstracts* (a monthly journal) with monthly bibliographies on epilepsy from MEDLARS over the period of a year (1968) *showed that Epilepsy Abstracts* provided more citations more quickly than MEDLARS. Specifically, *Epilepsy Abstracts* retrieved 1,116 citations with an average delay (based on a subset of 100 abstracts) between publication date of the article and appearance of the abstract of 5.41 months, while MEDLARS retrieved 1,006 citations (no more than 1 year old) with an average delay of 6.45 months.   **(684)**

Ibid. . . . *showed that* the overlap between the citations retrieved by the 2 services was relatively small. Only citations to 316 articles were duplicated by the 2 services, representing 28.3% of the citations retrieved by *Epilepsy Abstracts* and 31.4% of the citations retrieved by MEDLARS. This lack of overlap was not due to indexing or abstracting a different set of journals, since only 37% of the citations not retrieved by MEDLARS and 20% of the citations not retrieved by *Epilepsy Abstracts* were due to the journals not being covered by that particular service. The main reason for lack of more overlap was conjectured to be indexing or abstracting and retrieval procedures.

(684)

Ibid. . . . *showed that* "approximately 10%" of the MEDLARS citations were irrelevant, compared to .1% of the *Epilepsy Abstracts* citations.

(684)

■ A 1971 study comparing MEDLINE bibliographic retrieval (data base of 1,100 journal titles) with SUNY Biomedical Communication Network bibliographic retrieval (data base of 2,300 journal titles) by duplicating 165 search requests on the 2 systems *showed that* the SUNY system retrieved 5,529 citations from 1,163 different journal titles, compared to 4,353 citations from 641 unique journal titles for the MEDLINE system. MEDLINE retrieved 78.7% of the citations retrieved by the SUNY system. Further, "almost half" of the 21.3% citations not retrieved by the MEDLINE system were from foreign-language journals. **(693)**

■ A study reported in 1982 of time lag between receipt of indexed journal issue and receipt of the index that covered the first article (or in the case of the online index the time lag between receipt of the journal issue and the date when the first article in that issue became available online) involving 4 indexes (*Current Contents: Life Sciences, Science Citation Index,* SDILINE/MEDLINE, and *Index Medicus*) and 51 journals *showed that* the lag was:

Current Contents: Life Sciences	31 day lag
SDILINE/MEDLINE	86 day lag
Science Citation Index	110 day lag
Index Medicus	129 day lag **(439)**

■ A study reported in 1983 investigating consistency of indexing in MEDLINE, based on 760 articles published between 1974 and 1980 that were indexed twice in *Index Medicus, showed that* MeSH headings and subheadings were applied with more consistency to central concepts than to peripheral points, that the addition of subheadings to main headings lowered consistency, and that "floating" subheadings were more consistent than attached subheadings. The degree of consistency for different types of headings and subheadings was as follows:

checktags	74.7% consistency
central concept main headings	61.1% consistency

continued

geographics	56.6% consistency
descriptors	55.4% consistency
central concept subheadings	54.9% consistency
subheadings	48.7% consistency
main headings	48.2% consistency
central concept main headings/ subheadings combinations	43.1% consistency
main heading/subheading combinations	33.8% consistency **(748)**

Ibid. . . . *showed that* inconsistency in the use of geographic terms was not caused by different geographic terms applied to the same item but whether a geographic term was used at all. In other words, some indexers would use a geographic heading for an article, and some would not. In order to retrive all relevant articles, therefore, care should be taken when using a geographic heading.   **(748)**

Ibid. . . . *showed that* length of article, language of article, and journal indexing priority had no statistically significant effect on consistency. Further, in all 9 categories of index terms, the average number of terms used (depth of indexing) showed no statistically significant differences.   **(748)**

Quality of Tools—Periodicals

General

■ A comparison reported in 1978 of 3 guides (*Ulrich's International Periodicals Directory*, Katz's *Magazines for Libraries*, and *Chicorel Index to Abstracting and Indexing Services*) that identify where periodicals are indexed or abstracted, based on a study of 46 periodical titles written in or translated into English and 6 indexing/abstracting tools (*Sociological Abstracts, Social Sciences and Humanities Index, Abstracts for Social Workers, Public Affairs Information Service, Social Sciences Citation Index*, and *Psychological Abstracts*), *showed that*, of 46 titles, Katz gave correct information on where the journals were indexed or abstracted in 13 instances (28%); of the 43 titles covered by *Ulrich's*, the correct information was provided in 7 instances (16%); and of the 44 titles covered by *Chicorel*, the correct information was given in 3 cases (6%).   **(153)**

Ibid. . . . *showed that* the number of times 1 of the 6 indexing/abstracting tools indicated coverage by one of the 46 titles when this fact was not reported by 1 of the 3 guides was 63 times in *Chicorel*, 41 times in *Ulrich's*, and 39 times in Katz. **(153)**

Ibid. . . . *showed that* the number of times 1 of the 3 guides reported a title as indexed or abstracted in 1 of the 6 indexing/abstracting tools when in fact it was not was 16 times in *Ulrich's*, 13 times in Katz, and 5 times in *Chicorel*. **(153)**

Ibid. . . . *showed that* indexing in *Sociological Abstracts* was most frequently omitted by the 3 guides (55 times), compared to an average of 18 omissions each for the other 5 indexing/abstracting tools, while *Public Affairs Information Service* was the indexing/abstracting tool that was most often credited with indexing or abstracting 1 of the 46 titles when in fact it did not (20 instances compared to a mode of 2 for the other 5 indexing/abstracting tools). **(153)**

Ibid. . . . *showed that* a check of the front matter of half of the 46 periodical titles indicated that only 8 of the 23 included indexing and abstracting information and that none of these 8 gave completely accurate information on where they were indexed and abstracted, judging from the coverage reported by the 6 indexing/abstracting tools. **(153)**

■ An evaluation reported in 1980 of the degree to which the 17th edition of *Ulrich's* correctly reported journal indexing and abstracting, based on a study of 31 frequently cited journals in health and related fields *showed that Ulrich's* reported correctly only 28% of the indexes and abstracts that covered the 31 journals. *Ulrich's* reported a total of 177 references to indexes/abstracts for the 31 journals. 8 of these references were incorrect, and *Ulrich's* missed a total of 224 references to indexes/abstracts that it reportedly covers. A further 191 references were missed by *Ulrich's* in indexes and abstracts it does not cover. **(159)**

■ A 1982 investigation to identify a core group of business journals, by selecting those periodicals that were listed in at least 3 of 4 business reference tools (ABI/INFORM, *Business Index, Business Periodicals Index*, and the *F and S Index United States*) or that were cited more than the median number of times business and business-related journals were cited in the 1981 *Social Sciences Citation Index Journal Reports showed that* the percentage of the 283 business periodicals indexed in each of the 4 tools was as follows:

Business Index	91% of the core periodicals
Business Periodicals Index	84% of the core periodicals
ABI/INFORM	81% of the core periodicals
F and S Index United States	43% of the core periodicals **(561)**

Ibid. . . . *showed that* the number of the core periodicals as a percentage of the total periodicals indexed in each of the 4 tools was as follows:

Business Periodicals Index	78% of total periodicals indexed
Business Index	46% of total periodicals indexed
ABI/INFORM	42% of total periodicals indexed
F and S Index United States	22% of total periodicals indexed **(561)**

Ibid. . . . *showed that* the number of unique titles in each of the 4 tools, i.e., the number of titles indexed by each of the tools that were not indexed in any of the other tools, was as follows:

F And S Index United States	71% of periodicals indexed
ABI/INFORM	30% of periodicals indexed
Business Index	26% of periodicals indexed
Business Periodicals Index	8% of periodicals indexed **(561)**

■ A study reported in 1983 comparing the OCLC data base and *New Serial Titles* as information resources for serials, based on searching 200 titles randomly selected from OCLC in *New Serial Titles* and 200 titles randomly selected from *New Serial Titles* in OCLC *showed that* there was only a moderate amount of overlap between the 2 tools. Specifically, a total of 217 (54.3%) titles were found in both. Further, 96 (48%) of the OCLC titles were found in *New Serial Titles*, while 121 (60.5%) of the *New Serial Titles* were found in OCLC. **(776)**

Ibid. . . . *showed that* different information appeared to be contributed by OCLC and NST for the 217 serial titles they reported in common. For example, bibliographic information present in the NST record but absent in the OCLC record was as follows:

ISSN	21 (9.7%) records
Dewey number	127 (58.5%) records

continued

beginning date/number	21 (9.7%) records
place of publication	4 (1.8%) records
publisher's address	24 (11.1%) records
price	10 (4.6%) records
frequency	9 (4.1%) records **(776)**

Ibid. . . . *showed that* information absent from both the OCLC and NST for the 217 records held in common was as follows:

ISSN	absent from 108 (49.8%) records
beginning date/number	absent from 76 (35.0%) records
publisher's address	absent from 119 (54.8%) records
price	absent from 161 (74.2%) records
frequency	absent from 89 (41.0%) records **(776)**

Ibid. . . . *showed that*, of the 217 titles held in common, OCLC records contained 273 notes, while NST records held 220 notes. 102 (37.4%) of the OCLC notes supplied information not contained in the NST notes, while 15.9% [no raw number given] of the NST notes provided information not contained in the OCLC notes. **(776)**

Academic

■ A survey reported in 1976 of 179 journals cited by political science books and journals *showed that* only 29.05% of the cited journals were classified by *Ulrich's International Periodicals Directory* as political science. **(053)**

Quality of Tools—Subject Area (Agricultural Economics)

Academic

■ A study reported in 1969 of the bibliographic coverage of a stratified sample of 1,527 agricultural economics publications (20%), taken from a population of 7,624 publications reported published by U.S. agricultural economists during the 3-year period 1961-63 *showed that* 44.54% of the sample publications were indexed in 1 or more of 8 bibliographic services used in the agricultural economics field. Specifically, the *Bibliography of Agriculture* referenced 39.40% of the sample publications; *Agricultural Index* (now *Biological and Agricultural Index*) referenced 17.83%; *World Agricultural Economics and Rural Sociology Abstracts* referenced 8.71%; *Public Affairs Information Service* referenced 3.58%; *International Bibliography of Economics* referenced 2.6%; *Dairy Science Abstracts* referenced 0.44%; *Journal of Economics Abstracts* referenced 0.16%; and *Business Periodicals Index* referenced 0.13%.   **(245)**

Ibid. . . . *showed that* if a publication appeared as a part of a series or in a periodical it had a statistically significantly better chance (significant at the .01 level) of being indexed than if it appeared as a separate publication. For example, while 72% of the research monographs in a series were indexed, only 13% of the separate research reports were indexed.   **(245)**

Ibid. . . . *showed that* national-level publications were more likely to be indexed than state- or regional-level publications. For example, 65.29% of the U.S. federal publications and 54.13% of the national or regional organization or society publications were indexed, compared to 21.58% of the state government agency publications and 10.94% of the local or state organization publications.   **(245)**

Quality of Tools—Subject Area (Agriculture)

General

■ A study reported in 1981 comparing the duplication rates of periodical titles among 3 agricultural data bases (AGRICOLA, U.S. National Agricultural Library; CAB, Commonwealth Agricultural Bureaux, United Kingdom; and AGRIS, International Information for the Agricultural Sciences and Technology, Food and Agriculture Organization, United Nations) *showed that* only 10.01% of the combined periodical titles were common to all 3 data bases.   **(644)**

Ibid. . . . *showed that* AGRICOLA covered 6,079 periodical titles (97 countries), from which 120,000 articles a year were indexed; that AGRIS covered 5,365 periodical titles (97 countries), from which 180,000 articles a year were indexed; and that CAB covered 8,500 periodical titles (115 countries), from which 120,000 articles a year were indexed.   **(644)**

Quality of Tools—Subject Area (Biology)

Academic

■ A study reported in 1972 of the author indexes of *Biological Abstracts* for 1968 and 1969 in comparison with the author cards of *Index to American Botanical Literature* for the same period *showed that*, of a 10% sample of *IABL* articles for 1968 (176 articles), 21 (12%) were not found in the subsequent 4 years of *BA*. Of another 10% sample of *IABL* articles for 1969 (195 articles), 43 (22%) were not found in the subsequent 3 years of *BA*.   **(137)**

■ A study reported in 1972 of the articles abstracted in *Biological Abstracts* in 1968 (sample size: 11,853 citations or 8.5% of total) and 1969 (sample size: 13,008 citations or 9.6% of total) *showed that* half a year or more usually elapsed between publication of an article and its appearance in *Biological Abstracts*. Further, while the overwhelming majority of articles were abstracted in *BA* within 1-2 years following their publication, a few take as long as a decade to be abstracted.   **(137)**

Quality of Tools—Subject Area (Botany)

Academic

■ A study reported in 1972 of the author indexes of *Biological Abstracts* for 1968 and 1969 in comparison with the author cards of *Index to American Botanical Literature* for the same period *showed that*, of a 10% sample of *IABL* articles for 1968 (176 articles), 21 (12%) were not found in the subsequent 4 years of *BA*. Of another 10% sample of *IABL* articles for 1969 (195 articles), 43 (22%) were not found in the subsequent 3 years of *BA*.   **(137)**

■ A study reported in 1972 of the articles abstracted in *Biological Abstracts* in 1968 (sample size: 11,853 citations or 8.5% of total) and 1969 (sample size: 13,008 citations or 9.6% of total) *showed that* half a year or more usually elapsed between publication of an article and its appearance in *Biological Abstracts*. Further, while the overwhelming majority of articles were abstracted in *BA* within 1-2 years following their publication, a few take as long as a decade to be abstracted.   **(137)**

Quality of Tools—Subject Area (Business)

General

■ A 1982 investigation to identify a core group of business journals, by selecting those periodicals that were listed in at least 3 of 4 business reference tools (ABI/INFORM, *Business Index*, *Business Periodicals Index*, and the *F and S Index United States*) or that were cited more than the median number of times business and business-related journals were cited in the 1981 *Social Sciences Citation Index Journal Reports*, *showed that* the percentage of the 283 business periodicals indexed in each of the 4 tools was as follows:

Business Index	91% of the core periodicals
Business Periodicals Index	84% of the core periodicals
ABI/INFORM	81% of the core periodicals
F and S Index United States	43% of the core periodicals **(561)**

Ibid. . . . *showed that* the number of the core periodicals as a percentage of the total periodicals indexed in each of the 4 tools was as follows:

Business Periodicals Index	78% of total periodicals indexed
Business Index	46% of total periodicals indexed
ABI/INFORM	42% of total periodicals indexed
F and S Index United States	22% of total periodicals indexed **(561)**

Ibid. . . . *showed that* the number of unique titles in each of the 4 tools, i.e., the number of titles indexed by each of the tools that were not indexed in any of the other tools, was as follows:

F And S Index United States	71% of periodicals indexed
ABI/INFORM	30% of periodicals indexed
Business Index	26% of periodicals indexed
Business Periodicals Index	8% of periodicals indexed **(561)**

Quality of Tools—Subject Area
(Economics)

Academic

■ A study reported in 1976 of the bibliographic coverage of 1,972 social science (psychology, sociology, political science, and economics) books and government publications (primarily 1971 and 1972 imprints searched in the bibliographic sources for the subsequent 3-4 years) *showed that* in economics, of 258 books and 54 government documents, the *International Bibliography of Economics* covered 140 (54%) of the books and 8 (15%) of the documents; the *Journal of Economic Literature* covered 80 (31%) of the books and none of the documents; *Economic Abstracts* covered 40 (16%) of the books and none of the documents; and *PAIS* covered none of the books and 26 (48%) of the documents.						**(410)**

Ibid. . . . *showed that* books reviewed in a discipline's journals are more likely than nonreviewed books to be cited in the bibliographic services. For example:

in psychology, 115 of 170 books (68%) were reviewed overall, while 57 of 77 (74%) cited books were reviewed;

in sociology, 108 of 270 books (40%) were reviewed overall, while 72 of 136 (53%) cited books were reviewed;

in political science, 44 of 105 (42%) books were reviewed overall, while 42 of 86 (49%) cited books were reviewed;

in economics, 44 of 149 (30%) books were reviewed overall, while 43 of 116 (37%) cited books were reviewed.			**(410)**

Quality of Tools—Subject Area (Education)

Academic

■ A 1974 study of indexing overlap among *Education Index* (218 titles), *Current Index to Journals in Education* (702 titles), and *Psychological Abstracts* (866 titles) *showed that CIJE* duplicated 180 (83%) of the titles indexed by *Education Index*. However, *Education Index* fully indexed all of its 218 titles (cover-to-cover indexing), while *CIJE* fully indexed only 159

(23%) of its titles. Of these fully indexed titles, 101 are indexed also by *Education Index*, for a 46% overlap.   **(453)**

Ibid. . . . *showed that Psychological Abstracts* fully indexed 138 or 16% of its titles. 70 titles (8%) in *Psychological Abstracts* were also covered by both *CIJE* and *Education Index*, but only 6 of the *Psychological Abstracts* titles that were fully indexed (cover-to-cover) were also fully indexed in both *CIJE* and *Education Index*. However, 160 titles (18%) in *Psychological Abstracts* were also covered in either *CIJE* or *Education Index* of which 19 titles were fully indexed in either *CIJE* or *Education Index*.   **(453)**

■ A study reported in 1975 of the reading level of abstracts compared to the reading level of the source document of 48 ERIC documents (12 each from 4 different clearinghouses) as determined by the Flesch Reading Ease formula *showed that* the abstracts had a statistically significantly higher reading level than their source documents (significant at the .001 level). Nevertheless, the reading levels of even the most highly scoring abstracts (score of 14.59) appeared within the range of the intended audience (new teachers, graduate students, and librarians) as described in the *ERIC Operating Manual*.   **(612)**

Quality of Tools—Subject Area (Geochemistry)

Academic

■ A study reported in 1975 of index control and overlap in the area of geochemistry, involving 879 citations of materials published between 1960 and 1966 taken from selected bibliographies and searched in *Chemical Abstracts, Bibliography of North American Geology, Bibliography and Index of Geology Exclusive of North America*, and *Geoscience Abstracts*, *showed that* 135 (15%) were not found in any of the 4 indexing and abstracting tools, while 560 (64%) were found in *Chemical Abstracts*, 258 (29%) were found in *Bibliography and Index of Geology Exclusive of North America*, 250 (28%) were found in *Geoscience Abstracts*, and 220 (25%) were found in *Bibliography of North American Geology*.   **(408)**

Ibid. . . . *showed that* considerable overlap exists in the coverage of the 4 indexing and abstracting tools, with 42% of the citations found in more than 1 of the tools. Further, 62% of the citations found in *Bibliography of North American Geology* and *Bibliography and Index of Geology Exclusive of North America* were also found in *Chemical Abstracts*, while 79% of the citations found in *Geoscience Abstracts* were also found in *Bibliography of North American Geology* and *Bibliography and Index of Geology Exclusive of North America.* **(408)**

Quality of Tools—Subject Area (Library Science)

General

■ A study reported in 1973 based on the journal articles listed in the 1967 volume of *Library Literature* (4,418 journal articles in 247 journals) *showed that* 136 (55%) journals were listed in *Library Literature*'s regular list of library-oriented journals, while 111 (45%) journals were nonlibrary journals. Of the 4,418 articles, 1,162 (26%) were 1 page or less in length. **(610)**

■ A study reported in 1974 of citations in the 1972 volumes of *Library and Information Science Abstracts* (10% sample or 318 citations) and *Library Literature* (10% sample or 1,607 citations) *showed that* the average time lag between publication date of an article and appearance of a citation in either *LISA* or *Liblit* was 6.2 months; the range of the lag ran from 0-53 months; and the mode was 2.0 months. **(143)**

Ibid. . . . *showed that* 60% of the sample citations were from North American sources, 16% from United Kingdom sources, 15% from European sources, 6% from Australia-New Zealand sources, and 2% each from Asian and African sources. **(143)**

Ibid. . . . *showed that* there was a statistically significant shorter time lag between publication date and citation in *Library and Information Science Abstracts* as compared to *Library Literature*. From each of 6 major world regions, *LISA* cited articles more quickly than *LibLit*: from North America (3.6 vs. 4.5 months lag), United Kingdom (2.4 vs. 5.7 months), Australia-New Zealand (1.9 vs. 6.6 months), Europe (4.4 vs. 19.0 months), Asia (8.1 vs. 8.2 months), and Africa (3.6 vs. 11.8 months). **(143)**

Academic

■ A study reported in 1973 based on the journal articles listed in the 1967 volume of *Library Literature* (4,418 journal articles in 247 journals) *showed that* 136 (55%) journals were listed in *Library Literature*'s regular list of library-oriented journals, while 111 (45%) journals were nonlibrary

journals. Of the 4,418 articles, 1,162 (26%) were 1 page or less in length.
(610)

■ A study reported in 1974 of citations in the 1972 volumes of *Library and Information Science Abstracts* (10% sample or 318 citations) and *Library Literature* (10% sample or 1,607 citations) *showed that* the average time lag between publication date of an article and appearance of a citation in either *LISA* or *Liblit* was 6.2 months; the range of the lag ran from 0-53 months; and the mode was 2.0 months.   **(143)**

Ibid. . . . *showed that* 60% of the sample citations were from North American sources, 16% from United Kingdom sources, 15% from European sources, 6% from Australia-New Zealand sources, and 2% each from Asian and African sources.   **(143)**

Ibid. . . . *showed that* there was a statistically significant shorter time lag between publication date and citation in *Library and Information Science Abstracts* as compared to *Library Literature*. From each of 6 major world regions, *LISA* cited articles more quickly than *LibLit*: from North America (3.6 vs. 4.5 months lag), United Kingdom (2.4 vs. 5.7 months), Australia-New Zealand (1.9 vs. 6.6 months), Europe (4.4 vs. 19.0 months), Asia (8.1 vs. 8.2 months), and Africa (3.6 vs. 11.8 months). **(143)**

Quality of Tools—Subject Area (Marine Biology)

Academic

■ A study reported in 1977 at Rutgers University comparing 240 marine biology citations found in 6 1975 issues of *Oceanic Abstracts* with coverage in *Biological Abstracts* and *Bioresearch Index* from 1973 through the first half of 1976 *showed that*, overall, 69.6% of the 240 citations were found in either *Biological Abstracts* or *Bioresearch Index*.   **(418)**

Ibid. . . . *showed that* a comparison of time lag between publication date of the original article and citation in either *Oceanic Abstracts* or *Biological Abstracts/Bioresearch Index* in 24 time periods between 1972 and 1975 revealed that in all but 1 time period the time lag was shorter for citations found in either *Biological Abstracts* or *Bioresearch Index* than for citations found in *Oceanic Abstracts*.   **(418)**

Quality of Tools—Subject Area (Medicine)

Academic

■ A study reported in 1968 concerning bibliographic control of the proceedings and reports of biomedical congresses, conferences, symposia, etc., from the regional to the international level and involving investigation of 120 bibliographic tools *showed that* 28 tools "gave some consideration to conferences and meetings," while 5 tools dealt totally with conferences and symposia (reporting some 1,821 biomedical conferences). The 5 were:

1. *Directory of Published Proceedings*
2. *Symposia and Conferences Published in Serials Recieved at Wayne State University Medical Library*
3. *Proceedings in Print*
4. *Bibliographical Current List of Papers, Reports and Proceedings of International Meetings*
5. *Technical Meetings Index*   **(676)**

■ A study reported in 1970 of the cardiovascular literature, involving 78 journals "solely concerned with publishing papers dealing with some aspect of the heart and/or blood vessels, i.e. c-v speciality journals" plus 789 journals that published the findings of National Heart Institute grantees in fiscal 1967 (5,860 papers) *showed that* the coverage given to the 78 cardiovascular speciality journals by the major indexing and abstracting services was as follows:

Index Medicus	48 (62%) journals
Excerpta Medica	47 (60%) journals
Biological Abstracts	35 (45%) journals
Chemical Abstracts	33 (42%) journals
Science Citation Index	15 (19%) journals

(607)

■ A study reported in 1970 comparing *Epilepsy Abstracts* (a monthly journal) with monthly bibliographies on epilepsy from MEDLARS over the period of a year (1968) *showed that Epilepsy Abstracts* provided more citations more quickly than MEDLARS. Specifically, *Epilepsy Abstracts* retrieved 1,116 citations with an average delay (based on a subset of 100 abstracts) between publication date of the article and appearance of the abstract of 5.41 months, while MEDLARS retrieved 1,006 citations (no more than 1 year old) with an average delay of 6.45 months.   **(684)**

Ibid. . . . *showed that* the overlap between the citations retrieved by the 2 services was relatively small. Only citations to 316 articles were duplicated by the 2 services, representing 28.3% of the citations retrieved by *Epilepsy Abstracts* and 31.4% of the citations retrieved by MEDLARS. This lack of overlap was not due to indexing or abstracting a different set of journals, since only 37% of the citations not retrieved by MEDLARS and 20% of the citations not retrieved by *Epilepsy Abstracts* were due to the journals not being covered by that particular service. The main reason for lack of more overlap was conjectured to be indexing or abstracting and retrieval procedures.   **(684)**

Ibid. . . . *showed that* "approximately 10%" of the MEDLARS citations were irrelevant, compared to .1% of the *Epilepsy Abstracts* citations.
                                                                      (684)

■ A study reported in 1974 of 3,347 biomedical book reviews (2,067 titles) taken from the 1970 issues of 54 English-language biomedical journals (excluding *Science* and *Nature*) that contained "bona fide" book reviews *showed that* the average time lag (difference between publication date of a book and the date of the journal issue containing the review of the book) for the 54 journals varied widely, ranging from 5.8 months for *Lancet* to 42 months for *Acta Radiologica: Therapy, Physics, Biology*. 29.7% of the 3,347 reviews appeared in the same year as the book was published.   **(700)**

Ibid. . . . *showed that* the length of the reviews ranged from 50 words to 1,650 words with "most . . . over 265 words." Further, reviews in all but 3 of the 54 journals were signed.   **(700)**

Ibid. . . . *showed that* the lag time for individual reviews ranged from 0 months to 108 months (9 years). The modal lag for individual reviews was 8 months, while the average lag was 10.43 months.   **(700)**

■ A study reported in 1974 of 3,347 biomedical book reviews (2,067 titles) taken from the 1970 issues of 54 English-language biomedical journals (excluding *Science* and *Nature*) that contained "bona fide" book reviews *showed that* 5 journals covered 680 (93.53%) of the books reviewed more than once and 1,131 titles (54.71%) of the total titles reviewed. These journals were:

British Medical Journal	375 (18.1%) total titles
Annals of Internal Medicine	243 (11.8%) total titles
Lancet	212 (10.3%) total titles

continued

> *Journal of the American Medical*
> *Association*   184 (8.9%) total titles
> *New England Journal of Medicine*   117 (5.7%) total titles   **(703)**

■ A study reported in 1982 investigating *Science Citation Index*'s coverage of preclinical science literature (5,795 references to articles published between 1964-77 taken from 70 dissertations written during 1973-77 in anatomy, biochemistry, immunology, microbiology, pathology, pharmacology, and physiology) *showed that* 5,495 (94.8%) of the cited articles were indexed by *Science Citation Index*. Of the 300 citations not indexed, 282 were in journals not indexed by *SCI*. Only 18 (0.3%) citations were to journals that *SCI* indexed.   **(656)**

Ibid. . . . *showed that SCI* coverage of the cited articles by discipline (see above) was consistently good, with only a 2.5% difference separating the best (microbiology, 96.75% of articles cited) from the worst (pathology, 94.2% of articles cited).   **(656)**

■ A study reported in 1983 investigating consistency of indexing in MEDLINE, based on 760 articles published between 1974 and 1980 that were indexed twice in *Index Medicus, showed that* MeSH headings and subheadings were applied with more consistency to central concepts than to peripheral points, that the addition of subheadings to main headings lowered consistency, and that "floating" subheadings were more consistent than attached subheadings. The degree of consistency for different types of headings and subheadings was as follows:

checktags	74.7% consistency
central concept main headings	61.1% consistency
geographics	56.6% consistency
descriptors	55.4% consistency
central concept subheadings	54.9% consistency
subheadings	48.7% consistency
main headings	48.2% consistency
central concept main headings/ subheadings combinations	43.1% consistency
main heading/subheading combinations	33.8% consistency **(748)**

Ibid. . . . *showed that* inconsistency in the use of geographic terms was not caused by different geographic terms applied to the same item but whether a geographic term was used at all. In other words, some indexers would use a geographic heading for an article, and some would not. In order to retrive all relevant articles, therefore, care should be taken when using a geographic heading. **(748)**

Ibid. . . . *showed that* length of article, language of article, and journal indexing priority had no statistically significant effect on consistency. Further, in all 9 categories of index terms, the average number of terms used (depth of indexing) showed no statistically significant differences.

(748)

Special

■ A study reported in 1968 concerning bibliographic control of the proceedings and reports of biomedical congresses, conferences, symposia, etc., from the regional to the international level and involving investigation of 120 bibliographic tools *showed that* 28 tools "gave some consideration to conferences and meetings," while 5 tools dealt totally with conferences and symposia (reporting some 1,821 biomedical conferences). The 5 were:

1. *Directory of Published Proceedings*
2. *Symposia and Conferences Published in Serials Recieved at Wayne State University Medical Library*
3. *Proceedings in Print*
4. *Bibliographical Current List of Papers, Reports and Proceedings of International Meetings*
5. *Technical Meetings Index* **(676)**

■ A study reported in 1970 of the cardiovascular literature, involving 78 journals "solely concerned with publishing papers dealing with some aspect of the heart and/or blood vessels, i.e. c-v speciality journals" plus 789 journals that published the findings of National Heart Institute grantees in fiscal 1967 (5,860 papers) *showed that* the coverage given to the 78 cardiovascular speciality journals by the major indexing and abstracting services was as follows:

Index Medicus	48 (62%) journals
Excerpta Medica	47 (60%) journals
Biological Abstracts	35 (45%) journals
Chemical Abstracts	33 (42%) journals
Science Citation Index	15 (19%) journals **(607)**

■ A study reported in 1970 comparing *Epilepsy Abstracts* (a monthly journal) with monthly bibliographies on epilepsy from MEDLARS over the period of a year (1968) *showed that Epilepsy Abstracts* provided more citations more quickly than MEDLARS. Specifically, *Epilepsy Abstracts* retrieved 1,116 citations with an average delay (based on a subset of 100 abstracts) between publication date of the article and appearance of the abstract of 5.41 months, while MEDLARS retrieved 1,006 citations (no more than 1 year old) with an average delay of 6.45 months.

(684)

Ibid. . . . *showed that* the overlap between the citations retrieved by the 2 services was relatively small. Only citations to 316 articles were duplicated by the 2 services, representing 28.3% of the citations retrieved by *Epilepsy Abstracts* and 31.4% of the citations retrieved by MEDLARS. This lack of overlap was not due to indexing or abstracting a different set of journals, since only 37% of the citations not retrieved by MEDLARS and 20% of the citations not retrieved by *Epilepsy Abstracts* were due to the journals not being covered by that particular service. The main reason for lack of more overlap was conjectured to be indexing or abstracting and retrieval procedures.

(684)

Ibid. . . . *showed that* "approximately 10%" of the MEDLARS citations were irrelevant, compared to .1% of the *Epilepsy Abstracts* citations.

(684)

■ A study reported in 1974 of 3,347 biomedical book reviews (2,067 titles) taken from the 1970 issues of 54 English-language biomedical journals (excluding *Science* and *Nature*) that contained "bona fide" book reviews *showed that* the average time lag (difference between publication date of a book and the date of the journal issue containing the review of the book) for the 54 journals varied widely, ranging from 5.8 months for *Lancet* to 42 months for *Acta Radiologica: Therapy, Physics, Biology.* 29.7% of the 3,347 reviews appeared in the same year as the book was published.

(700)

Ibid. . . . *showed that* the length of the reviews ranged from 50 words to 1,650 words with "most . . . over 265 words." Further, reviews in all but 3 of the 54 journals were signed.

(700)

Ibid. . . . *showed that* the lag time for individual reviews ranged from 0 months to 108 months (9 years). The modal lag for individual reviews was 8 months, while the average lag was 10.43 months.

(700)

■ A study reported in 1974 of 3,347 biomedical book reviews (2,067 titles) taken from the 1970 issues of 54 English-language biomedical journals (excluding *Science* and *Nature*) that contained "bona fide" book reviews *showed that* 5 journals covered 680 (93.53%) of the books reviewed more than once and 1,131 titles (54.71%) of the total titles reviewed. These journals were:

British Medical Journal	375 (18.1%) total titles
Annals of Internal Medicine	243 (11.8%) total titles
Lancet	212 (10.3%) total titles
Journal of the American Medical Association	184 (8.9%) total titles
New England Journal of Medicine	117 (5.7%) total titles **(703)**

■ A study reported in 1982 investigating *Science Citation Index*'s coverage of preclinical science literature (5,795 references to articles published between 1964-77 taken from 70 dissertations written during 1973-77 in anatomy, biochemistry, immunology, microbiology, pathology, pharmacology, and physiology) *showed that* 5,495 (94.8%) of the cited articles were indexed by *Science Citation Index*. Of the 300 citations not indexed, 282 were in journals not indexed by *SCI*. Only 18 (0.3%) citations were to journals that *SCI* indexed.   **(656)**

Ibid. . . . *showed that SCI* coverage of the cited articles by discipline (see above) was consistently good, with only a 2.5% difference separating the best (microbiology, 96.75% of articles cited) from the worst (pathology, 94.2% of articles cited).   **(656)**

■ A study reported in 1983 investigating consistency of indexing in MEDLINE, based on 760 articles published between 1974 and 1980 which were indexed twice in *Index Medicus*, *showed that* MeSH headings and subheadings were applied with more consistency to central concepts than to peripheral points, that the addition of subheadings to main headings lowered consistency, and that "floating" subheadings were more consistent than attached subheadings. The degree of consistency for different types of headings and subheadings was as follows:

checktags	74.7% consistency
central concept main headings	61.1% consistency
geographics	56.6% consistency
descriptors	55.4% consistency
central concept subheadings	54.9% consistency
subheadings	48.7% consistency
main headings	48.2% consistency

continued

central concept main headings/
   subheadings combinations   43.1% consistency
main heading/subheading
   combinations   33.8% consistency   **(748)**

Ibid. . . . *showed that* inconsistency in the use of geographic terms was not caused by different geographic terms applied to the same item but whether a geographic term was used at all. In other words, some indexers would use a geographic heading for an article, and some would not. In order to retrive all relevant articles, therefore, care should be taken when using a geographic heading.   **(748)**

Ibid. . . . *showed that* length of article, language of article, and journal indexing priority had no statistically significant effect on consistency. Further, in all 9 categories of index terms, the average number of terms used (depth of indexing) showed no statistically significant differences.   **(748)**

Quality of Tools—Subject Area (Music)

Academic

■ A study reported in 1972 of the 1967 *RILM Abstracts (Repertoire International de la Litterature Musicale)* involving every tenth entry from the subject index (158 items) *showed that* the 3 most popular languages were English (72.5 or 46% articles), German (20 or 12.5% articles), and French (15 or 9.5% articles). Articles published in 2 languages were counted as .5 in each language.   **(401)**

Ibid. . . . *showed that* an examination of every twelfth entry in the 1967 cumulative index (1,125 entries) indicated that the 4 most common publication forms were: articles from periodicals (612 or 54.4%), monographs (145 or 13.7%), articles from Festschriften (75 or 6.7%), and book reviews (72 or 6.4%).   **(401)**

Ibid. . . . *showed that* a comparison of potential descriptors for the 158 sample items with the actual index terms used by *RILM* revealed that overall 13.5% of important terms were overlooked. This was considered a low number.   **(401)**

Quality of Tools—Subject Area
(Political Science)

Academic

■   A study of 2,801 articles in a core group of 25 political science journals published in the period 1968-70 and the related indexing and abstracting services *showed that* 3 indexing/abstracting tools covered 100% of the articles published in the journals they covered. These were *Social Science and Humanities Index, ABC/POLSCI*, and *British Humanities Index*. The remaining 7 tools indexed or abstracted selectively with the range of selectivity as follows:

International Political Science Abstracts	96.00% coverage
Universal Reference System	63.11% coverage
International Bibliography of Political Science	58.79% coverage
PAIS	51.18% coverage
Bulletin Analytique de Documentation Politique	35.85% coverage
Historical Abstracts	4.20% coverage (053)

■   A study reported in 1976 of the bibliographic coverage of 1,972 social science (psychology, sociology, political science, and economics) books and government publications (primarily 1971 and 1972 imprints searched in the bibliographic sources for the subsequent 3-4 years) *showed that* in political science, of 159 books and 33 government documents, the *International Bibliography of Political Science* covered 84 (53%) of the books and 3 (9%) of the documents; the *Universal Reference System* covered 58 (36%) of the books and none of the documents; and *PAIS* covered none of the books and 21 (64%) of the documents.   (410)

Ibid. . . . *showed that* books reviewed in a discipline's journals are more likely than nonreviewed books to be cited in the bibliographic services. For example:

in psychology, 115 of 170 books (68%) were reviewed overall, while 57 of 77 (74%) cited books were reviewed;

in sociology, 108 of 270 books (40%) were reviewed overall, while 72 of 136 (53%) cited books were reviewed;

in political science, 44 of 105 (42%) books were reviewed overall, while 42 of 86 (49%) cited books were reviewed;

in economics, 44 of 149 (30%) books were reviewed overall, while 43 of 116 (37%) cited books were reviewed. **(410)**

■ A survey reported in 1976 of 179 journals cited by political science books and journals *showed that* only 29.05% of the cited journals were classified by *Ulrich's International Periodicals Directory* as political science. **(053)**

Quality of Tools—Subject Area (Psychology)

Academic

■ A 1974 study of indexing overlap among *Education Index* (218 titles), *Current Index to Journals in Education* (702 titles), and *Psychological Abstracts* (866 titles) *showed that* CIJE duplicated 180 (83%) of the titles indexed by *Education Index*. However, *Education Index* fully indexed all of its 218 titles (cover-to-cover indexing), while *CIJE* fully indexed only 159 (23%) of its titles. Of these fully indexed titles, 101 are indexed also by *Education Index*, for a 46% overlap. **(453)**

Ibid. . . . *showed that Psychological Abstracts* fully indexed 138 or 16% of its titles. 70 titles (8%) in *Psychological Abstracts* were also covered by both *CIJE* and *Education Index*, but only 6 of the *Psychological Abstracts* titles that were fully indexed (cover-to-cover) were also fully indexed in both *CIJE* and *Education Index*. However, 160 titles (18%) in *Psychological Abstracts* were also covered in either *CIJE* or *Education Index*, of which 19 titles were fully indexed in either *CIJE* or *Education Index*. **(453)**

■ A study reported in 1976 of the bibliographic coverage of 1,972 social science (psychology, sociology, political science, and economics) books and government publications (primarily 1971 and 1972 imprints searched in the bibliographic sources for the subsequent 3-4 years) *showed that* in psychology, of 170 books and 19 government documents, *Psychological Abstracts* covered 68 (40%) of the total books and 5 (26%) of the total documents; *American Behavioral Scientist's Recent Publications in the Social and Behavioral Sciences* covered 10 (6%) of the total books and none of the documents; and *PAIS* covered none of the books and 2 (11%) of the documents.   **(410)**

Ibid. . . . *showed that* books reviewed in a discipline's journals are more likely than nonreviewed books to be cited in the bibliographic services. For example:

in psychology, 115 of 170 books (68%) were reviewed overall, while 57 of 77 (74%) cited books were reviewed;

in sociology, 108 of 270 books (40%) were reviewed overall, while 72 of 136 (53%) cited books were reviewed;

in political science, 44 of 105 (42%) books were reviewed overall, while 42 of 86 (49%) cited books were reviewed;

in economics, 44 of 149 (30%) books were reviewed overall, while 43 of 116 (37%) cited books were reviewed.   **(410)**

■ A study reported in 1980 comparing the coverage of *Psychological Abstracts* and *Index Medicus* of the journal literature on the topic of operant conditioning, based on all citations in the 2 indexes under that topic for the year 1978 (351 articles in 96 different journals) *showed that* for 1978 only 21 (6%) of the 351 articles were found in both indexes. However, a comprehensive check of earlier and later volumes of both indexes revealed 127 (36%) articles were found in both tools.   **(624)**

Ibid. . . . *showed that*, of 288 articles that carried monthly dates, the time lag between publication of the article in the journal and the time the article appeared in an index averaged 5.76 months for *Index Medicus* and 11.8 months for *Psychological Abstracts*. This difference did not appear to be due to a greater time lag between the date of a journal issue and its actual appearance for psychology journals, since median time lag in this regard for both the psychology and medical journals was the same—1 month.
                                                                       (624)

Quality of Tools—Subject Area (Sociology)

Academic

■ A study reported in 1976 of the bibliographic coverage of 1,972 social science (psychology, sociology, political science, and economics) books and government publications (primarily 1971 and 1972 imprints searched in the bibliographic sources for the subsequent 3-4 years) *showed that* in sociology, of 280 books and 48 government documents, the *International Bibliography of Sociology* covered 90 (32%) of the books and 24 (50%) of the documents; *Sociological Abstracts* covered 2 (0.7%) of the books and none of the documents; and *PAIS* covered none of the books and 20 (42%) of the documents. **(410)**

Ibid. . . . *showed that* books reviewed in a discipline's journals are more likely than nonreviewed books to be cited in the bibliographic services. For example:

in psychology, 115 of 170 books (68%) were reviewed overall, while 57 of 77 (74%) cited books were reviewed;

in sociology, 108 of 270 books (40%) were reviewed overall, while 72 of 136 (53%) cited books were reviewed;

in political science, 44 of 105 (42%) books were reviewed overall, while 42 of 86 (49%) cited books were reviewed;

in economics, 44 of 149 (30%) books were reviewed overall, while 43 of 116 (37%) cited books were reviewed. **(410)**

Quality of Tools—Time Lag of Reviewing

General

■ A 1967 study comparing *Cumulative Book Index* (CBI) with *Canadiana* in terms of its coverage of English-language books published in Canada (209 titles from the first 3 months of 1966 *Canadiana* searched in CBI for 1965-66-67) *showed that*, of the 154 titles located in CBI, 17 (11%) of the titles appeared in CBI before they appeared in *Canadiana*; 22 (14%) titles appeared in CBI within a month or 2 of their appearance in *Canadiana*; and 115 (75%) appeared in CBI at least 2 months after appearing in *Canadiana*. Further, 93 (60.4%) of the titles found in CBI appeared 4-5 months after appearing in *Canadiana*. **(595)**

■ A study of 4 major book review journals *showed that* the time lag between publishing date and appearance of the review for 11 notable books during the period 1973-75 was 1.5 days for the *New York Times Book Review*, 16.6 days for the *Library Journal*, 57.6 days for *Booklist*, and 127.7 days for *Choice*. **(157)**

■ A study reported in 1974 of citations in the 1972 volumes of *Library and Information Science Abstracts* (10% sample or 318 citations) and *Library Literature* (10% sample or 1,607 citations) *showed that* the average time lag between publication date of an article and appearance of a citation in either *LISA* or *Liblit* was 6.2 months; the range of the lag ran from 0-53 months; and the mode was 2.0 months. **(143)**

Ibid. . . . *showed that* there was a statistically significant shorter time lag between publication date and citation in *Library and Information Science Abstracts* as compared to *Library Literature*. From each of 6 major world regions, *LISA* cited articles more quickly than *LibLit*: from North America (3.6 vs. 4.5 months lag), United Kingdom (2.4 vs. 5.7 months), Australia-New Zealand (1.9 vs. 6.6 months), Europe (4.4 vs. 19.0 months), Asia (8.1 vs. 8.2 months), and Africa (3.6 vs. 11.8 months). **(143)**

■ A study reported in 1980 comparing the *Book Review Digest, Book Review Index*, and *Cuurent Book Review Citations*, *showed that* the time lag in publishing the reviews [presumably the time between the publication date of the book and the publication of the reviewing issue of the tool] was as follows:

Current Book Review Citations: 50% of the reviews were 6 months old or less, 33% of the reviews were between 6-9 months old, and 17% of the reviews were more than 9 months old;

Book Review Index: 100% of the reviews were 6 months old or less;

Book Review Digest: 46% of the reviews were 6 months old or less, 34% of the reviews were 6-9 months old, and 20% of the reviews were more than 9 months old. **(790)**

Academic

■ A study reported in 1970 comparing *Epilepsy Abstracts* (a monthly journal) with monthly bibliographies on epilepsy from MEDLARS over the period of a year (1968) *showed that Epilepsy Abstracts* provided more citations more quickly than MEDLARS. Specifically, *Epilepsy Abstracts* retrieved 1,116 citations with an average delay (based on a subset of 100 abstracts) between publication date of the article and appearance of the abstract of 5.41 months, while MEDLARS retrieved 1,006 citations (no more than 1 year old) with an average delay of 6.45 months. **(684)**

Ibid. . . . *showed that* the overlap between the citations retrieved by the 2 services was relatively small. Only citations to 316 articles were duplicated by the 2 services, representing 28.3% of the citations retrieved by *Epilepsy Abstracts* and 31.4% of the citations retrieved by MEDLARS. This lack of overlap was not due to indexing or abstracting a different set of journals, since only 37% of the citations not retrieved by MEDLARS and 20% of the citations not retrieved by *Epilepsy Abstracts* were due to the journals not being covered by that particular service. The main reason for lack of more overlap was conjectured to be indexing or abstracting and retrieval procedures.   **(684)**

Ibid. . . . *showed that* "approximately 10%" of the MEDLARS citations were irrelevant, compared to .1% of the *Epilepsy Abstracts* citations.
                                                                    (684)

■ A study reported in 1972 of the bibliographic control of doctoral dissertations in the areas of sociology, psychology, biology, and education, involving 3,012 dissertations selected from *American Doctoral Dissertations*, *showed that*, of those dissertations abstracted in *Dissertation Abstracts* and available on microfilm, 1,604 (90.5%) were abstracted within 2 years of the date of degree issuance. However, this comprised only 53.4% of the total number of dissertations issued.   **(400)**

■ A study reported in 1972 of the articles abstracted in *Biological Abstracts* in 1968 (sample size: 11,853 citations or 8.5% of total) and 1969 (sample size: 13,008 citations or 9.6% of total) *showed that* half a year or more usually elapsed between publication of an article and its appearance in *Biological Abstracts*. Further, while the overwhelming majority of articles were abstracted in *BA* within 1-2 years following their publication, a few take as long as a decade to be abstracted.   **(137)**

■ A study reported in 1974 of 3,347 biomedical book reviews (2,067 titles) taken from the 1970 issues of 54 English-language biomedical journals (excluding *Science* and *Nature*) that contained "bona fide" book reviews *showed that* the average time lag (difference between publication date of a book and the date of the journal issue containing the review of the book) for the 54 journals varied widely, ranging from 5.8 months for *Lancet* to 42 months for *Acta Radiologica: Therapy, Physics, Biology*. 29.7% of the 3,347 reviews appeared in the same year as the book was published.   **(700)**

Ibid. . . . *showed that* the lag time for individual reviews ranged from 0 months to 108 months (9 years). The modal lag for individual reviews was 8 months, while the average lag was 10.43 months.   **(700)**

■ A study reported in 1974 of citations in the 1972 volumes of *Library and Information Science Abstracts* (10% sample or 318 citations) and *Library Literature* (10% sample or 1,607 citations) *showed that* the average time lag between publication date of an article and appearance of a citation in either *LISA* or *Liblit* was 6.2 months; the range of the lag ran from 0-53 months; and the mode was 2.0 months.   **(143)**

Ibid. . . . *showed that* there was a statistically significant shorter time lag between publication date and citation in *Library and Information Science Abstracts* as compared to *Library Literature*. From each of 6 major world regions, *LISA* cited articles more quickly than *LibLit*: from North America (3.6 vs. 4.5 months lag), United Kingdom (2.4 vs. 5.7 months), Australia-New Zealand (1.9 vs. 6.6 months), Europe (4.4 vs. 19.0 months), Asia (8.1 vs. 8.2 months), and Africa (3.6 vs. 11.8 months).
                                                                                    (143)

■ A study reported in 1977 at Rutgers University comparing 240 marine biology citations found in 6 1975 issues of *Oceanic Abstracts* with coverage in *Biological Abstracts* and *Bioresearch Index* from 1973 through the first half of 1976 *showed that* a comparison of time lag between publication date of the original article and citation in either *Oceanic Abstracts* or *Biological Abstracts/Bioresearch Index* in 24 time periods between 1972 and 1975 revealed that in all but 1 time period the time lag was shorter for citations found in either *Biological Abstracts* or *Bioresearch Index* than for citations found in *Oceanic Abstracts*.   **(418)**

■ A study reported in 1980 comparing the coverage of *Psychological Abstracts* and *Index Medicus* of the journal literature on the topic of operant conditioning, based on all citations in the 2 indexes under that topic for the year 1978 (351 articles in 96 different journals), *showed that*, of 288 articles that carried monthly dates, the average time lag between publication of the article in the journal and the time the article appeared in an index averaged 5.76 months for *Index Medicus* and 11.8 months for *Psychological Abstracts*. This difference did not appear to be due to a greater time lag between the date of a journal issue and its actual appearance for psychology journals, since median time lag in this regard for both the psychology and medical journals was the same—1 month.
                                                                                    (624)

■ A study reported in 1982 of time lag between receipt of indexed journal issue and receipt of the index that covered the first article (or in the case of the online index the time lag between receipt of the journal issue and the date when the first article in that issue became available online), involving 4 indexes (*Current Contents: Life Sciences, Science Citation Index,*

SDILINE/MEDLINE, and *Index Medicus*) and 51 journals, *showed that* the lag was:

Current Contents: Life Sciences	31 day lag
SDILINE/MEDLINE	86 day lag
Science Citation Index	110 day lag
Index Medicus	129 day lag **(439)**

Special

■ A study reported in 1970 comparing *Epilepsy Abstracts* (a monthly journal) with monthly bibliographies on epilepsy from MEDLARS over the period of a year (1968) *showed that Epilepsy Abstracts* provided more citations more quickly than MEDLARS. Specifically, *Epilepsy Abstracts* retrieved 1,116 citations with an average delay (based on a subset of 100 abstracts) between publication date of the article and appearance of the abstract of 5.41 months, while MEDLARS retrieved 1,006 citations (no more than 1 year old) with an average delay of 6.45 months. **(684)**

Ibid. . . . *showed that* the overlap between the citations retrieved by the 2 services was relatively small. Only citations to 316 articles were duplicated by the 2 services, representing 28.3% of the citations retrieved by *Epilepsy Abstracts* and 31.4% of the citations retrieved by MEDLARS. This lack of overlap was not due to indexing or abstracting a different set of journals, since only 37% of the citations not retrieved by MEDLARS and 20% of the citations not retrieved by *Epilepsy Abstracts* were due to the journals not being covered by that particular service. The main reason for lack of more overlap was conjectured to be indexing or abstracting and retrieval procedures. **(684)**

Ibid. . . . *showed that* "approximately 10%" of the MEDLARS citations were irrelevant, compared to .1% of the *Epilepsy Abstracts* citations. **(684)**

■ A study reported in 1974 of 3,347 biomedical book reviews (2,067 titles) taken from the 1970 issues of 54 English-language biomedical journals (excluding *Science* and *Nature*) that contained "bona fide" book reviews *showed that* the average time lag (difference between publication date of a book and the date of the journal issue containing the review of the book) for the 54 journals varied widely, ranging from 5.8 months for *Lancet* to 42 months for *Acta Radiologica: Therapy, Physics, Biology.* 29.7% of the 3,347 reviews appeared in the same year as the book was published. **(700)**

Ibid. . . . *showed that* the lag time for individual reviews ranged from 0 months to 108 months (9 years). The modal lag for individual reviews was 8 months, while the average lag was 10.43 months.   **(700)**

■ A study reported in 1982 of time lag between receipt of indexed journal issue and receipt of the index that covered the first article (or in the case of the online index the time lag between receipt of the journal issue and the date when the first article in that issue became available online), involving 4 indexes (*Current Contents: Life Sciences, Science Citation Index, SDILINE/MEDLINE,* and *Index Medicus*) and 51 journals, *showed that* the lag was:

Current Contents: Life Sciences	31 day lag
SDILINE/MEDLINE	86 day lag
Science Citation Index	110 day lag
Index Medicus	129 day lag **(439)**

Quality of Tools—Translations

Academic

■ A study reported in 1978 comparing foreign-language scientific and technical articles that received *ad hoc* or selective translations to those that did not receive such translations (articles in journals receiving regular cover-to-cover translations were excluded from the study), involving 2 groups of 266 articles each selected from *Science Citation Index* and *Translations Register-Index, showed that* there was a statistically significant difference between the 2 groups on the basis of subject content. For example, 100% (14 articles) of the photography articles, 96% (25 articles) of the metallurgy articles, and 82% (18 articles) of the physics articles received *ad hoc* or selective translations, compared to 17% (4 articles) in general science, 26% (5 articles) in biology, and 32% (18 articles) in medicine (differences significant at beyond the .001 level; measure of association, eta = .50).   **(621)**

Ibid. . . . *showed that* there was a statistically significant difference between the 2 groups on the basis of original language of the article. For example, 94% (16 articles) of the Russian, 67% (2 articles) of the Polish, and 58% (84 articles) of the German articles received *ad hoc* or selective translations, compared to no translations of the Swedish/Norwegian (total of 2 articles) or Hungarian (total of 2 articles) and translations for only 18% (2 articles) of the Italian articles (differences significant at beyond the .001 level; measure of assocation, eta = .37).   **(621)**

Ibid. . . . *showed that* there was a statistically significant difference between the 2 groups on the basis of number of references cited by the
article, with the articles with more references more likely to receive *ad hoc*
or selective translations. For example, only 28% (12 articles) of the articles
with no references received *ad hoc* or selective translations, compared to
69% (22 articles) of the articles with more than 29 references (differences
significant at beyond the .001 level; measure of association, eta = .31).

(621)

Special

■ A study reported in 1978 comparing foreign-language scientific and
technical articles that received *ad hoc* or selective translations to those that
did not receive such translations (articles in journals receiving regular
cover-to-cover translations were excluded from the study), involving 2
groups of 266 articles each selected from *Science Citation Index* and
Translations Register-Index, *showed that* there was a statistically significant
difference between the 2 groups on the basis of subject content. For
example, 100% (14 articles) of the photography articles, 96% (25 articles)
of the metallurgy articles, and 82% (18 articles) of the physics articles
received *ad hoc* or selective translations, compared to 17% (4 articles) in
general science, 26% (5 articles) in biology and 32% (18 articles) in
medicine (differences significant at beyond the .001 level; measure of
association, eta = .50).

(621)

Ibid. . . . *showed that* there was a statistically significant difference between the 2 groups on the basis of original language of the article. For
example, 94% (16 articles) of the Russian, 67% (2 articles) of the Polish,
and 58% (84 articles) of the German articles received *ad hoc* or selective
translations, compared to no translations of the Swedish/Norwegian (total
of 2 articles) or Hungarian (total of 2 articles) and translations for only
18% (2 articles) of the Italian articles (differences significant at beyond the
.001 level; measure of assocation, eta = .37).

(621)

Ibid. . . . *showed that* there was a statistically significant difference between the 2 groups on the basis of number of references cited by the
article, with the articles with more references more likely to receive *ad hoc*
or selective translations. For example, only 28% (12 articles) of the articles
with no references received *ad hoc* or selective translations, compared to
69% (22 articles) of the articles with more than 29 references (differences
significant at beyond the .001 level; measure of association, eta = .31).

(621)

Reference Interview

Academic

■ A 1975 study at the University of Nebraska, Omaha, concerning student perceptions of academic librarians and involving a stratified sample of full-time students (sample size: 700; responding: 362 or 51.7%) *showed that* only 31.6% felt that the verbal interchange between student and librarian was "frequently" or "always" a learning experience; 22.5% of the students felt that librarians should not locate answers and materials for them (59.4% answered "sometimes"); and 11.6% "frequently" or "always" wished their questions answered briefly without additional information. **(449)**

■ A study reported in 1983 at the humanities reference desk of the Harold B. Lee Library, Brigham Young University, concerning the effect of librarian self-disclosure in the reference interview and based on 64 patron interviews (32 interviews involved librarian self-disclosure and 32 did not) *showed that* overall there was no statistically significant difference in patron response to librarian disclosure versus nondisclosure. **(802)**

Ibid. . . . *showed that* there did seem to be a statistically significant difference in patron responses to questions concerning public relations in that in those reference interviews in which the librarian was self-disclosing the librarians were rated as both "warm" and as "friendly" to a statistically significant higher degree than in those interviews in which the librarians were not self-disclosing (significant at the .05 level). However, there were no statistically significant differences between the 2 types of reference interviews in how well the patrons felt the librarians understood what they wanted, in whether the librarian's help was valuable or worthless, whether the reference interview process was easy or difficult, or whether they would approach the librarian again. **(802)**

Public

■ A study reported in 1976 in the Weld County Public Library *showed that* there was no statistically significant increase in user satisfaction with the transfer of information when librarians displayed immediate verbal-nonverbal behavior (eye contact, nodding, etc.) rather than nonimmediate behavior. However, a statistically significant increase in patron satisfaction was found both with the reference interview and with the patron's own performance in negotiating the reference question when the librarian involved used immediate verbal-nonverbal behavior (eye contact, nodding, etc.) rather than nonimmediate verbal-nonverbal behavior. **(051)**

■ A study reported in 1978 involving 18 reference librarians in 4 New Jersey public libraries and using a microphone to record approximately l6 hours of reference/patron interaction in each library (1,159 questions) *showed that*, out of 751 reference questions, the patron was interviewed in 366 (49%) of the cases. **(260)**

Ibid. . . . *showed that* 408 (35%) interactions were directional; 242 (21%) were holdings; 458 (40%) were substantive; and 51 (4%) were moving, i.e., moved from one level (e.g., directional) to another (e.g., substantive). **(260)**

Reference Statistics

General

■ An informal 1967 survey of reference statistical forms conducted by the ALA/LAD/LOMS Committee on Reference Statistics (a request for forms was published in 12 different library journals), with 101 libraries responding including academic, public, and special, *showed that* the top 4 uses of reference statistics were method of assessing service (16 libraries), justification of additional help at peak times or how time is spent (13 libraries), and justification of budget requests (11 libraries). **(150)**

Ibid. . . . *showed that* 3 types of data were collected by 50% of the libraries: type of reference transaction (e.g., ready reference, card catalog, instruction; 55 libraries); form of request (e.g., letter, telephone, in person; 54 libraries); and directional questions (50 libraries). **(150)**

SDI Services—General Issues

General

■ A 1970 survey by the Canadian National Science Library of users of its nationwide SDI system, involving bibliographies produced from the Chemical Abstracts Service, the Institute for Scientific Information, and the British Institution of Electrical Engineers (survey size: 604; responding: 406 or 67.2%) *showed that* the 3 most frequently mentioned shortcomings in the service (out of 17) were (multiple responses allowed): lack of retrospective searching (175 or 43.1%), obtaining hardcopy documents (91 or 22.4%), and low percentage of relevant references (73 or 18.0%).

(536)

Ibid. . . . *showed that* the 3 most frequently mentioned ways in which subscribers became aware of the service were local library (40%), National Science Library (23%), and professional colleague (17%).   **(536)**

Ibid. . . . *showed that* the number of colleagues with whom 377 respondents reported sharing the results of the SDI searches were as follows: no sharing (118 or 29.1%), share with 1 to 5 colleagues (248 or 61.1%), share with over 5 colleagues (34 or 8.4%).   **(536)**

Ibid. . . . *showed that*, of 361 respondents, 116 (32.1%) reported a time savings due to the service of 2 hours; 127 (35.2%) reported a time savings of 3 to 7 hours; 92 (25.5%) reported the same amount of time required; and 26 (7.2%) reported the service cost them more time.   **(536)**

■ A 1970 survey of psychiatrists randomly selected from the 1968 membership of the American Psychiatric Association (survey size: 394; responding: 290 or 74%) *showed that* library reference services were used as follows (multiple responses allowed):

guidance by the librarian	40% respondents	
recent acquisitions lists	38% respondents	
requested bibliographies	35% respondents	
MEDLARS	11% respondents	
other	11% respondents	**(690)**

Academic

■ A 1974 study of current awareness methods used by Canadian academic chemists in 34 institutions (survey size: 170; responding: 134 or 80%) *showed that* only 19% of the respondents subscribed to a selective dissemination of information service. Among the reasons given for not subscribing were ignorance of the existence of such services (15% respondents), not needed because of the nature of their work (15%), cost (25%), and personal preference (45%).   **(636)**

Ibid. . . . *showed that* the time spent on current awareness activities averaged 2-5 hours per week, with a distribution as follows:

0-1 hours per week	7 (5.2%) respondents
1-2 hours per week	30 (22.4%) respondents
2-5 hours per week	53 (39.6%) respondents
5-10 hours per week	38 (28.4%) respondents
10-20 hours per week	6 (4.5%) respondents **(636)**

■ A survey reported in 1974 at the Hershey Medical Center Library of Pennsylvania State University comparing medical faculty views of a manually generated selective dissemination of information service with SDILINE (Selective Dissemination of Information Online, from the National Library of Medicine) *showed that* SDILINE was not used as the only source of current awareness. Of the 13 faculty users of SDILINE, 55.5% reported use of *Current Contents* as well, and of the 8 faculty users who had used both systems, 66.7% reported that SDILINE was used as a backup to other forms of current awareness. **(705)**

■ A study of a pilot SDI program reported in 1975 at the University of Arkansas, Little Rock, involving 9 faculty members who had received grants for 7 different research studies, *showed that*, of 1,188 citations sent to the faculty members, 717 (60.4%) were directly used in the research projects, while an additional 255 citations (21%) were of general interest to the researchers but not incorporated into the research projects. **(145)**

■ A survey reported in 1977 concerning online searching at the U.S. Army Construction Engineering Research Laboratory library (Champaign, Illinois), involving both users of the service (sample size: 27; responding: 26 or 96.3%) and nonusers of the service (sample size: 19; responding: 13 or 68.4%), *showed that*, of 25 user respondents, 7 (28%) indicated an interest in periodic update searches on their research topic; 11 (44%) indicated they would not; and 7 (28%) indicated they were uncertain. **(416)**

■ A study reported in 1978 at Indiana University, Bloomington, of materials requested through a delivery service to faculty in the political science and economics departments during a 32-month period (October 1972-June 1975), involving 39 political scientists and 14 economists (40-50% of the faculty in the departments) and 5,478 articles from 620 different journals and newspapers, *showed that*, when the delivery service

supplied copies of contents pages, this current awareness service was used by 40 (64%) of the faculty, while materials listed in the contents pages accounted for 30.3% of all materials requested on the delivery service.
(421)

Public

■ A 1973 experimental project with SDI service in the Mideastern Michigan Library Cooperative (a random sample of 2,498 were invited to participate; 96 responded) *showed that* the most popular SDI topics were fiction with the following headings: fiction with a twentieth-century setting (50%), mystery-suspense (43%), historical fiction (38%). The 3 most popular nonfiction categories were drawing and decorative arts (35%), recreation (30%), and psychology (30%).   **(144)**

■ A 1973 study of an experimental SDI service in the Mideastern Michigan Library Cooperative (sample size: 96; responding: 42 or 44%) *showed that* 43% of the respondents indicated they found the service "very useful" while an additional 45% reported that they found the service "of some use." 52% indicated that they thought that at least half of the books suggested fit their interests.   **(144)**

Special

■ A 1974 user survey of the Bristol Laboratory library (Syracuse, New York) involving 32 individuals (14% sample size) from 21 departments, including 18 directors and 14 nondirectors, *showed that* 72% of the respondents rejected the need for a personalized selective dissemination of information service. The main reason given (38% respondents) was that interests were too broad and changing. 28% reported that their present method of keeping up with the literature was satisfactory, and 6% reported a need for personal contact with the literature.   **(407)**

■ A survey reported in 1974 at the Hershey Medical Center Library of Pennsylvania State University comparing medical faculty views of a manually generated selective dissemination of information service with SDILINE (Selective Dissemination of Information Online, from the National Library of Medicine) *showed that* SDILINE was not used as the only source of current awareness. Of the 13 faculty users of SDILINE,

55.5% reported use of *Current Contents* as well, and of the 8 faculty users who had used both systems, 66.7% reported that SDILINE was used as a backup to other forms of current awareness. **(705)**

■ A survey reported in 1977 concerning online searching at the U.S. Army Construction Engineering Research Laboratory library (Champaign, Illinois), involving both users of the service (sample size: 27; responding: 26 or 96.3%) and nonusers of the service (sample size: 19; responding: 13 or 68.4%), *showed that*, of 25 user respondents, 7 (28%) indicated an interest in periodic update searches on their research topic; 11 (44%) indicated they would not; and 7 (28%) indicated they were uncertain. **(416)**

SDI Services—Impact

General

■ A 1970 survey by the Canadian National Science Library of users of its nationwide SDI system, involving bibliographies produced from the Chemical Abstracts Service, the Institute for Scientific Information and the British Institution of Electrical Engineers (survey size: 604; responding: 406 or 67.2%), *showed that* the number of colleagues with whom 377 respondents reported sharing the results of the SDI searches were as follows: no sharing (118 or 29.1%), share with 1 to 5 colleagues (248 or 61.1%), share with over 5 colleagues (34 or 8.4%). **(536)**

Ibid. . . . *showed that*, of 361 respondents, 116 (32.1%) reported a time savings due to the service of 2 hours; 127 (35.2%) reported a time savings of 3 to 7 hours; 92 (25.5%) reported the same amount of time required; and 26 (7.2%) reported the service cost them more time. **(536)**

Academic

■ A study reported in 1970 at the Washington University School of Medicine Library comparing a commercial, automated selective dissemination of information system (ASCA III, provided by the Institute for Scientific Information, based on 1,989 periodicals) with a local, semimanual SDI system (based on 1,879 periodicals received by the library) in terms of retrieving citations for profiles developed by 6 faculty members *showed that* the automated service was a good supplement to the local service in that it increased the total number of useful citations provided to the 6 scientists from 346 to 725 (including 96 duplicate citations).   **(687)**

■ A 1974 study of current awareness methods used by Canadian academic chemists in 34 institutions (survey size: 170; responding: 134 or 80%) *showed that* there was a statistically significant relationship between time spent on current awareness and level of success reported in keeping up-to-date, with success increasing with amount of time spent (significant at the .01 level).   **(636)**

Ibid. . . . *showed that* there was a statistically significant relationship between time spent on current awareness and productivity (number of articles published in the past 5 years), with productivity increasing with amount of time spent on current awareness. For example, 9% of the respondents reporting 0-5 articles published spent 5-20 hours per week on current awareness, compared to 46% of the respondents publishing over 20 articles (significant beyond the .001 level).   **(636)**

Ibid. . . . *showed that* there was no statistically significant relationship (inverse) between perceived scatter of information and success in keeping up-to-date. The reason for this was the increased time spent on current awareness by respondents in specialities with high information scatter. There was a statistically significant inverse relationship between scatter of information and efficiency (success divided by time spent) in keeping up-to-date (significant at the .01 level).   **(636)**

Ibid. . . . *showed that* use of an SDI service reduced efficiency (success divided by time spent) for respondents in specialities with low information scatter but suggested it may increase efficiency for respondents in specialities with high information scatter. Specifically, in specialities with low information scatter subscribers to an SDI service had a statistically significant lower efficiency rate than nonsubscribers (significant at the .02 level). In specialities with high information scatter, subscribers to an SDI service did not have a statistically significant higher efficiency rate than nonsubscribers, but the data did show a "tendency" in this direction.

(636)

■ A survey reported in 1974 at the Hershey Medical Center Library of Pennsylvania State University comparing medical faculty views of a manually generated selective dissemination of information service with SDILINE (Selective Dissemination of Information Online, from the

National Library of Medicine) *showed that*, of 13 faculty users of SDI-LINE, an average of 3 users shared each subscription. **(705)**

Special

■ A survey reported in 1974 at the Hershey Medical Center Library of Pennsylvania State University comparing medical faculty views of a manually generated selective dissemination of information service with SDILINE (Selective Dissemination of Information Online, from the National Library of Medicine) *showed that*, of 13 faculty users of SDI-LINE, an average of 3 users shared each subscription. **(705)**

■ A survey reported in 1978 of the current awareness service provided at the General Electric Corporate Research and Development library (Schenectady, New York) involving the Chemical Abstracts CONDENSATES data base (sample size: 65; responding: 60.0% [no raw number given]) and the Engineering Index COMPENDEX data base (sample size: 68; responding: 38.2%) *showed that* 59.0% of the CONDENSATES users and 50.0% of the COMPENDEX users reported their literature searching time decreased; 20.5% of the CONDENSATES users and 38.5% of the COMPENDEX users reported no change in literature searching time; and 10.3% of the CONDENSATES users and none of the COMPENDEX users reported that their literature search time had increased. The remainder did not reply to the question. Further, 46.2% of both groups reported that they were reading more articles. **(424)**

Ibid. . . . *showed that* the 3 main professional benefits resulting from the current awareness service for CONDENSATES users were: made aware of others in the field (53.8% respondents), provided new research leads (43.6% respondents), and made more time available for research (25.6% respondents). **(424)**

Ibid. . . . *showed that* the 3 main professional benefits resulting from the current awareness service for COMPENDEX users were: made aware of others in the field (50.0% respondents), provided new research leads (30.7% respondents), and prevented duplication of research conducted elsewhere (19.2% respondents). **(424)**

Ibid. . . . *showed that* 76.9% of the CONDENSATES users and 41.0% of the COMPENDEX users shared their profile with colleagues; 61.5% of the CONDENSATES users and 69.2% of the COMPENDEX users told others about the service; and 12.8% of the CONDENSATES users and 7.7% of the COMPENDEX users suggested names of potential users. **(424)**

SDI Services—Need

General

■ A study reported in 1981 of citations to a "definitive clinical trial which demonstrated the beneficial effects of photocoagulation in treating diabetic retinopathy" that 18 months after its publication was still not widely known to physicians treating an appreciable number of diabetic patients *showed that* "a large number of citations in the literature to a clinically significant paper did not of itself ensure that the information reported would readily reach the appropriate practicing physician." Specifically, between 1976 (when the study was published) and 1979, *Science Citation Index* reported 70 citations to the original report. However, "not a single citation which appeared before 1978 came from a general American medical journal, unrestricted in geographic or subject scope." **(738)**

Academic

■ A survey reported in 1972 at the University of Saskatchewan of participants in the SELDOM service (a selective dissemination information service for new English-language monographs based on MARC records) (sample size: 121; responding: 77; usable: 71 or 58.6%) *showed that* 23.6% of the respondents reported that in most cases items of interest on the SELDOM lists were previously unknown to them, while 45.8% reported that items of interest from the list were frequently new to them. **(322)**

■ A 1974 study of current awareness methods used by Canadian academic chemists in 34 institutions (survey size: 170; responding: 134 or 80%) *showed that* the success in keeping up-to-date was as follows [135 responses given, no explanation]:

great difficulty	4 (3.0%) respondents
not too well	30 (22.2%) respondents
adequately	67 (49.6%) respondents
quite well	24 (17.8%) respondents
very well	10 (7.4%) respondents **(636)**

Ibid. . . . *showed that* there was a statistically significant relationship between time spent on current awareness and level of success reported in keeping up-to-date, with success increasing with amount of time spent (significant at the .01 level). **(636)**

Ibid. . . . *showed that* there was a statistically significant relationship between time spent on current awareness and productivity (number of articles published in the past 5 years), with productivity increasing with amount of time spent on current awareness. For example, 9% of the respondents reporting 0-5 articles published spent 5-20 hours per week on current awareness, compared to 46% of the respondents publishing over 20 articles (significant beyond the .001 level). **(636)**

Ibid. . . . *showed that* there was a statistically significant relationship between perception of scatter of information (number of different sources respondents felt it necessary to consult in order to stay up-to-date in a speciality) and time spent on current awareness, with time spent on current awareness higher in specialities where information was perceived as being more scattered (significant at beyond the .001 level). However, there was no statistically significant relationship between perception of scatter of information and subscribing to an SDI service. **(636)**

Ibid. . . . *showed that* there was no statistically significant relationship (inverse) between perceived scatter of information and success in keeping up-to-date. The reason for this was the increased time spent on current awareness by respondents in specialities with high information scatter. There was a statistically significant inverse relationship between scatter of information and efficiency (success divided by time spent) in keeping up-to-date (significant at the .01 level). **(636)**

Ibid. . . . *showed that* use of an SDI service reduced efficiency (success divided by time spent) for respondents in specialities with low information scatter but suggested it may increase efficiency for respondents in specialities with high information scatter. Specifically, in specialities with low information scatter, subscribers to an SDI service had a statistically significant lower efficiency rate than nonsubscribers (significant at the .02 level). In specialities with high information scatter, subscribers to an SDI service did not have a statistically significant higher efficiency rate than nonsubscribers, but the data did show a "tendency" in this direction. **(636)**

Special

■ A survey reported in 1978 of the current awareness service provided at the General Electric Corporate Research and Development library (Schenectady, New York) involving the Chemical Abstracts CONDENSATES data base (sample size: 65; responding: 60.0% [no raw number given]) and the Engineering Index COMPENDEX data base (sample size: 68; responding: 38.2%) *showed that* the 2 most highly rated features of the current awareness service were convenience (84.6% of CONDENSATES users; 88.5% of COMPENDEX users) and coverage of journals and other publications that respondent would normally not see (79.5% of CONDENSATES users; 84.6% of COMPENDEX users).   **(424)**

SDI Services—Patron Satisfaction

General

■ A 1970 survey by the Canadian National Science Library of users of its nationwide SDI system, involving bibliographies produced from the Chemical Abstracts Service, the Institute for Scientific Information and the British Institution of Electrical Engineers (survey size: 604; responding: 406 or 67.2%) *showed that* the 3 most frequently mentioned shortcomings in the service (out of 17) were (multiple responses allowed): lack of retrospective searching (175 or 43.1%), obtaining hardcopy documents (91 or 22.4%), and low percentage of relevant references (73 or 18.0%). **(536)**

Academic

■ A survey reported in 1972 at the University of Saskatchewan of participants in the SELDOM service (a selective dissemination information service for new English-language monographs based on MARC records) (sample size: 121; responding: 77; usable: 71 or 58.6%) *showed that* 25.8% of the respondents reported the SDI lists "very useful," 48.5% reported them "useful," while 8.5% reported them inconsequential for their purposes.   **(322)**

Ibid. . . . *showed that* 88.6% of the respondents wished the SDI service to continue, with 11.3% of the respondents rating the service "very high," 33.8% rating it "high," 42.2% rating it "medium," and 12.7% rating it "low."   **(322)**

■ A survey reported in 1974 at the Hershey Medical Center Library of Pennsylvania State University comparing medical faculty views of a manually generated selective dissemination of information service with

SDILINE (Selective Dissemination of Information Online, from the National Library of Medicine) *showed that*, of 8 faculty who had used both systems, 88.9% preferred SDILINE and reported that it covered their subject area best. **(705)**

Ibid. . . . *showed that*, of 13 faculty users of SDILINE, 46.1% reported it of major value; 46.1% reported it of moderate value; and only 1 (7.7%) reported it of minor value. Further, 76.9% respondents reported that "many of the articles were relevant," and 57% respondents reported satisfaction with the SDILINE results. However, 92.3% respondents reported without qualification that they would renew their subscription (the remaining respondent reported he would renew only if the rates did not increase). **(705)**

Special

■ A survey reported in 1974 at the Hershey Medical Center Library of Pennsylvania State University comparing medical faculty views of a manually generated selective dissemination of information service with SDILINE (Selective Dissemination of Information Online, from the National Library of Medicine) *showed that*, of 8 faculty who had used both systems, 88.9% preferred SDILINE and reported that it covered their subject area best. **(705)**

Ibid. . . . *showed that*, of 13 faculty users of SDILINE, 46.1% reported it of major value; 46.1% reported it of moderate value; and only 1 (7.7%) reported it of minor value. Further, 76.9% respondents reported that "many of the articles were relevant," and 57% respondents reported satisfaction with the SDILINE results. However, 92.3% respondents reported without qualification that they would renew their subscription (the remaining respondent reported he would renew only if the rates did not increase). **(705)**

■ A survey reported in 1978 of the current awareness service provided at the General Electric Corporate Research and Development library (Schenectady, New York) involving the Chemical Abstracts CONDENSATES data base (sample size: 65; responding: 60.0% [no raw number given]) and the Engineering Index COMPENDEX data base (sample size: 68; responding: 38.2%) *showed that* the 2 most highly rated features of the current awareness service were convenience (84.6% of CONDENSATES users; 88.5% of COMPENDEX users) and coverage of journals and other publications that respondent would normally not see (79.5% of CONDEN-

SATES users; 84.6% of COMPENDEX users).   **(424)**

Ibid. . . . *showed that* 84.6% of the CONDENSATES users and 88.5% of the COMPENDEX users reported that the service had a "major" or "moderate" value, while 87.2% of the CONDENSATES users and 84.6% of the COMPENDEX users reported that "many" or "most" of the references retrieved by their profiles were relevant.   **(424)**

SDI Services—Quality

Academic

■ A study reported in 1970 at the Washington University School of Medicine Library comparing a commercial, automated selective dissemination of information system (ASCA III, provided by the Institute for Scientific Information, based on 1,989 periodicals) with a local, semimanual SDI system (based on 1,879 periodicals received by the library) in terms of retrieving citations for profiles developed by 6 faculty members *showed that* the local SDI service appeared much more timely than the ASCA service. Specifically, of the 128 (16% of the total unique citations retrieved by both services) overlap citations retrieved by both services, the local SDI service retrieved 78% of the citations before the ASCA service, while the ASCA service retrieved only 10% of the citations before the local service. (12% of the citations were retrieved in the same week.)
                                                              (687)

Ibid. . . . *showed that*, while the ASCA service retrieved more citations (1,073 citations) than the local service (442 citations), this was largely offset by a much lower relevancy rate. Specifically, ASCA retrieved only 379 relevant citations, while the local service retrieved 346 relevant citations.   **(687)**

Ibid. . . . *showed that* 84% of all the citations came from a core of 664 journals common to both services. These core journals accounted for 86% of the citations generated by ASCA and 87% of the citations generated by the local service.   **(687)**

Ibid. . . . *showed that* the local service was more closely attuned to local needs. The ASCA service secured 11% of its citations from journals to which the library did not subscribe, while the library secured 5% of its citations from journals to which ASCA did not subscribe. However, only

11% of those citations to journals to which the library did not subscribe were considered relevant or partially relevant, while 67% of those citations to journals to which ASCA did not subscribe were considered relevant or partially relevant. **(687)**

Ibid. . . . *showed that* the automated service was a good supplement to the local service in that it increased the total number of useful citations provided to the 6 scientists from 346 to 725 (including 96 duplicate citations). **(687)**

■ A survey reported in 1972 at the University of Saskatchewan of participants in the SELDOM service (a selective dissemination information service for new English-language monographs based on MARC records) (sample size: 121; responding: 77; usable: 71 or 58.6%) *showed that* 83.5% of the respondents indicated that the information provided (MARC data only) was sufficient to determine whether they were interested in the item or not. The 3 most important data elements in making such determinations were, in decending order of importance: title, author/ editor, and subject headings. 55.8% of the respondents reported they needed no more than 10 minutes per week to scan the SDI printouts. **(322)**

■ A survey reported in 1974 at the Hershey Medical Center Library of Pennsylvania State University comparing medical faculty views of a manually generated selective dissemination of information service with SDILINE (Selective Dissemination of Information Online, from the National Library of Medicine) *showed that*, of 13 faculty users of SDI-LINE, 46.1% reported it of major value; 46.1% reported it of moderate value; and only 1 (7.7%) reported it of minor value. Further, 76.9% respondents reported that "many of the articles were relevant," and 57% respondents reported satisfaction with the SDILINE results. However, 92.3% respondents reported without qualification that they would renew their subscription (the remaining respondent reported he would renew only if the rates did not increase). **(705)**

Special

■ A study reported in 1970 at the Washington University School of Medicine Library comparing a commercial, automated selective dissemination of information system (ASCA III, provided by the Institute for Scientific Information, based on 1,989 periodicals) with a local, semimanual SDI system (based on 1,879 periodicals received by the library) in terms of retrieving citations for profiles developed by 6 faculty members

showed that the local SDI service appeared much more timely than the ASCA service. Specifically, of the 128 (16% of the total unique citations retrieved by both services) overlap citations retrieved by both services, the local SDI service retrieved 78% of the citations before the ASCA service, while the ASCA service retrieved only 10% of the citations before the local service. (12% of the citations were retrieved in the same week.)
(687)

Ibid. . . . *showed that*, while the ASCA service retrieved more citations (1,073 citations) than the local service (442 citations), this was largely offset by a much lower relevancy rate. Specifically, ASCA retrieved only 379 relevant citations, while the local service retrieved 346 relevant citations. **(687)**

Ibid. . . . *showed that* 84% of all the citations came from a core of 664 journals common to both services. These core journals accounted for 86% of the citations generated by ASCA and 87% of the citations generated by the local service. **(687)**

Ibid. . . . *showed that* the local service was more closely attuned to local needs. The ASCA service secured 11% of its citations from journals to which the library did not subscribe, while the library secured 5% of its citations from journals to which ASCA did not subscribe. However, only 11% of those citations to journals to which the library did not subscribe were considered relevant or partially relevant, while 67% of those citations to journals to which ASCA did not subscribe were considered relevant or partially relevant. **(687)**

Ibid. . . . *showed that* the automated service was a good supplement to the local service in that it increased the total number of useful citations provided to the 6 scientists from 346 to 725 (including 96 duplicate citations). **(687)**

■ A survey reported in 1974 at the Hershey Medical Center Library of Pennsylvania State University comparing medical faculty views of a manually generated selective dissemination of information service with SDILINE (Selective Dissemination of Information Online, from the National Library of Medicine) *showed that*, of 13 faculty users of SDI-LINE, 46.1% reported it of major value; 46.1% reported it of moderate value; and only 1 (7.7%) reported it of minor value. Further, 76.9% respondents reported that "many of the articles were relevant," and 57% respondents reported satisfaction with the SDILINE results. However, 92.3% respondents reported without qualification that they would renew their subscription (the remaining respondent reported he would renew only if the rates did not increase). **(705)**

Services—General Issues

General

■ A 1970 survey of psychiatrists randomly selected from the 1968 membership of the American Psychiatric Association (survey size: 394; responding: 290 or 74%) *showed that* library reference services were used as follows (multiple responses allowed):

guidance by the librarian	40% respondents
recent acquisitions lists	38% respondents
requested bibliographies	35% respondents
MEDLARS	11% respondents
other	11% respondents **(690)**

■ A survey reported in 1981 of chief administrators of U.S. theater collections concerning methods of cataloging nonbook theatrical memorabilia (survey size: 40 libraries; responding: 26; usable: 25 or 62.5%) *showed that*:

22 (88%) libraries reported having no complete accessing tools to the nonbook items in the collection;

22 (88%) libraries reported that their cataloging system was designed by the library staff for their particular collection (however, 6 or 24% libraries reported that they had adopted a pre-established system for the collection). **(769)**

Academic

■ A 1967 survey of medical school libraries concerning reference services (survey size: 93 libraries; responding: 85 or 91.4% libraries) *showed that* the libraries were open an average of 87.9 hours per week and provided reference services an average of 53.8 hours per week. **(682)**

Ibid. . . . *showed that* 68 (80%) libraries reported compiling bibliographies and/or literature searches, while 17 (20%) libraries reported they did not do so. Of those 68 libraries that compiled bibliographies, the patrons for whom they compiled them were as follows:

faculty	65 (95.6%) libraries
research personnel	57 (83.8%) libraries
house staff	50 (73.5%) libraries
medical students	6 (8.8%) libraries **(682)**

Ibid. . . . *showed that* the following number of libraries provided the following services (multiple responses allowed):

MEDLARS searchs	77 (90.6%) libraries
edit bibliographies for authors	37 (43.5%) libraries
current awareness service	15 (17.6%) libraries
recurring bibliographies	14 (16.5%) libraries
routing of current journals	11 (12.9%) libraries

Further, 3 (3.5%) libraries reported charging a fee for providing bibliographic services.   **(682)**

Ibid. . . . *showed that* 48 (56.5%) libraries maintained a file of local translators. Only 3 (3.5%) libraries provided "other than short spot translations."   **(682)**

■ A 1967 survey by the Institute of Higher Education at Teachers College, Columbia University, of innovative programs in libraries in academic institutions with liberal arts programs (sample size: 1,193; responding: 781 or 65%) *showed that* 41 responding libraries (6%) reported table of contents services and 91 (12%) reported selective dissemination of information services.   **(190)**

■ A 1967 survey of the 73 ARL members concerning their use of information desks (61 responding or 83.7%, with 37 usable responses due to their reporting the presence of information desks) *showed that* 29 libraries reported providing simple telephone reference service at the information desk; 19 libraries reported that the information desk is responsible for public relations duties such as conducting tours, speaking to groups on library orientation, etc.; and 15 libraries reported no reference books were kept at the information desk, while 10 reported more than 100 books were kept at the information desk.   **(192)**

■ A survey reported in 1980 of a representative sample of 100 Drexel University students using conjoint analysis to determine the relative importance of various elements of reference service to these students *showed that* reference service elements were ranked as follows, from most to least important: (1) completeness of answer, (2) data base service, (3) attitude of reference librarian, (4) hours of service, (5) interlibrary loans, (6) knowledge of reference librarian, (7) time needed to answer, (8) wait for service. **(263)**

Ibid. . . . *showed that* students' school level, subject discipline, sex, use of the library, and place of residence made no difference in which of the 3 elements of reference service they ranked most important or in the order in which they ranked them. **(263)**

■ A survey reported in 1983 of U.S. dental school libraries concerning their service to dental practitioners (population: 60 dental school libraries; responding: 53 or 88%) *showed that* 7 (14%) libraries reported participating in continuing education programs to some extent; 2 (3.8%) reported occasionally preparing bibliographies for instructors of continuing education classes but no further involvement; and 44 (83%) libraries reported no participation in continuing education. **(752)**

Ibid. . . . *showed that*, of 51 respondents, 22 (43%) libraries reported using at least 1 method (e.g., articles in local or state association journals, alumni bulletin, information given to graduating students, etc.) to promote library services to dental practitioners, while 29 (57%) reported they do not advertise such services at all. **(752)**

Ibid. . . . *showed that*, of 51 respondents, 36 (70.6%) libraries reported it important to offer library services to dental practitioners; 12 (23.5%) reported that offering such services was important but could not provide such services due to limited resources; and 3 (5.9%) reported that only faculty and students are served by the dental library. **(752)**

Public

■ A questionnaire survey of 3,500 public library cardholders in 5 medium-sized Pennsylvania cities in conjunction with interviews of a randomly selected sample of householders in one city by the Institute of Public Administration (at Pennsylvania State University) under contract to the Pennsylvania State Library in 1965 *showed that* the major service provided by the library was book borrowing (60%) of respondents, while reference/information was the next most important use made of the library (26% of respondents). **(084)**

■ A 1976 survey of 723 public libraries in communities of more than 10,000 and having a central labor council by the Joint Committee on Library Services to Labor Groups, RASD, ALA (385 or 53.2% responding) *showed that* 14 or 4% of the responding libraries reported that a staff member was assigned to work with labor organizations and/or labor-related materials. This compares to 22 or 6% of responding libraries (out of 384) in an unpublished 1967 survey. **(152)**

Special

■ A 1967 survey of medical school libraries concerning reference services (survey size: 93 libraries; responding: 85 or 91.4%) *showed that* the libraries were open an average of 87.9 hours per week and provided reference services an average of 53.8 hours per week. **(682)**

Ibid. . . . *showed that* 68 (80%) libraries reported compiling bibliographies and/or literature searches, while 17 (20%) libraries reported they did not do so. Of those 68 libraries that compiled bibliographies, the patrons for whom they compiled them were as follows:

faculty	65 (95.6%) libraries
research personnel	57 (83.8%) libraries
house staff	50 (73.5%) libraries
medical students	6 (8.8%) libraries **(682)**

Ibid. . . . *showed that* the following number of libraries provided the following services (multiple responses allowed):

MEDLARS searchs	77 (90.6%) libraries
edit bibliographies for authors	37 (43.5%) libraries
current awareness service	15 (17.6%) libraries
recurring bibliographies	14 (16.5%) libraries
routing of current journals	11 (12.9%) libraries

Further, 3 (3.5%) libraries reported charging a fee for providing bibliographic services. **(682)**

Ibid. . . . *showed that* 48 (56.5%) libraries maintained a file of local translators. Only 3 (3.5%) libraries provided "other than short spot translations." **(682)**

■ A 1976 survey of physicians associated with hospitals in a 17-county region of upstate New York (Health Service Area V) based on a systematic sample of "approximately 40%" of the physicians in each county (survey size: 592 physicians; responding: 258 or 45.6%) *showed that* physicians reported that the speed with which their information needs had to be met was as follows: 24 hours (39% physicians, including 5% who reported "immediately"), up to a week (54% physicians), and longer than a week (7% physicians). **(720)**

■ A survey reported in 1980 of the largest medical library in each state (sample size: 51; responding: 37) *showed that* 26 (91%) reported that they were open to the public; 8 (22%) reported they were partly open to the public; and 3 (8%) reported they were not open to the public. **(236)**

Ibid. . . . *showed that*, in terms of providing medical information to nonmedical or nonallied health professionals, patients, or laymen, 7 (20%) reported a completely open policy; 24 (65%) reported they were open to the public with limited services; 1 (3%) reported open to some of the public; 1 (3%) reported open to the public through the public library; and 3 (8%) reported not being open to the public at all. **(236)**

Ibid. . . . *showed that* 12 (32%) reported they would like to serve the public extensively; 7 (19%) reported they would perhaps like to serve the public extensively; and 10 (27%) reported they would not like to serve the public extensively. **(236)**

Ibid. . . . *showed that* 21 (57%) respondents referred questions from the public to public libraries; 8 (22%) referred questions to the local medical association; 10 (27%) referred questions to a physician; and 3 (8%) referred questions to other libraries. **(236)**

■ A survey reported in 1983 of U.S. dental school libraries concerning their service to dental practitioners (population: 60 dental school libraries; responding: 53 or 88%) *showed that* 7 (14%) libraries reported participating in continuing education programs to some extent; 2 (3.8%) reported occasionally preparing bibliographies for instructors of continuing education classes but no further involvement; and 44 (83%) libraries reported no participation in continuing education. **(752)**

Ibid. . . . *showed that*, of 51 respondents, 22 (43%) libraries reported using at least 1 method (e.g., articles in local or state association journals, alumni bulletin, information given to graduating students, etc.) to promote

library services to dental practitioners, while 29 (57%) reported they do
not advertise such services at all.   **(752)**

Ibid. . . . *showed that*, of 51 respondents, 36 (70.6%) libraries reported it
important to offer library services to dental practitioners; 12 (23.5%)
reported that offering such services was important but could not provide
such services due to limited resources; and 3 (5.9%) reported that only
faculty and students are served by the dental library.   **(752)**

Staff Attitudes

General

■ A 1976 survey of RASD members (population: 4,062; sample size:
738; usable responses: 542 or 73.4%) concerning their attitudes toward
automated information retrieval services *showed that* the 3 greatest
barriers to developing automated information retrieval sources in libraries
reported by respondents were costs (88.2%), lack of trained library
personnel (51.1%), and overworked staff (49.6%).   **(148)**

Academic

■ A survey of 49 university libraries (48 responding) in the North Central
Association of Colleges and Universities *showed that* 87% of the responding public service librarians felt that professional librarians should work
weekends.   **(017)**

Public

■ A study reported in 1978 concerning reference performance in Illinois
public libraries (population: 530 libraries; sample size: 60; responding: 51
or 85%), using one reference librarian from each library to answer 25 test
reference questions, *showed that* perceived adequateness of size of reference collection was related in a statistically significant manner to both
percentage of correctly answered questions (.50 with no significance level
given) and percentage of those questions that, given the reference tools

available, could have been answered correctly (.57 with no significance level given). **(259)**

Staffing Levels

Academic

■ A 1967 survey of medical school libraries concerning reference services (survey size: 93 libraries; responding: 85 or 91.4%) *showed that* the average staffing per library was as follows:

professional	5.2 FTE
nonprofessional	9.1 FTE
reference, professional	1.7 FTE
reference, nonprofessional	0.8 FTE	**(682)**

Special

■ A 1967 survey of medical school libraries concerning reference services (survey size: 93 libraries; responding: 85 or 91.4%) *showed that* the average staffing per library was as follows:

professional	5.2 FTE
nonprofessional	9.1 FTE
reference, professional	1.7 FTE
reference, nonprofessional	0.8 FTE	**(682)**

Time per Question

General

■ A report on a statewide Teletype reference service provided by library school students at the University of Iowa in an advanced reference course, involving 460 questions received in the first 6 months of 1974 from college libraries or public library regional centers *showed that* the average time spent searching for answers to the 460 questions was 1.9 hours, with 145 (31%) of the questions requiring a half hour or less to answer, 22 (48%)

requiring an hour or less to answer, and only 43 (9%) requiring more than 5 hours of searching. **(146)**

Academic

■ An analysis of 5,096 reference questions during 7 selected weeks in 1970-71 at the Sterling Library at Yale *showed that* the questions broke down into the following categories according to time required for answer:

TIME REQUIRED	% OF TOTAL	
negligible	25.3	
1-2 minutes	38.1	
3-5 minutes	26.2	
6-10 minutes	6.9	
11-60 minutes	2.7	
over 60 minutes	0.2	
not recorded	0.7	**(101)**

Type of Patron

Academic

■ A 1968 study of graduate students at the University of Michigan concerning their use of periodical literature (sample size: 399; responding: 338 or 85%) *showed that*, of those reporting use of the periodical literature during the term (284), 49.3% had the precise reference to the article before coming to the library, while 50% did not. **(195)**

■ An analysis of 5,096 reference questions during 7 selected weeks in 1970-71 at the Sterling Library at Yale *showed that* types of reference questions asked by graduate students were very similar to those asked by undergraduates and in general did not reveal a more sophisticated understanding of the library.

TYPE OF QUESTION (partial list)	% OF QUESTIONS Undergrads	Grads	
general information	11.1	8.9	
library directions	23.9	19.3	
use of card catalog	21.0	21.5	
bibliographic	18.9	22.0	**(101)**

■ A survey of reference services at the University of British Columbia during 1 week in October 1975 *showed that*, while 16.7% of the questions asked were from patrons external to the university, they required 25% of the total time.   **(022)**

Ibid. . . . *showed that*, of the patrons external to the university, over 37% were from other educational institutions; 24% were doing personal research; 10% were from business and industry; 9% from health science professions; and 8% from government departments. 35% of the patrons external to the university asked questions via phone compared to 10% of the university patrons.   **(022)**

■ A study of business students (undergraduate and graduate) at the University of Delaware, University of Maryland, and Wright State University in 1975 *showed that* they were infrequent users of almost all the recognized and commonly available sources of marketing information. For example, over 10% of the students reported they had never heard of *Business Periodical Index*.   **(049)**

■ A 1975-77 study of the use of a drug information service (including closed circuit TV capability for sending answers) originating from the Health Sciences Library at the University of Cincinnati to provide information about drugs, chemicals, and poisons to health professionals in 14 local hospitals (2,294 questions researched; TV used to help provide the answer in 460 instances) *showed that* types of users were as follows:

pharmacists accounted for 31.3% of the total queries and 29.3% of the queries with a TV response;

physicians accounted for 25.8% of the total queries and 22.6% of the queries with a TV response;

nurses accounted for 21.2% of the total queries and 24.8% of the queries with a TV response;

medical students accounted for 2.4% of the total queries and 3.5% of the queries with a TV response;

"other" accounted for 22.0% of the total queries and 24.1% of the queries with a TV response.   **(422)**

■ An analysis of reference questions asked during selected periods throughout the major part of the academic year 1976-77 at Albion College Library, using step categories where each step represents a "distinct and definable judgment leading to a decision, action or recommendation" and where roughly 1 step corresponds to directional questions, 2 steps corresponds to ready reference questions, and multistep corresponds to reference questions, *showed that* the proportion of 1-step, 2-step, and multistep questions asked by undergraduates was 62%, 22%, and 16%, respectively, while that of faculty was 41%, 25%, and 34%, respectively. **(154)**

■ An analysis of reference questions asked during fiscal year 1977-78 at the Engineering, Mathematics and Science Library at the University of Waterloo (Ontario), using step categories where each step represents a "distinct and definable judgment leading to a decision, action or recommendation" and where roughly 1 step corresponds to directional questions, 2 steps correspond to ready reference questions, and multistep corresponds to reference questions *showed that* the proportion of 1-step, 2-step, and multistep questions asked by undergraduates was 37%, 42%, and 21%, respectively, while that of graduates was 24%, 51%, and 25%, respectively. **(154)**

Special

■ A 1975-77 study of the use of a drug information service (including closed circuit TV capability for sending answers) originating from the Health Sciences Library at the University of Cincinnati to provide information about drugs, chemicals, and poisons to health professionals in 14 local hospitals (2,294 questions researched; TV used to help provide the answer in 460 instances) *showed that* types of users were as follows:

pharmacists accounted for 31.3% of the total queries and 29.3% of the queries with a TV response;

physicians accounted for 25.8% of the total queries and 22.6% of the queries with a TV response;

nurses accounted for 21.2% of the total queries and 24.8% of the queries with a TV response;

medical students accounted for 2.4% of the total queries and 3.5% of the queries with a TV response;

"other" accounted for 22.0% of the total queries and 24.1% of the queries with a TV response. **(422)**

■ A 1976 survey of physicians associated with hospitals in a 17-county region of upstate New York (Health Service Area V) based on a systematic sample of "approximately 40%" of the physicians in each county (survey size: 592 physicians; responding: 258 or 45.6%) *showed that* physicians working on a medical research project, engaged in medical education programs (as teachers), or with a hospital-based medical practice reported statistically significant greater use of library reference services (including requests for information from the medical librarian) and MEDLARS searches (all significant at the .05 level or greater). For example, 69% of the physicians engaged in medical research, 47% of the teachers, and 41% of the hospital-based physicians reported using MEDLARS at least once, compared to 27% of all respondents. Further, 82% of the teachers and 76% of the hospital-based physicians requested information from a medical librarian at least once in the past year, compared to 61% of all respondents. **(720)**

Ibid. . . . *showed that* physicians reported that the speed with which their information needs had to be met was as follows: 24 hours (39% physicians, including 5% who reported "immediately"), up to a week (54% physicians), and longer than a week (7% physicians). **(720)**

Type of Question

Academic

■ An analysis of 5,096 reference questions during 7 selected weeks in 1970-71 at the Sterling Library at Yale *showed that* the questions broke down into the following categories according to time required for answer:

TIME REQUIRED	% OF TOTAL	
negligible	25.3	
1-2 minutes	38.1	
3-5 minutes	26.2	
6-10 minutes	6.9	
11-60 minutes	2.7	
over 60 minutes	0.2	
not recorded	0.7	**(101)**

Ibid. . . . *showed that* the number of inquiries by type of inquiry was:

TYPE OF INQUIRY	% OF TOTAL
general information	11.2
library directions	19.4

continued

TYPE OF INQUIRY	% OF TOTAL	
card catalog	26.2	
bibliographic	16.4	
data	6.3	
miscellaneous	20.5	**(101)**

Ibid. . . . *showed that* types of reference questions asked by graduate students were very similar to those asked by undergraduates and in general did not reveal a more sophisticated understanding of the library.

TYPE OF QUESTION (partial list)	% OF QUESTIONS		
	Undergrads	Grads	
general information	11.1	8.9	
library directions	23.9	19.3	
use of card catalog	21.0	21.5	
bibliographic	18.9	22.0	**(101)**

■ A survey reported in 1972 of 1/3 of the social science and humanities faculty at Case Western Reserve University (sample size: 116; responding: 103 or 89%) concerning government document use *showed that*, of 39 users of the government document collection, the frequency with which respondents reported needing assistance from the staff was as follows: more than 50% of the time, 28% (11); 25-50% of the time, 10% (4); less than 25% of the time, 36% (14); never, 23% (9); no answer, 3% (1).   **(209)**

■ An analysis of questions asked at the reference desks at San Jose State University in 1975-76 *showed that* 74% were classified as directional or informational rather than as reference or search questions.   **(010)**

■ A study of reference questions (sample size: 25,588) encountered at the University of Nebraska, Omaha, during academic year 1975-76 *showed that*: 44.1% were directional, 18.0% instructional, 32.0% reference, and 5.90% extended reference.   **(005)**

■ An analysis of reference questions asked during selected periods throughout the major part of the academic year 1976-77 at Albion College Library, using step categories where each step represents a "distinct and definable judgment leading to a decision, action or recommendation" and where roughly 1 step corresponds to directional questions, 2 steps correspond to ready reference questions, and multistep corresponds to reference questions *showed that*, of 1,245 questions, 753 (60%) were 1-step, 271 (22%) were 2-step, and 221 (18%) were multistep. **(154)**

Ibid. . . . *showed that* the proportion of 1-step, 2-step, and multistep questions asked by undergraduates was 62%, 22%, and 16%, respectively, while that of faculty was 41%, 25%, and 34%, respectively. **(154)**

■ An analysis of reference questions asked during fiscal year 1977-78 at the Engineering, Mathematics and Science Library at the University of Waterloo (Ontraio), using step categories where each step represents a "distinct and definable judgment leading to a decision, action or recommendation" and where roughly 1 step corresponds to directional questions, 2 steps correspond to ready reference questions, and multistep corresponds to reference questions, *showed that*, of 5,761 questions which it was possible to code out of 5,969 asked: 1,800 (31%) were 1-step, 2,714 (47%) were 2-step, and 1,247 (22%) were multistep. **(154)**

Ibid. . . . *showed that* the proportion of 1-step, 2-step, and multistep questions asked by undergraduates was 37%, 42%, and 21%, respectively, while that of graduates was 24%, 51%, and 25%, respectively. **(154)**

■ A study reported in 1982 of 14,026 reference questions asked during randomly selected periods over 40 weeks at Virginia Polytechnic Institute and State University *showed that* 6,374 (45.5%) were locational; 3,387 (24.1%) were instructional; 2,879 (20.5%) were reference; and 1,386 (9.9%) were miscellaneous (how to operate equipment, special permissions, etc.). **(160)**

Ibid. . . . *showed that*, of the locational questions, the location of publications (54% of total) was the most frequent type of question, followed by finding items not in the stacks (20.6%) and seeking directions to facilities (restrooms, drinking fountains) (16.4%). **(160)**

Ibid. . . . *showed that*, of the instructional questions, the most frequent category was how to use bibliographic tools (48.8%), followed by how to find journals in the library (33.3%). **(160)**

Ibid. . . . *showed that* the 20.5% reference quetions consisted of 11.3% ready reference questions, 8.5% regular reference, and 0.7% in-depth reference questions. **(160)**

Public

■ A study reported in 1978 involving 18 reference librarians in 4 New Jersey public libraries and using a microphone to record approximately 16 hours of reference/patron interaction in each library (1.159 questions) *showed that* 408 (35%) interactions were directional; 242 (21%) were holdings; 458 (40%) were substantive; and 51 (4%) were moving, i.e., moved from one level (e.g., directional) to another (e.g., substantive).
(260)

Use of Tools—General Issues

General

■ A 1962 survey of 1,750 librarians (1,090 responding; 1,078 used) in academic, school, and public libraries who were asked to sort a list of 352 basic reference titles into 1 of 3 use categories (constant, regular, infrequent) *showed that* half or more of the respondents agreed on a "constant" rating for 73 (20.7%) of the titles and a "regular" rating for 69 (19.6%) of the titles. No title was unanimously selected for a "constant" rating. **(132)**

Use of Tools—Encyclopedias

Public

■ A 1978 survey of 100 (77 or 77% responding) U.S. public libraries of varying sizes concerning 37 general English-language encyclopedias *showed that* the following 5 encyclopedias were reported to be in "constant and heavy demand" by at least a third of the respondents: *World Book Encyclopedia* (76 respondents); *Encyclopedia Americana* (66 respondents); *New Encyclopedia Britannica* (30 respondents); *Collier's Encyclopedia* (28 respondents); and *Compton's Encyclopedia* (26 respondents).
(232)

Use of Tools—Government Documents

General

■ A survey of 50 depository libraies selected at random from the 1970 issues of the *Monthly Catalog* and reported in 1972 (36 or 72% responding) concerning subject access to government documents *showed that* 81% of responding libraries reported that the *Monthly Catalog* was their main source for subject retrieval of U.S. documents.   **(140)**

Ibid. . . . *showed that* 19% of the responding libraries compiled separate subject indexes or catalogs for their U.S. government documents.   **(140)**

Use of Tools—Indexing

General

■ A study reported in 1970 evaluating the potential value of a Keyword In Context (KWIK) index for *Library Literature* by comparing the keywords in the title of an article with the subject heading assigned to the article (survey size: 1,379 title/heading pairs selected from 4 1967 issues of *Library Literature*), *showed that* 483 (35.1%) pairs were identical terms; 144 (10.4%) pairs were synonyms; 138 (10.0%) pairs were related by 1 term being a more specific or more general version of the other (e.g., equipment and supplies/filing cabinets); and 614 (44.5%) pairs had no relationship with each other. Altogether 55% of the title/heading pairs were identical or related, which compares favorably with other indexing tools that have both subject and KWIK indexes.   **(605)**

■ A study reported in 1981 comparing author-assigned index terms with editorially assigned index terms in the field of mathematics, involving 138 articles, *showed that* both approaches retrieved the same number of articles (69 or 50%), although authors assigned an average of 1.87 index terms per article, while editors assigned an average of 1.47 index terms per article.   **(435)**

Ibid. . . . *showed that*, with author indexing, 72% of the articles with at least 3 index terms were retrieved, while only 43% of the articles with less than 3 terms were retrieved. With editorial indexing, 77% of the articles with at least 3 index terms were retrieved, while only 47% of the articles with less than 3 terms were retrieved.   **(435)**

■ A study reported in 1983 of the effectiveness of document retrieval through use of keyword in title indexes *showed that* overall 41% of the articles available were retrieved. In the social science area, 48% of the available articles were retrieved; in the science area, 42% of the available articles were retrieved; and in the arts and humanities area, 31% of the available articles were retrieved.   **(440)**

Academic

■ A study reported in 1981 comparing author-assigned index terms with editorially assigned index terms in the field of mathematics, involving 138 articles *showed that* both approaches retrieved the same number of articles (69 or 50%), although authors assigned an average of 1.87 index terms per article, while editors assigned an average of 1.47 index terms per article.
(435)

Ibid. . . . *showed that*, with author indexing, 72% of the articles with at least 3 index terms were retrieved, while only 43% of the articles with less than 3 terms were retrieved. With editorial indexing, 77% of the articles with at least 3 index terms were retrieved, while only 47% of the articles with less than 3 terms were retrieved.   **(435)**

Visibility

Academic

■ A survey reported in 1973 of the faculty of 6 institutions of higher education in the California system of state colleges and universities, involving 955 full-time faculty of the colleges (694 or 73% responding), *showed that* faculty from the humanities and education had a higher level of awareness of specific library reference services than other teaching areas, although only in relation to the science faculty was the difference statistically significant.   **(663)**

Ibid. . . . *showed that* the 3 reference services with which the most faculty were acquainted were:

advice and assistance in use of the library	95%
interlibrary borrowing	85%
library instruction for classes	65%

while the three reference services with which the least faculty were acquainted were:

lists of reference sources for specific classes	17%
answer requiring a search (i.e., answering questions that require a librarian to spend some time searching for the answer)	22%
answer to a factual question by phone	36% **(663)**

Ibid. . . . *showed that* the reference services that teaching faculty valued most highly (top 5) were:

REFERENCE SERVICE	FAVORABLE ATTITUDE
advice and assistance in use of the library	89%
interlibrary borrowing	89%
library bulletins and handbooks	87%
library instruction for classes	81%
answer to a factual question	81%

while the 2 reference services which the faculty valued least were:

| lists of reference sources for classes | 54% |
| answer requiring a search (i.e., answering questions that require a librarian to spend some time searching for the answer) | 60% **(663)** |

Ibid. . . . *showed that* the average teaching faculty member responding to the questionnaire was aware of only 50% of the reference services available to him from his college library. **(663)**

■ A 1975 telephone survey of a random stratified sample of undergraduates, graduates, and professional students at the University of Chicago to determine awareness of reference services (population: 7,940; sample size: 124; responding: 98) *showed that*, although 100% of the respondents had used the Regenstein Library, 22 (22.4%) reported that they did not know what the reference department did, and 33 (34%) reported that they had never used reference services there. **(151)**

Ibid. . . . *showed that* 75 (75.5%) of the respondents had not used Regenstein reference services in the previous month (October/November); that 10 (10.2%) had used reference services there once in the previous

month; and 8 (8.2%) reported using the reference services twice in the
previous month.   **(151)**

Ibid. . . . *showed that*, out of the 12 reference services available in
Regenstein, only 7 were known by 50% or more of the respondents. **(151)**

Volume

General

■ A study reported in 1983 of 3 surveys made by the American Medical
Association's Division of Library and Archival Services in 1969, 1973, and
1979 concerning the status of health sciences libraries in the U.S. (survey
size for each survey ran between 12,000-14,000 health-related organizations, with a response rate for each survey around 95%) *showed that* in
1979 hospital health science libraries averaged 631 reference transactions
per library annually (ranged from an average of 138 questions per year in
the smallest hospitals to 1,151 questions per year in the largest hospitals),
while the hospitals averaged 457 directional transactions per library
annually (ranged from 73 directional questions per year per library in the
smallest hospitals to 1,085 directional questions per year per library in the
largest hosptials).   **(747)**

Academic

■ A study of 1977 survey information gathered by the National Center
for Educational Statistics (U.S. Office of Education) concerning the degree
to which 1,146 college and university libraries (Liberal Arts Colleges I and
II; Comprehensive Universitites and Colleges I and II) met the 1975
Standards for College Libraries (ACRL) *showed that* the average number
of loans per FTE student per year was 24 with a median of 19 loans, while
the average number of directional and reference questions asked per FTE
student per week was .33 with a median of .17 questions.   **(486)**

■ A study reported in 1981 of data on 1,146 2-year colleges, as reported
in the 1977 Higher Education General Information Surveys and compared
to the 1979 Association of College and Research Libraries standards
showed that libraries in private schools averaged about 3 1/2 times as many
reference and directional transactions per student as libraries in public
schools. Specifically, overall the number of reference and directional
transactions per week per FTE student averaged .36 with a median of .13,
including for privately supported schools (197 reporting) an average of .82

and a median of .30 and for publicly supported schools (794 reporting) an average of .25 and a median of .11. **(500)**

■ A study reported in 1983 of 3 surveys made by the American Medical Association's Division of Library and Archival Services in 1969, 1973, and 1979 concerning the status of health sciences libraries in the U.S. (survey size for each survey ran between 12,000-14,000 health-related organizations, with a response rate for each survey around 95%) *showed that* in 1979 hospital health science libraries averaged 631 reference transations per library annually (ranged from an average of 138 questions per year in the smallest hospitals to 1,151 questions per year in the largest hospitals), while the libraries averaged 457 directional transactions per library annually (ranged from 73 directional questions per year per library in the smallest hospitals to 1,085 directional questions per year per library in the largest hospitals). **(747)**

Public

■ A study of the gross annual circulation statistics and gross annual reference statistics for the 30 large and medium-large public libraries for the years 1972-73-74 as reported in the *Bowker Annual, 1976, showed that* there was a fairly strong positive correlation between the 2 figures, with a correlation coefficient of +.80 for 1972, +.75 for 1973, and +.76 for 1974. No significance level was reported. **(156)**

■ An attempt reported in 1982 to establish 4 input measures and 4 output measures for public libraries, based on published statistical reports for 301 New Jersey public libraries over a 6-year period (1974-79) and survey data for 96 public libraries in New Jersey, *showed that* (per capita based on the population in the library's service area):

INPUT MEASURES

The proportion of budget spent on materials averaged 19.9%, with a standard deviation of .081 (based on 301 libraries).

The new volumes per capita averaged .181, with a standard deviation of .097 (based on 301 libraries).

The periodical titles per capita averaged .0094, with a standard deviation of .0054 (based on 301 libraries).

The circulation per volume averaged 1.79, with a standard deviation of .77 (based on 301 libraries).

OUTPUT MEASURES

The circulation per capita averaged 5.04, with a standard deviation of 3.07 (based on 301 libraries).

The patron visits per capita averaged 2.82, with a standard deviation of 1.82 (based on 96 libraries).

The reference questions per capita averaged 1.12, with a standard deviation of .79 (based on 96 libraries).

The in-library uses of materials per capita averaged 2.29, with a standard deviation of 2.02 (based on 96 libraries). **(576)**

Special

■ A study reported in 1983 of 3 surveys made by the American Medical Association's Division of Library and Archival Services in 1969, 1973, and 1979 concerning the status of health sciences libraries in the U.S. (survey size for each survey ran between 12,000-14,000 health-related organizations, with a response rate for each survey around 95%) *showed that* in 1979 hospital health science libraries averaged 631 reference transactions per library annually (ranged from an average of 138 questions per year in the smallest hospitals to 1,151 questions per year in the largest hospitals), while the hospitals averaged 457 directional transactions per library annually (ranged from 73 directional questions per year per library in the smallest hospitals to 1,085 directional questions per year per library in the largest hospitals). **(747)**

2.

Library Instruction

General Attitudes—Librarians

General

■ A survey reported in 1978 of 74 North American libraries providing point-of-use library instruction ("any presentation that informs the patron about the use of a particular reference/research tool and is found at the location of that tool") *showed that*, in response to the question of whether or not point-of-use instruction worked, the following answers were given:

it worked	46 (62%) libraries
it worked under certain conditions	15 (20%) libraries
uncertain	6 (8%) libraries
it did not work	5 (7%) libraries
[not accounted for	2 (3%) libraries]

However, only 40 (54%) respondents reported that they had employed any evaluation of their point-of-use instruction.   **(753)**

Ibid. . . . *showed that*, in response to the question of whether or not point-of-use instruction saved time for librarians, the following responses were given:

it saved time	28 (38%) libraries
it saved time under certain conditions	9 (12%) libraries
doubted that it saved time	17 (23%) libraries
it did not save time	13 (18%) libraries
[not accounted for	7 (9%) libraries] **(753)**

Academic

■ A survey reported in 1981 of bibliographic instruction in business school libraries (sample size: 120 libraries; responding: 65; usable: 61 or 50.8%) *showed that* respondents rated the overall effectiveness of the orientation/instruction methods used as follows: "highly successful" (5%), "moderately successful" (58.3%), "needs improvement" (30%), and "total failure" (1.7%).   **(436)**

School

■ A survey of teachers and librarians at 2 high schools (sample size: 133) reported in 1967 *showed that* the greatest areas of disagreement between teachers and school librarians were:

1. librarians should help students select research topics (teacher agreement, 58%; librarian agreement, 88%);

2. the librarian ought to establish separate resource centers equipped with pertinent equipment and supplies for every academic area (teacher agreement, 75%; librarian agreement, 44%);

3. librarians should visit classes and give book talks (teacher agreement, 63%; librarian agreement, 88%);

4. room libraries are more effective than resource centers as a central library (teacher agreement, 25%; librarian agreement, 0%).   **(083)**

Ibid. . . . *showed that* over 90% of the teachers and school librarians agreed with the following 8 statements:

1. school librarians should be considered part of the school's instructional staff;

2. high school students should be given instruction in library skills;

3. librarians should help direct student's leisure reading;

4. librarians should keep teachers informed of new materials available for their use;

5. many teachers don't use the library and its facilities effectively;

6. instruction in effective use of the library should be given as part of a teacher's in-service training;

7. the library staff should include someone to help teachers prepare audiovisual aids;

8. teachers would use the library more effectively if they knew more about what resources are available and how to locate them.   **(083)**

General Attitudes—Students

Academic

■ A study in 1975 of business students (undergraduate and graduate) at the University of Delaware, University of Maryland, and Wright State University *showed that* the students felt knowing how to use the library was necessary for academic success but not career success.   **(049)**

■ A survey reported in 1983 of students in freshman rhetoric classes concerning their choice library orientation formats [without necessarily having experienced the options] *showed that* 156 students at the University of Iowa chose the following as the "most interesting" format:

librarian-guided tour	95 (61%) students
audiotape tour	44 (28%) students
slide-tape or videotape tour	17 (11%) students

The same students chose the following as "most instructive" format:

librarian-guided tour	102 (65%) students
audiotape tour	39 (25%) students
slide-tape or videotape tour	15 (10%) students	**(786)**

Ibid. . . . *showed that* 112 students at the University of Missouri chose the following as the "most interesting" format:

| audiotape tour | 79 (71%) students |
| slide-tape or videotape tour | 33 (29%) students |

The same students chose the following as the "most instructive" format:

| audiotape tour | 86 (77%) students |
| slide-tape or videotape tour | 26 (23%) students | **(786)** |

General Attitudes—Teaching Faculty

School

■ A survey of teachers and librarians at 2 high schools (sample size: 133) reported in 1967 *showed that* the greatest areas of disagreement between teachers and school librarians were:

1. librarians should help students select research topics (teacher agreement, 58%; librarian agreement, 88%);

2. the librarian ought to establish separate resource centers equipped with pertinent equipment and supplies for every academic area (teacher agreement, 75%; librarian agreement, 44%);

3. librarians should visit classes and give book talks (teacher agreement, 63%; librarian agreement, 88%);

4. room libraries are more effective than resource centers as a central library (teacher agreement, 25%; librarian agreement, 0%). **(083)**

Ibid. . . . *showed that* over 90% of the teachers and school librarians agreed with the following 8 statements:

1. school librarians should be considered part of the school's instructional staff;

2. high school students should be given instruction in library skills;

3. librarians should help direct student's leisure reading;

4. librarians should keep teachers informed of new materials available for their use;

5. many teachers don't use the library and its facilities effectively;

6. instruction in effective use of the library should be given as part of a teacher's in-service training;

7. the library staff should include someone to help teachers prepare audiovisual aids;

8. teachers would use the library more effectively if they knew more about what resources are available and how to locate them.   **(083)**

General Practice

General

■ A survey reported in 1978 of 74 North American libraries providing point-of-use library instruction ("any presentation that informs the patron about the use of a particular reference/research tool and is found at the location of that tool") *showed that* the 4 most frequently mentioned tools with which point-of-use instruction was used were card catalog (34 or 45.9% libraries), *Reader's Guide* (12 or 16.2% libraries), and *Science Citation Index* and *Psychological Abstracts* (11 or 14.9% libraries each).
                                                                    (753)

Academic

■ A 1965 survey of libraries in colleges with enrollments generally between 500 and 5,000 (sample size: 200; responding: 157; usable because of offering a program in library instruction: 126 or 63%) *showed that* 89

(56.7%) provided a library tour; 46 (29%) provided an orientation week lecture; and 46 (29%) provided an orientation course, with 34 requiring the course and 18 granting credit for the course. **(188)**

■ A 1967 survey of medical school libraries concerning reference services (survey size: 93 libraries; responding: 85 or 91.4%) *showed that*, of 67 libraries, the following library instruction was provided:

conducted tours	51 (76.0%) libraries
lectures	41 (61.2%) libraries
orientation talks	40 (59.7%) libraries
semester courses	5 (7.5%) libraries **(682)**

■ A 1969 survey of the 71 ARL libraries (57 responding; 55 or 77.5% usable) concerning librarians as teachers *showed that* informal instructional programs were provided as follows:

conducts lectures, tours, conferences on request (39.8%);

offers planned orientation lectures and tours (30.1%);

offers bibliography course and/or lectures to beginning graduate students (12.9%);

provides videotape, film, or TV programs (4.3%);

checks theses for correct bibliographical format (1.1%);

offers no structured program of any kind (9.7%);

no response (2.1%). **(196)**

■ A 1973 survey of law school libraries listed in the *Directory of Law Teachers* (population: 156; responding: 124 or 80%) *showed that* only 4 (3.2%) respondents offered group library instruction to students in other than their first year, while 103 (83.1%) respondents reported that such instruction was provided to "first-year class only." **(394)**

■ A survey during the 1979-80 academic year of publicly supported, 2-year community colleges in Texas concerning library programs for developmental education students (disadvantaged students) (survey size: 52; responding: 46; usable: 43 or 82.7%) *showed that* 5 most frequently reported methods of assisting students in the use of the learning resource center (out of 10) were as follows (multiple responses allowed):

library tour	93.0% respondents
orientation lecture	83.7% respondents

continued

course-related instruction   69.8% respondents
handbooks   62.8% respondents
point-of-use aids   51.2% respondents   **(517)**

■ A survey reported in 1981 of bibliographic instruction in business school libraries (sample size: 120; responding: 65; usable: 61 or 50.8%) *showed that* the following use was made of printed materials for orientation and instruction:

handbook/guide   86.7% respondents
single-page handouts   70.0% respondents
subject bibliographies   70.0% respondents
information on specific sources 56.7% respondents
walking tour   51.7% respondents
map   50.0% respondents
library column   25.0% respondents   **(436)**

Ibid. . . . *showed that* the following use was made of lectures and separate bibliography classes (multiple responses allowed):

bibliographic instruction lectures by librarian to specific classes (88.3% respondents);

orientation lectures to new students (48.3% respondents);

separate bibliographic instruction class taught by librarian (16.7% respondents);

separate bibliographic instruction class taught by other faculty (5% respondents).   **(436)**

Special

■ A 1967 survey of medical school libraries concerning reference services (survey size: 93 libraries; responding: 85 or 91.4%) *showed that*, of 67 libraries, the following library instruction was provided:

conducted tours   51 (76.0%) libraries
lectures   41 (61.2%) libraries
orientation talks   40 (59.7%) libraries
semester courses   5 (7.5%) libraries   **(682)**

■ A 1973 survey of law school libraries listed in the *Directory of Law Teachers* (population: 156; responding: 124 or 80%) *showed that* only 4

(3.2%) respondents offered group library instruction to students in other than their first year, while 103 (83.1%) respondents reported that such instruction was provided to "first-year class only."   **(394)**

Impact—Attitude toward Instruction

Academic

■ A 1966 survey at the University of Windsor (Canada) of freshman students who had taken a compulsory 7-week library orientation course where the lectures were presented via videotape (population: "around 900"; responding: 832) *showed that*, when asked if they felt they had learned to use the library more effectively, 336 (40.4%) reported "yes," 317 (38.1%) reported "yes, with reservations," 169 (20.3%) reported no, and 10 (1.2%) were uncertain.   **(533)**

■ A review of 209 student responses to an engineering bibliographic instruction project at the University of Alabama in the Fall semester 1977 *showed that* 64.1% thought that participating in the project would have future value for other engineering courses, but only 21.1% indicated a wish for further library instruction.   **(026)**

■ A study reported in 1981 at Southern Illinois University, Carbondale, of responses by primarily upperclassmen and some graduate students to a 1 hour-1 credit library taught course in bibliographic instruction taken by most of them as freshmen (survey size: 659; responding: 169 or 25.64%) *showed that*:

> 88.8% [no raw number given] reported they were a "more confident library user" as a result of the course;

> 78.9% [no raw number given] reported they were "more comfortable in asking a librarian for help" as a result of the course;

> 69.5% [no raw number given] reported they had "recommended the course to someone else";

> 48.8% [no raw number given] reported they would be interested in an advanced course of bibliographic instruction.   **(488)**

Ibid. . . . *showed that* the 3 most frequently reported strengths of the course were (multiple response allowed): physical layout and location of material (30.8%); learned how much was available in the library (27.8%); and taught how to find material (24.9%).   **(488)**

Ibid. . . . *showed that* the 3 most frequently reported weaknesses of the course were (multiple responses allowed): too general, not specialized enough (18.9%); time, class should meet longer or more often (17.8%); and not stimulating (16.0%).   **(488)**

Ibid. . . . *showed that* there was some evidence that the importance of the course increased over time. Specifically, 68.4% of the sophomores, 84.1% of the juniors and 82.8% of the seniors reported that the course had been of help to them in other classes [no raw numbers given].   **(488)**

■ A study reported in 1982 at Bowling Green State University in Ohio that compared library instruction provided via a workbook (250 students) versus lecture (203 students) *showed that* instructor support of bibliographic instruction was an important influence on student attitudes toward such instruction. Specifically, students who "agreed" or "strongly agreed" that the course instructor was supportive of the bibliographic instruction program tended to "agree" or "strongly agree" that the "workbook was a useful assignment." These responses were associated with a gamma of .35. [No significance level was given.]   **(514)**

Impact—Attitude toward Library

Academic

■ A study reported in 1971 of library instruction involving "approximately 190" students in a general biology class at Earlham College *showed that* there was no statistically significant difference in students' ability to use the library or in their development of positive attitudes toward the library regardless of whether instruction was presented by a librarian in a 2-hour lecture/demonstration or via a guided self-paced exercise undertaken by individual students.   **(208)**

■ A study reported in 1979 at DePauw University comparing classes receiving bibliographic instruction with classes not receiving such instruction and involving 162 freshmen students in English composition courses (133 test subjects receiving instruction; 29 control-group subjects not receiving instruction) *showed that,* of those students who initially felt the library was not an unexpectedly interesting place to be, there was no net change among the control group (those students not receiving instruction), while there was a substantial positive net change (an increase of 24 out of 67) among those students who had received instruction.   **(472)**

■ A 1979 survey at the University of Illinois, Urbana, of 3 groups of freshman students (46 students who had received no bibliographic instruction; 28 students who had received bibliographic instruction from their rhetoric class teaching assistant; and 106 students who had received bibliographic instruction from the Undergraduate Library staff), based on student self-report, *showed that* both library- and TA-instructed students reported a statistically significant greater degree of confidence in their ability to locate materials in the Undergraduate Library than noninstructed students. Specifically, with 1 "strongly agree" and 4 "strongly disagree" that they felt confident, the average score for library-instructed students was 1.86, for TA-instructed students was 1.86, and for noninstructed students was 2.20. This difference was significant at the .05 level.   **(490)**

Ibid. . . . *showed that* both noninstructed and TA-instructed students reported a statistically significant higher degree of frustration in their use of the library than library-instructed students. Specifically, with 1 "strongly agree" and 4 "strongly disagree" that they found using the libraries frustrating, the average score for library-instructed students was 2.72, for TA-instructed students was 2.26, and for noninstructed students was 2.33. This difference was significant at the .05 level.   **(490)**

■ A study in 1980 of library instruction effectiveness over a 3-week period for a group of 43 precollege students at DePauw University *showed that* there was a statistically significant increase in scores on library skills (significant at the .01 level) but no significant change in attitudes toward libraries and librarians.   **(041)**

■ A study reported in 1981 at Southern Illinois University, Carbondale, of responses by primarily upperclassmen and some graduate students to a 1 hour-1 credit library taught course in bibliographic instruction taken by most of them as freshmen (survey size: 659; responding: 169 or 25.64%) *showed that*:

88.8% [no raw number given] reported they were a "more confident library user" as a result of the course;

78.9% [no raw number given] reported they were "more

comfortable in asking a librarian for help" as a result of the course;

69.5% [no raw number given] reported they had "recommended the course to someone else";

48.8% [no raw number given] reported they would be interested in an advanced course of bibliographic instruction.   **(488)**

Impact—Development of Library Skills

Academic

■ A study reported in 1971 of library instruction involving "approximately 190" students in a general biology class at Earlham College *showed that* there was no statistically significant difference in students' ability to use the library or in their development of positive attitudes toward the library regardless of whether instruction was presented by a librarian in a 2-hour lecture/demonstration or via a guided self-paced exercise undertaken by individual students.   **(208)**

■ A study reported in 1972 of 174 students at Brigham Young University concerning library instruction *showed that* students provided with audio-taped, programmed instruction scored statistically significantly higher on their instruction post-test than did those students given a written, nonprogrammed instruction document (significance level at .01 or better). Both groups scored statistically significantly higher than the control group (significance level at .01 or better).   **(214)**

Ibid. . . . *showed that* the mean score betweeen pretest and post-test for the audiotaped, programmed instruction method rose from 32% correct answers to 84%, while the mean score for the written, nonprogrammed instruction method rose from 32% to 72%. Both of these increases were statistically significant, while the slight increase in the mean score for the control group was not statistically significant.   **(214)**

■ A 1978 study of freshmen in English courses at Michigan Technological University and the University of Minnesota, Duluth, to compare the effects of bibliographic instruction and instruction techniques (survey size: 1,868; usable: 1,234 with 327 students in the lecture group, 302 in the programmed instruction group, and 605 in the control group) *showed that* students who had received instruction (regardless of method) made statistically significant increases in their scores on a library skills test, while noninstructed students did not. Specifically, instructed students averaged an increase from 19.88 on the pretest to 33.408 on the post-test (significant at the .01 level), while noninstructed students averaged an increase from 19.343 on the pretest to 21.084 on the post-test. **(506)**

■ A study of the effectiveness of 3 different approaches to the teaching of library skills at the University of Nebraska, Omaha, Spring semester 1978, *showed that* PLATO and a tutorial approach were almost equally effective and resulted in statistically significantly higher test scores on a library skills test than either the noninstructed control group or the group provided with a traditional library tour. However, the average scores for PLATO and tutorial instruction were only 51% and 52% correct, respectively. **(036)**

■ A study reported in 1979 at the Crouch Music Library in Baylor University of the effectiveness of music bibliographic instruction, involving 104 students in 4 groups, *showed that* there was a statistically significant improvement in library skills test scores in 3 of the 4 groups after bibliographic instruction (significant at the .05 level). The fourth group also improved, but the difference in average scores was not statistically significant. **(470)**

■ A study reported in 1979 *showed that* required completion of a library instruction workbook caused a statistically significant increase in test scores of library use skills [significance level not given; presumed to be .01]. **(023)**

■ A study reported in 1979 at DePauw University comparing classes receiving bibliographic instruction with classes not receiving such instruction and involving 162 freshman students in English composition courses (133 test subjects receiving instruction; 29 control-group subjects not receiving instruction) *showed that* the pretest/post-test increase in scores on a 20-question library test was .2 for for the control group and 2.7 for the test group. Although the change was not statistically significant for the control group, this was a statistically significant increase for the test group at the .001 significance level. **(472)**

Ibid. . . . *showed that*, of the 133 test group students (those receiving bibliographic instruction), the average increase in pretest/post-test scores was statistically significant regardless of their SAT verbal aptitude scores. Specifically, for those students with an SAT verbal score lower than 500 the average increase was 3.0 points; for students with SAT verbal scores between 500 and 549 the average increase was 2.4 points; and for students with SAT verbal scores of 550 or above the average increase was 3.2 points. All increases were statistically significant at the .001 level. **(472)**

■ A 1979-80 study at Erindale and Scarborough Colleges (satellite campuses of the University of Toronto, Canada) concerning the effectiveness of course-integrated instruction and a compulsory course-related library assignment in both biology and sociology classes (2 biology classes and 3 sociology classes involving 406 undergraduate students) *showed that* a compulsory library assignment may be an important element in providing library instruction:

> library skills test scores were statistically significantly higher for biology students given instruction and assignment (79.5% correct answers) than for students given neither instruction or assignment (63% correct answers), significant at the .05 level;

> library skills test scores were statistically significantly higher for sociology students given instruction and assignment (79.4% correct answers) than for students given neither instruction or assignment (70% correct answers), significant at the .05 level;

> library skills test scores were *not* statistically significantly higher for sociology students given instruction but no assignment (72% correct answers) than for sociology students given no instruction and no assignment (70% correct answers). **(558)**

■ A study in 1980 of library instruction effectiveness over a 3-week period for a group of 43 precollege students at DePauw University *showed that* there was a statistically significant increase in scores on library skills (significant at the .01 level) but no significant change in attitudes toward libraries and librarians. **(041)**

Ibid. . . . *showed that* library instruction alone could have accounted for the gains in library skills. Specifically, there were no statistically significant gains in library skills associated with students' reading skills, study habits and attitudes, scholastic aptitude, or previous academic achievement. **(041)**

■ A study reported in 1980 at the University of California, Irvine, concerning the effectiveness of 2 videotapes (1 dealing with online bibliographic data base searching; 1 dealing with using the library to write a research paper), involving 24 undergraduates in the experimental group and 26 students in the control group, *showed that* the average pretest and post-test score of the experimental group, which viewed the 2 tapes, increased from 13.00 to 15.04 correct answers (out of a possible 20), while average scores for the control group increased from 12.19 to 12.96 correct answers. This was a statistically significant difference in increase in scores (significant at the .05 level). **(489)**

■ A study reported in 1982 at DePauw University of 82 seniors who had received formal library instruction as freshmen as well as in subsequent courses *showed that*, of 4 factors expected to predict library use skill scores, exposure to bibliographic instruction was a much better predictor than SAT verbal scores or college GPA. Specifically, the 4 factors together accounted for .389 of the variance (r2), while the variances explained by the individual factors (Beta scores) were as follows:

total number of bibliographic instruction courses taken	.367 (Beta)
total number of upper-division courses taken that included bibliographic instruction	.262 (Beta)
SAT verbal score	.162 (Beta)
GPA	.159 (Beta)

The first 2 Beta scores were significant at the .001 level, and the second 2 Beta scores were significant at the .05 level. **(507)**

Special

■ A study reported in 1979 at the Crouch Music Library in Baylor University of the effectiveness of music bibliographic instruction, involving 104 students in 4 groups, *showed that* there was a statistically significant improvement in library skills test scores in 3 of the 4 groups after bibliographic instruction (significant at the .05 level). The fourth group also improved, but the difference in average scores was not statistically significant. **(470)**

Impact—Patron Use Patterns

Academic

■ A study of the effect of the library instruction program for all entering freshmen at Ohio State University *showed that* reference questions at the West Campus Learning Center and the Undergraduate Library in the first full year of the program (1978-79) increased by 35% and 14%, respectively, as compared to an average increase of 2% in the departmental libraries for this same period. Student population did not change significantly. **(042)**

Ibid. . . . *showed that* reshelving of reference materials in the UGL increased 13% in Fall 1978 (first term of the program) over Fall 1977 and by 84% in Fall 1979 over Fall 1978. **(042)**

■ A 1979 survey at the University of Illinois, Urbana, of 3 groups of freshman students (46 students who had received no bibliographic instruction; 28 students who had received bibliographic instruction from their rhetoric class teaching assistant; and 106 students who had received bibliographic instruction from the Undergraduate Library staff), based on student self-report, *showed that* there was no statistically significant difference between the 3 groups and their use of Undergraduate Library reference service, term-paper counseling service, Main Library reference service, or departmental libraries. **(490)**

Ibid. . . . *showed that*:

> there was no statistically significant difference between the 3 groups in their use of encyclopedias;

> the group of students receiving no bibliographic instruction made greater use of bibliographies (average of 1.56 per student) than students receiving instruction either from the library (.91 per student) or from their TA (.96 per student); this was a statistically significant difference at the .01 level;

> the students receiving no bibliographic instruction made less use of periodical indexes (average of 1.37 periodical index titles per student) than students receiving instruction from the library (2.42 titles per student) or from their TA (2.46 titles per student); this was a statistically significant difference at the .01 level. **(490)**

Ibid. . . . *showed that* students receiving bibliographic instruction from either the teaching assistant or library staff reported using statistically significantly more periodical articles and microform/media materials than students who had not received instruction. Specifically, average use of periodical articles for library-instructed students was 3.09 per student, for TA-instructed students was 3.39 per student, and for noninstructed students was 2.11 per student; average use of microforms/media materials for library-instructed students was .81 items per student, for TA-instructed students was 1.14 items per student, and for noninstructed students was .04 items per student. This difference was significant at the .01 level. **(490)**

Ibid. . . . *showed that* students who had received bibliographic instruction from library staff reported using statistically significantly fewer books than students receiving instruction from the teaching assistant or who had not received instruction. Specifically, average book use by library-instructed students was 3.50 books per student, by TA-instructed students was 4.43 books per student, and by noninstructed students was 4.20 books per student. The difference was significant at the .01 level. **(490)**

Ibid. . . . *showed that* there were no statistically significant differences between the 3 groups in their reported use of the card catalog. However, students receiving bibliographic instruction from library staff reported making statistically significantly more use of the Library Computer System than students in the other 2 groups. Specifically, library-instructed students averaged 1.30 uses of the Library Computer System per student; TA-instructed students averaged .50 uses per student; and noninstructed students averaged .59 uses per student. This difference was significant at the .05 level.   **(490)**

Prior Skill Level

Academic

■   A study in 1975 of business students (undergraduate and graduate) at the University of Delaware, University of Maryland, and Wright State University *showed that* they were infrequent readers of most business periodicals. For example, 21% of the undergrads and 8% of the M.B.A.'s reported never having read the *Wall Street Journal*.   **(049)**

■   A survey of 197 students participating in an engineering bibliographic instruction project at the University of Alabama in Fall semester 1977 *showed that* 26.4% of the students had not used *Reader's Guide* before (68.6% had used the *Guide* previously, and 5% gave no response).

(026)

■   A study reported in 1972 of 79 graduate business students at a large, accredited southeastern business school *showed that* 48% of the students could not list 1 index or abstract that they knew how to use, while only 11% were able to list more than 2 sources they knew how to use.   **(297)**

Ibid. . . . *showed that*, of those students who had taken a graduate business research course, 67% rated their knowledge of the library as good to excellent, with 33% rating their knowledge as poor to very poor. Of the students who had not taken the research course, 34% rated their knowledge of the library as good to excellent, while 66% rated their knowledge as poor to very poor.   **(297)**

Staffing—General Issues

Academic

■ A survey of 500 college and university library administrators throughout the U.S. (397 or 79% responding) in 1961 *showed that* 107 (27%)
reported that either reference librarians or a member of the library staff
was responsible for teaching a course in the use of the library to freshman
students.   **(117)**

Ibid. . . . *showed that* 221 (56%) of the libraries reported that a member of
the library staff gave 1 or more lectures on library use in connection with
English classes.   **(117)**

■ A 1969 survey of the 71 ARL libraries (57 responding; 55 or 77.5%
usable) concerning librarians as teachers *showed that* 61.8% of responding
libraries reported that their staffs were involved in the formal instructional
programs of their institutions, while another 16.4% stated that the
involvement was "intermittent" or "only occasional." There was no
involvement in teaching reported by 21.8% of the responding libraries.
                                                                         (196)

■ A 1973-74 survey of large library instruction programs in the U.S. and
Great Britain *showed that* libraries with a library instruction coordinator
had the most extensive instructional programs as indicated by credit
courses offered, class-related bibliographic lectures given, and self-guided
or programmed library instruction materials provided.   **(061)**

■ A study of the effect of the library instruction program for all entering
freshmen at Ohio State University *showed that* reference questions at the
West Campus Learning Center and the Undergraduate Library in the first
full year of the program (1978-79) increased by 35% and 14%, respectively, as compared to an average increase of 2% in the departmental
libraries for this same period. Student population did not change significantly.   **(042)**

Ibid. . . . *showed that* reshelving of reference materials in the UGL
increased 13% in Fall 1978 (first term of the program) over Fall 1977 and by
84% in Fall 1979 over Fall 1978.   **(042)**

■ A survey during the 1979-80 academic year of publicly supported, 2-year community colleges in Texas concerning library programs for developmental education students (disadvantaged students) (survey size: 52; responding: 46; usable: 43 or 82.7%) *showed that*, of 39 respondents, at least 1 member of the following ethnic groups was on the staff of the learning resource center:

Anglo	39 (100.0%)	LRCs
black	25 (64.1%)	LRCs
Mexican-American	23 (59.0%)	LRCs
Oriental	5 (12.8%)	LRCs
other	3 (7.7%)	LRCs	**(517)**

■ A 1980 survey of bibliographic instruction librarians with an M.L.S. degree and at least 2 years of bibliographic instruction in 18 selected college and university libraries in Pennsylvania (sample size: 133; responding: 120 or 90%) *showed that* 3 (3%) librarians reported full-time assignments in bibliographic instruction; 8 (7%) reported half-time assignments in bibliographic instruction; and 109 (91%) reported less than half-time assignments in bibliographic instruction.   **(510)**

Special

■ A 1976 survey of head law librarians in North American schools (sample size: 178; responding: 154 or 86.7%) *showed that*:

49 (32%) law school library directors taught law school legal bibliography courses only;

35 (23%) taught both legal bibliography and substantive courses in the law school;

16 (10%) taught courses in both the law school and library school;

13 (8%) taught substantive courses only in the law school;

2 (1%) taught library school legal bibliography courses only;

2 (1%) taught legal research courses outside of the law or library school;

37 (24%) taught no courses.   **(357)**

Ibid. . . . *showed that* the numbers of law school libraries where professional staff besides the director taught courses (entire courses only) were as follows:

23 (16%) libraries reported staff teaching law school legal bibliography course only;

4 (3%) reported staff teaching library school legal bibliography or substantive courses;

3 (2%) reported staff teaching law school substantive courses only;

2 (1%) reported staff teaching both law school legal bibliography and substantive courses;

2 (1%) reported staff teaching both law and library school courses;

1 reported staff teaching courses in other schools;

117 (76%) reported staff teaching no courses.   **(357)**

Staffing—Education and Experience

Academic

■ A 1980 survey of bibliographic instruction librarians with an M.L.S. degree and at least 2 years of bibliographic instruction in 18 selected college and university libraries in Pennsylvania (sample size: 133; responding: 120 or 90%) *showed that* the number of years of bibliographic instruction experience was as follows:

2-5 years	29 (25%) librarians
6-8 years	27 (22%) librarians
9-11 years	27 (22%) librarians
12 or more years	37 (31%) librarians

(510)

Ibid. . . . *showed that* 28 (23%) reported college-level teaching experience and 56 (47%) reported elementary- or secondary-level teaching experience before their involvement in bibliographic instruction.   **(510)**

Ibid. . . . *showed that* of 120 respondents the 2 most frequent methods of actually gaining training for bibliographic instruction reported by respondents were self-study (63 or 56%) and credit courses (34 or 30%). However, respondents' 4 most frequently recommended ways of preparing for bibliographic instruction were:

previous teaching experience	32 (28%) respondents
workshops	28 (25%) respondents

continued

| in-service programs | 22 (19%) respondents |
| credit courses | 20 (18%) respondents |

(510)

Techniques—General Issues

Academic

■ A 1967 random survey of 200 members of the American Association of Colleges for Teacher Education (94 colleges responding) seeking information on library user education practices *showed that* 19 (20%) used a combination of handbooks, lectures, and tours; 89 (95%) gave orientation of freshmen only; 8 (9%) offered a credit class; and 17 (18%) offered no library instruction at all. **(135)**

■ A 1969 survey of the 71 ARL libraries (57 responding; 55 or 77.5% usable) concerning librarians as teachers *showed that* informal instructional programs were provided as follows: conducts lectures, tours, conferences on request (39.8%); offers planned orientation lectures and tours (30.1%); offers bibliography courses and/or lectures to beginning graduate students 12.9%); provides videotape, film, or TV programs (4.3%); checks theses for correct bibliographical format (1.1%); offers no structured program of any kind (9.7%); no response (2.1%). **(196)**

■ A survey reported in 1981 of bibliographic instruction in business school libraries (sample size: 120 libraries; responding: 65; usable: 61 or 50.8%) *showed that* the 3 methods rated by respondents as most effective in bibliographic instruction and orientation were lectures to specific classes (48.3% respondents), printed materials (21.7% respondents), and tours (11.7% respondents). **(436)**

Ibid. . . . *showed that* the 2 methods rated by respondents as least effective in bibliographic instruction and orientation were: orientation lectures (20% respondents) and tours (15% respondents). **(436)**

Ibid. . . . *showed that* the following use was made of printed materials for orientation and instruction:

handbook/guide	86.7% respondents
single-page handouts	70.0% respondents
subject bibliographies	70.0% respondents
information on specific sources	56.7% respondents

continued

walking tour   51.7% respondents
map   50.0% respondents
library column   25.0% respondents   **(436)**

Techniques—Audiovisual

General

■ A survey reported in 1978 of 74 North American libraries providing point-of-use library instruction ("any presentation that informs the patron about the use of a particular reference/research tool and is found at the location of that tool") *showed that* the 2 most frequently reported nonprint formats for point-of-use instruction (multiple responses allowed) were slidetape (19 or 25.7% libraries) and audiotape (14 or 18.9% libraries), while the 3 most frequently reported print formats for point-of-use instruction were (multiple responses allowed) handouts (48 or 64.9% libraries), charts (23 or 31.1% libraries), and posters (19 or 25.7% libraries).   **(753)**

Academic

■ A 1965 survey of libraries in colleges with enrollments generally between 500 and 5,000 (sample size: 200; responding: 157; usable because of offering a program in library instruction: 126 or 63%) *showed that* no audiovisual aids were used in 94 (60%) institutions, while AV was used in 38% of the institutions.   **(188)**

■ A 1967 survey by the Institute of Higher Education at Teachers College, Columbia University, of innovative programs in libraries in academic institutions with liberal arts programs (sample size: 1,193 libraries; responding: 781 or 65%) *showed that* 30 (39%) of the libraries reported multimedia cards in their card catalogs; 193 (25%) have special catalogs for multimedia materials; and 170 (22%) reported using various media in programs of library instruction.   **(190)**

■ A 1966 survey at the University of Windsor (Canada) of freshman students who had taken a compulsory 7-week library orientation course where the lectures were presented via videotape (population: "around 900"; responding: 832) *showed that*, when asked whether they preferred the video to an instructor without the aid of television, 438 (52.6%) reported they preferred the video, 320 (38.5%) reported they preferred the instructor without the video, and 74 (8.9%) reported they had no preference. **(533)**

■ A study reported in 1972 of 174 students at Brigham Young University concerning library instruction *showed that* students provided with audio-taped, programmed instruction scored statistically significantly higher on their instruction post-test than did those students given a written, nonprogrammed instruction document (significance level at .01 or better). Both groups scored statistically significantly higher than the control group (significance level at .01 or better). **(214)**

Ibid. . . . *showed that* the mean score betweeen pretest and post-test for the audiotaped, programmed instruction method rose from 32% correct answers to 84%, while the mean score for the written, nonprogrammed instruction method rose from 32% to 72%. Both of these increases were statistically significant, while the slight increase in the mean score for the control group was not statistically significant. **(214)**

■ A questionnaire survey reported in 1975 of U.S. and Canadian libraries with student enrollments of 8,000 or more and known to have bibliographic instruction programs (sample size: 48 libraries; responding: 42; usable: 38 or 79.2%) *showed that* 80% of the respondents indicated use of AV equipment in some part of their instructional program. **(061)**

■ A study of the effectiveness of 3 different approaches to the teaching of library skills at the University of Nebraska, Omaha, Spring semester 1978, *showed that* PLATO and a tutorial approach were almost equally effective and resulted in statistically significantly higher test scores on a library skills test than either the noninstructed control group or the group provided with a traditional library tour. However, the average scores for PLATO and tutorial instruction were only 51% and 52% correct respectively. **(036)**

■ A study reported in 1979 at the University of Toledo comparing the effectiveness of presenting bibliographic instruction information by means of a slide-tape show versus a library tour to students in a freshman-level business report-writing course (slide-tape group, 76 students; tour group, 75 students) *showed that* there was no statistically significant difference in post-test scores between the groups. The tour group scores averaged 15.35, while the slide-tape scores averaged 13.75. **(468)**

■ A study reported in 1980 at the University of California, Irvine, concerning the effectiveness of 2 videotapes (1 dealing with online bibliographic data base searching; 1 dealing with using the library to write a research paper), involving 24 undergraduates in the experimental group and 26 students in the control group, *showed that* the average pretest and post-test score of the experimental group, which viewed the 2 tapes, increased from 13.00 to 15.04 correct answers (out of a possible 20), while average scores for the control group increased from 12.19 to 12.96 correct answers. This was a statistically significant difference in increase in scores (significant at the .05 level).   **(489)**

■ A survey reported in 1981 of bibliographic instruction in business school libraries (sample size: 120; responding: 65; usable: 61 or 50.8%) *showed that* the following use was made of audiovisual material for orientation and instruction:

slide-tape	23.3% respondents
audiotour	8.3% respondents
transparencies	8.3% respondents
videotape	3.3% respondents
television	1.7% respondents
other	5.0% respondents **(436)**

■ A survey reported in 1983 of students in freshman rhetoric classes concerning their choice library orientation formats [without necessarily having experienced the options] *showed that* 156 students at the University of Iowa chose the following as the "most interesting" format:

librarian-guided tour	95 (61%) students
audiotape tour	44 (28%) students
slide-tape or videotape tour	17 (11%) students

The same students chose the following as "most instructive" format:

librarian-guided tour	102 (65%) students
audiotape tour	39 (25%) students
slide-tape or videotape tour	15 (10%) students **(786)**

Ibid. . . . *showed that* 112 students at the University of Missouri chose the following as the "most interesting" format:

audiotape tour	79 (71%) students
slide-tape or videotape tour	33 (29%) students

The same students chose the following as the "most instructive" format:

audiotape tour	86 (77%) students
slide-tape or videotape tour	26 (23%) students **(786)**

Techniques—Comparison

Academic

■ A 1966 survey at the University of Windsor (Canada) of freshman students who had taken a compulsory 7-week library orientation course where the lectures were presented via videotape (population: "around 900"; responding: 832) *showed that*, when asked whether they preferred the video to an instructor without the aid of television, 438 (52.6%) reported they preferred the video, 320 (38.5%) reported they preferred the instructor without the video, and 74 (8.9%) reported they had no preference.   **(533)**

■ A study reported in 1971 of library instruction involving "approximately 190" students in a general biology class at Earlham College *showed that* there was no statistically significant difference in students' ability to use the library or in their development of positive attitudes toward the library regardless of whether instruction was presented by a librarian in a 2-hour lecture/demonstration or via a guided self-paced exercise undertaken by individual students.   **(208)**

■ A study reported in 1972 of 174 students at Brigham Young University concerning library instruction *showed that* students provided with audiotaped, programmed instruction scored statistically significantly higher on their instruction post-test than did those students given a written, nonprogrammed instruction document (significance level at .01 or better). Both groups scored statistically significantly higher than the control group (significance level at .01 or better).   **(214)**

Ibid. . . . *showed that* the mean score betweeen pretest and post-test for the audiotaped, programmed instruction method rose from 32% correct answers to 84%, while the mean score for the written, nonprogrammed instruction method rose from 32% to 72%. Both of these increases were statistically significant, while the slight increase in the mean score for the control group was not statistically significant.   **(214)**

■ A survey reported in 1973 at Portland State University Library (Oregon) of more than 200 students randomly assigned to 7 different types of library instruction groups *showed that* the slide-tape presentation was found to be more effective than either a tape presentation alone or the conventional library lectures at the .01 level of significance and more effective than a television presentation (which included a follow-along notebook) at the .05 level of significance.   **(090)**

Ibid. . . . *showed that* students who received a tape presentation followed by a 50-minute follow-up session by a librarian received statistically significantly higher scores than did students receiving only the slide-tape presentation.   **(090)**

■ A study in 1975-76 at the Wooster Agricultural Technical Institute of the Ohio State University of 161 freshmen *showed that* there was no statistically significant difference between using lecture method versus programmed instruction text in teaching use of periodical indexes.   **(023)**

■ A study of the effectiveness of 3 different approaches to the teaching of library skills at the University of Nebraska, Omaha, Spring semester 1978, *showed that* PLATO and a tutorial approach were almost equally effective and resulted in statistically significantly higher test scores on a library skills test than either the noninstructed control group or the group provided with a traditional library tour. However, the average scores for PLATO and tutorial instruction were only 51% and 52% correct, respectively.   **(036)**

■ A survey reported in 1983 of students in freshman rhetoric classes concerning their choice library orientation formats [without necessarily having experienced the options] *showed that* 156 students at the University of Iowa chose the following as the "most interesting" format:

librarian-guided tour	95 (61%) students
audiotape tour	44 (28%) students
slide-tape or videotape tour	17 (11%) students

The same students chose the following as "most instructive" format:

librarian-guided tour	102 (65%) students
audiotape tour	39 (25%) students
slide-tape or videotape tour	15 (10%) students **(786)**

Ibid. . . . *showed that* 112 students at the University of Missouri chose the following as the "most interesting" format:

audiotape tour	79 (71%) students
slide-tape or videotape tour	33 (29%) students

The same students chose the following as the "most instructive" format:

audiotape tour	86 (77%) students
slide-tape or videotape tour	26 (23%) students **(786)**

■ A 1978 study of freshmen in English courses at Michigan Technological University and the University of Minnesota, Duluth, to compare the effects of bibliographic instruction and instruction techniques (survey size: 1,868; usable: 1,234 with 327 students in the lecture group, 302 in the programmed instruction group, and 605 in the control group) *showed that* students provided with programmed instruction made statistically significantly higher scores on a library skills test than students provided with the traditional lecture. Specifically, students who received programmed instruction averaged a score of 36.759, while students who received the lecture approach averaged a score of 30.056 (significant at the .001 level). **(506)**

■ A study reported in 1979 at the University of Toledo comparing the effectiveness of presenting bibliographic instruction information by means of a slide-tape show versus a library tour to students in a freshman-level business report-writing course (slide-tape group, 76 students; tour group, 75 students) *showed that* there was no statistically significant difference in post-test scores between the groups. The tour group scores averaged 15.35, while the slide-tape scores averaged 13.75. **(468)**

■ A 1979 study at the University of Michigan comparing 2 groups of graduate students in an educational psychology class who compiled required bibliographies in 2 different ways (6 students used online searching; 8 students used conventional manual methods) *showed that* there were substantial differences of opinion about the 2 search processes:

66% of the online group versus 100% of the manual group ranked the literature as "highly responsive to information needs";

12% of the online group versus 80% of the manual group reported a "high proportion of total productive time spent in literature search";

50% of the online group versus 100% of the manual group reported a "high level of confidence about being able to find information in future searches";

12% of the online group versus 40% of the manual group reported that "search techniques provide a great deal of insight into topics considered." **(651)**

■ A 1979-80 study at Erindale and Scarborough Colleges (satellite campuses of the University of Toronto, Canada) concerning the effectiveness of course-integrated instruction and a compulsory course-related library assignment in both biology and sociology classes (2 biology classes and 3 sociology classes involving 406 undergraduate students) *showed that* a compulsory library assignment may be an important element in providing library instruction:

> library skills test scores were statistically significantly higher for biology students given instruction and assignment (79.5% correct answers) than for students given neither instruction or assignment (63% correct answers), significant at the .05 level;

> library skills test scores were statistically significantly higher for sociology students given instruction and assignment (79.4% correct answers) than for students given neither instruction or assignment (70% correct answers), significant at the .05 level;

> library skills test scores were *not* statistically significantly higher for sociology students given instruction but no assignment (72% correct answers) than for sociology students given no instruction and no assignment (70% correct answers).   **(558)**

■ A survey reported in 1981 of bibliographic instruction in business school libraries (sample size: 120 libraries; responding: 65; usable: 61 or 50.8%) *showed that* the 3 methods rated by respondents as most effective in bibliographic instruction and orientation were lectures to specific classes (48.3% respondents), printed materials (21.7% respondents), and tours (11.7% respondents).   **(436)**

Ibid. . . . *showed that* the 2 methods rated by respondents as least effective in bibliographic instruction and orientation were orientation lectures (20% respondents) and tours (15% respondents).   **(436)**

■ A study reported in 1982 at Bowling Green State University in Ohio that compared library instruction provided via a workbook (250 students) versus lecture (203 students) *showed that* generally students preferred the workbook. For example, 74.8% of the students "agreed" or "strongly agreed" that the workbook was "clear and understandable" compared to 63.2% of the students so responding for the lecture, while 48.0% of the students "agreed" or "strongly agreed" that the workbook helped them feel more confident in using the library compared to 43.6% of the students so responding to the lecture. Later revisions of the workbook used by another group of students (460 students) raised its "clear and understandable" rating to 85.6% and its "more confident in using the library" rating to 70.0%.   **(514)**

Techniques—Lecture

Academic

■ A 1965 survey of libraries in colleges with enrollments generally between 500 and 5,000 (sample size: 200; responding: 157; usable because of offering a program in library instruction: 126 or 63%) *showed that* the most common means of instruction was through library lectures in freshman English classes (reported in 98 or 62% institutions), with librarians providing lectures in 45 institutions and the English instructor providing the lectures in 53 institutions. **(188)**

■ A 1967 random survey of 200 members of The American Association of Colleges for Teacher Education (94 responding) seeking information on library user education practices *showed that* 19 (20%) used a combination of handbooks, lectures, and tours; 89 (95%) gave orientation for freshmen only; 8 (9%) offered a credit class; and 17 (18%) offered no library instruction at all. **(135)**

Techniques—Other

Academic

■ A 1967 random survey of 200 members of the American Association of Colleges for Teacher Education (94 colleges responding) seeking information on library user education practices *showed that* 54 (57%) sent lists of new acquisitions monthly or periodically to faculty; 29 (31%) used bulletin board displays and exhibits of new acquisitions; and 13 (14%) used new book shelves. 21 (22%) reported no notification at all. **(135)**

Techniques—Study Guides, Workbooks

General

■ A survey reported in 1978 of 74 North American libraries providing point-of-use library instruction ("any presentation that informs the patron about the use of a particular reference/research tool and is found at the location of that tool") *showed that* the 2 most frequently reported nonprint formats for point-of-use instruction (multiple responses allowed) were slide-tape (19 or 25.7% libraries) and audiotape (14 or 18.9% libraries), while the 3 most frequently reported print formats for point of use instruction were (multiple responses allowed) handouts (48 or 64.9% libraries), charts (23 or 31.1% libraries), and posters (19 or 25.7% libraries).   **(753)**

Academic

■ A 1967 random survey of 200 members of The American Association of Colleges for Teacher Education (94 responding) seeking information on library user education practices *showed that* 19 (20%) used a combination of handbooks, lectures, and tours; 89 (95%) gave orientation for freshmen only; 8 (9%) offered a credit class; and 17 (18%) offered no library instruction at all.   **(135)**

■ A study reported in 1979 at the University of Arizona of 487 entering students *showed that* required completion of a library instruction workbook caused a statistically significant increase in test scores of library use skills [significance level not given; presumed to be .01].   **(023)**

■ A review reported in 1979 of 16 study guides *showed that* they did not offer a fruitful or sophisticated approach to library research, made serious omissions in their recommendations of indexes and abstracts, and assigned librarians only a limited service role.   **(024)**

■ A survey reported in 1981 of bibliographic instruction in business school libraries (sample size: 120; responding: 65; usable: 61 or 50.8%) *showed that* the following use was made of printed materials for orientation and instruction:

handbook/guide	86.7% respondents
single-page handouts	70.0% respondents
subject bibliographies	70.0% respondents
information on specific sources	56.7% respondents
walking tour	51.7% respondents
map	50.0% respondents
library column	25.0% respondents **(436)**

■ A study reported in 1982 at Bowling Green State University in Ohio that compared library instruction provided via a workbook (250 students) versus lecture (203 students) *showed that* generally students preferred the workbook. For example, 74.8% of the students "agreed" or "strongly agreed" that the workbook was "clear and understandable" compared to

63.2% of the students so responding for the lecture, while 48.0% of the students "agreed" or "strongly agreed" that the workbook helped them feel more confident in using the library compared to 43.6% of the students so responding to the lecture. Later revisions of the workbook used by another group of students (460 students) raised its "clear and understandable" rating to 85.6% and its "more confident in using the library" rating to 70.0%. **(514)**

BIBLIOGRAPHY OF ARTICLES

Note: This Bibliography cites all articles summarized in the six-volume set of *Handbooks.* Entries in the Bibliography are sequentially arranged by the citation reference numbers that correspond to the numbers appearing at the end of each research summary throughout the six volumes. The numbers in boldface located at the end of some citations refer only to those research summaries contained in this volume. Alphabetic access to the Bibliography is provided through the Author Index.

1   Pamela Kobelski and Jean Trumbore. "Student Use of On-line Bibliographic Services," *Journal of Academic Librarianship* 4:1 (March 1978), 14-18. **(43, 55, 63, 79, 80, 100)**

2   John V. Richardson, Jr. "Readability and Readership of Journals in Library Science," *Journal of Academic Librarianship* 3:1 (March 1977), 20-22.

3   Elizabeth Gates Kesler. "A Campaign against Mutilation," *Journal of Academic Librarianship* 3:1 (March 1977), 29-30.

4   Bruce Miller and Marilyn Sorum. "A Two Stage Sampling Procedure for Estimating the Proportion of Lost Books in a Library," *Journal of Academic Librarianship* 3:2 (May 1977), 74-80.

5   Jeffrey St. Clair and Rao Aluri. "Staffing the Reference Desk: Professionals or Nonprofessionals," *Journal of Academic Librarianship* 3:3 (July 1977), 149-153. **(14, 218)**

6   Valentine DeBruin. "Sometimes Dirty Things Are Seen on the Screen," *Journal of Academic Librarianship* 3:5 (November 1977), 256-266.

7   Herbert S. White. "The View from the Library School," *Journal of Academic Librarianship* 3:6 (January 1970), 321.

8   Stella Bentley. "Collective Bargaining and Faculty Status," *Journal of Academic Librarianship* 4:2 (May 1978), 75-81.

9   Steven Seokho Chwe. "A Comparative Study of Job Satisfaction: Catalogers and Reference Librarians in University Libraries," *Journal of Academic Librarianship* 4:3 (July 1978), 139-143. **(31)**

10   Jo Bell Whitlatch and Karen Kieffer. "Service at San Jose State University: Survey of Document Availability," *Journal of Academic Librarianship* 4:4 (September 1978), 196-199. **(114, 218)**

11   Joan Grant and Susan Perelmuter. "Vendor Performance Evaluation," *Journal of Academic Librarianship* 4:5 (November 1978), 366-367.

12   Robert Goehlert. "Book Availability and Delivery Service," *Journal of Academic Librarianship* 4:5 (November 1978), 368-371.

13   Linda L. Phillips and Ann E. Raup. "Comparing Methods for Teaching Use of Periodical Indexes," *Journal of Academic Librarianship* 4:6 (January 1979), 420-423.

14   Margaret Johnson Bennett, David T. Buxton and Ella Capriotti. "Shelf Reading in a Large, Open Stack Library," *Journal of Academic Librarianship* 5:1 (March 1979), 4-8.

15   Sarah D. Knapp and C. James Schmidt. "Budgeting To Provide Computer-Based Reference Services: A Case Study," *Journal of Academic Librarianship* 5:1 (March 1979), 9-13. **(63)**

16   Herbert S. White. "Library Materials Prices and Academic Library Practices: Between Scylla and Charybdis," *Journal of Academic Librarianship* 5:1 (March 1979), 20-23.

17   Dorothy P. Wells. "Coping with Schedules for Extended Hours: A Survey of Attitudes and Practices," *Journal of Academic Librarianship* 5:1 (March 1979), 24-27. **(11, 13, 212)**

18   Johanna E. Tallman. "One Year's Experience with CONTU Guidelines for Interlibrary Loan Photocopies," *Journal of Academic Librarianship* 5:2 (May 1979), 71-74.

19   Robert Goehlert. "The Effect of Loan Policies on Circulation Recalls," *Journal of Academic Librarianship* 5:2 (May 1979), 79-82.

20   James R. Dwyer. "Public Response to an Academic Library Microcatalog," *Journal of Academic Librarianship* 5:3 (July 1979), 132-141.

21   Paul Metz. "The Role of the Academic Library Director," *Journal of Academic Librarianship* 5:3 (July 1979), 148-152.

22   Anne B. Piternick. "Problems of Resource Sharing with the Community: A Case Study," *Journal of Academic Librarianship* 5:3 (July 1979), 153-158. **(215)**

23   Shelley Phipps and Ruth Dickstein. "The Library Skills Program at the University of Arizona: Testing, Evaluation and Critique," *Journal of Academic Librarianship* 5:4 (September 1979), 205-214. **(239, 252, 256)**

24   Michael Stuart Freeman. "Published Study Guides: What They Say about Libraries," *Journal of Academic Librarianship* 5:5 (November 1979), 252-255. **(256)**

25   James H. Richards, Jr. "Missing Inaction," *Journal of Academic Librarianship* 5:5 (November 1979), 266-269.

26   Philip H. Kitchens. "Engineers Meet the Library," *Journal of Academic Librarianship* 5:5 (November 1979), 277-282. **(235, 243)**

27   Michael Rouchton. "OCLC Serials Records: Errors, Omissions, and Dependability," *Journal of Academic Librarianship* 5:6 (January 1980), 316-321.

28   Charles R. McClure. "Academic Librarians, Information Sources, and Shared Decision Making," *Journal of Academic Librarianship* 6:1 (March 1980), 9-15.

29   Marjorie E. Murfin. "The Myth of Accessibility: Frustration and Failure in Retrieving Periodicals," *Journal of Academic Librarianship* 6:1 (March 1980), 16-19.

30   Anthony W. Ferguson and John R. Taylor. "What Are You Doing? An Analysis of Activities of Public Service Librarians at a Medium-sized Research Library," *Journal of Academic Librarianship* 6:1 (March 1980), 24-29.

31   Regina Shelton. "Adaption: A One-Year Survey of Reserve Photocopying," *Journal of Academic Librarianship* 6:2 (May 1980), 74-76.

32   Dorothea M. Thompson. "The Correct Uses of Library Data Bases Can Improve Interlibrary Loan Efficiency," *Journal of Academic Librarianship* 6:2 (May 1980), 83-86.

33   Joan Repp and Julia A. Woods. "Student Appraisal Study and Allocation Formula: Priorities and Equitable Funding in a University Setting," *Journal of Academic Librarianship* 6:2 (May 1980), 87-90.

34   Elaine S. Friedman. "Patron Access to Online Cataloging Systems: OCLC in the Public Service Environment," *Journal of Academic Librarianship* 6:3 (July 1980), 132-139. **(158, 159)**

35   Edward C. Jestes. "Manual vs. Automated Circulation: A Comparison of Operating Costs in a University Library," *Journal of Academic Librarianship* 6:3 (July 1980), 144-150.

36   Kathleen A. Johnson and Barbara S. Plake. "Evaluation of PLATO Library Instructional Lessons: Another View," *Journal of Academic Librarianship* 6:3 (July 1980), 154-158. **(239, 249, 252)**

37   Priscilla C. Yu. "International Gift and Exchange: The Asian Experience," *Journal of Academic Librarianship* 6:6 (January 1981), 333-338.

38   George W. Black, Jr. "Estimating Collection Size Using the Shelf List in a Science Library," *Journal of Academic Librarianship* (January 1981), 339-341.

39   Beth Macleod. "*Library Journal* and *Choice*: A Review of Reviews," *Journal of Academic Librarianship* 7:1 (March 1981), 23-28. **(131, 132, 135, 136)**

40   Frank Wm. Goudy. "HEA, Title II-C Grant Awards: A Financial Overview from FY 1978-79 through FY 1981-82," *Journal of Academic Librarianship* 8:5 (November 1982), 264-269.

41 Larry Hardesty and John Wright. "Student Library Skills and Attitudes and Their Change: Relationships to Other Selected Variables," *Journal of Academic Librarianship* 8:4 (September 1982), 216-220. **(237, 240)**

42 Penelope Pearson and Virginia Teufel. "Evaluating Undergraduate Library Instruction at the Ohio State University," *Journal of Academic Librarianship* 7:6 (January 1982), 351-357. **(241, 242, 244)**

43 David S. Ferrioro. "ARL Directors as Proteges and Mentors," *Journal of Academic Librarianship* 7:6 (January 1982), 358-365.

44 Albert F. Maag. "So You Want to be a Director...," *Journal of Academic Librarianship* 7:4 (September 1981), 213-217.

45 Mary Noel Gouke and Sue Pease. "Title Searches in an Online Catalog and a Card Catalog: A Comparative Study of Patron Success in Two Libraries," *Journal of Academic Librarianship* 8:3 (July 1982), 137-143.

46 John K. Mayeski and Marilyn T. Sharrow. "Recruitment of Academic Library Managers: A Survey," *Journal of Academic Librarianship* 8:3 (July 1982), 151-154.

47 Linda K. Rambler. "Syllabus Study: Key to a Responsive Academic Library," *Journal of Academic Librarianship* 8:3 (July 1982), 155-159.

48 Marion T. Reid. "Effectiveness of the OCLC Data Base for Acquisitions Verification," *Journal of Academic Librarianship* 2:6 (January 1977), 303-326. **(145, 155)**

49 James D. Culley, Denis F. Healy and Kermit G. Cudd. "Business Students and the University Library: An Overlooked Element in the Business Curriculum," *Journal of Academic Librarianship* 2:6 (January 1977), 293-296. **(215, 230, 243)**

50 Edward Kazlauskas. "An Exploratory Study: A Kenesic Analysis of Academic Library Service Points," *Journal of Academic Librarianship* 2:3 (July 1976), 130-134. **(3)**

51 Helen Gothberg. "Immediacy: A Study of Communication Effect on the Reference Process," *Journal of Academic Librarianship* 2:3 (July 1976), 126-129. **(193)**

52 John Vasi. "Building Libraries for the Handicapped: A Second Look," *Journal of Academic Librarianship* 2:2 (May 1976), 82-83.

53 Elliot S. Palais. "The Significance of Subject Dispersion for the Indexing of Political Science Journals," *Journal of Academic Librarianship* 2:2 (May 1976), 72-76. **(167, 182, 183)**

54 Ruth Carol Cushman. "Lease Plans—A New Lease on Life for Libraries," *Journal of Academic Librarianship* 2:1 (March 1976), 15-19.

55 Charles R. McClure. "Subject and Added Entries as Access to Information," *Journal of Academic Librarianship* 2:1 (March 1976), 9-14.

56 Marilyn L. Miller and Barbara B. Moran. "Expenditures for Resources in School Library Media Centers FY '82-'83," *School Library Journal* 30:2 (October 1983), 105-114.

57 Karen Lee Shelley. "The Future of Conservation in Research Libraries," *Journal of Academic Librarianship* 1:6 (January 1976), 15-18.

58 Maryan E. Reynolds. "Challenges of Modern Network Development," *Journal of Academic Librarianship* 1:2 (May 1975), 19-22.

59 Marjorie E. Martin and Clyde Hendrick. "Ripoffs Tell Their Story: Interviews with Mutilators in a University Library," *Journal of Academic Librarianship* 1:2 (May 1975), 8-12.

60 Audrey Tobias. "The Yule Curve Describing Periodical Citations by Freshmen: Essential Tool or Abstract Frill?" *Journal of Academic Librarianship* 1:1 (March 1975), 14-16.

61 Allan J. Dyson. "Organizing Undergraduate Library Instruction," *Journal of Academic Librarianship* 1:1 (March 1975), 9-13. **(244, 249)**

62 David F. Kohl. "High Efficiency Inventorying through Predictive Data," *Journal of Academic Librarianship* 8:2 (May 1982), 82-84.

63 Eleanor Phinney. "Trends in Public Library Adult Services," *ALA Bulletin* 57:3 (March 1963), 262-266. **(17)**

64 Zelia J. French. "Library-Community Self-studies in Kansas," *ALA Bulletin* 56:1 (January 1962), 37-41.

65 Guy Garrison. "Nonresident Library Fees in Suburban Chicago," *ALA Bulletin* 55:6 (June 1961), 1013-1017.

66 James E. Bryan. "The Christmas Holiday Jam," *ALA Bulletin* 55:6 (June 1961), 526-530.

67 Joint Libraries Committee on Fair Use in Photocopying, American Library Association. "Fair Use in Photocopying: Report on Single Copies," *ALA Bulletin* 55:6 (June 1961), 571-573.

68 Henry J. Dubester. "Stack Use of a Research Library," *ALA Bulletin* 55:10 (November 1961), 891-893.

69 Mary Virginia Gaver. "Teacher Education and School Libraries," *ALA Bulletin* 60:1 (January 1966), 63-72.

70 Richard Waters. "Free Space: Can Public Libraries Receive It?" *ALA Bulletin* 58:3 (March 1964), 232-234.

71 Frank L. Schick. "Professional Library Manpower," *ALA Bulletin* 58:4 (April 1964), 315-317.

72 Milbrey Jones. "Socio-Economic Factors in Library Service to Students," *ALA Bulletin* 58:11 (December 1964), 1003-1006.

73 Elizabeth W. Stone. "Administrators Fiddle while Employees Burn or Flee," *ALA Bulletin* 63:2 (February 1969), 181-187.

74 Staff Organizations Round Table, American Library Association. "Opinions on Collective Bargaining," *ALA Bulletin* 63:6 (June 1969), 803-808.

75 Library Administration Division, American Library Association. "Library Employment of Minority Group Personnel," *ALA Bulletin* 63:7 (July-August 1969), 985-987.

76 Eli M. Oboler. "The Case for ALA Regional Annual Conferences," *ALA Bulletin* 63:8 (September 1969), 1099-1101.

77 Edward N. Howard. "Breaking the Fine Barrier," *ALA Bulletin* 63:11 (December 1969), 1541-1545.

78 Elin B. Christianson. "Variation of Editorial Material in Periodicals Indexed in *Reader's Guide*," *ALA Bulletin* 62:2 (February 1968), 173-182.

79 Insurance for Libraries Committee, American Library Association. "The Makings of a Nationwide Scandal," *ALA Bulletin* 62:4 (April 1968), 384-386.

80 George L. Gardiner. "Collective Bargaining: Some Questions Asked," *ALA Bulletin* 62:8 (September 1968), 973-976.

81 Barbara M. Conant. "Trials and Tribulations of Textbook Price Indexing," *ALA Bulletin* 61:2 (February 1967), 197-199.

82 Henry T. Drennan and Sarah R. Reed. "Library Manpower," *ALA Bulletin* 61:8 (September 1967), 957-965.

83 Jerry L. Walker. "Changing Attitudes toward the Library and the Librarian," *ALA Bulletin* 61:8 (September 1967), 977-981. **(230, 231, 232)**

84 William R. Monat. "The Community Library: Its Search for a Vital Purpose," *ALA Bulletin* 61:11 (December 1967), 1301-1310. **(209)**

85 Irene A. Braden. "Pilot Inventory of Library Holdings," *ALA Bulletin* 62:9 (October 1968), 1129-1131.

86 Genevieve Casey. "Library Manpower in the Detroit Metropolitan Region," *American Libraries* 1:8 (September 1970), 787-789.

87 Nora Cambier, Barton Clark, Robert Daugherty and Mike Gabriel. "Books in Print 1969: An Analysis of Errors," *American Libraries* 1:9 (October 1970), 901-902. **(131)**

88 Tom Childers and Beth Krevitt. "Municipal Funding of Library Services," *American Libraries* 3:1 (January 1972), 53-57.

89 Albert H. Rubenstein, David J. Werner, Gustave Rath, John A. Kernaghan, and Robert D. O'Keefe. "Search versus Experiment—the Role of the Research Librarian," *College and Research Libraries* 34:4 (July 1973), 280-286.

90 Frank F. Kuo. "A Comparison of Six Versions of Science Library Instruction," *College and Research Libraries* 34:4 (July 1973), 287-290. **(252)**

91 Laurence Miller. "The role of Circulation Services in the Major University Library," *College and Research Libraries* 34:6 (November 1973), 463-471.

92 Ruth Hyman and Gail Schlachter. "Academic Status: Who Wants It?" *College and Research Libraries* 34:6 (November 1973), 472-478.

93 Larry E. Harrelson. "Large Libraries and Information Desks," *College and Research Libraries* 35:1 (January 1974), 21-27. **(11, 12, 13, 14, 19, 20, 21, 22)**

94 Robert B. Downs. "Library Resources in the United States," *College and Research Libraries* 35:2 (March 1974), 97-108.

95 Richard J. Beeler. "Late-Study Areas: A Means of Extending Library Hours," *College and Research Libraries* 35:3 (May 1974), 200-203. **(19, 20)**

96 Rolland E. Stevens. "A Study of Interlibrary Loan," *College and Research Libraries* 35:5 (September 1974), 336-343.

97 Jay B. Clark. "An Approach to Collection Inventory," *College and Research Libraries* 35:5 (September 1974), 354-359.

98 Jan Baaske, Don Tolliver and Judy Westerberg. "Overdue Policies: A Comparison of Alternatives," *College and Research Libraries* 35:5 (September 1974), 354-359.

99 Clyde Hendrick and Marjorie E. Murfin. "Project Library Ripoff: A Study of Periodical Mutilation in a University Library," *College and Research Libraries* 35:6 (November 1974), 402-411.

100 Peter Marshall. "How Much, How Often?" *College and Research Libraries* 35:6 (November 1974), 453-456.

101 Robert Balay and Christine Andres. "Use of the Reference Service in a Large Academic Library," *College and Research Libraries* 36:1 (January 1975), 9-26. **(214, 217, 218)**

102 Guy Walker. "Preservation Efforts in Larger U.S. Academic Libraries," *College and Research Libraries* 36:1 (January 1975), 39-44.

103 Susanne Patterson Wahba. "Job Satisfaction of Librarians: A Comparison between Men and Women," *College and Research Libraries* 36:1 (January 1975), 45-51.

104 Grant T. Skelley. "Characteristics of Collections Added to American Research Libraries 1940-1970: A Preliminary Investigation," *College and Reseach Libraries* 36:1 (January 1975), 52-60.

105 Laura M. Boyer and William C. Theimer, Jr. "The Use and Training of Nonprofessional Personnel at Reference Desks in Selected College and University Libraries," *College and Research Libraries* 36:3 (May 1975), 193-200. (11, 13, 20)

106 Robert J. Greene. "LENDS: An Approach to the Centralization/Decentralization Dilemma," *College and Research Libraries* 36:3 (May 1975), 201-207.

107 Frances L. Meals and Walter T. Johnson. "We Chose Microfilm," *College and Research Libraries* 21:3 (May 1960), 223-228.

108 George Caldwell. "University Libraries and Government Publications: A Survey," *College and Research Libraries* 22:1 (January 1961), 30-34.

109 Allen Story. "Leo in Libraryland," *American Libraries* 7:9 (October 1976), 569-571.

110 Leslie R. Morris. "The Rise and Fall of the Library Job Market," *American Libraries* 12:9 (October 1981), 557-558.

111 Richard De Gennaro. "Escalating Journal Prices: Time To Fight Back," *American Libraries* 8:1 (January 1977), 69-74.

112 Joe A. Hewitt. "The Impact of OCLC," *American Libaries* 7:5 (May 1976), 268-275.

113 Fritz Veit. "Book Order Procedures in the Publicly Controlled Colleges and Universities of the Midwest," *College and Research Libraries* 23:1 (January 1962), 33-40.

114 Keyes D. Metcalf. "Compact Shelving," *College and Research Libraries* 23:2 (March 1962), 103-111.

115 Natalie N. Nicholson and Eleanor Bartlett. "Who Uses University Libraries," *College and Research Libraries* 23:3 (May 1962), 217-259.

116 H. William Axford. "Rider Revisited," *College and Research Libraries* 23:4 (July 1962), 345-347.

117   E.J. Josey. "The Role of the College Library Staff in Instruction in the Use of the Library," *College and Research Libraries* 23:6 (November 1962), 492-498. **(244)**

118   Edwin E. Williams. "Magnitude of the Paper-Deterioration Problems as Measured by a National Union Catalog Sample," *College and Research Libraries* 23:6 (November 1962), 499.

119   Stella Frank Mosborg. "Measuring Circulation Desk Activities Using a Random Alarm Mechanism," *College and Research Libraries* 41:5 (September 1980), 437-444.

120   Jean E. Koch and Judith M. Pask. "Working Papers in Academic Business Libraries," *College and Research Libraries* 41:6 (November 1980), 517-523.

121   Paul Metz. "Administrative Succession in the Academic Library," *College and Research Libraries* 39:5 (September 1978), 358-364.

122   Libby Trudell and James Wolper. "Interlibrary Loan in New England," *College and Research Libraries* 39:5 (September 1978), 365-371.

123   Richard M. Dougherty. "The Evaluation of Campus Library Document Delivery Service," *College and Research Libraries* 34:1 (January 1973), 29-39.

124   Ung Chon Kim. "A Comparison of Two Out-of-Print Book Buying Methods," *College and Research Libraries* 34:5 (September 1973), 258-264.

125   Ann Gwyn, Anne McArthur and Karen Furlow. "Friends of the Library," *College and Research Libraries* 36:4 (July 1975), 272-282.

126   John J. Knightly. "Library Collections and Academic Curricula: Quantitative Relationships," *College and Research Libraries* 36:4 (July 1975), 295-301.

127   Alice S. Clark and Rita Hirschman. "Using the 'Guidelines': A Study of the State-Supported Two-Year College Libraries in Ohio," *College and Research Libraries* 36:5 (September 1975), 364-370.

128   Virginia E. Yagello and Gerry Gutherie. "The Effect of Reduced Loan Periods on High Use Items," *College and Research Libraries* 36:5 (September 1975), 411-414.

129   George Piternick. "Library Growth and Academic Quality," *College and Research Libraries* 24:3 (May 1963), 223-229.

130   Robert N. Broadus. "An Analysis of Faculty Circulation in a University Library," *College and Research Libraries* 24:4 (July 1963), 323-325.

131   Perry D. Morrison. "The Personality of the Academic Librarian," *College and Research Libraries* 24:5 (September 1963), 365-368.

132   W.J. Bonk. "What is Basic Reference?" *College and Research Libraries* 25:3 (May 1964), 5-8. **(130, 220)**

133   Jean Legg "The Periodical Scene," *RQ* 7:3 (Spring 1968), 129-132. **(124)**

134   Richard H. Perrine. "Catalog Use Difficulties," *RQ* 7:4 (Summer 1968), 169-174. **(112)**

135   Thelma E. Larson. "A Survey of User Orientation Methods," *RQ* 8:3 (Spring 1969), 182-187. **(247, 255, 256)**

136   Phil Hoehn and Jean Hudson. "Academic Library Staffing Patterns," *RQ* 8:4 (Summer 1969), 242-244. **(10, 12, 18, 32)**

137   T.H. Milby. "Two Approaches to Biology," *RQ* 11:3 (Spring 1972), 231-235. **(169, 170, 187)**

138   James B. Way. "Loose Leaf Business Services," *RQ* 9:2 (Winter 1969), 128-133. **(125, 126)**

139   Mary Jane Swope and Jeffrey Katzer. "Why Don't They Ask Questions?" *RQ* 12:2 (Winter 1972), 161-165.

140   Robert M. Simmons. "Finding That Government Document," *RQ* 12:2 (Winter 1972), 167-171. **(221)**

141   Lee Regan. "Status of Reader's Advisory Service," *RQ* 12:3 (Spring 1973), 227-233.

142   Bruce Cossar. "Interlibrary Loan Costs," *RQ* 12:3 (Spring 1973), 243-246.

143   Mary R. Turtle and William C. Robinson. "The Relationship between Time Lag and Place of Publication in *Library and Information Science Abstracts* and *Library Literature*," *RQ* 14:1 (Fall 1974), 28-31. **(173, 174, 186, 188)**

144   Rosemary Magrill and Charles H. Davis. "Public Library SDI; A Pilot Study," *RQ* 14:2 (Winter 1974), 131-137. **(196)**

145   Steve Parker and Kathy Essary. "A Manual SDI System for Academic Libraries," *RQ* 15:1 (Fall 1975), 47-54. **(195)**

146   Carl F. Orgren and Barbara J. Olson. "Statewide Teletype Reference Service," *RQ* 15:3 (Spring 1976), 203-209. **(8, 14, 214)**

147   Anne S. Mavor, Jose Orlando Toro and Ernest R. Deprospo. "An Overview of the National Adult Independent Learning Project," *RQ* 15:4 (Summer 1976), 293-308.

148   Danuta A. Nitecki. "Attitudes toward Automated Information Retrieval Services among RASD Members," *RQ* 16:2 (Winter 1976), 133-141. **(32, 33, 41, 62, 107, 212)**

149   Rhoda Garoogian. "Library Use of the New York Times Information Bank: A Preliminary Survey," *RQ* 16:1 (Fall 1976), 59-64. **(55, 57, 87, 89)** ,

150 Marcella Ciucki. "Recording of Reference/Information Service Activities: A Study of Forms Currently Used," *RQ* 16:4 (Summer 1977), 273-283. **(193)**

151 Mollie Sandock. "A Study of University Students' Awareness of Reference Services," *RQ* 16:4 (Summer 1977), 284-296. **(223, 224)**

152 Kathleen Imhoff and Larry Brandwein. "Labor Collections and Services in Public Libraries throughout the United States, 1976," *RQ* 17:2 (Winter 1977), 149-158. **(210)**

153 Cynthia Swenk and Wendy Robinson. "A Comparison of the Guides to Abstracting and Indexing Services Provided by Katz, Chicorel and Ulrich," *RQ* (Summer 1978), 317-319. **(164, 165)**

154 John P. Wilkinson and William Miller. "The Step Approach to Reference Service," *RQ* (Summer 1978), 293-299. **(216, 219)**

155 Gerald Johoda, Alan Bayer and William L. Needham. "A Comparison of On-Line Bibliographic Searches in One Academic and One Industrial Organization," *RQ* 18:1 (Fall 1978), 42-49. **(35, 40, 56, 59, 80, 83)**

156 Stephen P. Harter and Mary Alice S. Fields. "Circulation, Reference and the Evaluation of Public Library Service," *RQ* 18:2 (Winter 1978), 147-152. **(225)**

157 Daniel Rearn. "An Evaluation of Four Book Review Journals," *RQ* 19:2 (Winter 1979), 149-153. **(185)**

158 Joseph W. Palmer. "Review Citations for Best-Selling Books," *RQ* 19:2 (Winter 1979), 154-158. **(136)**

159 "An Evaluation of References to Indexes and Abstracts in Ulrich's 17th Edition," *RQ* 20:2 (Winter 1980), 155-159. **(165)**

160 Victoria T. Kok and Anton R. Pierce. "The Reference Desk Survey: A Management Tool in an Academic Research Library," *RQ* 22:2 (Winter 1982), 181-187. **(219)**

161 Sheila S. Intner. "Equality of Cataloging in the Age of AACR2," *American Libraries* 14:2 (February 1983), 102-103.

162 Joseph W. Palmer. "The Future of Public Library Film Service," *American Libraries* 13:2 (February 1982), 140-142.

163 Robert Grover and Mary Kevin Moore. "Print Dominates Library Service to Children," *American Libraries* 13:4 (April 1982), 268-269.

164 Richard H. Evensen and Mary Berghaus Levering. "Services Are 500% Better," *American Libraries* 10:6 (June 1979), 373.

165 Judith Schick. "Job Mobility of Men and Women Librarians and How It Affects Career Advancement," *American Libraries* 10:11 (December 1979), 643-647.

166   Elizabeth Rountree. "Users and Nonusers Disclose Their Needs," *American Libraries* 10:8 (September 1979), 486-487. **(108)**

167   George Bobinski. "A Survey of Faculty Loan Policies," *College and Research Libraries* 24:6 (November 1963), 483-486. add

168   L. Miles Raisig and Frederick G. Kilgour. "The Use of Medical Theses as Demonstrated by Journal Citations, 1850-1960," *College and Research Libraries* 25:2 (March 1964), 93-102.

169   George H. Fadenrecht. "Library Facilities and Practices in Colleges of Veterinary Medicine," *College and Research Libraries* 25:4 (July 1964), 308-335.

170   Donald Thompson. "Working Conditions in Selected Private College Libraries," *College and Research Libraries* 25:4 (July 1964), 261-294.

171   Benedict Brooks and Frederick G. Kilgour. "Catalog Subject Searches in the Yale Medical Library," *College and Research Libraries* 25:6 (November 1964), 483-487. **(111)**

172   Patrick Barkey. "Patterns of Student Use of a College Library," *College and Research Libraries* 26:2 (March 1965), 115-118.

173   Genevieve Porterfield. "Staffing of Interlibrary Loan Service," *College and Research Libraries* 26:4 (July 1965), 318-320.

174   Harold Mathis. "Professional or Clerical: A Cross-Validation Study," *College and Research Libraries* 26:6 (November 1965), 525-531.

175   David H. Doerrer. 'Overtime' and the Academic Librarian," *College and Research Libraries* 27:3 (May 1966), 194-239.

176   Lois L. Luesing. "Church Historical Collections in Liberal Arts Colleges," *College and Research Libraries* 27:5 (July 1966), 291-317.

177   W.C. Blankenship. "Head Librarians: How Many Men? How Many Women?" *College and Research Libraries* 28:1 (January 1967), 41-48.

178   Morrison C. Haviland. "Loans to Faculty Members in University Libraries," *College and Research Libraries* 28:3 (May 1967), 171-174.

179   R. Vernon Ritter. "An Investigation of Classroom-Library Relationships on a College Campus as Seen in Recorded Circulation and GPA's," *College and Research Libraries* 29:1 (January 1968), 3-4.

180   Peter Spyers-Duran. "Faculty Studies: A Survey of Their Use in Selected Libraries," *College and Research Libraries* 29:1 (January 1968), 55-61.

181   Raymond Kilpela. "The University Library Committee," *College and Research Libraries* 29:2 (March 1968), 141-143.

182 W. Porter Kellam and Dale L. Barker. "Activities and Opportunities of University Librarians for Full Participation in the Educational Enterprise," *College and Research Libraries* 29:5 (May 1968), 195-199.

183 Lloyd A. Kramer and Martha B. Kramer. "The College Library and the Drop-Out," *College and Research Libraries* 29:4 (July 1968), 310-312.

184 Carl Hintz. "Criteria for Appointment to and Promotion in Academic Rank," *College and Research Libraries* 29:5 (September 1968), 341-346.

185 Desmond Taylor. "Classification Trends in Junior College Libraries," *College and Research Libraries* 29:6 (September 1968), 351-356.

186 Raj Madan, Eliese Hetler and Marilyn Strong. "The Status of Librarians in Four-Year State Colleges and Universities," *College and Research Libraries* 29:5 (September 1968), 381-386.

187 Victor Novak. "The Librarian in Catholic Institutions," *College and Research Libraries* 29:5 (September 1968), 403-410.

188 Barbara H. Phipps. "Library Instruction for the Undergraduate," *College and Research Libraries* 29:5 (September 1968), 411-423. **(233, 248, 255)**

189 Ashby J. Fristoe. "Paperbound Books: Many Problems, No Solutions," *College and Research Libraries* 29:5 (September 1968), 437-442.

190 Sidney Forman. "Innovative Practices in College Libraries," *College and Research Libraries* 29:6 (November 1968), 486-492. **(208, 248)**

191 Richard W. Trueswell. "Some Circulation Data from a Research Library," *College and Research Libraries* 29:6 (November 1968), 493-495.

192 Jane P. Kleiner. "The Information Desk: The Library's Gateway to Service," *College and Research Libraries* 29:6 (November 1968), 496-501. **(18, 21, 23, 208)**

193 J.E.G. Craig, Jr. "Characteristics of Use of Geology Literature," *College and Research Libraries* 3:3 (May 1969), 230-236.

194 Ronald A. Hoppe and Edward C. Simmel. "Book Tearing: The Bystander in the University Library," *College and Research Libraries* 3:3 (May 1969), 247-251.

195 Stephen L. Peterson. "Patterns of Use of Periodical Literature," *College and Research Libraries* 30:5 (September 1969), 422-430. **(214)**

196 Mary B. Cassata. "Teach-in: The Academic Librarian's Key to Status," *College and Research Libraries* 31:1 (January 1970), 22-27. **(233, 244, 247)**

197 E.J. Josey. "Community Use of Junior College Libraries—A Symposium," *College and Research Libraries* 31:3 (May 1970), 185-198.

198 Virgil F. Massman. "Academic Library Salaries in a Seven-State Area," *College and Research Libraries* 3:6 (November 1969), 477-482.

199   James Krikelas. "Subject Searches Using Two Catalogs: A Comparative Evaluation," *College and Research Libraries* 30:6 (November 1969), 506-517. **(112)**

200   James Wright. "Fringe Benefits for Academic Library Personnel," *College and Research Libraries* 31:1 (January 1970), 18-21.

201   Howard Clayton. "Femininity and Job Satisfaction among Male Library Students at One Midwestern University," *College and Research Libraries* 31:6 (November 1970), 388-398.

202   Philip V. Rzasa and John H. Moriarty. "The Types and Needs of Academic Library Users: A Case Study of 6,568 Responses," *College and Research Libraries* 31:6 (November 1970),403-409.

203   Bob Carmack and Trudi Loeber. "The Library Reserve System—Another Look," *College and Research Libraries* 32:2 (March 1971), 105-109.

204   C. James Schmidt and Kay Shaffer. "A Cooperative Interlibrary Loan Service for the State-Assisted University Libraries in Ohio," *College and Research Libraries* 32:3 (May 1971), 197-204.

205   Edward S. Warner. "A Tentative Analytical Approach to the Determination of Interlibrary Loan Network Effectiveness," *College and Research Libraries* 32:3 (May 1971), 217-221.

206   Irving Zelkind and Joseph Sprug. "Increased Control through Decreased Controls: A Motivational Approach to a Library Circulation Problem," *College and Research Libraries* 32:3 (May 1971), 222-226.

207   William E. McGrath. "Correlating the Subjects of Books Taken Out Of and Books Used Within an Open-Stack Library," *College and Research Libraries* 32:4 (July 1971), 280-285.

208   Thomas Kirk. "A Comparison of Two Methods of Library Instruction for Students in Introductory Biology," *College and Research Libraries* 32:6 (November 1971), 465-474. **(236, 238, 251)**

209   Dawn McCaghy and Gary Purcell. "Faculty Use of Government Publications," *College and Research Libraries* 33:1 (January 1972), 7-12. **(218)**

210   Joe A. Hewitt. "Sample Audit of Cards from a University Library Catalog," *College and Research Libraries* 33:1 (January 1972), 24-27. **(144, 145)**

211   William E. McGrath. "The Significance of Books Used According to a Classified Profile of Academic Departments," *College and Research Libraries* 33:3 (May 1972), 212-219.

212   Carlos A. Cuadra and Ruth J. Patrick. "Survey of Academic Library Consortia in the U.S.," *College and Research Libraries* 33:4 (July 1972), 271-283.

213   Marjorie Johnson. "Performance Appraisal of Librarians—A Survey," *College and Research Libraries* 33:5 (September 1972), 359-367.

214 Marvin E. Wiggins. "The Development of Library Use Instruction Programs," *College and Research Libraries* 33:6 (November 1972), 473-479. **(238, 249, 251)**

215 Margaret E. Monroe. "Community Development as a Mode of Community Analysis," *Library Trends* 24:3 (January 1976), 497-514.

216 Janet K. Rudd and Larry G. Carver. "Topographic Map Acquisition in U.S. Academic Libraries," *Library Trends* 29:3 Winter 1981), 375-390.

217 John Belland. "Factors Influencing Selection of Materials," *School Media Quarterly* 6:2 (Winter 1978), 112-119.

218 Virginia Witucke. "A Comparative Analysis of Juvenile Book Review Media," *School Media Quarterly* 8:3 (Spring 1980), 153-160. **(138, 139, 141)**

219 M. Carl Drott and Jacqueline C. Mancall. "Magazines as Information Sources: Patterns of Student Use," *School Media Quarterly* 8:4 (Summer 1980), 240-250.

220 Jerry J. Watson and Bill C. Snider. "Book Selection Pressure on School Library Media Specialists and Teachers," *School Media Quarterly* 9:2 (Winter 1981), 95-101.

221 Jerry J. Watson and Bill C. Snider. "Educating the Potential Self-Censor," *School Media Quarterly* 9:4 (Summer 1981), 272-276.

222 Lucy Anne Wozny. "Online Bibliographic Searching and Student Use of Information: An Innovative Teaching Approach," *School Library Media Quarterly* 11:1 (Fall 1982), 35-42. **(72, 110)**

223 Carol A. Doll. "School and Public Library Collection Overlap and the Implications for Networking," *School Library Media Quarterly* 11:3 (Spring 1983), 193-199.

224 Arthur Tannenbaum and Eva Sidhom. "User Environment and Attitudes in an Academic Microform Center," *Library Journal* 101:18 (October 15, 1976), 2139-2143.

225 Timothy Hays, Kenneth D. Shearer and Concepcion Wilson. "The Patron Is Not the Public," *Library Journal* 102:16 (September 15, 1977), 1813-1818. **(129)**

226 Wilma Lee Woolard. "The Combined School and Public Library: Can It Work?" *Library Journal* 103:4 (February 15, 1978), 435-438.

227 David C. Genaway. "Bar Coding and the Librarian Supermarket: An Analysis of Advertised Library Vacancies," *Library Journal* 103:3 (February 1, 1978), 322-325.

228 Hoyt Galvin. "Public Library Parking Needs," *Library Journal* 103:2 (November 15, 1978), 2310-2313.

229   Harold J. Ettelt. "Book Use at a Small (Very) Community College Library," *Library Journal* 103:2 (November 15, 1978), 2314-2315.

230   Frederick G. Kilgour. "Interlibrary Loans On-Line," *Library Journal* 104:4 (February 15, 1979), 460-463.

231   Paul Little. "The Effectiveness of Paperbacks," *Library Journal* 104:2 (November 15, 1979), 2411-2416.

232   Ken Kister. "Encyclopedias and the Public Library: A National Survey," *Library Journal* 104:8 (April 15, 1979), 890-893. **(150, 220)**

233   Arlene T. Dowell. "Discrepancies in CIP: How Serious Is the Problem," *Library Journal* 104:19 (November 1, 1979), 2281-2287.

234   Gary D. Byrd, Mary Kay Smith and Norene McDonald. "MINET in K.C.," *Library Journal* 104:17 (October 1, 1979), 2044-2047. **(33, 86, 98, 103)**

235   Ray L. Carpenter. "The Public Library Patron," *Library Journal* 104:3 (February 1, 1979), 347-351.

236   Cathy Schell. "Preventive Medicine: The Library Prescription," *Library Journal* 105:8 (April 15, 1980), 929-931. **(211)**

237   Michael Gonzalez, Bill Greeley and Stephen Whitney. "Assessing the Library Needs of the Spanish-speaking," *Library Journal* 105:7 (April 1, 1980), 786-789.

238   Thomas Childers. "The Test of Reference," *Library Journal* 105:8 (April 15, 1980), 924-928. **(15)**

239   Mary Noel Gouke and Marjorie Murfin. "Periodical Mutilization: The Insidious Disease," *Library Journal* 105:16 (September 15, 1980), 1795-1797.

240   Sheila Creth and Faith Harders. "Requirements for the Entry Level Librarian," *Library Journal* 105:18 (October 15, 1980), 2168-2169.

241   Kathleen M. Heim and Leigh S. Estabrook. "Career Patterns of Librarians," *Drexel Library Quarterly* 17:3 (Summer 1981), 35-51.

242   Margaret Peil. "Library Use by Low-Income Chicago Families," *Library Quarterly* 33:4 (October 1963), 329-333.

243   Herbert Goldhor and John McCrossan. "An Exploratory Study of the Effect of a Public Library Summer Reading Club on Reading Skills," *Library Quarterly* 36:1 (June 1966), 14-24.

244   Robert Sommer. "Reading Areas in College Libraries," *Library Quarterly* 38:3 (July 1968), 249-260.

245   Isaac T. Littleton. "The Literature of Agricultural Economics: Its Bibliographic Organization and Use," *Library Quarterly* 39:2 (April 1969), 140-152. **(125, 168)**

246 G. Edward Evans. "Book Selection and Book Collection Usage in Academic Libraries," *Library Quarterly* 40:3 (July 1970), 297-308.

247 Marilyn Werstein Greenberg. "A Study of Reading Motivation of Twenty-Three Seventh-Grade Students," *Library Quarterly* 40:3 (July 1970), 309-317.

248 Ben-Ami Lipetz. "Catalog Use in a Large Research Library," *Library Quarterly* 42:1 (January 1972), 129-130. **(113, 114)**

249 John Aubry. "A Timing Study of the Manual Searching of Catalogs," *Library Quarterly* 42:4 (October 1972), 399-415.

250 Kenneth H. Plate and Elizabeth W. Stone. "Factors Affecting Librarians' Job Satisfaction: A Report of Two Studies," *Library Quarterly* 44:2 (April 1974), 97-109.

251 Elizabeth Warner McElroy. "Subject Variety in Adult Reading: I. Factors Related to Variety in Reading," *Library Quarterly* 38:1 (April 1968), 154-167.

252 James C. Baughman. "A Structural Analysis of the Literature of Sociology," *Library Quarterly* 44:4 (October 1974), 293-308.

253 Edd E. Wheeler. "The Bottom Lines: Fifty Years of Legal Footnoting in Review," *Law Library Journal* 72:2 (Spring 1979), 245-259.

254 Daniel O'Connor and Phyllis Van Orden. "Getting into Print," *College and Research Libraries* 39:5 (September 1978), 389-396.

255 Howard Fosdick. "Library Education in Information Science: Present Trends," *Special Libraries* 69:3 (March 1978), 100-108.

256 Paula de Simone Watson. "Publication Activity among Academic Librarians," *College and Research Libraries* 38:5 (September 1977), 375-384.

257 Susan Andriette Ariew. "The Failure of the Open Access Residence Hall Library," *College and Research Libraries* 39:5 (September 1978), 372-380.

258 Mary Ellen Soper. "Characteristics and Use of Personal Collections," *Library Quarterly* (October 1976), 397-415.

259 Ronald R. Powell. "An Investigation of the Relationships Between Quantifiable Reference Service Variables and Reference Performance in Public Libraries," *Library Quarterly* 48:1 (January 1978), 1-19. **(9, 16, 213)**

260 Mary Jo Lynch. "Reference Interviews in Public Libraries," *Library Quarterly* 48:2 (April 1978), 119-142. **(193, 220)**

261 William A. Satariano. "Journal Use in Sociology: Citation Analysis versus Readership Patterns," *Library Quarterly* 48:3 (July 1978), 293-300.

262   Paul Metz. "The Use of the General Collection in the Library of Congress," *Library Quarterly* 49:4 (October 1979), 415-434.

263   Michael Halperin and Maureen Strazdon. "Measuring Students' Preferences for Reference Service: A Conjoint Analysis," *Library Quarterly* 50:2 (April 1980), 208-224. **(209)**

264   Herbert S. White. "Factors in the Decisions by Individuals and Libraries To Place or Cancel Subscriptions to Scholarly and Research Journals," *Library Quarterly* 50:3 (July 1980), 287-309.

265   George D'Elia. "The Development and Testing of a Conceptual Model of Public Library User Behavior," *Library Quarterly* 50:4 (October 1980), 410-430.

266   Donald A. Hicks. "Diversifying Fiscal Support by Pricing Public Library Services: A Policy Impact Analysis," *Library Quarterly* 50:4 (October 1980), 453-474.

267   Theodora Hodges and Uri Block. "Fiche or Film for COM Catalogs: Two Use Tests," *Library Quarterly* 52:2 (April 1982), 131-144. **(118, 119)**

268   Terry L. Weech and Herbert Goldhor. "Obtrusive versus Unobtrusive Evaluation of Reference Service in Five Illinois Public Libraries: A Pilot Study," *Library Quarterly* 52:4 (October 1982), 305-324. **(17)**

269   Stephen E. Wiberley, Jr. "Journal Rankings From Citation Studies: A Comparison of National and Local Data From Social Work," *Library Quarterly* 52:4 (October 1982), 348-359.

270   George D'Elia and Sandra Walsh. "User Satisfaction with Library Service— A Measure of Public Library Performance?" *Library Quarterly* 53:2 (April 1983), 109-133.

271   Edward A. Dyl. "A Note on Price Discrimination by Academic Journals," *Library Quarterly* 53:2 (April 1983), 161-168.

272   Michael R. Kronenfeld and James A. Thompson. "The Impact of Inflation on Journal Costs," *Library Journal* 106:7 (April 1,1981), 714-717.

273   George D'Elia and Mary K. Chelton. "Paperback Books," *Library Journal* 107:16 (September 15, 1982), 1718-1721.

274   Patsy Hansel and Robert Burgin. "Hard Facts about Overdues," *Library Journal* 108:4 (February 15, 1983), 349-352.

275   Robert Dale Karr. "Becoming a Library Director," *Library Journal* 108:4 (February 15, 1983), 343-346.

276   Mary V. Gaver. "The Science Collection—New Evidence To Consider," *Junior Libraries* (later *School Library Journal*) 7:6 (February 1961), 4-7.

277   Dorothy G. Petersen. "Teachers' Professional Reading," *School Library Journal* 9:8 (April 1963), 24-27.

278 Linda Kraft. "Lost Herstory: The Treatment of Women in Children's Encyclopedias," *School Library Journal* 19:5 (January 1973), 26-35. **(150, 152)**

279 John Stewig and Margaret Higgs. "Girls Grow Up: A Study of Sexism in Children's Literature," *School Library Journal* 19:5 (January 1973), 44-49.

280 W. Bernard Lukenbill. "Fathers in Adolescent Novels," *School Library Journal* 20:6 (February 1974), 26-30.

281 Jacqueline C. Mancall and M. Carl Drott. "Tomorrow's Scholars: Patterns of Facilities Use," *School Library Journal* 20:7 (March 1980), 99-103.

282 John McCrossan. "Education of Librarians Employed in Small Public Libraries," *Journal of Education for Librarianship* 7:4 (Spring 1967), 237-245.

283 Gail Schlachter and Dennis Thomison. "The Library Science Doctorate: A Quantitative Analysis of Dissertations and Recipients," *Journal of Education for Librarianship* 15:2 (Fall 1974), 95-111.

284 Constance Rinehart and Rose Mary Magrill. "Characteristics of Applicants for Library Science Teaching Positions," *Journal of Education for Librarianship* 16:3 (Winter 1976), 173-182.

285 George W. Whitbeck. "Grade Inflation in the Library School—Myth or Reality," *Journal of Education for Librarianship* 17:4 (Spring 1977), 214-237.

286 Charles H. Davis. "Computer Programming for Librarians," *Journal of Education for Librarianship* 18:1 (Summer 1977), 41-52.

287 Helen M. Gothberg. "A Study of the Audio-Tutorial Approach to Teaching Basic Reference," *Journal of Education for Librarianship* 18:3 (Winter 1978), 193-202.

288 J. Periam Danton. "British and American Library School Teaching Staffs: A Comparative Inquiry," *Journal of Education for Librarianship* 19:2 (Fall 1978), 97-129.

289 Lucille Whalen. "The Role of the Assistant Dean in Library Schools," *Journal of Education for Librarianship* 20:1 (Summer 1979), 44-54.

290 A. Neil Yerkey. "Values of Library School Students, Faculty and Librarians: Premises for Understanding," *Journal of Education for Librarianship* 21:2 (Fall 1980), 122-134.

291 Judith B. Katz. "Indicators of Success: Queens College Department of Library Science," *Journal of Education for Librarianship* 19:2 (Fall 1978), 130-139.

292 Lawrence Auld, Kathleen H. Heim and Jerome Miller. "Market Receptivity for an Extended M.L.S.," *Journal of Education for Librarianship* 21:3 (Winter 1981), 235-245.

293   John Richardson, Jr. and Peter Hernon. "Theory vs. Practice: Student Preferences," *Journal of Education for Librarianship* 21:4 (Spring 1981), 287-300.

294   Richard I. Blue and James L. Divilbiss. "Optimizing Selection of Library School Students," *Journal of Education for Librarianship* 21:4 (Spring 1981), 301-312.

295   David H. Jonassen and Gerald G. Hodges. "Student Cognitive Styles: Implications for Library Educators," *Journal of Education for Librarianship* 22:3 (Winter 1982), 143-153.

296   Mary Kingsbury. "How Library Schools Evaluate Faculty Performance," *Journal of Education for Librarianship* 22:4 (Spring 1982), 219-238.

297   John W. Lee and Raymond L. Read. "The Graduate Business Student and the Library," *College and Research Libraries* 33:5 (September 1972), 403-407. **(243)**

298   Carol Steer. "Authors Are Studied," *Canadian Library Journal* 39:3 (June 1982), 151-155.

299   Rashid Tayyeb. "Implementing AACR 2—A National Survey," *Canadian Library Journal* 39:6 (December 1982), 373-376.

300   Dick Matzek and Scott Smith. "Online Searching in the Small College Library—The Economics and the Results,"   *Online* (March 1982), 21-29. **(49, 101)**

301   Mary Lee Bundy. "Metropolitan Public Library Use," *Wilson Library Bulletin* 41:9 (May 1967), 950-961. **(108)**

302   John Shipman. "Signifying Renewal as Well as Change: One Library's Experience with the Center for Research Libraries," *Library Acquisitions: Practice and Theory* 2:5 (1978), 243-248.

303   Nathan R. Einhorn. "The Inclusion of the Products of Reprography in the International Exchange of Publications," *Library Acquisitions: Practice and Theory* 2:5 (1978), 227-236

304   Nancy J. Williamson. "Education for Acquisitions Librarians: A State of the Art Review," *Library Acquisitions: Practice and Theory* 2:3-4 (1978), 199-208.

305   Janet L. Flowers. "Time Logs for Searchers: How Useful?" *Library Acquisitions: Practice and Theory* 2:2 (1978), 77-83.

306   D.N. Wood. "Current Exchange of Serials at the British Library Lending Division," *Library Acquisitions: Practice and Theory* 3:2 (1979), 107-113.

307   Robert Goehlert. "Journal Use Per Monetary Unit: A Reanalysis of Use Data," *Library Acquisitions: Practice and Theory* 3:2 (1979), 91-98.

308 Margaret Landesman and Christopher Gates. "Performance of American Inprint Vendors: A Comparison at the University of Utah," *Library Acquisitions: Practice and Theory* 4:3-4 (1980), 187-192.

309 Kenton Pattie and Mary Ernst. "Chapter II Grants: Libraries Gain," *School Library Journal* 29:5 (January 1983), 17-19.

310 John Erlandson and Yvonne Boyer. "Acquistions of State Documents," *Library Acquisitions: Practice and Theory* 4:2 (1980), 117-127.

311 George V. Hodowanec. "Analysis of Variables Which Help To Predict Book and Periodical Use," *Library Acquisitions: Practice and Theory* 4:1 (1980), 75-85.

312 Darrell L. Jenkins. "Acquiring Acquisitions Librarians," *Library Acquisitions: Practice and Theory* 5:2 (1981), 81-87.

313 Steven E. Maffeo. "Invoice Payment by Library Acquisitions: A Controlled Time Study," *Library Acquisitions: Practice and Theory* 5:2 (1981), 67-71.

314 Joyce G. McDonough, Carol Alf O'Connor and Thomas A. O'Connor. "Moving the Backlog: An Optimum Cycle for Searching OCLC," *Library Acquisitions: Practice and Theory* 6:3 (1982), 265-270.

315 Paul B. Wiener. "Recreational Reading Services in Academic Libraries: An Overview," *Library Acquisitions: Practice and Theory* 6:1 (1982), 59-70.

316 Peter Hernon. "Use of Microformatted Government Publications," *Microform Review* 11:4 (Fall 1982), 237-252. **(123)**

317 Charles R. McClure. "Online Government Documents Data Base Searching and the Use of Microfiche Documents Online by Academic and Public Depository Librarians," *Microfilm Review* 10:4 (Fall 1981), 245-259. **(36, 37, 38, 60, 61, 72, 88, 89, 92, 105, 106)**

318 Peter Hernon and George W. Whitbeck. "Government Publications and Commercial Microform Publishers: A Survey of Federal Depository Libraries," *Microform Review* 6:5 (September 1977), 272-284.

319 Robert F. Jennings and Hathia Hayes. "The Use of Microfiche Copies of Children's Trade Books in Selected Fourth-Grade Classrooms," *Microform Review* 3:3 (July 1974), 189-193.

320 E.R. Norten. "New Books in Microform: A Survey," *Microform Review* 1:4 (October 1972), 284-288.

321 Renata Tagliacozzo, Manfred Kochen and Lawrence Rosenberg. "Orthographic Error Patterns of Author Names in Catalog Searches," *Journal of Library Automation* 3:2 (June 1970), 93-101. **(112, 113)**

322 Lorne R. Buhr. "Selective Dissemination of MARC: A User Evaluation," *Journal of Library Automation* 5:1 (March 1972), 39-50. **(202, 205)**

323 Gerry D. Guthrie and Steven D. Slifko. "Analysis of Search Key Retrieval on a Large Bibliographic File," *Journal of Library Automation* 6:2 (June 1972), 96-100. **(200)**

324 Alan L. Landgraf and Frederick G. Kilgour. "Catalog Records Retrieved by Personal Author Using Derived Search Keys," *Journal of Library Automation* 6:2 (June 1973), 103-108.

325 Martha E. Williams. "Data Element Statistics for the MARC II Data Base," *Journal of Library Automation* 6:2 (June 1976), 89-100.

326 Michael D. Cooper and Nancy A. DeWath. "The Cost of On-Line Bibliographic Searching," *Journal of Library Automation* 9:3 (September 1976), 195-209. **(37, 49, 70, 73, 74, 76, 84, 89, 95, 96)**

327 Edward John Kazlauskas. "The Application of the Instrumental Development Process to a Module on Flowcharting," *Journal of Library Automation* 9:3 (September 1976), 234-244.

328 Lawrence K. Legard and Charles P. Bourne. "An Improved Title Word Search Key for Large Catalog Files," *Journal of Library Automation* 9:4 (December 1976), 318-327.

329 Ryan E. Hoover. "Patron Appraisal of Computer-Aided On-Line Bibliographic Retrieval Services," *Journal of Library Automation* 9:4 (December 1976), 335-350. **(34, 43, 55, 75, 87, 93, 100, 104)**

330 T.D.C. Kuch. "Analysis of the Literature of Library Automation through Citations in the *Annual Review of Information Science and Technology*," *Journal of Library Automation* 10:1 (March 1977), 82-84.

331 Isobel Jean Mosley. "Cost-Effectiveness Analysis of the Automation of a Circulation System," *Journal of Library Automation* 10:3 (September 1977), 240-254.

332 Michael D. Cooper and Nancy A. DeWath. "The Effect of User Fees on the Cost of On-Line Searching in Libraries," *Journal of Library Automation* 10:4 (December 1977), 304-319. **(50, 66, 67, 71, 74, 76, 85, 89, 96, 105)**

333 James W. Bourg, Douglas Lacy, James Llinas and Edward T. O'Neill. "Developing Corporate Author Search Keys," *Journal of Library Automation* 11:2 (June 1978), 106-125.

334 Cynthia C. Ryans. "A Study of Errors Found in Non-MARC Cataloging in a Machine-Assisted System," *Journal of Library Automation* 11:2 (June 1978), 125-132.

335 Joselyn Druschel. "Cost Analysis of an Automated and Manual Cataloging and Book Processing System," *Journal of Library Automation* 14:1 (March 1981), 24-49.

336 Kunj B. Bastogi and Ichiko T. Morita. "OCLC Search Key Usage Patterns in a Large Research Library," *Journal of Library Automation* 14:2 (June 1981), 90-99.

337 Georgia L. Brown. "AACR 2: OCLC's Implementation and Database Conversion," *Journal of Library Automation* 14:3 (September 1981), 161-173. **(145, 155)**

338 James R. Martin. "Automation and the Service Attitudes of ARL Circulation Managers," *Journal of Library Automation* 14:3 (September 1981), 190-194.

339 University of Oregon Library. "A Comparison of OCLC, RLG/RLIN and WLN," *Journal of Library Automation* 14:3 (September 1981), 215-217.

340 Terence Crowley. "Comparing Fiche and Film: A Test of Speed," *Journal of Library Automation* 14:4 (December 1981), 292-294. **(119)**

341 Public Service Satellite Consortium. "Cable Library Survey Results," *Journal of Library Automation* 14:4 (December 1981), 304-313.

342 Dennis Reynolds. "Entry of Local Data on OCLC: The Options and Their Impact on the Processing of Archival Tapes," *Information Technology and Libraries* 1:1 (March 1982), 5-14. **(146, 147, 157)**

343 Joseph Ford. "Network Service Centers and Their Expanding Role," *Information Technology and Libraries* 1:1 (March 1982), 28-35. **(41)**

344 Carolyn A. Johnson. "Retrospective Conversion of Three Library Collections," *Information Technology and Libraries* 1:2 (June 1982), 133-139. **(159)**

345 Lynn L. Magrath. "Computers in the Library: The Human Element," *Information Technology and Libraries* 1:3 (September 1982), 266-270. **(117, 121)**

346 Izabella Taler. "Automated and Manual ILL: Time Effectiveness and Success Rate," *Information Technology and Libraries* 1:3 (September 1982), 277-280.

347 Martha E. Williams, Stephen W. Barth and Scott E. Preece. "Summary of Statistics for Five Years of the MARC Data Base," *Journal of Library Automation* 12:4 (December 1979), 314-337.

348 Susan U. Golden and Gary A. Golden. "Access to Periodicals: Search Key versus Keyword," *Information Technology and Libraries* 2:1 (March 1983), 26-32. **(134)**

349 Ray R. Larson and Vicki Graham. "Monitoring and Evaluating MELVYL," *Information Technology and Libraries* 2:1 (March 1983), 93-104. **(119, 120)**

350 Barbara E. Carr. "Improving the Periodicals Collection through an Index Correlation Study," *Reference Services Review* 9:4 (October/December 1981), 27-31.

351 I.N. Sengupta. "Impact of Scientific Serials on the Advancement of Medical Knowledge: An Objective Method of Analysis," *International Library Review* 4:2 (April 1972), 169-195.

352 June L. Stewart. "The Literature of Politics: A Citation Analysis," *International Library Review* 2:3 (July 1970), 329-353.

353 I.N. Sengupta. "The Literature of Microbiology," *International Library Review* 6:3 (July 1974), 353-369.

354 I.N. Sengupta. "The Literature of Pharmacology," *International Library Review* 6:4 (October 1974), 483-504.

355 A.W. Hafner. "Citation Characteristics of Physiology Literature, 1970-72," *International Library Review* 8:1 (January 1976), 85-115.

356 Hans Hanan Wellisch. "Script Conversion Practices in the World's Libraries," *International Library Review* 8:1 (January 1976), 55-84.

357 Christine Anderson Brock and Gayle Smith Edelman. "Teaching Practices of Academic Law Librarians," *Law Library Journal* 71:1 (February 1978), 96-107. **(245, 246)**

358 Charles B. Wolfe. "Current Problems Facing State Law Libraries," *Law Library Journal* 71:1 (February 1978), 108-114).

359 Mindy J. Myers. "The Impact of Lexis on the Law Firm Library: A Survey," *Law Library Journal* 71:1 (February 1978), 158-169. **(40, 52, 61, 62, 107)**

360 Nancy P. Johnson. "Legal Periodical Usage Survey: Method and Application," *Law Library Journal* 71:1 (February 1978), 177-186.

361 Ann M. Carter. "Budgeting in Private Law Firm Libraries," *Law Library Journal* 71:1 (February 1978), 187-194.

362 James F. Bailey, III and Oscar M. Trelles, II. "Autonomy, Librarian Status, and Librarian Tenure in Law School Libraries: The State of the Art, 1978," *Law Library Journal* 71:3 (August 1978), 425-462.

363 Frank Wm. Goudy. "Funding Local Public Libraries: FY 1966 to FY 1980," *Public Libraries* 21:2 (Summer 1982), 52-54.

364 Guy Garrison. "A Look At Research on Public Library Problems in the 1970's," *Public Libraries* 19:1 (Spring 1980), 4-8.

365 Terry L. Weech. "School and Public Library Cooperation—What We Would Like To Do, What We Do," *Public Libraries* 18:2 (Summer 1979), 33-34.

366 Patricia L. Piper and Cecilia Hing Ling Kwan. "Cataloging and Classification Practices in Law Libraries: Results of a Questionnaire," *Law Library Journal* 71:3 (August 1978), 481-483.

367 Christian M. Boissonnas. "The Quality of OCLC Bibliographic Records: The Cornell Law Library Experience," *Law Library Journal* 72:1 (Winter 1979), 80-85.

368 Kent Schrieffer and Linnea Christiani. "Ballots at Boalt," *Law Library Journal* 72:3 (Summer 1979), 497-512.

369 Ermina Hahn. "Survey of Technical Services Practices at Fifty Large Law School Libraries," *Law Library Journal* 73:3 (Summer 1980), 715-725.

370 Lana Caswell Garcia. "Legal Services Law Librarianship—An Investigation of Salary and Benefits in a Pioneer Field," *Law Library Journal* 73:3 (Summer 1980), 731-733.

371 Reynold J. Kosek. "Faculty Status and Tenure for Nondirector, Academic Law Librarians" a section within "Status of Academic Law Librarians," *Law Library Journal* 73:4 (Fall 1980), 892-905.

372 Martha C. Adamson and Gloria J. Zamora. "Authorship Characteristics in *Law Library Journal*: A Comparative Study," *Law Library Journal* 74:3 (Summer 1981), 527-533.

373 David G. Badertscher. "An Examination of the Dynamics of Change in Information Technology as Viewed from Law Libraries and Information Centers," *Law Library Journal* 75:2 (Spring 1982), 198-211. (135)

374 Donald J. Dunn. "The Law Librarian's Obligation To Publish," *Law Library Journal* 75:2 (Spring 1982), 225-231.

375 Audio-Visual Committee, American Association of Law Libraries. "Summary of Audio-Visual Materials Used in Legal Education: Audio-Visual Committee Report—June 1967," *Law Library Journal* 60:3 (August 1967), 272-276.

376 Cameron Allen. "Duplicate Holding Practices of Approved American Law School Libraries." *Law Library Journal* 62:2 (May 1969), 191-200.

377 Margaret Shediac. "Private Law Libraries Special Interest Section 1980 Salary Survey," *Law Library Journal* 74:2 (Spring 1981), 444-457.

378 Bettie H. Scott. "Price Index for Legal Publications," *Law Library Journal* 75:1 (Winter 1982), 171-174.

379 Silvia A. Gonzalez. "County Law Library Survey," *Law Library Journal* 74:3 (Summer 1981), 654-691.

380 Silvia A. Gonzalez. "Survey of State Law Libraries," *Law Library Journal* 74:1 (Winter 1981), 160-201.

381 Silvia A. Gonzalez. "Survey of Court Law Libraries," *Law Library Journal* 74:2 (Spring 1981), 458-494.

382 David A. Thomas. "1980 Statistical Survey of Law School Libraries and Librarians," *Law Library Journal* 74:2 (Spring 1981), 359-443.

383 Marija Hughes. "Sex-Based Discrimination in Law Libraries," *Law Library Journal* 64:1 (February 1971), 13-22.

384 Oscar M. Trelles. "Law Libraries and Unions," *Law Library Journal* 65:2 (May 1972), 158-180.

385 Claudia Sumler, Kristine Barone and Art Goetz. "Getting Books Faster and Cheaper: A Jobber Acquisitions Study," *Public Libraries* 19:4 (Winter 1980), 103-105.

386 Vernon A. Rayford. "A Black Librarian Takes a Look at Discrimination: by a Law School Library Survey," *Law Library Journal* 65:2 (May 1972), 183-189.

387 Audio-Visual Committee, American Association of Law Libraries. "The Use of Audio-Visual Teaching Aids and Library Microforms in American Legal Education," *Law Library Journal* 66:1 (February 1973), 84-87.

388 Cameron Allen. "Whom We Shall Serve: Secondary Patrons of the University Law School Library," *Law Library Journal* 66:2 (May 1973), 160-171.

389 O. James Werner. "The Present Legal Status and Conditions of Prison Law Libraries," *Law Library Journal* 66:3 (August 1973), 259-269.

390 George S. Grossman. "Clinical Legal Education and the Law Library," *Law Library Journal* 67:1 (February 1974), 60-78.

391 Kurt Schwerin and Igor I. Kavass. "Foreign Legal Periodicals in American Law Libraries 1973 Union List," *Law Library Journal* 67:1 (February 1974), 120-126.

392 Bethany J. Ochal. "County Law Libraries," *Law Library Journal* 67:2 (May 1974), 177-234.

393 Peter Enyingi. "Subject Cataloging Practices in American Law Libraries: A Survey," *Law Library Journal* 68:1 (February 1975), 11-17.

394 Sandra Sadow and Benjamin R. Beede. "Library Instruction in American Law Schools," *Law Library Journal* 68:1 (February 1975), 27-32. (**233, 235**)

395 Michael L. Richmond. "Attitudes of Law Librarians to Theft and Mutilation Control Methods," *Law Library Journal* 68:1 (February 1975), 60-81.

396 Ellin B. Christianson. "Mergers in the Publishing Industry, 1958-1970," *Journal of Library History, Philosophy and Comparative Librarianship* 7:1 (January 1972), 5-32.

397 Eugene E. Graziano. "Interlibrary Loan Analysis: Diagnostic for Scientific Serials Backfile Acquisitions," *Special Libraries* 53:5 (May/June 1962), 251-257.

398 John E. James. "Library Technician Program: The Library Technician Graduates' Point of View," *Special Libraries* 62:6 (July/August 1971), 268-278.

399 James M. Matarazzo. "Scientific Journals: Page or Price Explosion?" *Special Libraries* 63:2 (February 1972), 53-58.

400 Julie L. Moore. "Bibliographic Control of American Doctoral Dissertations," *Special Libraries* 63:7 (July 1972), 285-291. (**148, 149, 187**)

401 Robert T. Bottle and William W. Chase. "Some Characteristics of the Literature on Music and Musicology," *Special Libraries* 63:10 (October 1972), 469-476. (**181**)

402 William P. Koughan and John A. Timour. "Are Hospital Libraries Meeting Physicians' Information Needs?" *Special Libraries* 64:5/6 (May/June 1972), 222-227.

403 Jean M. Ray. "Who Borrows Maps from a University Library Map Collection —And Why?" *Special Libraries* 65:3 (March 1974), 104-109.

404 Ching-Chih Chen. "How Do Scientists Meet Their Information Needs?" *Special Libraries* 65:7 (July 1974), 272-280. (**127**)

405 Katherine C. Owen. "Productive Journal Titles in the Pharmaceutical Industry," *Special Libraries* 65:10/11 (October/November 1974), 430-439.

406 Stanley A. Elman. "Cost Comparison of Manual and On-Line Computerized Literature Searching," *Special Libraries* 66:1 (January 1975), 12-18. (**50, 96**)

407 Jerome P. Fatcheric. "Survey of Users of a Medium-Sized Technical Library," *Special Libraries* 66:5/6 (May/June 1975), 245-251. (**196**)

408 Bahaa El-Hadidy. "Bibliographic Control among Geoscience Abstracting and Indexing Services," *Special Libraries* 66:5/6 (May/June 1975), 260-265. (**172, 173**)

409 Ruth W. Wender. "Hospital Journal Title Usage Study," *Special Libraries* 66:11 (November 1975), 532-537.

410 Thelma Freides. "Bibliographic Gaps in the Social Science Literature," *Special Libraries* 67:2 (February 1976), 68-75. (**171, 182, 183, 184, 185**)

411 Eileen E. Hitchingham. "MEDLINE Use in a University without a School of Medicine," *Special Libraries* 67:4 (April 1976), 188-194. (**51, 54, 79, 93**)

412   David Hull and Henry D. Fearnley. "The Museum Library in the United States: A Sample," *Special Libraries* 67:7 (July 1976), 289-298.

413   Amelia Breiting, Marcia Dorey and Deirdre Sockbeson. "Staff Development in College and University Libraries," *Special Libraries* 67:7 (July 1976), 305-309.

414   Arley L. Ripin and Dorothy Kasman. "Education for Special Librarianship: A Survey of Courses Offered in Accredited Programs," *Special Libraries* 67:11 (November 1976), 504-509.

415   George W. Black, Jr. "Selected Annaul Bound Volume Production," *Special Libraries* 67:11 (November 1976), 534-536.

416   Howard Fosdick. "An SDC-Based On-Line Search Service: A Patron Evaluation Survey and Implications," *Special Libraries* 68:9 (September 1977), 305-312.   (**35, 39, 43, 46, 51, 52, 55, 58, 64, 68, 71, 72, 75, 76, 79, 82, 195, 197**)

417   Diane M. Nelson. "Methods of Citation Analysis in the Fine Arts," *Special Libraries* 68:11 (November 1977), 390-395.

418   Annette Corth. "Coverage of Marine Biology Citations,"*Special Libraries* 68:12 (December 1977), 439-446. (**174, 188**)

419   Jean K. Martin. "Computer-Based Literature Searching: Impact on Interlibrary Loan Service," *Special Libaries* 69:1 (January 1978), 1-6. (**51**)

420   Jean M. Ray. "Who Borrows Maps from a University Library Map Collection —and Why? Report II," *Special Libraries* 69:1 (January 1978), 13-20.

421   Robert Goehlert. "Periodical Use in an Academic Library: A Study of Economists and Political Scientists," *Special Libraries* 69:2 (February 1978), 51-60. (**196**)

422   Sandra J. Springer, Robert A. Yokel, Nancy M. Lorenzi, Leonard T. Sigell and E. Don Nelson. "Drug Information to Patient Care Areas via Television: Preliminary Evaluation of Two Years' Experience," *Special Libraries* 69:4 (April 1978), 155-163. (**24, 27, 215, 216**)

423   Martha J. Bailey. "Requirement for Middle Managerial Positions," *Special Libraries* 69:9 (September 1978), 323-331.

424   Carolyn L. Warden. "An Industrial Current Awareness Service: A User Evaluation Study," *Special Libraries* 69:12 (December 1978), 459-467. (**199, 202, 204**)

425   Charles H. Davis. "Programming Aptitude as a Function of Undergraduate Major," *Special Libraries* 69:12 (December 1978), 482-485.

426   Jean Mace Schmidt. "Translation of Periodical Literature in Plant Pathology," *Special Libraries* 70:1 (January 1979), 12-17. (**127**)

427 Susan Dingle-Cliff and Charles H. Davis. "Collection Overlap in Canadian Addictions Libraries," *Special Libraries* 70:2 (February 1979), 76-81.

428 John J. Knightly. "Overcoming the Cirterion Problem in the Evaluation of Library Performance," *Special Libraries* 70:4 (April 1979), 173-178.

429 Ruth W. Wender. "Counting Journal Title Usage in the Health Sciences," *Special Libraries* 70:5/6 (May/June 1975), 219-226.

430 John Steuben. "Interlibrary Loan of Photocopies of Articles under the New Copyright Law," *Special Libraries* 70:5/6 (May/June 1979), 227-232.

431 John Kok and Edward G. Strable. "Moving Up: Librarians Who Have Become Officers of Their Organization," *Special Libraries* 71:1 (January 1980), 5-12.

432 Rebecca J. Jensen, Herbert D. Asbury and Radford G. King. "Costs and Benefits to Industry of Online Literature Searches," *Special Libraries* 71:7 (July 1980), 291-299. **(77, 82, 83)**

433 C. Margaret Bell. "The Applicability of OCLC and Inforonics in Special Libraries," *Special Libraries* 71:9 (September 1980), 398-404.

434 A. Neil Yerkey. "The Psychological Climate of Librarianship: Values of Special Librarians," *Special Libraries* 72:3 (July 1981), 195-200.

435 Virgil P. Diodato. "Author Indexing," *Special Libraries* 72:4 (October 1981), 361-369. **(221, 222)**

436 Judith M. Pask. "Bibliographic Instruction in Business Libraries," *Special Libraries* 72:4 (October 1981), 370-378. **(229, 234, 247, 248, 250, 254, 256)**

437 Ann T. Dodson, Paul P. Philbin and Kunj B. Rastogi. "Electronic Interlibrary Loan in the OCLC Library: A Study of its Effectiveness," *Special Libraries* 73:1 (January 1982), 12-20.

438 Gloria J. Zamora and Martha C. Adamson. "Authorship Characteristics in *Special Libraries*: A Comparative Study," *Special Libraries* 73:2 (April 1982), 100-107.

439 Robert K. Poyer. "Time Lag in Four Indexing Services," *Special Libraries* 73:2 (April 1982), 142-146. **(161, 163, 189, 190)**

440 Pauline R. Hodges. "Keyword in Title Indexes: Effectiveness of Retrieval in Computer Searches," *Special Libraries* 74:1 (January 1983), 56-60. **(222)**

441 D.K. Varma. "Increased Subscription Costs and Problems of Resource Allocation," *Special Libraries* 74:1 (January 1983), 61-66.

442 Michael Halperin and Ruth A. Pagell. "Searchers' Perceptions of Online Database Vendors," *Special Libraries* 74:2 (April 1973), 119-126. **(86, 87)**

443   Michael E.D. Koenig. "Education for Special Librarianship," *Special Librar-ies* 74:2 (April 1983), 182-196.

444   Powell Niland and William H. Kurth. "Estimating Lost Volumes in a University Library Collection," *College and Research Libraries* 37:2 (March 1976), 128-136.

445   Rush G. Miller. "The Influx of Ph.D.s into Librarianship: Intrusion or Transfusion?" *College and Research Libraries* 37:2 (March 1976), 158-165.

446   Steven Leach. "The Growth Rates of Major Academic Libraries: Rider and Purdue Reviewed," *College and Research Libraries* 37:6 (November 1976), 531-542.

447   T. Saracevic, W.M. Shaw, Jr. and P.B. Kantor. "Causes and Dynamics of User Frustration in an Academic Library," *College and Research Libraries* 38:1 (January 1977), 7-18.

448   R.W. Meyer and Rebecca Panetta. "Two Shared Cataloging Data Bases: A Comparison," *College and Research Libraries* 38:1 (January 1977), 19-24.

449   Peter Hernon and Maureen Pastine. "Student Perceptions of Academic Librarians," *College and Research Libraries* 38:2 (March 1977), 129-139. **(108, 128, 192)**

450   Catherine V. Von Schon. "Inventory 'By Computer'," *College and Research Libraries* 38:2 (March 1977), 147-152.

451   David C. Genaway and Edward B. Stanford. "Quasi-Departmental Librar-ies," *College and Research Libraries* 38:3 (May 1977), 187-194.

452   Elizabeth W. Matthews. "Trends Affecting Community College Library Administrators," *College and Research Libraries* 38:3 (May 1977), 210-217.

453   Lawrence J. Perk. "Secondary Publications in Education: A Study of Duplication," *College and Research Libraries* 38:3   (May 1977), 221-226. **(172, 183)**

454   Geraldine Murphy Wright. "Current Trends in Periodical Collections," *College and Research Libraries* 38:3 (May 1977), 234-240.

455   Lawrence J. Perk and Noelle Van Pulis. "Periodical Usage in an Education-Psychology Library," *College and Research Libraries* 38:4 (July 1977), 304-308.

456   Egill A. Halldorsson and Marjorie E. Murfin. "The Performance of Profes-sionals and Nonprofessionals in the Reference Interview," *College and Research Libraries* 38:5 (September 1977), 385-395. **(15)**

457   Susan A. Lee. "Conflict and Ambiguity in the Role of the Academic Library Director," *College and Research Libraries* 38:5 (September 1977), 396-403.

458 Glenn R. Wittig. "Dual Pricing of Periodicals," *College and Research Libraries* 38:5 (September 1977), 412-418.

459 Miriam A. Drake. "Attribution of Library Costs," *College and Research Libraries* 38:6 (November 1977), 514-519.

460 Harry M. Kriz. "Subscriptions vs. Books in a Constant Dollar Budget," *College and Research Libraries* 39:2 (March 1978), 105-109.

461 Charles J. Popovich. "The Characteristics of a Collection for Research in Business/Management," *College and Research Libraries* 39:2 (March 1978), 117.

462 Jean A. Major. "The Visually Impaired Reader in the Academic Library," *College and Research Libraries* 39:3 (May 1978), 191-196.

463 Herbert S. White and Karen Momenee. "Impact of the Increase in Library Doctorates," *College and Research Libraries* 39:3 (May 1978), 207-214.

464 James Michalko and Toby Heidtmann. "Evaluating the Effectiveness of an Electronic Security System," *College and Research Libraries* 39:4 (July 1978), 263-267.

465 William M. McClellan. "Judging Music Libraries," *College and Research Libraries* 39:4 (July 1978), 281-286.

466 Rita Hoyt Smith and Warner Granade. "User and Library Failures in an Undergraduate Library," *College and Research Libraries* 39:6 (November 1978), 467-473.

467 Linda Ann Hulbert and David Stewart Curry. "Evaluation of an Approval Plan," *College and Research Libraries* 39:6 (November 1978), 485-491.

468 Julia F. Baldwin and Robert S. Rudolph. "The Comparative Effectiveness of a Slide/Tape Show and a Library Tour," *College and Research Libraries* 40:1 (January 1979), 31-35. **(249, 253)**

469 Melissa D. Trevvett. "Characteristics of Interlibrary Loan Requests at the Library of Congress," *College and Research Libraries* 40:1 (January 1979), 36-43.

470 Elaine Zaremba Jennerich and Bessie Hess Smith. "A Bibliographic Instruction Program in Music," *College and Research Libraries* 40:3 (May 1979), 226-233. **(239, 241)**

471 William J. Maher and Benjamin F. Shearer. "Undergraduate Use Patterns of Newspapers on Microfilm," *College and Research Libraries* 40:3 (May 1979), 254-260.

472 Larry Hardesty, Nicholas P. Lovrich, Jr. and James Mannon. "Evaluating Library-Use Instruction," *College and Research Libraries* 40:4 (July 1979), 309-317. **(237, 239, 240)**

473 Seymour H. Sargent. "The Uses and Limitations of Trueswell," *College and Research Libraries* 40:5 (September 1979), 416-425.

474 Patricia Stenstrom and Ruth B. McBride." Serial Use by Social Science Faculty: A Survey," *College and Research Libraries* 40:5 (September 1979), 426-431.

475 Elaine C. Clever. "Using Indexes as 'Memory Assists'," *College and Research Libraries* 40:5 (September 1979), 444-449. **(124, 133, 134)**

476 William E. McGrath, Donald J. Simon and Evelyn Bullard. "Ethnocentricity and Cross-Disciplinary Circulation," *College and Research Libraries* 40:6 (November 1979), 511-518.

477 Michael Gorman and Jami Hotsinpiller. "ISBD: Aid or Barrier to Understanding," *College and Research Libraries* 40:6 (November 1979), 519-526.

478 Jinnie Y. Davis and Stella Bentley. "Factors Affecting Faculty Perceptions of Academic Libraries," *College and Research Libraries* 40:6 (November 1979), 527-532. **(129)**

479 Dennis J. Reynolds. "Regional Alternatives for Interlibrary Loan: Access to Unreported Holdings," *College and Research Libraries* 41:1 (January 1980), 33-42.

480 Ronald Rayman and Frank William Goudy. "Research and Publication Requirements in University Libraries," *College and Research Libraries* 41:1 (January 1980), 43-48.

481 John N. Olsgaard and Jane Kinch Olsgaard. "Authorship in Five Library Periodicals," *College and Research Libraries* 41:1 (January 1980), 49-53.

482 Albert F. Maag. "Design of the Library Director Interview: The Candidate's Perspective," *College and Research Libraries* 41:2 (March 1980), 112-121.

483 Thomas M. Gaughan. "Resume Essentials for the Academic Librarian," *College and Research Libraries* 41:2 (March 1980), 122-127.

484 Harold B. Shill. "Open Stacks and Library Performance," *College and Research Libraries* 41:3 (May 1980), 220-225.

485 Robert L. Turner, Jr. "Femininity and the Librarian—Another Test," *College and Research Libraries* 41:3 (May 1980), 235-241.

486 Ray L. Carpenter. "College Libraries: A Comparative Analysis in Terms of the ACRL Standards," *College and Research Libraries* 42:1 (January 1981), 7-18. **(224)**

487 George V. Hodowanec. "An Acquisition Rate Model for Academic Libraries," *College and Research Libraries* 39:6 (September 1978), 439-442.

488 Roland Person. "Long-Term Evaluation of Bibliographic Instruction: Lasting Encouragement," *College and Research Libraries* 42:1 (January 1981), 19-25. **(235, 236, 238)**

489 Laslo A. Nagy and Martha Lou Thomas. "An Evaluation of the Teaching Effectiveness of Two Library Instructional Videotapes," *College and Research Libraries* 42:1 (January 1981), 26-30. **(241, 250)**

490 David N. King and John C. Ory. "Effects of Library Instruction on Student Research: A Case Study," *College and Research Libraries* 42:1 (January 1981), 31-41. **(237, 242, 243)**

491 Herbert S. White. "Perceptions by Educators and Administrators of the Ranking of Library School Programs," *College and Research Libraries* 42:3 (May 1981), 191-202.

492 Russ Davidson, Connie Capers Thorson and Margo C. Trumpeter. "Faculty Status for Librarians in the Rocky Mountain Region: A Review and Analysis," *College and Research Libraries* 42:3 (May 1981), 203-213.

493 M. Kathy Cook. "Rank, Status, and Contribution of Academic Librarians as Perceived by the Teaching Faculty at Southern Illinois University, Carbondale," *College and Research Libraries* 42:3 (May 1981), 214-223.

494 John N. Olsgaard and Jane Kinch Olsgaard. "Post-MLS Educational Requirements for Academic Librarians," *College and Research Libraries* 42:3 (May 1981), 224-228.

495 Ronald Rayman. "Employment Opportunities for Academic Librarians in the 1970's: An Analysis of the Past Decade," *College and Research Libraries* 42:3 (May 1981), 229-234.

496 Martha C. Adamson and Gloria J. Zamora. "Publishing in Library Science Journals: A Test of the Olsgaard Profile," *College and Research Libraries* 42:3 (May 1981), 235-241.

497 Charles Sage, Janet Klass, Helen H. Spalding and Tracey Robinson. "A Queueing Study of Public Catalog Use," *College and Research Libraries* 42:4 (July 1981), 317-325.

498 Doris Cruger Dale. "Cataloging and Classsification Practices in Community College Libraries," *College and Research Libraries* 42:4 (July 1981), 333-339.

499 Dana Weiss. "Book Theft and Book Mutilation in a Large Urban University Library," *College and Research Libraries* 42:4 (July 1981), 341-347.

500 Raymond L. Carpenter. "Two-Year College Libraries: A Comparative Analysis in Terms of the ACRL Standards," *College and Research Libraries* 42:5 (September 1981), 407-415.

501 Paul D. Luyben, Leonard Cohen, Rebecca Conger and Selby U. Gration. "Reducing Noise in a College Library," *College and Research Libraries* 42:5 (September 1981), 470-481.

502   Prabha Sharma. "A Survey of Academic Librarians and Their Opinions
      Related to Nine-Month Contracts and Academic Status Configurations in
      Alabama, Georgia and Mississippi," *College and Research Libraries* 42:6
      (November 1981), 561-570.

503   Priscilla Geahigan, Harriet Nelson, Stewart Saunders and Lawrence Woods.
      "Acceptability of Non-Library/Information Science Publications in the Pro-
      motion and Tenure of Academic Librarians," *College and Research Libraries*
      42:6 (November 1981), 571-575.

504   Barbara Moore, Tamara J. Miller and Don L. Tolliver. "Title Overlap: A
      Study of Duplication in the University of Wisconsin System Libraries,"
      College and Research Libraries 43:1 (January 1982), 14-21.

505   Gary A. Golden, Susan U. Golden and Rebecca T. Lenzini. "Patron
      Approaches to Serials: A User Study," *College and Research Libraries* 43:1
      (January 1982), 22-30. **(121, 122)**

506   Thomas T. Surprenant. "Learning Theory, Lecture, and Programmed In-
      struction Text: An Experiment in Bibliographic Instruction," *College and
      Research Libraries* 43:1 (January 1982), 31-37. **(239, 253)**

507   Larry Hardesty, Nicholas P. Lovrich, Jr. and James Mannon. "Library-Use
      Instruction: Assessment of the Long-Term Effects," *College and Research
      Libraries* 43:1 (January 1982), 38-46. **(241)**

508   Robert Swisher and Peggy C. Smith. "Journals Read by ACRL Academic
      Librarians, 1973 and 1978," *College and Research Libraries* 43:1 (January
      1982), 51-58.

509   William Caynon. "Collective Bargaining and Professional Development of
      Academic Librarians," *College and Research Libraries* 43:2 (March 1982),
      133-139.

510   Barbara J. Smith. "Background Characteristics and Education Needs of a
      Group of Instruction Librarians in Pennsylvania," *College and Research
      Libraries* 43:3 (May 1982), 199-207. **(245, 246, 247)**

511   Gloria S. Cline. "*College and Research Libraries*: Its First Forty Years,"
      College and Research Libraries 43:3 (May 1982), 208-232.

512   John B. Harer and C. Edward Huber. "Copyright Policies in Virginia
      Academic Library Reserve Rooms," *College and Research Libraries* 43:3
      (May 1982), 233-241.

513   Laurie S. Linsley. "Academic Libraries in an Interlibrary Loan Network,"
      College and Research Libraries 43:4 (July 1982), 292-299.

514   Timothy D. Jewell. "Student Reactions to a Self-Paced Library Skills
      Workbook Program: Survey Evidence," *College and Research Libraries* 43:5
      (September 1982), 371-378. **(236, 254, 257)**

515 Mary Baier Wells. "Requirements and Benefits for Academic Librarians: 1959-1979," *College and Research Libraries* 43:6 (November 1982), 450-458.

516 Marjorie A. Benedict, Jacquelyn A. Gavryck and Hanan C. Selvin. "Status of Academic Librarians in New York State," *College and Research Libraries* 44:1 (January 1983), 12-19.

517 Carol Truett. "Services to Developmental Education Students in the Community College: Does the Library Have a Role?" *College and Research Libraries* 44:1 (January 1983), 20-28. **(234, 245)**

518 Gene K. Rinkel and Patricia McCandless. "Application of a Methodology Analyzing User Frustration," *College and Research Libraries* 44:1 (January 1983), 29-37.

519 Jo Bell Whitlatch. "Library Use Patterns Among Full- and Part-Time Faculty and Students," *College and Research Libraries* 44:2 (March 1983), 141-152.

520 Madeleine Stern. "Characteristics of the Literature of Literary Scholarship," *College and Research Libraries* 44:4 (July 1983), 199-209.

521 Philip Schwarz. "Demand-Adjusted Shelf Availability Parameters: A Second Look," *College and Research Libraries* 44:4 (July 1983), 210-219.

522 Paul M. Anderson and Ellen G. Miller. "Participative Planning for Library Automation: The Role of the User Opinion Survey," *College and Research Libraries* 44:4 (July 1983), 245-254. **(115, 116, 122)**

523 Raymond W. Barber and Jacqueline C. Mancall. "The Application of Bibliometric Techniques to the Analysis of Materials for Young Adults," *Collection Management* 2:3 (Fall 1978), 229-245.

524 Kenneth C. Kirsch and Albert H. Rubenstein. "Converting from Hard Copy to Microfilm: An Administrative Experiment," *Collection Management* 2:4 (Winter 1978), 279-302.

525 Herbert Goldhor. "U.S. Public Library Adult Non-Fiction Book Collections in the Humanities," *Collection Management* 3:1 (Spring 1979), 31-43.

526 Sally F. Williams. "Construction and Application of a Periodical Price Index," *Collection Management* 2:4 (Winter 1978), 329-344.

527 Mary Jane Pobst Reed. "Identification of Storage Candidates among Monographs," *Collection Management* 3:2/3 (Summer/Fall 1979), 203-214.

528 Ung Chon Kim. "Participation of Teaching Faculty in Library Book Selection," *Collection Management* 3:4 (Winter 1979), 333-352.

529 Glenn R. Lowry. "A Heuristic Collection Loss Rate Determination Methodology: An Alternative to Shelf-Reading," *Collection Management* 4:1/2 (Spring/Summer 1982), 73-83.

530 Stewart Saunders. "Student Reliance on Faculty Guidance in the Selection of Reading Materials: The Use of Core Collections," *Collection Management* 4:4 (Winter 1982), 9-23.

531 Ralph M. Daehn. "The Measurement and Projection of Shelf Space," *Collection Management* 4:4 (Winter 1982), 25-39.

532 Igor I. Kavass. "Foreign and International Law Collections in Selected Law Libraries of the United States: Survey, 1972-73," *International Journal of Law Libraries* 1:3 (November 1973), 117-133.

533 Robert J. Garen. "Library Orientation on Television," *Canadian Library Journal* 24:2 (September 1967), 124-126. **(235, 249, 251)**

534 D.W. Miller. "Non-English Books in Canadian Public Libraries," *Canadian Library Journal* 27:2 (March/April 1970), 123-129.

535 Robert H. Blackburn. "Canadian Content in a Sample of Photocopying," *Canadian Library Journal* 27:5 (September/October 1970), 332-340.

536 Peter H. Wolters and Jack E. Brown. "CAN/SDI System: User Reaction to a Computer Information Retrieval System for Canadian Scientists and Technologists," *Canadian Library Journal* 28:1 (January/ February), 20-23. **(194, 197, 202)**

537 M. Jamil Qureshi. "Academic Status, Salaries and Fringe Benefits in Community College Libraries of Canada," *Canadian Library Journal* 28:1 (January/February 1971), 41-45.

538 George J. Snowball. "Survey of Social Sciences and Humanities Monograph Circulation by Random Sampling of the Stack," *Canadian Library Journal* 28:5 (September/October 1971), 352-361.

539 Roop K. Sandhu and Harjit Sandhu. "Job Perception of University Librarians and Library Students," *Canadian Library Journal* 28:6 (November/ December 1971), 438-445.

540 Brian Dale and Patricia Dewdney. "Canadian Public Libraries and the Physically Handicapped," *Canadian Library Journal* 29:3 (May/June 1972), 231-236.

541 R.G. Wilson. "Interlibrary Loan Experiments at the University of Calgary," *Canadian Library Journal* 30:1 (January/February 1973), 38-40.

542 Peter Simmons. "Studies in the Use of the Card Catalogue in a Public Library," *Canadian Library Journal* 31:4 (August 1974), 323-337. **(116, 117)**

543 L.J. Amey and R.J. Smith. "Combination School and Public Libraries: An Attitudinal Study," *Canadian Library Journal* 33:3 (June 1976), 251-261.

544 John Wilkinson. "The Library Market for Canadian Juvenile Fiction: A Further Analysis," *Canadian Library Journal* 34:1 (February 1977), 5-15.

545 Larry Orten and John Wiseman. "Library Service to Part-time Students," *Canadian Library Journal* 34:1 (February 1977), 23-27.

546 Esther L. Sleep. "Whither the ISSN? A Practical Experience," *Canadian Library Journal* 34:4 (August 1977), 265-270.

547 Sarah Landy. "Why Johnny Can Read...but Doesn't," *Canadian Library Journal* 34:5 (October 1977), 379-387.

548 Sharon Mott. "An Edmonton High School Reduces Book Losses," *Canadian Library Journal* 35:1 (February 1978), 45-49.

549 Fotoula Pantazis. "Library Technicians in Ontario Academic Libraries," *Canadian Library Journal* 35:2 (April 1978), 77-91.

550 Dorothy Ryder. "Canadian Reference Sources—A 10 Year Overview," *Canadian Library Journal* 35:4 (August 1978), 289-293. **(9, 132)**

551 Laurent-G. Denis. "Full-time Faculty Survey Describes Educators," *Canadian Library Journal* 36:3 (June 1979), 107-121.

552 Marie Foster. "Philosophy of Librarianship," *Canadian Library Journal* 36:3 (June 1979), 131-137.

553 Kenneth H. Plate and Jacob P. Seigel. "Career Patterns of Ontario Librarians," *Canadian Library Journal* 36:3 (June 1979), 143-148.

554 Mavis Cariou. "Liaison Where Field and Faculty Meet," *Canadian Library Journal* 36:3 (June 1979), 155-163.

555 Norman Horrocks. "Encyclopedias and Public Libraries: A Canadian Survey," *Canadian Library Journal* 38:2 (April 1981), 79-83. **(10, 151, 152)**

556 Stephen B. Lawton. "Diffusion of Automation in Post-Secondary Institutions," *Canadian Library Journal* 38:2 (April 1980), 93-97. **(42, 49, 66, 88, 104)**

557 Mary Ann Wasylycia-Coe. "Profile: Canadian Chief Librarians by Sex," *Canadian Library Journal* 38:3 (June 1981), 159-163.

558 Margaret Currie, Elaine Goettler and Sandra McCaskill. "Evaluating the Relationship between Library Skills and Library Instruction," *Canadian Library Journal* 39:1 (February 1982), 35-37. **(240, 254)**

559 Esther L. Sleep. "Periodical Vandalism: A Chronic Condition," *Canadian Library Journal* 39:1 (February 1982), 39-42.

560 Kenneth Setterington. "The Ph.D. in Library Administration: A Report of Research," *Library Research* (after Spring 1983 called *Library and Information Science Research*) 5:2 (Summer 1983), 177-194.

561 Robert F. Rose. "Identifying a Core Collection of Business Periodicals for
     Academic Libraries," *Collection Management* 5:1/2 (Spring/Summer 1983),
     73-87. **(159, 160, 166, 170)**

562 Raymond Kilpela. "A Profile of Library School Deans, 1960-81," *Journal of
     Education for Librarianship* 23:3 (Winter 1983), 173-191.

563 Charlene Renner and Barton M. Clark. "Professional and Nonprofessional
     Staffing Patterns in Departmental Libraries," *Library Research* 1 (1979),
     153-170.

564 Jacqueline C. Mancall and M. Carl Drott. "Materials Used by High School
     Students in Preparing Independent Study Projects: A Bibliometric Ap-
     proach," *Library Research* 1 (1979), 223-236.

565 Alan R. Samuels. "Assessing Organizational Climate in Public Libraries,"
     Library Research 1 (1979), 237-254.

566 Diane Mittermeyer and Lloyd J. Houser. "The Knowledge Base for the
     Administration of Libraries," *Library Research* 1 (1979), 255-276.

567 Michael V. Sullivan, Betty Vadeboncoeur, Nancy Shiotani and Peter Stangl.
     "Obsolescence in Biomedical Journals: Not an Artifact of Literature
     Growth," *Library Research* 2 (1980-81), 29-46.

568 Robert V. Williams. "Sources of the Variability in Level of Public Library
     Development in the United States: A Comparative Analysis," *Library
     Research* 2 (1980-81), 157-176.

569 Bluma C. Peritz. "The Methods of Library Science Research: Some Results
     from a Bibliometric Survey," *Library Research* 2 (1980-81), 251-268.

570 Nancy Van House DeWath. "Fees for Online Bibliographic Search Services
     in Publicly-Supported Libraries," *Library Research* 3 (1981), 29-45. **(36, 37,
     65, 66, 67, 68)**

571 Bluma C. Peritz. "Citation Characteristics in Library Science: Some Further
     Results from a Bibliometric Survey," *Library Research* 3 (1981), 47-65.

572 Gary Moore. "Library Long-Range Planning: A Survey of Current Prac-
     tices," *Library Research* 3 (1981), 155-165.

573 Larry Hardesty. "Use of Library Materials at a Small Liberal Arts College,"
     Library Research 3 (1981), 261-282.

574 Stewart Saunders, Harriet Nelson and Priscilla Geahigan. "Alternatives to
     the Shelflist Measure for Determining the Size of a Subject Collection,"
     Library Research 3 (1981), 383-391.

575 P. Robert Paustian. "Collection Size and Interlibrary Loan in Large Aca-
     demic Libraries," *Library Research* 3 (1981), 393-400.

576 Daniel O. O'Connor. "Evaluating Public Libraries Using Standard Scores:
     The Library Quotient," *Library Research* 4 (1982), 51-70. **(226)**

577 Snunith Shoham. "A Cost-Preference Study of the Decentralization of Academic Library Services," *Library Research* 4 (1982), 175-194.

578 A.S. Pickett. "San Franscisco State College Library Technical Services Time Study," *Library Resources and Technical Services* 4:1 (Winter 1960), 45-46.

579 Rosamond H. Danielson. "Cornell's Area Classification: A Space-Saving Device for Less-Used Books," *Library Resources and Technical Services* 5:2 (Spring 1961), 139-141.

580 Miriam C. Maloy. "Reclassification for the Divisional Plan," Library Resources and Technical Services 6:3 (Summer 1962), 239-242.

581 Andre Nitecki. "Costs of a Divided Catalog," *Library Resources and Technical Services* 6:4 (Fall 1962), 351-355.

582 Donald V. Black. "Automatic Classification and Indexing, for Libraries?" *Library Resources and Technical Services* 9:1 (Winter 1965), 35-52.

583 Perry D. Morrison. "Use of Library of Congress Classsification Decisions in Academic Libraries—An Empirical Study," *Library Resources and Technical Services* 9:2 (Spring 1965), 235-242.

584 Manuel D. Lopez. "Subject Catalogers Equal to the Future?" *Library Resources and Technical Services* 9:3 (Summer 1965), 371-375.

585 Ashby J. Fristoe. "The Bitter End," *Library Resources and Technical Services* 10:1 (Winter 1966), 91-95.

586 Ole V. Groos. "Less-Used Titles and Volumes of Science Journals: Two Preliminary Notes," *Library Resources and Technical Services* 10:3 (Summer 1966), 289-290.

587 Paula M. Strain. "A Study of the Usage and Retention of Technical Periodicals," *Library Resources and Technical Services* 10:3 (Summer 1966), 295-304.

588 William R. Nugent. "Statistics of Collection Overlap at the Libraries of the Six New England State Universities," *Library Resources and Technical Services* 12:1 (Winter 1968), 31-36.

589 Walter R. Stubbs and Robert N. Broadus. "The Value of the Kirkus Service for College Libraries," *Library Resources and Technical Services* 13:2 (Spring 1969), 203-205. **(137)**

590 Barton R. Burkhalter and LaVerne Hoag. "Another Look at Manual Sorting and Filing: Backwards and Forwards," *Library Resources and Technical Services* 14:3 (Summer 1970), 445-454.

591 "More on DC Numbers on LC Cards: Quantity and Quality," *Library Resources and Technical Services* 14:4 (Fall 1970), 517-527.

592   Carol A. Nemeyer. "Scholarly Reprint Publishing in the United States: Selected Findings from a Recent Survey of the Industry," *Library Resources and Technical Services* 15:1 (Winter 1971), 35-48.

593   Betty J. Mitchell and Carol Bedoian. "A Systematic Approach to Performance Evaluation of Out-of-Print Book Dealers: The San Fernando Valley State College Experience," *Library Resources and Technical Services* 15:2 (Spring 1971), 215-222.

594   Barbara Schrader and Elaine Orsini. "British, French and Australian Publications in the National Union Catalog: A Study of NPAC's Effectiveness," *Library Resources and Technical Services* 15:3 (Summer 1971), 345-353. **(154, 155)**

595   Joel Levis. "Canadian Publications in the English Language: CBI vs. *Canadiana*," *Library Resources and Technical Services* 15:3 (Summer 1971), 354-358. **(131, 185)**

596   Zubaidah Isa. "The Entry-Word in Indonesian Names and Titles," *Library Resources and Technical Services* 15:3 (Summer 1971), 393-398.

597   Richard J. Hyman. "Access to Library Collections: Summary of a Documentary and Opinion Survey on the Direct Shelf Approach and Browsing," *Library Resources and Technical Services* 15:4 (Fall 1971), 479-491.

598   Robert L. Mowery. "The Cryptic Other," *Library Resources and Technical Services* 16:1 (Winter 1972), 74-78.

599   Ann Craig Turner. "Comparative Card Production Methods," *Library Resources and Technical Services* 16:3 (Summer 1972), pp. 347-358.

600   Edmund G. Hamann. "Expansion of the Public Card Catalog in a Large Library," *Library Resources and Technical Services* 16:4 (Fall 1972), 488-496.

601   Ernest R. Perez. "Acquisitions of Out-of-Print Materials," *Library Resources and Technical Services* 17:1 (Winter 1973), 42-59.

602   E. Dale Cluff and Karen Anderson. "LC Card Order Experiment Conducted at University of Utah Marriott Library," *Library Resources and Technical Services* 17:1 (Winter 1973), 70-72.

603   Betty J. Mitchell. "Methods Used in Out-of-Print Acquisition; A Survey of Out-of-Print Book Dealers," *Library Resources and Technical Services* 17:2 (Spring 1973), 211-215.

604   George Piternick. "University Library Arrearages," *Library Resources and Technical Services* 13:1 (Winter 1969), 102-114.

605   Nancy E. Brodie. "Evaluation of a KWIC Index for *Library Literature*," *Journal of the American Society for Information Science* 21:1 (January-February 1970), 22-28. **(221)**

606 William S. Cooper. "The Potential Usefulness of Catalog Access Points Other than Author, Title and Subject," *Journal of the American Society for Information Science* 21:2 (March-April 1970), 112-127. (114)

607 Barbara F. Frick and John M. Ginski. "Cardiovascular Serial Literature: Characteristics, Productive Journals, and Abstracting/Indexing Coverage," *Journal of the American Society for Information Science* 21:5 (September-October 1970), 338-344. (175, 178)

608 Ching-Chih Chen. "The Use Patterns of Physics Journals in a Large Academic Research Library," *Journal of the American Society for Information Science* 23:4 (July-August 1972), 254-265.

609 Janet Friedlander. "Clinician Search for Information," *Journal of the American Society for Information Science* 24:1 (January-February 1973), 65-69.

610 Tefko Saracevic and Lawrence J. Perk. "Ascertaining Activities in a Subject Area through Bibliometric Analysis," *Journal of the American Society for Information Science* 24:3 (March-April 1973), 120-134. (173, 174)

611 Ruth Kay Maloney. "Title versus Title/Abstract Text Searching in SDI Systems," *Journal of the American Society for Information Science* 25:6 (November-December 1974), 370-373. (58)

612 Gladys B. Dronberger and Gerald T. Kowitz. "Abstract Readability as a Factor in Information Systems," *Journal of the American Society for Information Science* 26:2 (March-April 1975), 108-111. (133, 172)

613 Jerry R. Byrne. "Relative Effectiveness of Titles, Abstracts and Subject Headings for Machine Retrieval from the COMPENDEX Services," *Journal of the American Society for Information Science* 26:4 (July-August 1975), 223-229. (53, 55)

614 Joseph D. Smith and James E. Rush. "The Relationship between Author Names and Author Entries in a Large On-Line Union Catalog as Retrieved Using Truncated Keys," *Journal of the American Society for Information Science* 28:2 (March 1977), 115-120.

615 Marcia J. Bates. "Factors Affecting Subject Catalog Search Success," *Journal of the American Society for Information Science* 28:3 (May 1977), 161-169. (115)

616 Terry Noreault, Matthew Koll and Michael J. McGill. "Automatic Ranked Output from Boolean Searches in SIRE," *Journal of the American Society for Information Science* 28:6 (November 1977), 333-339. (34)

617 Chai Kim and Eui Hang Shin. "Sociodemographic Correlates of Intercounty Variations in the Public Library Output," *Journal of the American Society for Information Science* 28:6 (November 1977), 359-365.

618 Harold E. Bamford, Jr. "Assessing the Effect of Computer Augmentation on Staff Productivity," *Journal of the American Society for Information Science* 30:3 (May 1979), 136-142.

619 Charles H. Davis and Deborah Shaw. "Collection Overlap as a Function of Library Size: A Comparison of American and Canadian Public Libraries," *Journal of the American Society for Information Science* 30:1 (January 1979), 19-24.

620 M. Carl Drott and Belver C. Griffith. "An Empirical Examination of Bradford's Law and the Scattering of Scientific Literature," *Journal of the American Society for Information Science* 29:5 (September 1978), 238-246.

621 James D. Anderson. "*Ad hoc* and Selective Translations of Scientific and Technical Journal Articles: Their Characteristics and Possible Predictability," *Journal of the American Society for Information Science* 29:3 (May 1978), 130-135. **(190, 191)**

622 Richard C. Anderson, Francis Narin and Paul McAllister. "Publication Ratings versus Peer Ratings of Universities," *Journal of the American Society for Information Science* 29:2 (March 1978), 91-103.

623 Dennis R. Eichesen. "Cost-Effectiveness Comparison of Manual and On-line Retrospective Bibliographic Searching," *Journal of the American Society for Information Science* 29:2 (March 1978), 56-66. **(44, 45, 47, 48, 49, 50, 56, 59, 94, 95, 97)**

624 Topsy N. Smalley. "Comparing *Psychological Abstracts* and *Index Medicus* for Coverage of the Journal Literature in a Subject Area in Psychology," *Journal of the American Society for Information Science* 31:3 (May 1980), 144-146. **(184, 188)**

625 Paul R. McAllister, Richard C. Anderson and Francis Narin. "Comparison of Peer and Citation Assessment of the Influence of Scientific Journals," *Journal of the American Society for Information Science* 31:3 (May 1980), 148-152.

626 Jerry Specht. "Patron Use of an Online Circulation System in Known-Item Searching," *Journal of the American Society for Information Science* 31:5 (September 1980), 335-346. **(109, 110)**

627 Guilbert C. Hentschke and Ellen Kehoe. "Serial Acquisition as a Capital Budgeting Problem," *Journal of the American Society for Information Science* 31:5 (September 1980), 357-362.

628 G. Edward Evans and Claudia White Argyres. "Approval Plans and Collection Development in Academic Libraries," *Library Resources and Technical Services* 18:1 (Winter 1974), 35-50.

629 Doris E. New and Retha Zane Ott. "Interlibrary Loan Analysis as a Collection Development Tool," *Library Resources and Technical Services* 18:3 (Summer 1974), 275-283.

630 H. William Axford. "The Validity of Book Price Indexes for Budgetary Projections," *Library Resources and Technical Services* 19:1 (Winter 1975), 5-12.

631 Geza A. Kosa. "Book Selection Tools for Subject Specialists in a Large Research Library: An Analysis," *Library Resources and Technical Services* 19:1 (Winter 1975), 13-18.

632 George P. D'Elia. "The Determinants of Job Satisfaction among Beginning Librarians," *Library Quarterly* 49:3 (July 1979), 283-302.

633 Tim LaBorie and Michael Halperin. "Citation Patterns in Library Science Dissertations," *Journal of Education for Librarianship* 16:4 (Spring 1976), 271-283.

634 Anne Woodsworth and Victor R. Neufeld. "A Survey of Physician Self-education Patterns in Toronto. Part 1: Use of Libraries," *Canadian Library Journal* 29:1 (January-February 1972), 38-44. **(111)**

635 Richard Eggleton. "The ALA Duplicates Exchange Union—A Study and Evaluation," *Library Resources and Technical Services* 19:2 (Spring 1975), 148-163.

636 Katherine H. Packer and Dagobert Soergel. "The Importance of SDI for Current Awareness in Fields with Severe Scatter of Information," *Journal of the American Society for Information Science* 30:3 (May 1979), 125-135. **(194, 195, 198, 200, 201)**

637 Doris M. Carson. "The Act of Cataloging," *Library Resources and Technical Services* 20:2 (Spring 1976), 149-153.

638 Robert L. Mowery. "The Cutter Classification: Still at Work," *Library Resources and Technical Services* 20:2 (Spring 1976), 154-156.

639 Kelly Patterson, Carol White and Martha Whittaker. "Thesis Handling in University Libraries," *Library Resources and Technical Services* 21:3 (Summer 1977), 274-285.

640 Sandra L. Stokley and Marion T. Reid. "A Study of Performance of Five Book Dealers Used by Louisiana State University Library," *Library Resources and Technical Services* 22:2 (Spring 1978), 117-125.

641 Hans H. Wellisch. "Multiscript and Multilingual Bibliographic Control: Alternatives to Romanization," *Library Resources and Technical Services* 22:2 (Spring 1978), 179-190.

642 Bert R. Boyce and Mark Funk. "Bradford's Law and the Selection of High Quality Papers," *Library Resources and Technical Services* 22:4 (Fall 1978), 390-401.

643 Susan Dingle-Cliff and Charles H. Davis. "Comparison of Recent Acquisitions and OCLC Find Rates for Three Canadian Special Libraries," *Journal of the American Society for Information Science* 32:1 (January 1981), 65-69.

644 Rose Mary Juliano Longo and Ubaldino Dantas Machado. "Characterization of Databases in the Agricultural Sciences," *Journal of the American Society for Information Science* 32:2 (March 1981), 83-91. **(161, 168, 169)**

645   Edward S. Warner. "The Impact of Interlibrary Access to Periodicals on Subscription Continuation/Cancellation Decision Making," *Journal of the American Society for Information Science* 32:2 (March 1981), 93-95.

646   Charles T. Payne and Robert S. McGee. "Comparisons of LC Proofslip and MARC Tape Arrival Dates at the University of Chicago Library," *Journal of Library Automation* 3:2 (June 1970), 115-121.

647   Wanda V. Dole and David Allerton. "University Collections: A Survey of Costs," *Library Acquistions: Practice and Theory* 6:2 (1982), 25-32.

648   Silvia A. Gonzalez. "1976 Statistical Survey of Law Libraries Serving a Local Bar," *Law Library Journal* 70:2 (May 1977), 222-237.

649   Carole J. Mankin and Jacqueline D. Bastille. "An Analysis of the Differences between Density-of-Use Ranking and Raw-Use Ranking of Library Journal Use," *Journal of the American Society for Information Science* 32:3 (May 1981), 224-228.

650   Katherine W. McCain and James E. Bobick. "Patterns of Journal Use in a Departmental Library: A Citation Analysis," *Journal of the American Society for Information Science* 32:4 (July 1981), 257-267.

651   Manfred Kochen, Victoria Reich and Lee Cohen. "Influence on [sic] Online Bibliographic Services on Student Behavior," *Journal of the American Society for Information Science* 32:6 (November 1981), 412-420. **(45, 253)**

652   Mark P. Carpenter and Francis Narin. "The Adequacy of the *Science Citation Index* (SCI) as an Indicator of International Scientific Activity," *Journal of the American Society for Information Science* 32:6 (November 1981), 430-439. **(135)**

653   Chai Kim. "Retrieval Languages of Social Sciences and Natural Sciences: A Statistical Investigation," *Journal of the American Society for Information Science* 33:1 (January 1982), 3-7. **(135)**

654   Ann H. Schabas. "Postcoordinate Retrieval: A Comparison of Two Indexing Languages," *Journal of the American Society for Information Science* 33:1 (January 1982), 32-37.

655   Miranda Lee Pao. "Collaboration in Computational Musicology," *Journal of the American Society for Information Science* 33:1 (January 1982), 38-43.

656   Robert K. Poyer. "*Science Citation Index*'s Coverage of the Preclinical Science Literature," *Journal of the American Society for Information Science* 33:5 (September 1982), 333-337. **(177, 180)**

657   Stephen M. Lawani and Alan E. Bayer. "Validity of Citation Criteria for Assessing the Influence of Scientific Publications: New Evidence with Peer Assessment," *Journal of the American Society for Information Science* 34:1 (January 1983), 59-66.

658 Edward G. Summers, Joyce Matheson and Robert Conry. "The Effect of Personal, Professional and Psychological Attributes, and Information Seeking Behavior on the Use of Information Sources by Educators," *Journal of the American Society for Information Science* 34:1 (January 1983), 75-85.

659 Bluma C. Peritz. "A Note on 'Scholarliness' and 'Impact,'" *Journal of the American Society for Information Science* 34:5 (September 1983), 360-362.

660 Michael D. Cooper. "Response Time Variations in an Online Search System," *Journal of the American Society for Information Science* 34:6 (November 1983), 374-380. **(85, 86)**

661 Richard S. Marcus. "An Experimental Comparison of the Effectiveness of Computers and Humans as Search Intermediaries," *Journal of the American Society for Information Science* 34:6 (November 1983), 381-404. **(53, 93)**

662 Michael J. Simonds, "Work Attitudes and Union Membership," *College and Research Libraries* 36:2 (March 1975), 136-142.

663 Jerold Nelson. "Faculty Awareness and Attitudes toward Academic Library Reference Services: A Measure of Communication," *College and Research Libraries* 34:5 (September 1973), 268-275. **(222, 223)**

664 Andre Nitecki, "Polish Books in America and the Farmington Plan," *College and Research Libraries* 27:6 (November 1966), 439-449.

665 Leslie R. Morris. "Projections of the Number of Library School Graduates," *Journal of Education for Librarianship* 22:4 (Spring 1982), 283-291. **(153)**

666 Thomas J. Galvin and Allen Kent. "Use of a University Library Collection," *Library Journal* 102:20 (November 1977), 2317-2320. [For further and more complete information see Allen Kent, et al. *Use of Library Materials: The University of Pittsburgh Study.* New York: Marcel Dekker, 1979.]

667 Allen Kent. "Library Resource Sharing Networks: How To Make a Choice," *Library Acquisitions: Practice and Theory* 2 (1978), 69-76. [For further and more complete information see Allen Kent, et al. *Use of Library Materials: The University of Pittsburgh Study.* New York: Marcel Dekker, 1979.]

668 Leigh S. Estabrook and Kathleen M. Heim. "A Profile of ALA Personal Members," *American Libraries* 11:11 (December 1980), 654-659. [For a fuller and more complete description of this study see Kathleen M. Heim and Leigh S. Estabrook. *Career Profiles and Sex Discrimination in the Library Profession.* Chicago: American Library Association, 1983.]

669 Mary Lee DeVilbiss. "The Approval-Built Collection in the Medium-Sized Academic Library," *College and Research Libraries* 36:6 (November 1975), 487-492.

670 Thomas P. Fleming and Frederick G. Kilgour. "Moderately and Heavily Used Biomedical Journals," *Bulletin of the Medical Library Association* 52:1 (January 1964), 234-241.

671 Richard J. Hyman. "Medical Interlibrary Loan Patterns," *Bulletin of the Medical Library Association* 53:2 (April 1965), 215-224.

672 L. Miles Raisig, Meredith Smith, Renata Cuff and Frederick G. Kilgour. "How Biomedical Investigators Use Library Books," *Bulletin of the Medical Library Association* 54:2 (April 1966), 104-107. **(109, 110, 112, 117, 118)**

673 Helen Crawford. "Centralization vs. Decentralization in Medical School Libraries," *Bulletin of the Medical Library Association* 54:2 (April 1966), 199-205.

674 Peter Stangl and Frederick G. Kilgour. "Analysis of Recorded Biomedical Book and Journal Use in the Yale Medical Library," *Bulletin of the Medical Library Association* 55:3 (July 1967), 290-300.

675 Peter Stangl and Frederick G. Kilgour. "Analysis of Recorded Biomedical Book and Journal Use in the Yale Medical Library," *Bulletin of the Medical Library Association* 55:3 (July 1967), 301-315.

676 Gwendolyn S. Cruzat. "Keeping Up with Biomedical Meetings," *Bulletin of the Medical Library Association* 56:2 (April 1968), 132-137. **(175, 178)**

677 Joan B. Woods, Sam Pieper and Shervert H. Frazier. "Basic Psychiatric Literature: I. Books," *Bulletin of the Medical Library Association* 56:3 (July 1968), 295-309.

678 Joan B. Woods, Sam Pieper and Shervert H. Frazier. "Basic Psychiatric Literature: II. Articles and Article Sources," *Bulletin of the Medical Library Association* 56:4 (October 1968), 404-427.

679 Reva Pachefsky. "Survey of the Card Catalog in Medical Libraries," *Bulletin of the Medical Library Association* 57:1 (January 1969), 10-20.

680 Janet Barlup. "Mechanization of Library Procedures in the Medium-sized Medical Library: VII. Relevancy of Cited Articles in Citation Indexing," *Bulletin of the Medical Library Association* 57:3 (July 1969), 260-263.

681 Wilhelm Moll. "Basic Journal List for Small Hospital Libraries," *Bulletin of the Medical Library Association* 57:3 (July 1969), 267-271.

682 Lois Ann Colainni and Robert F. Lewis. "Reference Services in U.S. Medical School Libraries," *Bulletin of the Medical Library Association* 57:3 (July 1969), 272-274. **(17, 18, 20, 41, 42, 63, 68, 207, 208, 210, 213, 233, 234)**

683 Vern M. Pings and Joyce E. Malin. "Access to the Scholarly Record of Medicine by the Osteopathic Physicians of Southeastern Michigan," *Bulletin of the Medical Library Association* 58:1 (January 1970), 18-22.

684 D.J. Goode, J.K. Penry and J.F. Caponio. "Comparative Analysis of *Epilepsy Abstracts* and a MEDLARS Bibliography," *Bulletin of the Medical Library Association* 58:1 (January 1970), 44-50. **(160, 162, 163, 175, 176, 179, 186, 187, 189)**

685 Robert Oseasohn. "Borrower Use of a Modern Medical Library by Practicing Physicians," *Bulletin of the Medical Library Association* 59:1 (January 1970), 58-59.

686 Joan M.B. Smith. "A Periodical Use Study at Children's Hospital of Michigan," *Bulletin of the Medical Library Association* 58:1 (January 1970), 65-67.

687 Jean K. Miller. "Mechanization of Library Procedures in the Medium-sized Medical Library: XI. Two Methods of Providing Selective Dissemination of Information to Medical Scientists," *Bulletin of the Medical Library Association* 58:3 (July 1970), 378-397. **(198, 204, 205, 206)**

688 Stella S. Gomes. "The Nature and the Use and Users of the Midwest Regional Medical Library," *Bulletin of the Medical Library Association* 58:4 (October 1970), 559-577.

689 Donald A. Windsor. "Publications on a Drug before the First Report of Its Administration to Man," *Bulletin of the Medical Library Association* 59:3 (July 1971), 433-437.

690 Charles L. Bowden and Virginia M. Bowden. "A Survey of Information Sources Used by Psychiatrists," *Bulletin of the Medical Library Association* 59:4 (October 1971), 603-608. **(108, 111, 118, 194, 207)**

691 Ruth E. Fenske. "Mechanization of Library Procedures in the Medium-sized Medical Library: XIV. Correlations between National Library of Medicine Classification Numbers and MeSH Headings," *Bulletin of the Medical Library Association* 60:2 (April 1972), 319-324.

692 Anne Brearley Piternick. "Measurement of Journal Availability in a Biomedical Library," *Bulletin of the Medical Library Association* 60:4 (October 1972), 534-542.

693 Isabel Spiegel and Janet Crager. "Comparison of SUNY and MEDLINE Searches," *Bulletin of the Medical Library Association* 61:2 (April 1973), 205-209. **(52, 161, 163)**

694 Fred W. Roper. "Special Programs in Medical Library Education, 1957-1971: Part II: Analysis of the Programs," *Bulletin of the Medical Library Association* 61:4 (October 1973), 387-395.

695 Norma Jean Lodico. "Physician's Referral Letter Bibliographic Service: A New Method of Disseminating Medical Information," *Bulletin of the Medical Library Association* 61:4 (October 1973), 422-432.

696 Wilhelm Moll. "MEDLINE Evaluation Study," *Bulletin of the Medical Library Association* 62:1 (January 1974), 1-5. **(43, 46, 63, 68, 78, 79, 82)**

697 Pamela Tibbetts. "A Method for Estimating the In-House Use of the Periodical Collection in the University of Minnesota Bio-Medical Library," *Bulletin of the Medical Library Association* 62:1 (January 1974), 37-48.

698 Joan Ash. "Library Use of Public Health Materials: Description and Analysis," *Bulletin of the Medical Library Association* 62:2 (April 1974), 95-104.

699 Ching-Chih Chen. "Current Status of Biomedical Book Reviewing: Part I. Key Biomedical Reviewing Journals with Quantitative Significance," *Bulletin of the Medical Library Association* 62:2 (April 1974), 105-112.

700 Ching-Chih Chen. "Current Status of Biomedical Book Reviewing: Part II. Time Lag in Biomedical Book Reviewing," *Bulletin of the Medical Library Association* 62:2 (April 1974), 113-119.(**137, 144, 176, 179, 187, 189, 190**)

701 George Scheerer and Lois E. Hines. "Classification Systems Used in Medical Libraries," *Bulletin of the Medical Library Association* 62:3 (July 1974), 272-280.

702 Jo Ann Bell. "The Academic Health Sciences Library and Serial Selection," *Bulletin of the Medical Library Association* 62:3 (July 1974), 281-290.

703 Ching-Chih Chen. "Current Status of Biomedical Book Reviewing: Part III. Duplication Patterns in Biomedical Book Reviewing," *Bulletin of the Medical Library Association* 62:3 (July 1974), 296-301.(**138, 144, 177, 180**)

704 Ching-Chih Chen. "Current Status of Biomedical Book Reviewing: Part IV. Major American and British Biomedical Book Publishers," *Bulletin of the Medical Library Association* 62:3 (July 1974), 302-308.

705 M. Sandra Wood and Robert S. Seeds. "Development of SDI Services from a Manual Current Awareness Service to SDILINE," *Bulletin of the Medical Library Association* 62:4 (October 1974), 374-384. (**195, 197, 199, 203, 205, 207**)

706 Margaret Butkovich and Robert M. Braude. "Cost-Performance of Cataloging and Card Production in a Medical Center Library," *Bulletin of the Medical Library Association* 63:1 (January 1975), 29-34.

707 Donald A. Windsor. "Science-Speciality Literatures: Their Legendary-Contemporary Parity, Based on the Transmission of Information between Generations," *Bulletin of the Medical Library Association* 63:2 (April 1975), 209-215.

708 Helen J. Brown, Jean K. Miller and Diane M. Pinchoff. "Study of the Information Dissemination Service—Health Sciences Library, State University of New York at Buffalo," *Bulletin of the Medical Library Association* 63:3 (July 1975), 259-271.

709 Rachel K. Goldstein and Dorothy R. Hill. "The Status of Women in the Administration of Health Science Libraries," *Bulletin of the Medical Library Association* 63:4 (October 1975), 386-395.

710 Janet G. Schnall and Joan W. Wilson. "Evaluation of a Clinical Medical Librarianship Program at a University Health Sciences Library," *Bulletin of the Medical Library Association* (July 1976), 278-283.(**3, 4, 6**)

711 Anne B. Piternick. "Effects of Binding Policy and Other Factors on the Availability of Journal Issues," *Bulletin of the Medical Library Association* 64:3 (July 1976), 284-292.

712 Richard B. Fredericksen and Helen N. Michael. "Subject Cataloging Practices in North American Medical School Libraries," *Bulletin of the Medical Library Association* 64:4 (October 1976), 356-366.

713 Paul M. McIlvaine and Malcolm H. Brantz. "Audiovisual Materials: A Survey of Bibliographic Controls in Distributors' Catalogs," *Bulletin of the Medical Library Association* 65:1 (January 1977), 17-21. **(153)**

714 Bette Greenberg, Robert Breedlove and Wendy Berger. "MEDLINE Demand Profiles: An Analysis of Requests for Clinical and Research Information," *Bulletin of the Medical Library Association* 65:1 (January 1977), 22-28. **(33, 38, 99, 100, 101, 102, 103, 104, 106)**

715 Renata Tagliacozzo. "Estimating the Satisfaction of Information Users," *Bulletin of the Medical Library Association* 65:2 (April 1977), 243-249. **(54, 58, 78, 81)**

716 Ruth W. Wender, Ester L. Fruehauf, Marilyn S. Vent and Constant D. Wilson. "Determination of Continuing Medical Education Needs of Clinicians from a Literature Search Study: Part I. The Study," *Bulletin of the Medical Library Association* 65:3 (July 1977), 330-337. **(34, 38)**

717 Ruth W. Wender, Ester L. Fruehauf, Marilyn S. Vent and Constant D. Wilson. "Determination of Continuing Medical Education Needs of Clinicians from a Literature Search Study: Part II. Questionnaire Results," *Bulletin of the Medical Library Association* 65:3 (July 1977), 338-341. **(34, 39)**

718 Donald J. Morton. "Analysis of Interlibrary Requests by Hospital Libraries for Photocopied Journal Articles," *Bulletin of the Medical Library Association* 65:4 (October 1977), 425-432,

719 Patrick W. Brennen and W. Patrick Davey. "Citation Analysis in the Literature of Tropical Medicine," *Bulletin of the Medical Library Association* 66:1 (January 1978), 24-30.

720 Theresa C. Strasser. "The Information Needs of Practicing Physicians in Northeastern New York State," *Bulletin of the Medical Library Association* 66:2 (April 1978), 200-209. **(130, 211, 217)**

721 Inci A. Bowman, Elizabeth K. Eaton and J. Maurice Mahan. "Are Health Science Faculty Interested in Medical History? An Evaluative Case Study," *Bulletin of the Medical Library Association* 66:2 (April 1978), 228-231. **(25, 28)**

722 Maurice C. Leatherbury and Richard A. Lyders. "Friends of the Library Groups in Health Sciences Libraries," *Bulletin of the Medical Library Association* 66:3 (July 1978), 315-318.

723   Bette Greenberg, Sara Battison, Madeleine Kolisch and Martha Leredu.
      "Evaluation of a Clinical Medical Librarian Program at the Yale Medical
      Library," *Bulletin of the Medical Library Association* 66:3 (July 1978),
      319-326. (4, 5, 7)

724   Gloria Werner. "Use of On-Line Bibliographic Retrieval Services in Health
      Sciences Libraries in the United States and Canada," *Bulletin of the Medical
      Library Association* 67:1 (January 1979), 1-14.   (35, 36, 39, 40, 44, 46, 47,
      51, 52, 64, 65, 69, 70, 71, 73, 89, 90, 91, 92, 94, 97, 100, 102, 104, 106, 107,
      129, 130)

725   B. Tommie Usdin. "Core Lists of Medical Journals: A Comparison," *Bulletin
      of the Medical Library Association* 67:2 (April 1979), 212-217.

726   John A. Timour. "Brief Communications: Use of Selected Abstracting and
      Indexing Journals in Biomedical Resource Libraries," *Bulletin of the Medical
      Library Association* 67:3 (July 1979), 330-335. (87, 90)

727   Rachel K. Goldstein and Dorothy R. Hill. "The Status of Women in the
      Administration of Health Sciences Libraries: A Five-Year Follow-Up Study,
      1972-1977," *Bulletin of the Medical Library Association* 68:1 (January 1980),
      6-15.

728   Richard T. West and Maureen J. Malone. "Communicating the Results of
      NLM Grant-supported Library Projects," *Bulletin of the Medical Library
      Association* 68:1 (January 1980), 33-39.

729   James A. Thompson and Michael R. Kronenfeld. "The Effect of Inflation on
      the Cost of Journals on the Brandon List," *Bulletin of the Medical Library
      Association* 68:1 (January 1980), 47-52.

730   Carol C. Spencer. "Random Time Sampling with Self-observation for
      Library Cost Studies: Unit Costs of Reference Questions," *Bulletin of the
      Medical Library Association* 68:1 (January 1980), 53-57. (10)

731   Justine Roberts. "Circulation versus Photocopy: Quid pro Quo?" *Bulletin of
      the Medical Library Association* 68:3 (July 1980), 274-277.

732   Dick R. Miller and Joseph E. Jensen. "Dual Pricing of Health Sciences
      Periodicals: A Survey," *Bulletin of the Medical Library Association* 68:4
      (October 1980), 336-347.

733   Jacqueline D. Bastille. "A Simple Objective Method for Determining a
      Dynamic Journal Collection," *Bulletin of the Medical Library Association*
      68:4 (October 1980), 357-366.

734   Mary H. Mueller. "An Examination of Characteristics Related to Success of
      Friends Groups in Medical School Rare Book Libraries," *Bulletin of the
      Medical Library Association* 69:1 (January 1981), 9-13.

735   Scott Davis, Lincoln Polissar and Joan W. Wilson. "Continuing Education in
      Cancer for the Community Physician: Design and Evaluation of a Regional

Table of Contents Service," *Bulletin of the Medical Library Association* 69:1 (January 1981), 14-20. (**28, 29**)

736 Gary D. Byrd. "Copyright compliance in Health Sciences Libraries: A Status Report Two Years after the Implementation of PL 94-553," *Bulletin of the Medical Library Association* 69:2 (April 1981), 224-230.

737 Ester L. Baldinger, Jennifer P.S. Nakeff-Plaat and Margaret S. Cummings. "An Experimental Study of the Feasibility of Substituting Chemical Abstracts Online for the Printed Copy in a Medium-Sized Medical Library," *Bulletin of the Medical Library Association* 69:2 (April 1981), 247-251. (**45, 46, 48**)

738 Doris R.F. Dunn. "Dissemination of the Published Results of an Important Clinical Trial: An Analysis of the Citing Literature," *Bulletin of the Medical Library Association* 69:3 (July 1981), 301-306. (**200**)

739 Cynthia H. Goldstein. "A Study of Weeding Policies in Eleven TALON Resource Libraries," *Bulletin of the Medical Library Association* 69:3 (July 1981), 311-316.

740 K. Suzanne Johnson and E. Guy Coffee. "Veterinary Medical School Libraries in the United States and Canada, 1977-78," *Bulletin of the Medical Library Association* 70:1 (January 1982), 10-20. (**36, 42, 60, 62, 88, 90**)

741 Suzanne F. Grefsheim, Robert H. Larson, Shelley A. Bader and Nina W. Matheson. "Automation of Internal Library Operations in Academic Health Sciences Libraries: A State of the Art Report," *Bulletin of the Medical Library Association* 70:2 (April 1982), 191-200.

742 Elizabeth R. Lenz and Carolyn F. Walz. "Nursing Educators' Satisfaction with Library Facilities," *Bulletin of the Medical Library Association* 70:2 (April 1982), 201-206.

743 Ruth Traister Morris, Edwin A. Holtum and David S. Curry. "Being There: The Effect of the User's Presence on MEDLINE Search Results," *Bulletin of the Medical Library Association* 70:3 (July 1982), 298-304. (**57, 59, 60, 73, 74, 75, 76, 77, 80, 81, 84, 95, 98, 100, 102**)

744 James K. Cooper, Diane Cooper and Timothy P. Johnson. "Medical Library Support in Rural Areas," *Bulletin of the Medical Library Association* 71:1 (January 1983), 13-15. (**25, 30**)

745 Susan Crawford. "Health Science Libraries in the United States: I. Overview of the Post-World War II Years," *Bulletin of the Medical Library Association* 71:1 (January 1983), 16-20.

746 Susan Crawford and Alan M. Rees. "Health Sciences Libraries in the United States: II. Medical School Libraries, 1960-1980," *Bulletin of the Medical Library Association* 71:1 (January 1983), 21-29.

747 Susan Crawford. "Health Science Libraries in the United States: III. Hospital Health Science Libraries, 1969-1979," *Bulletin of the Medical Library Association* 71:1 (January 1983), 30-36. (**224, 225, 226**)

748 Mark E. Funk and Carolyn Anne Reid. "Indexing Consistency in MED-LINE," *Bulletin of the Medical Library Association* 71:2 (April 1983), 176-183. **(162, 164, 177, 178, 181)**

749 Michael R. Kronenfeld and Sarah H. Gable. "Real Inflation of Journal Prices: Medical Journals, U.S. Journals and Brandon List Journals," *Bulletin of the Medical Library Association* 71:4 (October 1983), 375-379.

750 Jane McCarthy. "Survey of Audiovisual Standards and Practices in Health Sciences Libraries," *Bulletin of the Medical Library Association* 71:4 (October 1983), 391-395.

751 Rajia C. Tobia and David A. Kronick. "A Clinical Information Consultation Service at a Teaching Hospital," *Bulletin of the Medical Library Association* 71:4 (October 1983), 396-399. **(5, 6, 7, 8, 26, 30, 31)**

752 Elizabeth R. Ashin. "Library Service to Dental Practitioners," *Bulletin of the Medical Library Association* 71:4 (October 1983), 400-402. **(209, 211, 212)**

753 Peter P. Olevnik. "Non-Formalized Point-of-Use Library Instruction: A Survey," *Catholic Library World* 50:5 (December 1978), 218-220. **(123, 229, 232, 248, 256)**

754 Susan A. Stussy. "Automation in Catholic College Libraries," *Catholic Library World* 53:3 (October 1981), 109-111.

755 R.M. Longyear. "Article Citations and 'Obsolescence' in Musicological Journals," *Notes* 33:3 (March 1977), 563-571.

756 Ann Basart. "Criteria for Weeding Books in a University Music Library," *Notes* 36:4 (June 1980), 819-836.

757 Richard P. Smiraglia and Arsen R. Papakhian. "Music in the OCLC Online Union Catalog: A Review," *Notes* 38:2 (December 1981), 257-274.

758 William Gray Potter. "When Names Collide: Conflict in the Catalog and AACR 2," *Library Resources and Technical Services* 24:1 (Winter 1980), 3-16.

759 Rose Mary Magrill and Constance Rinehart. "Selection for Preservation: A Service Study," *Library Resources and Technical Services* 24:1 (Winter 1980), 44-57.

760 Sally Braden, John D. Hall and Helen H. Britton. "Utilization of Personnel and Bibliographic Resources for Cataloging by OCLC Participating Libraries," *Library Resources and Technical Services* 24:2 (Spring 1980), 135-154.

761 Cynthia C. Ryans. "Cataloging Administrators' Views on Cataloging Education," *Library Resources and Technical Services* 24:4 (Fall 1980), 343-351.

762 Thomas Schadlich. "Changing from Sears to LC Subject Headings," *Library Resources and Technical Services* 24:4 (Fall 1980), 361-363.

763 Elizabeth L. Tate. "For Our 25th Anniversary...," *Library Resources and Technical Services* 25:1 (January/March 1981), 3-7.

764 Barbara Moore. "Patterns in the Use of OCLC by Academic Library Cataloging Departments," *Library Resources and Technical Services* 25:1 (January/March 1981), 30-39.

765 Judith J. Johnson and Clair S. Josel. "Quality Control and the OCLC Data Base: A Report on Error Reporting," *Library Resources and Technical Services* 25:1 (January/March 1981), 40-47.

766 Edward T. O'Neill and Rao Aluri. "Library of Congress Subject Heading Patterns in OCLC Monographic Records," *Library Resources and Technical Services* 25:1 (January/March 1981), 63-80.

767 Elizabeth H. Groot. "A Comparison of Library Tools for Monograph Verification," *Library Resources and Technical Services* 25:2 (April/June 1981), 149-161. **(132, 133, 145, 146, 156)**

768 Elizabeth G. Mikita. "Monographs in Microform: Issues in Cataloging and Bibliographic Control," *Library Resources and Technical Services* 25:4 (October/December 1981), 352-361. **(154)**

769 Lee R. Nemchek. "Problems of Cataloging and Classification in Theater Librarianship," *Library Resources and Technical Services* 25:4 (October/December 1981), 374-385. **(207)**

770 John Hostage. "AACR 2, OCLC, and the Card Catalog in the Medium-Sized Library," *Library Resources and Technical Services* 26:1 (January/March 1982), 12-20.

771 Robert H. Hassell. "Revising the Dewey Music Schedules: Tradition vs. Innovation," *Library Resources and Technical Services* 26:2 (April/June 1982), 192-203.

772 Patricia Dwyer Wanninger. "Is the OCLC Database Too Large? A Study of the Effect of Duplicate Records in the OCLC System," *Library Resources and Technical Services* 26:4 (October/December 1982), 353-361. **(147, 157)**

773 Stephen R. Salmon. "Characteristics of Online Public Catalogs," *Library Resources and Technical Services* 27:1 (January/March 1983), 36-67.

774 Thomas E. Nisonger. "A Test of Two Citation Checking Techniques for Evaluating Political Science Collections in University Libraries," *Library Resources and Technical Services* 27:2 (April/June 1983), 163-176.

775 John Rutledge and Willy Owen. "Changes in the Quality of Paper in French Books, 1860-1914: A Study of Selected Holdings of the Wilson Library, University of North Carolina," *Library Resources and Technical Services* (April/June 1983), 177-187.

776   Jim Williams and Nancy Romero. "A Comparison of the OCLC Database and *New Serial Titles* as an Information Resource for Serials," *Library Resources and Technical Services* 27:2 (April/June 1983), 177-187. **(147, 148, 158, 166, 167)**

777   Mary E. Clack and Sally F. Williams. "Using Locally and Nationally Produced Periodical Price Indexes in Budget Preparation," *Library Resources and Technical Services* 27:4 (October/December 1983), 345-356.

778   Victoria Cheponis Lessard and Jack Hall. "Vocational Technical Collection Building: Does it Exist?" *Collection Building* 4:2 (1982), 6-18.

779   Virginia Witucke. "The Reviewing of Children's Science Books," *Collection Building* 4:2 (1982) 19-30. **(139, 140, 142, 143)**

780   Margaret F. Stieg. "The Information Needs of Historians," *College and Research Libraries* 42:6 (November 1981), 549-560. **(126, 127)**

781   Howard D. White. "Library Censorship and the Permissive Minority," *Library Quarterly* 51:2 (1981), 192-207.

782   Judith Serebnick. "Book Reviews and the Selection of Potentially Controversial Books in Public Libraries," *Library Quarterly* 51:4 (1981), 390-409.

783   Richard W. Scamell and Bette Ann Stead. "A Study of Age and Tenure as it Pertains to Job Satisfaction," *Journal of Library Administration* 1:1 (Spring 1980), 3-18.

784   Robert M. Hayes. "Citation Statistics as a Measure of Faculty Research Productivity," *Journal of Education for Librarianship* 23:3 (Winter 1983), 151-172.

785   William Skeh Wong and David S. Zubatsky. "The First-Time Appointed Academic Library Director 1970-1980: A Profile," *Journal of Library Administration* 4:1 (Spring 1983), 41-70.

786   James Rice, Jr. "An Assessment of Student Preferences for Method of Library Orientation," *Journal of Library Administration* 4:1 (Spring 1983), 87-93. **(231, 250, 252)**

787   Frank William Goudy. "Affirmative Action and Library Science Degrees: A Statistical Overview, 1973-74 through 1980-81," *Journal of Library Administration* 4:3 (Fall 1983), 51-60.

788   Thomas G. English. "Librarian Status in the Eighty-Nine U.S. Academic Institutions of the Association of Research Libraries: 1982," *College and Research Libraries* 44:3 (May 1983), 199-211.

789   Nathan M. Smith and Veneese C. Nelson. "Burnout: A Survey of Academic Reference Librarians," *College and Research Libraries* 44:3 (May 1983), 245-250. **(31)**

790 Floris W. Wood. "Reviewing Book Review Indexes," *Reference Services Review* (April/June 1980), 47-52. **(136, 137, 186)**

791 Herbert Goldhor. "Public Library Circulation up 3%; Spending Jumps 11%," *American Libraries* 14:8 (September 1983), 534.

792 Laura N. Gasaway and Steve Margeton. "Continuing Education for Law Librarianship," *Law Library Journal* 70:1 (February 1977), 39-52.

793 Michael L. Renshawe. "The Condition of the Law Librarian in 1976," *Law Library Review* 69:4 (November 1976), 626-640.

794 Susanne Patterson Wahba. "Women in Libraries," *Law Library* Journal 69:2 (May 1976), 223-231.

795 Jean Finch and Lauri R. Flynn. "An Update on Faculty Libraries," *Law Library Journal* 73:1 (Winter 1980), 99-106.

796 Robert D. Swisher, Peggy C. Smith and Calvin J. Boyer. "Educational Change Among ACRL Academic Librarians," *Library Research* (*Library and Information Science Research* since Spring 1983) 5:2 (Summer 1983), 195-205.

797 Michael D. Cooper. "Economies of Scale in Academic Libraries," *Library Research* (*Library and Information Science Research* after Spring 1983) 5:2 (Summer 1983), 207-219.

798 Virgil Diodato. "Faculty Workload: A Case Study," *Journal of Education for Librarianship* 23:4 (Spring 1983), 286-295.

799 Jerry D. Saye. "Continuing Education and Library School Faculty," *Journal of Education for Librarianship* 24:1 (Summer 1983), 3-16.

800 Maurice P. Marchant and Carolyn F. Wilson. "Developing Joint Graduate Programs for Librarians," *Journal of Education for Librarianship* 24:1 (Summer 1983), 30-37.

801 Barbara L. Stein and Herman L. Totten. "Cognitive Styles: Similarities Among Students," *Journal of Education for Librarianship* 24:1 (Summer 1983), 38-43.

802 Marilyn J. Markham, Keith H. Stirling and Nathan M. Smith. "Librarian Self-Disclosure and Patron Satisfaction in the Reference Interview," *RQ* 22:4 (Summer 1983), 369-374.

803 June L. Engle and Elizabeth Futas. "Sexism in Adult Encyclopedias," *RQ* 23:1 (Fall 1983), 29-39.

804 David F. Kohl. "Circulation Professionals: Management Information Needs and Attitudes," *RQ* 23:1 (Fall 1983), 81-86.

805   Kevin Carey. "Problems and Patterns of Periodical Literature Searching at an
      Urban University Research Library," *RQ* 23:2 (Winter 1983), 211-218. **(192)**

806   Beverly P. Lynch and Jo Ann Verdin. "Job Satisfaction in Libraries:
      Relationships of the Work Itself, Age, Sex, Occupational Group, Tenure,
      Supervisory Level, Career Commitment and Library Department," *Library
      Quarterly* 53:4 (October 1983), 434-447. **(149)**

807   Louise W. Diodato and Virgil P. Diodato. "The Use of Gifts in a Medium
      Sized Academic Library," *Collection Management* 5:1/2 (Spring/Summer
      1983), 53-71.

AUTHOR INDEX
TO BIBLIOGRAPHY OF ARTICLES

Note: The index is arranged alphabetically, word by word. All characters or groups of characters separated by spaces, dashes, hyphens, diagonal slashes or periods are treated as separate words. Acronyms not separated by spaces or punctuation are alphabetized as though they are single words, while initials separated by spaces or punctuation are treated as if each letter is a complete word. Personal names beginning with capital Mc, M' and Mac are all listed under Mac as though the full form were used, and St. is alphabetized as if spelled out.

Moriarty, John H., **202**
Morita, Ichiko T., **336**
Morris, Leslie R., **110, 665**
Morris, Ruth Traister, **743**
Morrison, Perry D., **131, 583**
Morton, Donald J., **718**
Mosborg, Stella Frank, **119**
Mosley, Isobel Jean, **331**
Mott, Sharon, **548**
Mowery, Robert L., **598, 638**
Mueller, Mary H., **734**
Murfin, Marjorie E., **29, 99, 239, 456**
Myers, Mindy J., **359**

Nagy, Laslo A., **489**
Nakeff-Plaat, Jennifer P.S., **737**
Narin, Francis, **622, 625, 652**
Needham, William L., **155**
Nelson, Diane M., **417**
Nelson, E. Don, **422**
Nelson, Harriet, **503, 574**
Nelson, Jerold, **663**
Nelson, Veneese C., **789**
Nemchek, Lee R., **769**
Nemeyer, Carol A., **592**
Neufeld, Victor R., **634**
New, Doris E., **629**
Nicholson, Natalie N., **115**
Niland, Powell, **444**
Nisonger, Thomas E., **774**
Nitecki, Andre, **581, 664**
Nitecki, Danuta A., **148**
Noreault, Terry, **616**
Norten, E.R., **320**
Novak, Victor, **187**
Nugent, William R., **588**

Oboler, Eli M., **76**
Ochal, Bethany J., **392**
O'Connor, Carol Alf, **314**
O'Connor, Daniel O., **254, 576**
O'Connor, Thomas A., **314**
O'Keefe, Robert, **89**
Olevnik, Peter P., **753**
Olsgaard, Jane Kinch, **481, 494**
Olsgaard, John N., **481, 494**
Olson, Barbara J., **146**
O'Neill, Edward T., **333, 766**
Orgren, Carl F., **146**
Orsini, Elaine, **594**
Orten, Larry, **545**
Ory, John C., **490**

Oseasohn, Robert, **685**
Ott, Retha Zane, **629**
Owen, Katherine C., **405**
Owen, Willy, **775**

Pachefsky, Reva, **679**
Packer, Katherine H., **636**
Pagell, Ruth A., **442**
Palais, Elliot S., **53**
Palmer, Joseph W., **158, 162**
Panetta, Rebecca, **448**
Pantazis, Fotoula, **549**
Pao, Miranda Lee, **655**
Papakhian, Richard P., **757**
Parker, Steve, **145**
Pask, Judith M., **120, 436**
Pastine, Maureen, **449**
Patrick, Ruth J., **212**
Patterson, Kelly, **639**
Pattie, Kenton, **309**
Paustian, P. Robert, **575**
Payne, Charles T., **646**
Pearson, Penelope, **42**
Pease, Sue, **45**
Peil, Margaret, **242**
Penry, J.K., **684**
Perelmuter, Susan, **11**
Perez, Ernest R., **601**
Peritz, Bluma C., **569, 571, 659**
Perk, Lawrence J., **453, 455, 610**
Perrine, Richard H., **134**
Person, Roland, **488**
Petersen, Dorothy G., **277**
Peterson, Stephen L., **195**
Philbin, Paul P., **437**
Phillips, Linda L., **13**
Phinney, Eleanor, **63**
Phipps, Barbara H., **188**
Phipps, Shelley, **23**
Pickett, A.S., **578**
Pieper, Sam, **677-678**
Pierce, Anton R., **160**
Pinchoff, Diane M., **708**
Pings, Vern M., **683**
Piper, Patricia L., **366**
Piternick, Anne Brearley, **22, 692, 711**
Piternick, George, **129, 604**
Plake, Barbara S., **36**
Plate, Kenneth H., **250, 553**
Polissar, Lincoln, **735**
Popovich, Charles J., **461**
Porterfield, Genevieve, **173**

ABOUT THE AUTHORS

DAVID F. KOHL is currently Undergraduate Librarian and Assistant Director for Undergraduate Libraries and Instructional Services at the University of Illinois-Urbana, with the rank of Associate Professor. Dr. Kohl did his graduate work at the University of Chicago. He has taught library administration at the University of Illinois Graduate School of Library and Information Science and has published numerous articles and monographs on library management and automation. His wide range of service in library management includes active participation in the ARL/OMS Library Consultant Program, the Washington State University's Managing for Productivity Program, and the Assessment Center Program for Potential Managers, sponsored jointly by the University of Washington Graduate Library School and the Washington State Library.

PETER G. WATSON is Assistant University Librarian for Programs and Services at California State University, Chico. He holds a bachelor's degree from Manchester University in England, and masters' degrees in English and Librarianship from the University of California, Santa Barbara and the University of California, Los Angeles, respectively. Mr. Watson has authored and coauthored numerous publications examining the impact of automation upon library reference service, including *Computer-Based Reference Service* (American Library Association, 1973) and several chapters in *Online Catalog: The Inside Story* (Ryan Research International, 1983), which he also coedited. He is also one of the founders of MARS (ALA's Machine Assisted Reference Section).